W9-CUZ-487

THE
ROCKLOPEDIA
FAKEBANDICA

THE
ROCKLOPEDIA
FAKEBANDICA

ILLUSTRATED BY JASON TORCHINSKY

T. MIKE CHILDS

ST. MARTIN'S GRIFFIN · NEW YORK

THOMAS DUNNE BOOKS.
An imprint of St. Martin's Press.

www.stmartins.com

All photos courtesy of The Kobal Collection

Book design by Jonathan Bennett

Library of Congress Cataloging-in-Publication Data

Childs, T. Mike.
    Rocklopedia Fakebandica/T. Mike Childs.—1st ed.
        p. cm.
    ISBN 0-312-32944-X
    EAN 978-0312-32944-0
    1. Rock music—Dictionairies. I. Title.

    ML102.R6C45 2004
    781.66—dc22
                                                                                    2004009860

First Edition: November 2004

10 9 8 7 6 5 4 3 2 1

'LEDGMENTS

I would like t

My moth

My fathe

My girlfr

Comedy   :mber: Alan Thomas Benson, Galen Karl

Black, Char   i Dana Torchinsky. I especially thank Alan

and Charle

Colomb

My frie   ιat helped turn this thing into a book.

My age   ιd especially for handling all the pictures.

My edi

I woul   Ͻ Westwood for its liberal rental policy, and

the Los /

I wou   ιiled a suggestion to the Rocklopedia Fake-

bandica   them all! The Web site and this book would

not be n

I wou   lowing Web sites, which all proved to be ex-

tremely

The

The

The

Th

Th

Th   ideo 1/ROCKVIDEO60s.html

Tł   .nds.com

Tł

Tl   :om/us6070s/fuzz.html

I   Ͻ on rockin' in the fake world!

Checklist for Gift Book Searching

NM_____   BPCL M_____   BPCL PM_____

NON-BPCL M __X__   NON-BPCL PM _____

PUBLICATION DATE ___2004___

CALL NUMBER:

REF ML102 .R6 C45 2004

LOC. (1) __Music__   #COPIES __1__

LOC. (2) _____   #COPIES _____

LOC. (3) _____   #COPIES _____

__X__ TITLE

__X__ AUTHOR(S)

__X__ PUBLISHER

__X__ DATE OF PUBLICATION

(Compare the date for the edition of the gift book you are searching and the date in the catalog.

__X__ NUMBER OF PAGES

(Should vary by fewer than five Pages.)

SEARCHER'S INITIALS: ___GB___

DATE: __9/27/24__

SEARCHING GUIDE

(Full instructions in Gift Book Searching folder)

Search catalog by title. If this results in a "no" match, re-search the book by author and/or series. If no title match can be found, write "0" on the line beside "Title" and draw an arrow through the remaining lines, (Author through Number of Pages.) Check "NM" on this form and write the date of publication of the book you are searching. If a search results in a title and author match, note whether the book and the record match for each point of information listed above ("X = match; "0" = no match). For partial matches note the information from the catalog record that varies from the book being searched. For partial matches, check "BPCL PM" or "NON-BPCL PM and write call number and the date of publication. Exact Match = M

INTRODUCTION

At the very beginning, before you read another word, let me admit, confess, and impress upon you that this volume is completely and utterly incomplete. There are many more fictional bands and artists from movies and television than are listed here, or, probably, could be. If you are unable to find what you seek, do not despair. The reasons for your particular picked nit's absence could be one, or a combination of, the following:

- This book is about fictional bands and musicians from AMERICAN television shows and movies. There are some exceptions for imported programs or movies that received significant exposure in the United States. I'm sure there are many worthy entries from languages and cultures I can't even begin to pronounce or spell.
- This book is about fictional bands and musicians from American Television SHOWS AND MOVIES. This includes TV specials, theatrically released cartoon shorts, movies-of-the-week, and miniseries. It does not include television commercials, advertising campaigns, infomercials, local access shows, student films, radio shows, albums, songs, spoken-word recordings, video games, Web sites, books, short stories, poems, plays, magazines, fanzines, zines, pamphlets, or anything you just made up.
- This book is about FICTIONAL bands and musicians from American television shows and movies. This does not include fictional portrayals of real bands or musicians, bio-pics, real documentaries, bands or artists playing themselves or fictionalized versions of themselves if they retain their real name, recording or performing pseudonyms used by real artists, or any band you think is fake just because you never heard of them.
- This book is about fictional BANDS and MUSICIANS from American television shows and movies. This does not include characters from musicals that burst into song, unless that character is also a musician, or a member of a band. This does not include a nonmusician character playing or singing in a nonprofessional setting, such as around their house, an open mic night, or singing "Happy Birthday" at a party. The transition from nonmusician to musician is as simple as declaring it so. But if they didn't make or imply that declaration, they are not included.
- The band or musician was never named. There are plenty of unnamed, unsung bands and musicians who perform in the backgrounds of movies and shows. There are more than enough ones that are named and sung to fill this book a dozen times over, so I'm not going to worry about the ones so minor that they didn't get a name.
- I never heard of them. Sorry, but this happens. I can't write about what I haven't got the slightest inkling. I may have never heard of that particularly obscure movie or television show. Or perhaps I have one band from a show and not another from another episode of the same show. I was not able to watch every episode and movie referenced herein, much less every movie and every episode of every show.
- I got tired. I had to stop at some point, didn't I? In compiling this compendium, I initially cast my net wide rather than deep. I have tried to round up the usual suspects and a few unusual ones as well.

If for any reason you are unable to find the band or artist you are looking for in these pages, please buy a second copy of this book and check that. It's probably in there.

You can also visit this book's official Web site at www.fakebands.com, which is always in progress, updated reasonably frequently, and contains fictional bands and musicians from all the types of sources I got all snotty about above. You can also submit entry suggestions and information about your favorites.

How to Read *The Rocklopedia Fakebandica*

Entries are arranged in alphabetical order, by the name of the band. If the first word of a band's name is "the," it is ignored, no matter what language it's in ("los" or "les" for example). Individual artists are listed by their last name first. Bands whose names start with a number are alphabetized as though the number was spelled out. Thus the band 2 Fine is alphabetized as though it were written "Two fine."

Bands whose names begin with the name of a person are alphabetized by the first word of the band name, and not the last name of the person, in order to hopefully reduce confusion. Or at least generate an entirely new kind of confusion. Thus the band Sid Knishes and the Mosh Pit-tatoes is alphabetized under "S" for "Sid" and not "K" for "Knishes."

Band or artist names that start with abbreviations, such as "Dr." or "Mr." are alphabetized as though the abbreviation was spelled out (doctor, mister). Thus, Dr. Dazzle comes before Dogs in Space, and not after.

In the rare instances where there are two fake bands or artists with the exact same name, they are designated (I) and (II), in chronological order of their appearance.

Sample Entry

Name of band. — **NON-DAIRY CREAMERS, THE**—This trio of English rockers hail from the "Hey You! Get Offa My Cow!" episode (10/26/87) of STV's sketch comedy show *Off the Cuff* (1986–present). The members are leader and lead singer John Lemmon (Rodney Honeycutt), guitarist Arnold McTinkering (James Parrish), and percussionist Dave "Galen" Mountcastle (Galen Black). The entire show is taken up with their improvised antics in faux documentary style as the band cuts its *Lasakadaisical Days* [sic] album, and it's obvious the participants just saw *This Is Spinal Tap* too many damn times. The band was wisely allowed only a few minutes in their next outing in "The Day After" episode (02/29/88), singing their new, pro-CIA song, "The CIA." The band then broke up on an unnamed talk show skit in the "A Cheap Host" episode (03/28/88), as Lemmon went solo as John Lemmon and Milk, and feuded with the others over the ownership of the band's name. *TRIVIA TIME!* Rodney Honeycutt now teaches school in North Carolina. See also **Beelzebobby Joe; Kiss the Lizard; Larry Loveday**.

Episode titles are given in quotes.

Show names are italicized.

Album titles are italicized.

Reference to another movie; movie titles are italicized.

Other appearances by the same band.

Interesting facts about the band or the actors/actresses involved come at the end of the entry in this section.

The origninal, first-run air date in the format: month/day/year.

Original network or channel the show aired on.

Years the show originally ran, not always present.

Character name; the actor's/actress's name is usually in parentheses unless otherwise noted.

"See also" lists additional related bands; they may be from the same episode/movie, or perhaps starring the same actors or actresses, or perhaps from a different episode of the same show, or perhaps related only thematically. Several pieces of unrelated data may be here.

THE
ROCKLOPEDIA
FAKEBANDICA

ACE TONES, THE—Traditional Scottish music band from Ferness, Scotland in the charming 1983 movie *Local Hero*. Played by Mark Winchester, Alan Clark, Alan Darby, Brian Rowan, Roddy Murray and Dale Winchester. The movie's score was done by guitar hero Mark Knopfler of Dire Straits.

AFRODISIACS, THE—In "The Music Man" episode (04/06/82) of biracial sitcom *Diff'rent Strokes*, older brother Willis Drummond (Todd Bridges) has this kinda sorta funkish/R&B-ish band. He is auditioning singers, which pits his black girlfriend Charlene (THE Janet Jackson!) versus his white stepsister Kimberly Drummond (Dana Plato). The solution? The two gals sing a horrible duet covering Paul McCartney and Stevie Wonder's "Ebony and Ivory," proving beyond a doubt there was a curse on the show.

AGAR—A genetically bred boy band in a *Saturday Night Live* skit (03/09/02), named for the gelatinous medium in which they were spawned. They appear on a parody of MTV's *Total Request Live* where Carson Daly (Jimmy Fallon) interviews their manager/creator, creepy Lou Perlstein (guest star Jon Stewart). Kyle (Seth Meyers) is the shy one, Chadddd (Dean Edwards) the cute one, Greg (Chris Parnell) is allergic to light, Jeremy (Horatio Sanz) has lobster claws and gills, and then there's Ass Face, about whom the less said the better. They sing "Thinkin' 'Bout Love," a song in which Jeremy pleads to be put out of his hellish existence.

AKINO, YOKO—Asian singer and celebrity judge (Molly Shannon) in a parody of *The Iron Chef* show

on *Saturday Night Live* (01/13/01). One contestant's (guest star Charlie Sheen) mini shark-head pizzas remind her of her hit song "Blue Jeans on Fire."

ALABAMA PORCH MONKEYS, THE—From director Spike Lee's racially charged mess of a movie, *Bamboozled* (2000). (Of course, that's redundant—all of Spike Lee's movies are racially charged.) This is the deliberately offensively named house band of the controversial hit Continental Network System TV show *Mantan: The New Millennium Minstrel Show*. They're costumed in old-style striped prison uniforms with ball and chain. And yes, the set they play on is a porch in Alabama. Played by real hip-hop band The Roots: Ahmir-Khalib Thompson, James "Kamal" Gray, Tariq Trotter, Leonard "Hub" Hubbard, and Kyle "Scratch" Jones. See also **The Mau Maus**.

ALAN TWITTY PROJECT, THE—From the "Battle of the Bands" episode (11/24/00) of the Disney Channel's sitcom *Even Stevens*. The name's probably a takeoff on The Alan Parsons Project. Twitty (A. J. Trauth) is auditioning lead singers (a batch of one-joke ponies), but manager Louis Stevens (Shia LaBeouf) rejects his sister Ren Stevens (Christy Carlson Romano) when she tries out. The rest of the band want her, and force Louis out. So, naturally, he goes and starts a rival band, The Louis Stevens Experience. When they compete to play a party thrown by Jason Bagwell (Artie Ryan), they are both rejected in a typical sitcom move. Just so there's no hard feelings, the two bands unite at the end into The Twitty-Stevens Connection. *TRIVIA TIME!* In a later episode, "Starstruck" (06/15/01), Twitty got to hand a tape of TATP to featured guest stars, the Britpop band BBMak, playing themselves. See also **The Twitty-Stevens Connection**.

ALI G—Yellow-clad gangsta rap whigger, played by

English comedian Sacha Baron Cohen. In his own 2003 HBO show, *Da Ali G Show*, he manages to talk himself into interviews with real famous people like Newt Gingrich and Donald Trump. During the interviews, he makes complete asses out of them, and—here's the good part—without them even suspecting that Ali G is not for real! Cohen originated the character on the 1998 English program *The 11 O'clock Show*.

ALICE BOWIE—Dope-oriented comedians Cheech and Chong throw together this band in their 1978 vehicle *Up in Smoke*, one of the seemingly endless series of dope-oriented movies they made in the 70s and 80s. They appear in a battle of the bands against real L.A. punkers, The Dils, The Whores, and The Berlin Brats, at a real L.A. punk club, The Roxy. In reality, C and C recorded the song "Earache My Eye" by "Alice Bowie" four years earlier, for their *Cheech and Chong's Wedding Album*, where it rose to #9 on the U.S. *Billboard* charts.

Anthony Stillman (Tommy Chong) (r) and Pedro DePacas (Cheech Marin) of Alice Bowie

ALIEN AUTOPSY—From the movie *Ghost World* (2001). A passing guy (Brett Gilbert) handing out flyers for an alternative rock show says he's in this band, to the disdain of main character Enid (Thora Birch). See also **Blueshammer; Fred Chatman; Vanilla, Jade, and Ebony**.

ALLIGATOR SHOES—A band whose schtick was that they all wore alligator shoes. They were mentioned in the "Guitarmageddon" (10/27/02) episode of somewhat animated show *Home Movies*. Coach McGuirk (voiced by H. Jon Benjamin) was a roadie for this band in his previous, pre-show existence. Well, not really a roadie. See, they never went on the road, so Coach McGuirk said he was more of a "helpie." See also **Brendon Poppins and the Chimminy Sweeps; Scäb**.

ALPHIE AND BIBI—Sweet, innocent folkie duo who would have all-American good looks if they weren't from Moosejaw, Canada. They play the World-Vision Song Festival in the craptacular spectacle that is the 1980 movie *The Apple*. In fact, the word "craptacle" was invented to describe it. Just now. Set in the terrifying future of 1994, where cars look suspiciously like 1960s station wagons with bubble domes haphazardly stuck on them, Bibi Phillips (Catherine Mary Stewart) is quickly corrupted by evil rock Svengali Mr. Boogalow (Vladek Sheybal) and turned into a glam rock bitch queen. But suspicious Alphie (George Gilmore) refuses to sell out and sign up, and so hits skid row, getting beat up and worked over by Boogalow's goons. Alphie eventually gets Bibi away from Mr. Boogalow, but not before Boogalow has crossed that oh-so-fine line from evil record company exec to 1984-style world dictator. He hunts them down in their hippie park commune and is ready to exterminate the lot of them, when the movie climaxes in a twist so bizarre it leaves not a jaw undropped. Oh, all right: GOD

HIMSELF COMES DOWN TO EARTH IN A COSMIC CADILLAC and saves Alphie, Bibi, and their hippie pals. Boogalow is revealed as Satan himself, and God pretty much GIVES UP ON PLANET EARTH, taking the hippies to start over on some other planet! See also **Dandi and Pandi**.

AMAZING MARVIN SUGGS AND HIS MUPPAPHONE, THE— From the Rita Moreno–hosted episode (10/09/76) of *The Muppet Show*. Voiced by Frank Oz with an Italian accent, this artiste "plays" "Lady of Spain" by hitting the tribble-shaped muppets (some named Lucy, Bernard, Marvin) with mallets as they go "ow" in key (noises of pain by Jim Henson and Jerry Nelson). Payback's a bitch, though, as a giant hammer slugs Suggs at the finale. You can find the song on *The Muppet Show Album* (1977) and the CD *Muppet Hits* (1993). The Muppaphone gag is awfully similar to Arthur Ewing and His Musical Mice, from *Monty Python's Flying Circus*. Marvin Suggs also shows up again in the Steve Martin–hosted episode (10/31/77) with a new act as Marvin Suggs and His All-Food Glee Club, which sings "Yes, We Have No Bananas." See also **Dr. Teeth and the Electric Mayhem; Mahna Mahna and the Two Snowths; Miss Piggy; Rowlf the Dog; Wayne and Wanda**.

A MEN, THE— From the episode "Reborn to Be Wild" (11/09/03) of the FOX show *King of the Hill*. They're an unseen Christian rock act playing the local Messiah Fest. Their roadie is Jessie (voiced by KISS frontman Gene Simmons!), who has the Ten Commandments tattooed on his back. See also **The Bluegrass Brothers; Cane and the Stubborn Stains; The Dale Gribble Bluegrass Experience; 4 Skore; The Harris Twins; John Redcorn and Big Mountain Fudge Cake; Pastor K; Pimp Franklin**.

AND AND AND— From *The Commitments* (1991). Crappy Irish New Wave wedding band trio featuring Ray (Philip Bredin) and future Commitments members Derek Scully (Kenneth McCluskey) and Outspan Foster (Glen Hansard). The threesome was considering a name change (Ray wanted to put an exclamation point after the second "and" because "it'd look deadly on the posters"), when Scully and Foster ran into Jimmy Rabbitte (Robert Arkins) at a wedding. He convinced them to ditch Ray and form the nucleus of The Commitments. See also **The Commitments**.

ANDROMEDA— Future rock band from the "Space Rockers" episode (02/21/80) of that shiny-spandexed glimpse of the future, *Buck Rogers in the 25th Century*. Their evil manager, Lars Mangros (Jerry Orbach), tries to put a mind control signal in their music during a concert broadcast from Musicworld to cause youth to riot everywhere. One may safely assume Buck (Gil Gerard) saves the day. Lineup: Karana (Nancy Frangione), Joanna (Judy Landers), and Cirus (Leonard Lightfoot).

ANGST, AGNUS— Comedienne Lily Tomlin's one-woman show, *The Search for Signs of Intelligent Life in the Universe* (co-written with Jane Wagner) first opened on Broadway in 1985, a showcase for her many and varied characters, including this fifteen-year-old punk-rock harridan, screeching at an unfair world that just stole her parakeet. Her parents change the locks on her, she clashes with her grandparents, and she rants onstage at the Unclub, riffing on a line she read in G. Gordon Liddy's book *Will*. The show was turned into a book in 1986 and finally into a film in 1991. See also **Purvis Hawkins; Linnea Reese; Tommy Velour**.

ANNE, ELIZABETH— Never-seen 60s female singer in *That Thing You Do* (1996). She's performing at Boss

Vic Koss the Mattress King's (Kevin Pollack) rock and roll show at the Pittsburgh Orpheum, which opens with a less-than-stellar performance by The Wonders. But you never actually SEE her or anything, her name is just briefly glimpsed on the marquee. See also **Blue Spot Trio; The Chantrellines; Diane Dane; The Echoes; Freddy Fredrickson; The G Men; The Heardsmen; The Hollyhocks; Jon D and the Walkers; Legends of Brass; Marilyn Lovell and the Geminis; The Norm Wooster Singers; Del Paxton; The Saturn 5; The Tempos; The Trends; Two Eriks; The Vicksburgs; The Wonders**.

ANN-MARGROCK—The prehistoric cartoon version of the vivacious and pneumatic Ann-Margret from the "Ann-Margrock Presents" episode (09/19/63) of *The Flintstones*. The cartoon version is a singer rather than an actress/singer. Ann-Margret, naturally, was the voice of Ann-Margrock. See also **The Beau Brummelstones; Jimmy Darrock; The Flintstone Canaries; "Hot Lips" Hannigan; Hi-Fye; Pebbles and Bamm-Bamm; Rock Roll**.

ANTIMATTER—From the "Amazon Hot Wax" episode (02/16/79) of TV show *Wonder Woman*. A pop-rock band on the Phoenix Records label, they help Diana Prince (Lynda Carter) decipher clues hidden in songs and an album cover (à la The Beatles) that find missing-presumed-dead Phoenix folkie Billy Dero. Lineup: Jerry (Danil Torppe), Anton (real rocker Rick Springfield), and Kim (Michael Botts). *TRIVIA TIME!* Rick Springfield also played fake rocker James Roberts in *Hard to Hold*. See also **Billy Dero; Jeff and Barbi Gordon; Lane Kinkaid; Kathy Meadows; Hamlin Rule**.

APOLLONIA—See **The Kid**.

ARCHIES, THE—The Monkees were fake band Colum-

buses, Edisons, and Henry Fords. They had sailed to the new world and proven you could successfully mass market youth rebellion. They also established the template: wacky adventures, zany humor, and three minutes of pure bubblegum pop. Now it was time to send in the clones. Enter The Archies. Filmation Associates, the animation company, had great success turning superhero comic book characters into cheap kids' programs. So why not non-superhero comic book character Archie Andrews, who had been around since the 40s? Sure, but how do you kick it up a notch? Norm Prescott of Filmation, a former radio DJ, knew Don Kirshner, who was behind The Monkees. Bingo, Archie and his pals were given a garage band. Archibald "Archie" Andrews was the band's leader and played guitar and sang. "Jughead" Jones played drums, Reginald "Reggie" Mantle played guitar, Veronica Lodge and Elizabeth "Betty" Cooper played keyboards and tambourine, respectively. On September 14, 1968, CBS Saturday morning kids program *The Archie Show* debuted to great success. It would expand to an hour the next year, becoming *The Archie Comedy Hour* and then *Archie's Fun House*, Don Kirshner provided the synergy: four albums of pure pop—*Everything's Archie* (1969), *Jingle Jangle* (1970), *Sunshine* (1970), and *This Is Love* (1971). The Archies' single "Sugar, Sugar" took the #1 slot in 1969 for four weeks. An oh-so-appropriate song title for the king of bubblegum groups. The team behind the music consisted of producer Jeff Barry and unsung bubblegum hero Ron Dante, who did the male vocals. Jeanie Thomas did the female vocals until she was replaced by Toni Wine. Barry and Andy Kim (songwriter and backing vocalist) co-wrote "Sugar, Sugar." Another *Archie* comic-book character, spunky teen witch Sabrina, got her own spinoff shows, *Sabrina and the Groovie Goolies* and *Sabrina, the Teenage Witch*. See also **The Groovie Goolies**.

ABSOLUTELY THE BEST
OF THE ARCHIES
(2001, VARÈSE SARABANDE)

THE ARCHIES' ALBUMS have been sliced and diced into best of and greatest hits collections almost since the group began. You find them in bargain bins and truck stops. One clue to the quality therein—do Archie and Co. actually appear on the cover? If not, avoid, it's probably a cheap, poor-quality compilation thrown together strictly to milk money from chumps like you. However, if they could afford to pay Archie Comics to put Archie on the cover, then obviously some thought went into it. So it is with the 2001 Varèse Sarabande compilation, *Absolutely the Best of The Archies*. This is one of the best Archies compilations out there, though fans may think sixteen tracks aren't enough, especially since The Archies' songs are typically shorter than three minutes. Which works in The Archies' favor—their sunny, bubblegum pop doesn't wear out its welcome. Producer Jeff Barry, who also wrote or cowrote most of the band's songs, knew how to keep the songs engaging all the way through, and then when to end them, a trait sorely lacking these days. All the band's hits are here, with good sound quality, including "Sugar, Sugar," "Jingle Jangle," "Bang-Shang-A-Lang," and "Who's Your Baby." One of the more interesting omissions, however, is "Seventeen Ain't Young," a righteous, non-PC paean to underage lust, er love. That song was probably easy to eliminate. "Over and Over" shamelessly cribs from "Little Bit O' Soul" by fellow bubblegummers The Music Explosion. If the choogling bass line of "Get on the Line" doesn't get your foot tapping, then there's something wrong with you. In fact, if Ron Dante's pure sunshine vocals and Barry's simple catchy songwriting can't get you to at least crack a smile, call your doctor, you may be dead.

ARCOLA, CHARLES "CHACHI"—The 1982–83 *Happy Days* spinoff *Joanie Loves Chachi* bombed bad. But the real bombshell was that the band around whose struggles the show was based HAD NO NAME! It never came up! Direct quote from Robert Pierce, who played Bingo, the drummer, confirms this: "I don't have a clue what we called ourselves!" It's probably a sly homage to its parent sitcom, in which the band Richie, Ralph, and Potsie were in never got a name, either. Darn irritating, isn't it? Lineup: Erin Moran played Joanie Cunningham, Scott Baio played Charles "Chachi" Arcola, Derrel Maury played Chachi's cousin Mario, and Winifred Freedman played Annette, another cousin of Chachi's. Scott Baio tried to capitalize on the show, releasing the 1982 album *The Boys Are Out Tonight* which limped to # 181 on the charts.

ARIEL—A gloomy singer attempting a comeback in the "Ariel's Comeback" skit on the 06/21/87 episode of *The Tracy Ullman Show*. Her big hit was titled "Slit My Wrists." And she actually did that the day it was released. Unfortunately, after her comeback, Ariel (Tracey Ullman) falls in love with a nice guy (show regular Sam McMurray) and only writes and sings upbeat songs that totally alienate her depressed female fanbase. She even has his baby! See also **Gulliver Dark**; **Kristy Muldoon**; **The Nice Neighbors**.

ARMADA—A crappy garage band trio with delusions of adequacy in several skits of the genius Canadian sketch comedy series, *The Kids in the Hall* (1989–94). Usually the drummer and bassist would gang up on the leader and browbeat him into things like renaming the band Rod Torfulson's Armada Featuring Herman Menderchuck, or adding backup singers and renaming the band Rod Torfulson's Armada Featuring Herman Menderchuk and the Dudettes. They had the songs "Camera Man" and

"She Watches," but "Trampoline Girl" was their, um, "hit." In the final *Kids in the Hall* episode (01/16/95) (where they've renamed themselves The New Rod Torfulson's Armada Featuring Herman Menderchuck), Chris Robinson of real band The Black Crowes plays a rock and roll angel who shows them their future, still practicing in the same damn garage when they're all wheezing seniors. Lineup: Rod Torfulson (Bruce McCulloch) on drums, Herman Menderchuck (Mark McKinney) on bass, and an unnamed Kevin McDonald on guitar and vocals. See also **Cancer Boy; Death Lurks; Mississippi Gary; The Noodles; Tammy**.

ARPEGGIO, VIC—Sax-playing private investigator who appeared in two extended skits, both black-and-white film-noir-ish detective movie parodies, on sketch comedy series *SCTV*. In "Vic Arpeggio Private Investigator" (02/11/83) set in 1960, Vic explains how he got fired from real Pittsburgh band The Joe Negri Trio when someone planted reefer in his locker, which is especially bad when you consider that Joe Negri was a regular on *Mister Roger's Neighborhood*. In "Vic Arpeggio Private Investigator: Black Like Vic" (03/13/84), Vic goes undercover in blackface as a butler in the Deep South. Joe Flaherty was Vic Hedges as Vic Arpeggio. See also **Big Momma; 5 Neat Guys; Happiness Unlimited; The Happy Wanderers; Lola Heatherton; The Lemon Twins; Linsk Minyk; Tom Munroe; The Queenhaters; The Ramblers; The Recess Monkeys; Russ Riley; Jackie Rogers Jr.; Jackie Rogers Sr.; Speed of Light; Dusty Towne; The Wally Hung Trio**.

ARTHUR EWING AND HIS MUSICAL MICE—From the "Sex and Violence" episode (10/12/69) of now-legendary BBC sketch show *Monty Python's Flying Circus*. This madman (Terry Jones) has trained mice to squeak at selected musical pitches, so that they can squeak tunes when "played" in the proper order. Unfortunately for the mice, "playing" means "hitting with large wooden mallets." He's allegedly playing "The Bells of St. Mary's," but it sounds uncannily like someone killing mice with a mallet. He is roundly castigated by the horrified audience and hauled off by the floor manager. This gag was later duplicated by the Muppets for The Amazing Marvin Suggs and his Muppaphone. See also **Bolton Choral Society; Johann Gambolputty de von Ausfern-schplenden-schlitter-crasscrenbon-fried-digger-dingle-dangle-dongle-dungle-burstein-von-knacker-thrasher-apple-banger-horowitz-ticolensic-grander-knotty-spelltinkle-grandlich-grumblemeyer-spelterwasser-kurstlich-himbleeisen-bahnwagen-gutenabend-bitte-ein-nürnburger-bratwustle-gerspurten-mitz-weimache-luber-hundsfut-gumberaber-shönendanker-kalbsfleisch-mittler-aucher von Hautkopft of Ulm; The Herman Rodriguez Four; The Hunlets; Jackie Charlton and the Tonettes; Arthur "Two Sheds" Jackson; Not Noel Coward; Not Tony Bennett; Rachel Toovey Bicycle Choir; Inspector Jean-Paul Zatapathique**.

ARTHUR HODGESON AND THE KNEECAPS—One of the other musical groups managed by The Rutles' manager Leggy Mountbatten (Terence Bayler) in the 60s, according to the 1978 TV mockumentary, *All You Need Is Cash*. See also **Les Garçons de la Plage; The Machismo Brothers; Ruttling Orange Peel; Punk Floyd; Blind Lemon Pye; The Rutles**.

AUDEN—Former Velvet Underground member Lou Reed (!) played this ultrareclusive rock star who hasn't left his house in years, in the underrated 1983 comedy *Get Crazy*. He finally leaves to play the big

New Year Eve's concert but arrives too late. Once there, he sings anyway ("Little Sister") to the delight of one fan. See also **King Blues; Nada; Reggie Wanker.**

AUTOBAHN — From the 1998 Coen Brothers movie *The Big Lebowski.* The three German nihilists (played by Peter Stormare, Torsten Voges, and Red Hot Chili Peppers bassist Flea) were said to have been in this techno-pop band, an obvious Kraftwerk rip-off. They had one album in the late 70s, called *nagelbett*, which is German for "bed of nails."

AVENUE GHETTO STREET BOYS, THE — From the "Something You Can Do with Your Finger" episode (07/12/00) of Comedy Central animated show *South Park.* This is the boy band that superceded The Ghetto Avenue Boys. After all, The Ghetto Avenue Boys were getting long in the tooth. One of them was already nineteen, for crying out loud! See also **Faith + 1; Fingerbang; Getting Gay with Kids; The Ghetto Avenue Boys; Jerome "Chef" McElroy; MOOP; Raging Pussies; Reach for the Skyler; Sanctified; Sisters of Mercy Hold No Pain Against the Dark Lord; Timmy! and the Lords of the Underworld; Trinity.**

AVERAGE JOE BAND, THE — In the "Cold Slither" episode (12/02/85) of jingoistic Reagan fantasy cartoon show *G.I. Joe*, terrorist group COBRA finances the rock band Cold Slither, putting hypnotic subliminal messages in their songs. The G.I. Joe team naturally foils their evil scheme, which climaxes midway through a Cold Slither concert. To pacify the freed and now confused crowd, the multitalented Joes grab the instruments and do an impromptu song (the show's theme music), introducing themselves as The Average Joe Band. See as **Cold Slither.**

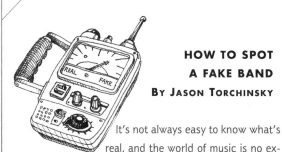

HOW TO SPOT A FAKE BAND
By Jason Torchinsky

It's not always easy to know what's real, and the world of music is no exception. Fake bands abound, and it is a worthwhile skill for anyone to be able to discern what is genuine and what is a clever pastiche. While a listing of all known fake bands could fill a book (such as the one you're holding), there are other methods for determining a band's authenticity. Ask yourself the following questions about a given band. If you can answer yes to all of them, the band is likely fake.

1. Is the band animated, or perhaps made of clay?

2. Are all the band's songs about hamburgers, or some other commercially available product?

3. Is the band's manager unabashedly evil? Warning signs: cackling, hand-rubbing, suddenly whipping around and acting all innocent when you enter the room.

4. Are one or more of the band members animals, or perhaps aliens?

5. Does the group tour and/or perform with an animal mascot wearing a trademark garment, like a hat or an ascot?

6. If the group has an animal, is it blessed with the power of speech?

7. Are all the members of the band well-known television or movie actors?

(continued)

8. Are you sure?

9. Does the band have matching uniforms whose cost is inconsistent with the band's disposable income?

10. Are the band members all over the age of forty and yet playing to a crowd of screaming, adoring teenagers?

11. Is the band utilizing pyrotechnics in their stage show even though it's only a high school dance?

12. Is Christopher Guest or Harry Shearer in the band?

13. Does the band solve crimes in addition to playing gigs?

14. Are they a teenage garage band with an expensive, professionally custom-painted touring van?

15. Did you make up the band just now?

B-RABBIT — Or Bunny Rabbit aka Rabbit. Controversial rapper Eminem plays poor white-trash rapper wannabe Jimmy "Rabbit" Smith Jr. in the semi-autobiographical movie *8 Mile* (2002) set in 1995 Detroit. He struggles for self-respect and a way out of grinding, GRINDING, GRINDING poverty at the weekly rap contest at The Shelter, hosted by his much-dreadlocked buddy and cheerleader, Future (Mekhi Phifer). After completely choking, he spends the next week watching his life slide downhill as he has to move back into his pathetic mom's (a completely unrecognizable Kim Basinger) trailer home. He has to put up with her Skynyrd-loving loser boyfriend who's no older than

he is, a dying car, a dead-end job in the exciting field of metal stamping, a pissed-off boss who can't wait to fire him, and run-ins with The Free World—successful rappers, jerks, and bullies. It all comes boiling back up at the next week's contest, as he cleverly defeats the competition by becoming the self-deprecating rapper! Which is practically apostasy in the brag, boast, and dis world of rap. How can your opponent attack you when you use all his best insults yourself, on yourself?! This movie's great triumph is to be enjoyable AND believable, despite having such hack touchstones as a "battle of the bands" with a rival "evil band" and the protagonist succeeding despite poor odds and the rivals' dirty tricks. How'd they do it? Just like rap, ya gots to keep it real. Gritty, in-yo'-face street life and poverty are shoved in your every orifice constantly. Detroit looks like a war zone and all the characters like refugees. Plus, the contest raps are actually clever, funny, and entertaining. If you learn one thing from this movie, it's stay the hell out of Detroit. See also **The Free World**.

B-RAD — Brad Gluckman (Jamie Kennedy) is a white-bread and white-bred wannabe rapper from Malibu, California, in the 2003 comedy *Malibu's Most Wanted*. His dad is trying to run for governor and doesn't need the embarrassment of his boy attempting to emulate black street culture. Frankly, you don't, either. So, dad (Ryan O'Neal) hires some black gangsta goons to kidnap his son in an attempt to scare B-Rad straight. Or, rather scare him white again.

BABY DOLL AND THE CRYSTALS — See **The Five Heartbeats**.

BABY JOEY — See **Generation O!**

BAD BILLY AND THE BAIL JUMPERS — From the 1992 action flick *Under Siege*. This rock band is really a cover for a team of CIA mercenaries gone bad—they play a show onboard the USS *Missouri* and take it over to secure the nukes for their own nefarious purposes. Possibly nuking something. Bad Billy himself is William Stranix (Tommy Lee Jones). It's up to Steven Seagal to kick all their asses. Or is it Jean-Claude Van Damme? No, no, it was Seagal. The rest of the band/team were played by Gene Barge, Anthony G. Brown, Hiram Bullock, Christopher Alan Cameron, Richard Davis, Tad Robinson, and Wendall Wayne Stewart.

William Stranix (Tommy Lee Jones) of Bad Billy and the Bail Jumpers

BAD NEWS—"The worst heavy metal band in the world" from the British TV show *The Comic Strip Presents*. They appeared in the episodes "Bad News Tour" (01/24/83) and "More Bad News" (02/27/88). In the first episode, this strictly small-time metal band can barely draw a crowd as they are the inexplicable subject of some documentary filmmakers. In the second, the band is acrimoniously reunited after five years to record, and climaxes with their brief performance at the real Monsters of Rock festival at Castle Donington. They also had a U.S. album, *Bad News*, on Rhino Records in 1989, which collected their British material, including their jaw-droppingly bad version of Queen's "Bohemian Rhapsody." Lineup: egomaniac Vim Fuego whose real name is Alan Metcalfe (Adrian Edmondson) on lead guitar and vocals, appallingly dim Den

Dennis (Nigel Planer) on rhythm guitar, appallingly pathetic Colin Grigson (Rik Mayall) on bass, and space case "Spider" Webb (Peter Richardson) on drums.

BADDERLY, FERN—From the "Too Many Girls" episode (12/19/66) of *The Monkees*. She's the daughter of crazy gypsy lady Mrs. Badderly (Reta Shaw) who flimflams the band to get Davy hooked up with her daughter Fern (Kelly Jean Peters) as her ticket into showbiz. She strong-arms Davy and Fern into a singing team and puts them on a TV amateur hour hosted by Mr. Hack (Jeff Debenning). The Monkees do everything they can to sabotage the show and break Davy and Fern up to get Davy back. Mike Nesmith competes disguised as hillbilly singer Billy Roy Hodstetter singing a sped-up version of "Different Drum." See also **Irene Chomsky; The Foreign Agents; The Four Martians; The Four Swine; Honey and the Bear; The Jolly Green Giants (I); Lester Crabtree and the Three Crabs; Sven Helstrom and the Swedish Rhythm Kings; The Swinging Android; The West Minstrel Abbies**.

BAILEY, BOBBY—Old-time 50s rock and roller from the "Old Meets New" episode (11/15/86) of cartoon *Jem!* He doesn't appreciate what modern rockers Jem and the Holograms have done to his song "Rock and Roll Forever." But they become friends anyway, especially when the gals' nemesis, Eric Raymond (voiced by Charles Adler), tries to have Bailey's building torn down. Bailey and the band team up to sing "Let's Not Forget the Past." See also **The Ben Tiller Orchestra; Jem and the Holograms; The Limp Lizards; The Misfits, The Stingers; The Tapps Tucker Quartet**.

BALTIMORE, BILLY—Mysteriously reclusive (or maybe just dead) former legend of the electric guitar in the "The Legendary Billy B." episode (03/31/87) of

HBO's R-rated *Twilight Zone* ripoff, *The Hitch-hiker*. Nosy journalist Jane (Kirstie Alley) breaks into Billy's estate to find out the truth—which is that Billy is a brain-dead freak-show exhibit, and that his handlers REALLY don't like nosy journalists. *TRIVIA TIME!* Andy Summers of real band The Police composed the music, and also had a role as Hodie, the photographer.

BANANA CONVENTION, THE—Greg Brady (Barry Williams) joins this teen garage band in the "Where There's Smoke" episode (01/08/71) of 70s ur-sitcom *The Brady Bunch*. It sparks one of the most serious crises to ever hit the Brady family, as Greg is caught SMOKING, a habit he gets talked into by his bandmates. Confronted by his stern but loving parents, he promises to quit, but later a pack of the dreaded weed falls out of his jacket—which he borrowed from the band's drummer (and smoker) Tommy Johnson (Craig Hundley). *TRIVIA TIME!* The song that Greg writes for the band, "Till I Met You," really was composed by Barry Williams. Alas, it's not hard rock enough for the band, and neither is Greg. See also **The Brady Kids; The Brady Six; Johnny Bravo; Phlegm; The Silver Platters**.

BANANA SPLITS, THE—Bubblegum rockers Fleegle (dog, guitar), Bingo (gorilla, drums), Drooper (lion, guitar), and Snorky (elephant, keyboard) hosted their own NBC Saturday morning kids show, *The Banana Splits Adventure Hour* (1968–70). Four likely very, very sweaty men in full-body animal suits ran around a lot, made goofy jokes, constantly slammed into each other and fell down, and frequently stopped to introduce a hodgepodge of cartoons and live action showlets. Try to imagine a lobotomized Monkees on nitrous. They were occasionally threatened by a gang of tough little girls called the Sour Grapes. They would also occasionally tool around in kick-ass, six-wheeled dune buggies, not to mention

rocking out to their own brand of sunny bubblegum psychedelia. They released one album, *We're the Banana Splits* (1968), on Decca. But there were also a pair of EPs only obtainable by saving and sending in cereal box tops (appropriate, as the show was sponsored by Kellogg's), as well as a slew of other, now highly collectible merchandise. Their goofy voices were done by some of the kings of cartoon voices: Paul Winchell (Tigger, Gargamel) voiced Fleegle; Daws Butler (Huckleberry Hound, Yogi Bear) voiced Bingo, Allan Melvin (Magilla Gorilla) voiced Drooper, and Don Messick (Scooby-Doo, Bamm-Bamm) voiced Snorky. Between them these guys have done different cartoon voices more times than you've had hot dinners! Or even thought about having hot dinners! But let us not forget the poor forgotten shlubs in the suits: Jeffrey Brock (Fleegle), Terence Henry (Bingo), Dan Owen (Drooper), and Jay Larrimore (Snorky). *TRIVIA TIME!* While the characters were invented by Hanna-Barbera (which made the show), the mascots-meet-Sgt.-Pepper-style costumes were designed by the brothers Sid and Marty Krofft, who would later make mascot suit–type psychedelic kids shows an art form.

WE'RE THE BANANA SPLITS
(1968, DECCA)

THE BANANA SPLITS made some of the weaker bubblegum of the bubblegum era, alas. Their single album, *We're the Banana Splits*, yielded not a single hit for the band. Weak songwriting and a lack of hooks and catchy melodies lurk behind its cheery veneer. The musicianship is fine, and the singer is trying so hard you worry he's going to hurt himself, but there's only so much you can do with a poorly written song. Take the title song, an attempt at a "(Theme from) The Monkees"-type song. It starts off on the wrong foot with an annoying chirping organ that won't shut up, and stays on the wrong foot, lurching along with a club-footed melody, a hookless chorus, a confusing rhyming scheme, a creepy flute solo, and sub par lyrics, even for this group—"Hello and good morning, we're here to give you a chuckle-loo. We're giving you warning, sit back and loosen your buckle." Songwriting tip: if you're going to rhyme "chuckle" with "buckle" don't add "loo" to the end of "chuckle," 'cause then they don't RHYME ANYMORE! The best song is the opening track, their TV-show theme, "The Tra La Song," which kicks pop-rock ass, and is the required soundtrack for any six-wheeled dune buggy ride you might go on. Unfortunately, it's only ninety seconds long, which leaves a whole lot of filler on this album to wade through. One of the more listenable numbers is the uptempo R&B jam "Doin' the Banana," which has a heavy James Brown feel, as whichever Split is singing is seriously feeling the groove—"ow!" Their tribute to fat chicks, "Two-Ton Tessie" might raise a few eyebrows these days. Or roll a few eyes, especially with its pseudo–Roaring Twenties instrumentation. In the same vein is the instrumental "Toy Piano Melody" a rinky-tink piece of ricky-ticky tinkling faux twenties jazz/ragtime that just makes you want to take an ax to the toy piano already. The album's closer "Don't Go Away—Go Go Girl" sounds like The Small Faces on anti-depressants, starting off with a promising cool period organ, which is then forced to smile a big cheesy grin and caper like an organ grinder's monkey. The most interesting things about this album are its odd hippie touches, like the fuzzed-out guitar on "I'm Gonna Find Me a Cave" or the droning sitar in "In New Orleans." In fact, "In New Orleans" doesn't feel like it should be on a kids' record at all. With the line "If you can't find it in New Orleans, well it ain't nowhere to be found" and its trippy, spaced-out blues feel, they manage to imply a seedy unwholesomeness that rivals the classic tune "House of the Rising Sun." Whereas The Archies expressed their fun and happy viewpoint with clean production focusing on the guitar, The Splits' messy, cluttered, everything-but-the-kitchen-sink production is more obsessed with the organ. That, combined with some of the overreaching histrionics of the singer gives the album a crazed, maddening, merry-go-round quality that makes you think the hippies the producers hired to play and sing on this album couldn't wait to get back to the Spahn ranch.

BANNER, JOHNNY—Real rocker Roy Orbison starred as this singer/Confederate spy with a gun in his guitar in the unlikely movie *The Fastest Guitar Alive* (1967). Banner posed as a singer in a plot to heist a shipment of Yankee gold. *TRIVIA TIME!* The movie also featured a small role by Domingo Samudio, better known as Sam the Sham of "Woolly Bully" fame.

BARBIE AND THE ROCKERS—When Jem and the Holograms hit the airwaves (1985), with matching dolls by rival Hasbro, the Barbie department at Mattel must have hit the panic button. Why else turn out the crappy, failed, *Jem!*-like animated pilot *Barbie and the Rockers: Out of This World* (1987)? Get this, Barbie (voiced by Sharon Lewis) and her band go to a SPACE STATION to sing for WORLD PEACE. Talk about overreaching! It also must have been a stretch to have to create new characters to be Barbie's bandmates. Sure, there's good old reliable Ken, but after that, they had to invent Dana, Dee Dee, Diva, and Derek out of whole cloth. Perhaps most damning is that this animated . . . thing . . . hired one of the art directors from *Jem!* Naturally, a *Barbie and the Rockers* version of Barbie, complete with cassette, was released. Truth be told, though, Mattel has issued Barbie records for years, before and after. Their long wait to try an animated show could be ascribed to the fact that Barbie has zero personality. See also **Jem and the Holograms**.

BARBUSTERS, THE — Hard-rockin' Cleveland bar band from the 1987 movie *Light of Day*. Real rocker Joan Jett and *Family Ties'* Michael J. Fox play working-class siblings Joe and Patti Rasnick, the heart of the band. Joe tries to keep the family together, despite Patti's and their mom's animosity. Things fall apart when Mom gets cancer and Joe kicks Patti's boyfriend out of the band and Patti leaves to sing for metal band The Hunzz. But the band, which includes Spïnal Tapper Michael McKean, comes back together to rock out at the end. *TRIVIA TIME!* Bruce Springsteen wrote the title track. Trent Reznor of Nine Inch Nails has a small role here in a band called The Problems!

BARLOW, EDUARDO — Jazz composer who passed away of leukemia at age fifty-six in a brief and utterly irrelevant news story at the very beginning of *The Dead Pool* (1988). He was best known for his compositions "Just for You" and "Midnight Hearts." Don't waste your time with this entry, go to the entry for **Johnny Squares** from the same movie.

BARNACLE BILL AND THE SEVEN SEAS — See **The Bird Brains**.

BARRY, BUZZ — At the beginning of his career, real singer and second-string teen idol Jimmy Darren played this rocker in the "April Fool" episode (04/01/59) of *The Donna Reed Show*. Naturally, all the teen girls have got their knickers in knots over his upcoming show. But sitcom teen Mary Stone (Shelley Fabares) gets hers twisted extra tight when Barry gets the measles on show night and is brought to her doctor dad's (Carl Betz) house for treatment. *TRIVIA TIME!* Darren also appeared on *The Flintstones* as Jimmy Darrock, and on *Star Trek: Deep Space Nine* as hologram Sinatra-wannabe Vic Fontaine. See also **Jimmy Darrock; Vic Fontaine**.

BARRY JIVE AND THE UPTOWN FIVE — From the 2000 movie *High Fidelity*, based on Nick Hornby's 1995 novel of the same name. Championship Vinyl record-store clerk and obnoxious music snob Barry (Jack Black) forms this band when a long-haired, metal-freak-lookin' guy (Daniel Lee Smith) finally responds to his ancient flyer at the store. They play The Kinky Wizards' EP release party, thrown by Barry's boss, Rob Gordon (John Cusack). Rob is so sure they're going to suck that he tries to bribe Barry not to play the show. That failing, he tries to get The Kinky Wizards not to show up. That failing, he surrenders and intros the band as Sonic Death Monkey (their original name) only to learn from Barry, "We're no longer called Sonic Death Monkey. We're on the verge of becoming Kathleen Turner Overdrive, but just for tonight, we are Barry Jive and the Uptown Five." Barry then launches into an impressively soulful rendition of Marvin Gaye's "Let's Get It On," which is Rob and his girlfriend's "our song" (and on the soundtrack album). See also **Marie deSalle; The Kinky Wizards; Licorice Comfits**.

Barry (Jack Black) of Barry Jive and the Uptown Five

BC-52S, THE — From *The Flintstones* (1994), a strange, live-action version of the modern Stone Age cartoon family. Real band The B-52s appear at a club in prehistoric drag as this band, covering the song "The Bedrock Twitch" by Rock Roll from the original series. Interestingly, earlier in the movie we see Fred (John Goodman) and Barney (Rick Moranis) rocking out to the car radio on the drive home to the original version of the song from the TV show ("The Twitch" episode, 10/12/62), presented as though it were an oldie-goldie! See also **Mick Jagged and the Stones.**

BE SHARPS, THE — Homer's barbershop quartet in the "Homer's Barbershop Quartet" (9/30/93) episode of *The Simpsons.* They hit the charts in the summer of 1985 and win a Grammy with the song "Baby on Board," and manage to release two albums (*Meet the Be Sharps* and *Bigger than Jesus*) before breaking up due to group tensions, Barney's new Japanese conceptual-artist girlfriend, and the evergreen "creative differences." The original lineup was Homer Simpson, Principal Seymour Skinner, Apu Nahasapeemapetilon, and Police Chief Clancy Wiggum. But their manager Nigel made them ditch Wiggum and change Apu's name, so the lineup that hit the big time was Homer Simpson, Principal Seymour Skinner, Barney Gumble and Apu D'Beaumarchais. See also **The Beach Boys Experience; Johnny Bobby; Johnny Calhoun; Captain Bart and the Tequila Mockingbirds; The Crazy Old Man Singers; Cyanide; Gulliver Dark; Ferl Dixon and His Second Helping Boys; Funky C Funky Do; Garfunkel, Messina, Oates, and Lisa; Hooray for Everything; Kovenant; Krusty and the Krums; The Larry Davis Experience; Little Timmy and the Shebangs; Loggins and Oates; Lurleen Lumpkin; M.C. Safety and the Caution Crew; Melvin and the Squirrels; "Bleeding Gums" Murphy; The Party Posse; The Rappin' Rabbis; Red Breem and His Band of Some Esteem; The Satin Knights; The Steve Sax Trio; Testament; Blind**

Willie Witherspoon; The Ya-Hoo Recovering Alcoholic Jug Band; Yodelin' Zeke.

THE SIMPSONS: SONGS IN THE KEY OF SPRINGFIELD
(1997, RHINO RECORDS)

THIS CD FELT long overdue upon its release in 1997. The show's previous musical output was 1990's self-indulgent *The Simpsons Sing the Blues*, which featured the cast singing in character, but no music actually from the show. Seven years later, this album gave the fans what they wanted, in spades. The show's musical highlights are neatly strung together here as Alf Clausen, *The Simpsons* unsung musical arranger and composer is slowly revealed as the genius and jack-of-all-styles he is. The album is jam-packed with good stuff. You get *The Simpsons* theme played more than a half dozen different ways, from Australian, spooky, Latin, Big Band, Renaissance, to homages of the themes from *Hill Street Blues, Dragnet*, and *It's a Mad, Mad, Mad, Mad World*. You get guest appearances by Tony Bennett, Robert Goulet, Tito Puente. You get Lurleen Lumpkin's "Your Wife Don't Understand You" and "Bagged Me and Homer" from "Colonel Homer," as well as the full version of The Be Sharps' "Baby on Board." And all the music from Springfield's musical production of "Oh Streetcar!" Great, classic bits of musical parody and satire are present, as well as hilarious bits of the show's dialogue. Stick with this baby and its sequel, *Go Simpsonic with The Simpsons* (1999), which fills any holes left by *Songs in the Key of Springfield*, and be sure to avoid *The Yellow Album*, an even weaker in-character album put out in 1998.

BEACH BOYS EXPERIENCE, THE — In the "Today, I Am a Clown" episode (12/07/03) of late-era, not-so-good

The Simpsons, kids' show host Krusty the Clown (voiced by Dan Castellaneta) reveals he never had a bar mitzvah. So he throws himself one in a FOX TV special, *Krusty the Klown's Wet 'n' Wild Bar Mitzvah!* Playing on the special is this band of sound-alikes, singing a Jewish-themed parody of the Beach Boys song "Kokomo." Of course, the Brian Wilson–less, "Kokomo"-era Beach Boys were already their own cover band version of themselves. See also **The Be Sharps; Johnny Bobby; Johnny Calhoun; Captain Bart and the Tequila Mockingbirds; The Crazy Old Man Singers; Cyanide; Gulliver Dark; Ferl Dixon and His Second Helping Boys; Funky C Funky Do; Garfunkel, Messina, Oates, and Lisa; Hooray for Everything; Kovenant; Krusty and the Krums; The Larry Davis Experience; Little Timmy and the Shebangs; Loggins and Oates; Lurleen Lumpkin; M. C. Safety and the Caution Crew; Melvin and the Squirrels; "Bleeding Gums" Murphy; The Party Posse; The Rappin' Rabbis; Red Breem and His Band of Some Esteem; The Satin Knights; The Steve Sax Trio; Testament; Blind Willie Witherspoon; The Ya-Hoo Recovering Alcoholic Jug Band; Yodelin' Zeke.**

BEACH BUMS, THE — An obvious Beach Boys parody group from the 1974 movie *Phantom of the Paradise.* They sing "Upholstery," a spoof of all those damn Beach Boys songs about cars—"Carburetors, man—that's what it's all about." The band was played by Archie Hahn, Jeffrey Commanor, and Harold Oblong. Jeffrey Commanor sang lead on "Upholstery." *TRIVIA TIME!* This bizarre rock version of *Faust* was directed by Brian De Palma. See also **The Juicy Fruits; Phoenix; The Undead.**

BEAGLES, THE — In 1966, Total Television Productions (the company that also made cartoon *Underdog*) introduced this Beatle-esque duo of animated canines in their self-titled show. Actually, Beatle-esque is too generous. Chad and Jeremy–esque or perhaps Peter and Gordon–esque is more accurate. Stringer (voiced by Sandy Becker) and Tubby (voiced by Allen Swift) were the pooches in question, who were sent on adventures by their manager. Although they were cancelled by CBS after a year, they lasted long enough to release the album *Here Come the Beagles.* Tragically, this obscure cartoon may be lost forever, as the master negatives got ignominiously tossed.

BEARDED CLAMS, THE — Punk band that crash lands along with the rest of the passengers on an island harboring a terrorist training camp. From the 1988 shoot-'em-up spoof *Troma's War,* by Troma Films, the little studio that tried to make bad movies fun again.

BEAU BRUMMELSTONES, THE — The prehistoric version of 60s folk-rock band The Beau Brummels, in the "Shinrock-a-Go-Go" episode (12/03/65) of animated show *The Flintstones.* Then popular dance show *Shindig* and its host Jimmy O'Neill are caricatured with typical *Flintstones* naming flair as *Shinrock* and Jimmy O'Neillstone. Hanna-Barbera sticks it to teen novelty dances as Fred hurts his foot and later sits on a pin, only to have Jimmy O'Neillstone (voiced by Jimmy O'Neill) proclaim his spasms of pain the new dance crazes—"the Frantic" and "the Flintstone Flop," respectively. Meanwhile, The Beau Brummelstones play their hit "Laugh Laugh," while around them, teens contort themselves in imitation of Mr. Flintstone's pain and suffering. See also **Ann-Margrock; Jimmy Darrock; The Flintstone Canaries; "Hot Lips" Hannigan; Hi-Fye; Pebbles and Bamm-Bamm; Rock Roll.**

BEAVIS AND BUTT-HEAD — A cappella teen duo (and Bunghole recording artists) who kick-started the boy band craze with their grunted versions of classic metal tunes. Sadly, they only played part of a single Houston show before Butt-head woke up. From "The Butt-head Experience" episode (06/07/93), MTV's *Beavis and Butt-head* cartoon (1993–97). In a genius move, when these two idiots (both voiced by Mike Judge) fantasize about being metal stars, they don't even have the imagination to gift themselves with talent, ability, or an instrument, they just vocalize the riffs—dunh dunh dunh!

BEDBUGS, THE — A 60s-style rock and roll band in the Civil War? No time traveling, just please willingly suspend your disbelief. It's only goofy historical sitcom *F-Troop*, anyway. In the "That's Showbiz" episode (02/09/67), this band played acoustic instruments but got a (dubbed) electric sound. They're popular enough that huckster Corporal Agarn (Larry Storch) goes civilian to manage the band. At least temporarily. Yet another 60s insect-named Beatles spoof band, this one was played by real band The Factory Rock Quartet, which later just became The Factory. It featured Lowell George, who would go on to play with Frank Zappa's Mothers of Invention and Little Feat. Impressed with the popularity of visiting band The Bedbugs, a bunch of the Fort Courage regulars form their own band, The Termites!

BEDROCK ROCKERS, THE — Hanna-Barbera cartoon characters Pebbles Flintstone (voiced by Sally Struthers) and Bamm-Bamm Rubble (voiced by Jay North), mere infants in the original *Flintstones* show (1960–66), were aged up into teens and given their own program in 1971, *The Pebbles and Bamm-Bamm Show*. They were also given this Archies-sounding bubblegum band with their friends Moonrock Crater (voiced by Lennie Weinrib), Penny Pillar (voiced by Mitzi McCall), and Wiggy Rockstone (voiced by Gay Hartweg). Pebbles gets Bamm-

Bamm to sing lead after hearing him in the shower in "The Golden Voice" episode (10/02/71). Unfortunately, he only sings well while IN the shower. Like father, like son—this same plotline was used in "The Flintstone Canaries" episode (10/24/64) of the original series with Bamm-Bamm's father, Barney. Only it makes NO sense, as Bamm-Bamm is adopted! A couple of the band's songs are "Yabba-Dabba Doozie" and "Sunshine Man." *TRIVIA TIME!* If you know your *Flintstones*, you'll recall that Pebbles and Bamm-Bamm become famous as infant musicians in the "No Biz Like Show Biz" episode (09/17/65) of the original series. Then you'll also recall it was all a dream Fred had. See also **Mick Jadestone and the Rolling Boulders; Pebbles and Bamm-Bamm.**

BEETLETOWN PLAYERS, THE — Unseen band from a skit in the "Flattop Tony and the Purple Canoes" episode (10/10/97) of HBO's *Mr. Show*. They are credited with playing the ridiculously Beatles-derivative instrumental "Got a Good Thing Going" on Beatles-Esque Records while show stars Bob Odenkirk and David Cross flee angry feminists. The *Hard Day's Night* parody video was directed by fake director Famous Mortimer. See also **Larry Black; Livingston Brewster; Willips Brighton; Dickie Crickets; Indomitable Spirit; Kid Jersey; Kill or Be Killed; C. S. Lewis Jr.; Horace Loeb; Marilyn Monster; Norma Jean Monster; John Baptiste Philouza; Professor Murder; Puscifer; Salini; Smoosh; Old Swerdlow; Three Times One Minus One; Titannica; Sir Lloyd Wilson Webber; Wyckyd Sceptre; Daffy "Mal" Yinkleyankle.**

BEETS, THE — This rock band with generic Limey accents figured in several episodes of Nickelodeon's animated show *Doug*. The titular preteen Doug Funnie (voiced by Billy West) was a big fan. They were introduced in the "Doug Rocks" episode (09/01/91), singing "Killer Tofu." In "Doug Meets RoboBone" (06/14/92), Principal Bone won't let the band play a show at Doug's school, until Doug negotiates a deal to let Bone's yodeling oompah band also play. The band rocks out with that immortal tween anthem "I Need More Allowance." "Doug's Hot Ticket" (06/28/92) has Doug and pal Skeeter going to a Beets show (featuring the song "Shout Your Lungs Out") and ending up as temporary roadies. In 1996, the show switched to ABC, as *Brand Spanking New Doug* (later renamed *Disney's Doug*). They retooled the show slightly, aged all the characters a year, and had The Beets break up after their *Let It Beet* album in the first episode ("Doug's Last Birthday," 09/07/96). Boo! But they get back together by the time of "Quailman VII: Quaildad" (10/03/98). Lineup: Monroe Yoder (bass/vocals), Clyde "Chap" Lipman (drums), Wendy Nespot (keyboards), and Flounder (guitar).

BELLYFLOP — Talked-about-but-never-seen band in the "Too Good to be Truant" episode (10/23/99) of the animated series *Detention*. Shareena Wicket (voiced by Tara Charendoff) wants to see the band, "the ultimate in alt-rock," but has to stay late in the titular detention and the concert is sold out by the time she gets to the ticket booth (the guy before her buys the last tickets, natch).

BEN TILLER ORCHESTRA, THE — The cartoon *Jem!* really pushes it when, in the "Journey Through Time" episode (01/06/88), Jem and the Holograms travel BACK IN TIME to meet this famous 40s swing band (an obvious stand-in for the Glen Miller Orchestra). Past meets present as they team to sing "We're Makin' It Happen." In the same episode they also meet Mozart and hippie guitar legend Johnny Bendrix (a Jimi Hendrix stand-in). See also **Bobby Bailey**; **Jem and the Holograms**; **The Limp**

Lizards; **The Misfits**; **The Stingers**; **The Tapps Tucker Quartet**.

BENDRIX, JOHNNY — See **The Ben Tiller Orchestra**.

BENNETT, STONY — See **Mick Jagged and the Stones**.

BENNY — Tough, straight-to-the-point, hardball-playing S.O.B. who just happens to be a millionaire mulleted kid singer (Billy Lombardo). Benny's even hired his adoring mother (Mary Louise Wilson) to be his maid. And he smokes! He sold 22 million records in 1985, and was *Billboard*'s artist of the year. Also a client of music accountant Walter Fielding (Tom Hanks). Fielding comes to him to borrow the $200,000 he needs to buy his dream house, which quickly turns into the titular problematic nightmare of *The Money Pit* (1986). Benny probably has a last name, but it's never given. *TRIVIA TIME!* Tom Hanks would later create the fake bandstravaganza *That Thing You Do* (1996). See also **The Cheap Girls**.

BENNY AND THE BEEFEATERS — From the "I Do, I Do" episode (02/24/81) of classic sitcom *Laverne and Shirley*. This unseen band is mentioned as having married American girls to obtain U.S. citizenship to avoid harsh English taxes, which gives London (Peter Noone) and Derek (Eric Idle) of band London's Bridges the not-so-bright idea of trying to get Laverne DeFazio (Penny Marshall) and Shirley Feeney (Cindy Williams) to marry them for the same reason. See also **Lenny and the Squigtones**; **London's Bridges**.

BERKO — A singer/guitarist and the coolest employee at record store and movie *Empire Records* (1995), mainly by default, alas, as all the other employees are self-absorbed twits. Played by Coyote Shivers, he has the near-magical ability to produce a drummer out of thin air when the final scene calls for a big, wacky rooftop concert. He wrote and sang "SugarHigh," the song his character sings on the roof. *TRIVIA TIME!* Shivers also wrote *The Kids in the Hall* theme song ("Having an Average Weekend") as a member of real band Shadowy Men on a Shadowy Planet. See also **Rex Manning**.

Berko (Coyote Shivers)

BERNICE AND HER MAMMALS — A circus act? A perverted sex show? No, just another band on the roster of Starspun Records that's mentioned in passing by Jerome (Will Mackenzie) during the "On the Flip Side" episode (12/07/66) of anthology show *ABC Stage 67*. Jerome, the manager of Starspun Records pop star Carlos O'Conner (Ricky Nelson), is trying to convince Carlos that groups are all the rage these days and that Carlos should get one of his own. His evidence? Bernice and Her Mammals. You're convinced, right? See also **The Celestials; Chuck Roast and the Rares; The Harpoons; Heinrich and the West Berlin Nine; The Hors D'Oeuvres; Carlos O'Conner**.

BEYOND GRAVITY — Band from the 2000 VH1 movie *At Any Cost*. Singer/songwriter Lance (Eddie Mills), his younger brother and lead guitarist Mike

(James Franco), and Lance's wife, Chelsea (Maureen Flannigan on bass), head out to L.A. to sign with Rage Records. Then, of course, everything goes to hell: Mike dies of a heroin OD, Chelsea quits to watch the kid, their manager Ben (Glenn Quinn) gets all corrupt, and although Lance gets replacements, the magic's gone and blah blah blah, it used to be about the music, maaaan! Oh, and there's a cameo by Gene Simmons of KISS.

BIBI — See **Alphie and Bibi**.

BIG DAN AND THE SAND DOLLARS — Four female friends (Luanne, Pudge, Melaina, and Carson) sneak down to Myrtle Beach, South Carolina, for one last fling before college and Carson's marriage break them apart in the 1989 movie *Shag*. Before your brain goes any further, shag is a type of dance that was huge in South Carolina in 1963, when the story takes place and still is today. Big Dan and company play The Pavillion, where the gals hang out and meet the men who turn their lives upside down, all to the laid-back brand of 60s R&B that is shag music. Pudge (Annabeth Gish) hooks up with Chip (Scott Coffey), Luanne's (Page Hannah) parents' vacation house is trashed in a huge party, Melaina (Bridget Fonda) hooks up with celeb Jimmy Valentine (Jeff Yagher) and his manager, and Carson (Phoebe Cates) ends up throwing over her dull fiancé Harley Ralston (Tyrone Power Jr.) for "sweet potato" Buzz Ravenel (Robert Rusler). The ending shag dance contest is more of a coda than anything else. The band was played by real band The Voltage Brothers: Jim Kelly Jr., Garry Goins, John Lewis Jr., Douglas Smith, and Lawrence Whitaker. *TRIVIA TIME!* This movie was cowritten by Terry Sweeney, better known for his 1985–86 stint on *Saturday*

Night Live, where he did a frighteningly believable impersonation of First Lady Nancy Reagan. See also **Jimmy Valentine**.

Big Dan and the Sand Dollars

BIG FUN—Never-seen pop band from the 1989 black comedy *Heathers*. Their big hit was "Teenage Suicide (Don't Do It)." It was especially appropriate, as the local high school seemed to be suffering a rash of teen suicides. In reality, students Veronica Sawyer (Winona Ryder) and her psycho boyfriend Jason Dean (Christian Slater) were offing them and making it look like suicides. J.D. went too far when he hatched a crazy-ass scheme to blow up the school and make it look like mass suicide, complete with a note signed by the entire school. He pulled that trick off by disguising the note as a petition to get this band to come play the school! *TRIVIA TIME!* Big

Fun's cheesy song was actually written and performed by producer/singer Don Dixon and, unfortunately, does not appear on the soundtrack album. It can be found on Dixon's 1992 *If I'm a Ham, Well You're a Sausage* album.

BIG MOMMA—Singer from the extended "Polynesiantown" sketch (a *Chinatown* parody) on the 05/22/81 episode of *SCTV*. This is the opening act for real musical guest Dr. John that Johnny LaRue (John Candy) hired at the opening night of his new Polynesian restaurant. Big Momma (played by Andrea Martin) bombs. She also shows up at the beginning of the "Star Is Born" parody (01/28/83). See also **Vic Arpeggio**; **5 Neat Guys**; **Happiness Unlimited**; **The Happy Wanderers**; **Lola Heatherton**; **The Lemon Twins**; **Linsk Minyk**; **Tom Munroe**; **The Queenhaters**; **The Ramblers**; **The Recess Monkeys**; **Russ Riley**; **Jackie Rogers Jr.**; **Jackie Rogers Sr.**; **Speed of Light**; **Dusty Towne**; **The Wally Hung Trio**.

BIKINI BOTTOM SUPER BAND, THE—Sourpuss octopus Squidward Tentacles (voiced by Rodger Bumpass) formed this impromptu marching/rock band in the "Band Geeks" episode (09/07/01) of Nickelodeon cartoon series *SpongeBob SquarePants*. They played one known gig at the Bubble Bowl. See also **The Bird Brains**.

BILLY BOB AND THE NOCTURNAL EMISSIONS—Fifties dance band that appears briefly in the "If I'm Dyin', I'm Lyin'" episode (04/04/00) of animated sitcom *Family Guy*. The band is onstage during a flashback to Peter's cousin Rufus's blaxploitation flick *Black to the Future*. It's pretty much a straight parody of the *Back to the Future* prom band scene, except that Marty McSuperfly plays funk, and the band leader calls Isaac Hayes, not Chuck Berry. See also **Pearl Burton**; **Stewie and the Cowtones**.

BINKY — From the "Binky Rules" and "Meet Binky" episodes (both 11/09/98) of the animated PBS children's show *Arthur*. In the first, one of the kids, Binky Barnes (voiced by Bruce Dinsmore), gets in trouble because someone's been painting "Binky Rules" on the school walls. The kids turn detective to find out whodunit, but the answer turns out to be a few overzealous promoters the local DJ hired to promote Finnish band BINKY. The DJ makes it up to them by giving them free copies of the BINKY album, which has their big radio hit (the title is never given), as well as the songs "Goodbye Baxter Norland" and "Snowy Snowy, Slushy Slushy." In "Meet Binky" the kids are all excited to go to a BINKY concert. Arthur Read (voiced by Michael Yarmush) gets a crappy seat in the nosebleed section but then finds out his dad is doing the band's catering and gets a free backstage pass. Bitter and vindictive, the usually goody-goody Arthur doesn't invite any of his friends. Backstage he finds out the band is just a bunch of holograms! Manager Svern Smith and his technowizard Winston put the band together with the "Troglodyte 5000" computer and synthesizers. BINKY also made a brief appearance in a fantasy sequence in the "To Beat or Not to Beat" episode (10/18/99). The untitled radio hit is really the song "Matalij Ja Mustii," done by real Finnish band Värttinä. See also **Piccolo Pete**; **The Squabs**; **U Stink**; **We Stink**.

BIRD AND THE MIDNIGHT FALCONS — This mid-60s soul/R&B vocal group, fronted by preening, scheming Bird (Roy Fegan), is introduced trying to sabotage a performance by their rival Five Heartbeats in the 1991 Robert Townsend movie of the same name. Their girlfriends are front and center to boo the 'Beats and scream for their boys. Worse, Bird's cousin, the house manager, forces The Five Heartbeats to use the house pianist, who deliberately ham-fists his way through their song. Fed up, Heartbeat Duck (Robert Townsend) pushes the pianist away, takes over, and fires up the band. Bird and the Midnight Falcons eventually tour with The Five Heartbeats, their fellow Big Red Records label-mates. Later, Bird makes the mistake of accusing Big Red himself (Hawthorne James) of shortchanging him on royalties. Big Red has him beat up and dangled off a hotel balcony. But when Big Red has the Heartbeats' manager killed, Bird joins with the Heartbeats to testify and put Big Red in prison. The rest of the Falcons were played by Gregory "Popeye" Alexander, Roger Rose, and Jimmy Woodard. See also **The Five Heartbeats**; **The Five Horsemen**; **Flash and the Ebony Sparks**.

BIRD BRAINS, THE — Exceptionally loud four-piece all-bird puppet band that plays Patchy the Pirate's party in the "SpongeBob's House Party" episode (05/17/02) of cartoon *SpongeBob SquarePants*. The quartet was hired by Patchy's pet parrot Polly, but Patchy (voiced by Tom Kenny) would have preferred hearing from The First Mates, Barnacle Bill and the Seven Seas, or Rusty Hinges and the Boys From the Brig. He has the band walk the plank, forgeting they're birds and can just fly away. See also **The Bikini Bottom Super Band**.

BIRDIE, CONRAD — Rock star from the 1960 Broadway musical and later 1963 movie *Bye Bye Birdie*. Conrad Birdie (Jesse Pearson) was an Elvis parody with some Conway Twitty thrown in (i.e., his name), centering on the title character's being drafted for the army. The skimpy plot revolved around a promotional stunt of picking a girl to give Conrad his "One Last Kiss" (with song of the same name) before he goes into service. Obviously, the writers forgot about the many brothels that gladly open their doors to our boys in uniform. Dick Van Dyke stars as songwriter Albert Peterson. The songs were written by Charles Strouse and Lee Adams.

There was also a 1995 ABC TV remake, with *Seinfeld* star Jason Alexander as Peterson and Marc Kudisch as Birdie. ***TRIVIA TIME!*** Charles Strouse also wrote the songs for the musical *Annie*, and the opening theme for sitcom *All in the Family*.

Conrad Birdie (Jessie Pearson) and Kim McAfee (Ann-Margret)

BIZARRE, BENITA — See **The Bugaloos**.

BLACK, JENNIFER — Wacky Judge Harry Stone (Harry Anderson) dates this rock star (played by Kristin DeBell) in the aptly—or unimaginatively—named episode "Harry and the Rock Star" (03/24/84) of 80s sitcom *Night Court*. Alas, reporters and fans cause chaos and confusion in the court, and their breakup leaves Stone with just his memories and her album of screeching.

BLACK, LARRY — Very Caucasian "soul-singing sensation" and obvious Barry White parody who performs "We'll Make Love Tonight" at his concert—especially for the ladies. Only Larry (Bob Odenkirk) checks his schedule midsong to discover he's busy tonight, maybe tomorrow—no, his brother's coming into town . . . dammit! From the "We Regret to Inform You" episode (11/17/95) of HBO's sketch comedy program *Mr. Show*. On the DVD commentary, Odenkirk apologizes for his crappy singing! See also **The Beetletown Players; Livingston Brewster; Willips Brighton; Dickie Crickets; Indomitable Spirit; Kid Jersey; Kill or Be Killed; C. S. Lewis Jr.; Horace Loeb; Marilyn Monster; Norma Jean Monster; John Baptiste Philouza; Professor Murder; Puscifer; Salini; Smoosh; Old Swerdlow; Three Times One Minus One; Titannica; Sir Lloyd Wilson Webber; Wyckyd Sceptre; Daffy "Mal" Yinkleyankle.**

BLACK PLAGUE — Heavy metal band in the 1990 Andrew Dice Clay vehicle, *The Adventures of Ford Fairlane*. Lead singer Bobby Black (Mötley Crüe's Vince Neil) dies onstage after being poisoned by Julian Grendel (singer Wayne Newton), the evil head of Grendel Records. The rest of Black Plague (played by Phil Soussan, Carlos Cavazo, and Randy Castillo) carry on, even playing at Black's midnight funeral. See also **Disco Express; F. F. & Captain**

John; The Pussycats; Slam; Kyle Troy.

BLACK ROSES—A truly satanic metal band from the 1988 movie of the same name. Let's call it the "metal-sploitation" subgenre of horror flicks. For once, the local PMRC types are absolutely right! The concert happens and the teen fans of the small town of Mill Basin turn into no-goodniks, then into murderers, then into demons! Or whatever the hell weirdo things the special effects department could whip up for cheap. Lead singer Damian (Sal Viviano) eventually turns into a big lizard. (Insert your own "Lizard King" joke here.) Well, at least there's gratuitous nudity. *TRIVIA TIME!* The band's drummer, Vinny Apache, was played by Carmine Appice, who was the real drummer for Vanilla Fudge and co-wrote Rod Stewart's smash hit "Do Ya Think I'm Sexy?" Other band members were played by Ron Mazza (guitar) and Paul Phenomenon (keyboards).

BLEACH BOYS, THE—From a *Saturday Night Live* skit (03/22/97). This was Bill Forrest's (Mark McKinney) college band when he went prematurely gray. It was made up of students who had all gone prematurely gray. Which would explain why the skit's name is "Prematurely Gray," a talk show that "celebrates being prematurely gray."

BLEEDING EARDRUM—From the Roger Corman–created schlock Sci Fi Channel show *Black Scorpion*. The sexy-babe heroine (Michelle Lintel) of the title, who fights crime by running around in bondage gear kicking people in the face, goes up against another one of TV's damned "musical villains" in the "Face the Music" episode (06/16/01). This band blows so bad the only way they can sell albums is by putting subliminal messages in them. But lead singer Vox Populi (Shannon Whirry) crosses that razor-thin line between rock star and supervillain and uses her now-violent, brainwashed fans to go on

a crime spree. The other band members were Screech (Elan Carter) and Shriek (Angelica Bridges).

BLENDER CHILDREN, THE—Typical 80s hair metal band from the 1988 movie *Tapeheads*. When the band dies in a plane crash, discount music-video makers Josh Tager (Tim Robbins) and Ivan Alexeev (John Cusack) accidentally dub some geezer's funeral footage over the original video for the band, and the result becomes a hit! Punk semilegend Stiv Bators played the lead singer, Dick Slammer. The rest of the band was played by Nick Turner, Brian James, and Alistare Symons. Their song in the movie was "Mr. MX-7." *TRIVIA TIME!* Lead singer of punk band The Dead Kennedys, Jello Biafra, has a bit role as an FBI agent. See also **Cube Squared**; **Ranchbone**; **The Swanky Modes**.

BLIND FISH—Way successful current rock band that doesn't have the time to chat with 70s comeback trail hitters Strange Fruit, the focus of the 1998 Brit flick *Still Crazy*. Already platinum in the States, they are kicking off their European tour in the Netherlands when they waltz by the Fruits—a quick snub, and they're away! See also **Strange Fruit**; **Thumbscrew**.

BLITZ, JIMMY—Hotel-trashing rock star in VH1 anthology movie *Strange Frequency* (2001), which was turned into a TV series. A rock and roll *Twilight Zone* rip, the "Room Service" segment features Duran Duran member John Taylor versus a perniciously neat hotel room that won't stay trashed. The supernatural room has its revenge on him in the end, though.

BLOCK ROCKERS, THE—See **The Gumbies**.

BLOOD POLLUTION—From the 2001 movie *Rock Star*.

Chris Cole's (Mark Wahlberg) rock and roll dreams come true after he is plucked from being the lead singer of this local Steel Dragon cover band to fronting the real Steel Dragon! Then the usual rock and roll problems come up and he quits. Cole's singing voice was Jeff Scott Soto (Yngwie J. Malmsteen's lead singer) and/or Mike Matijevic (Steelheart vocalist). The rest of the band was mostly played by real musicians: guitarist Rob (Timothy Olyphant), Donny (Blas Elias of Slaughter), guitarist Xander Cummins (Nick Catanese of Black Label Society), and bassist Ricki (Brian Vander Ark of The Verve Pipe). See also **Steel Dragon**.

BLOODLUST—Unseen band sweet-seventeen Mari Collingwood (Sandra Cassel) goes off to sea at the beginning of horror flick *The Last House on the Left* (1972). Horror is a misnomer, really; it's more of an emotionally disturbing trauma. The band is known for onstage chicken killing, so you know they've gotta be good. On the way to the concert, however, Mari and her pal Phyllis Stone (Lucy Grantham) get sidetracked trying to score some weed, which leads to their kidnapping by nasty loon Krug Stillo (David Hess) and his entourage: Weasel Podowski (Fred Lincoln, later a porn director), Krug's sadist girlfriend Sadie (Jeramie Rain), and Krug's ineffectual, heroin-addicted son, Junior Stillo (Marc Sheffler). Krug and Ko. then end up at Mari's parents house by a staggering coincidence. More effective than a dozen "Just Say No" PSAs!

BLOW GOES, THE—Number seven artist on the top-ten board in the record shop scene in the 1971 dystopian science fiction classic *A Clockwork Orange*. The song title is "Downy." See also **Bread Brothers; Comic Strips; Cyclops; Goggly Gogol; The Heaven Seventeen; The Humpers; The Legend; The Sharks; Johnny Zhivago.**

BLOWHOLES, THE—Nickelodeon's 1993–96 live action comedy *The Adventures of Pete and Pete* (about two brothers both named Pete) was a minor masterpiece of surreal humor. It frequently attracted hip, sorta-underground guest stars like Michael Stipe, LL Cool J, Steve Buscemi and Iggy Pop. The "Hard Day's Pete" episode attracted musicians Syd Straw (as math teacher Miss Fingerwood) and Marshall Crenshaw (as a meter reader), specifically. They combine forces with little Pete (Danny Tamberelli) and another kid to briefly form this band to re-create a song little Pete heard by another, unnamed garage band. The unnamed band was played by Polaris, aka Miracle Legion, who wrote and performed the show's theme, "Hey Sandy." A Polaris three-song promotional cassingle was once offered via cereal box. "Blowhole" was a favorite insult used by little Pete. See also **Kreb Zeppelin.**

BLUE BOYS, THE—From the "The Night They Raided Daddy's" episode (02/19/70) of *That Girl*. Ann Marie (Marlo Thomas) hires this band to improve business at her dad's restaurant, but gets more for her money than expected when the band plays in the buff, to show they're the hippest, happeningest thing in music. The Blue Boys were played by Jeff Brock, Joe Duckett, and Rayburn Wallace.

BLUE SPOT TRIO—Their name is never mentioned in *That Thing You Do* (1996), but this hot/cool piano/drums/standup-bass jazz threesome playing at Los Angeles Blue Spot Club is listed in the credits as the Blue Spot Trio. So maybe it's not really their name but more of a description. But what the heck, let's count it anyway. This African-American trio was played by Barth Beasley, James Leary, and Alphonse Mouzon; the latter also composed the instrumental they are shown playing, "Blue Spot." It is at this club where Guy (Tom Everett Scott) meets his idol, jazz pianist Del Paxton (Bill Cobbs). See also **Elizabeth Anne**; **The Chantrellines**; **Diane Dane**; **The Echoes**; **Freddy Fredrickson**; **The G Men**; **The Heardsmen**; **The Hollyhocks**; **Jon D and the Walkers**; **Legends of Brass**; **Marilyn Lovell and the Geminis**; **The Norm Wooster Singers**; **Del Paxton**; **The Saturn 5**; **The Tempos**; **The Trends**; **Two Eriks**; **The Vicksburgs**; **The Wonders**.

BLUEGRASS BROTHERS, THE—From "The Bluegrass Is Always Greener" episode (02/24/02) of FOX animated show *King of the Hill*. This bluegrass band stares and twiddles their beards at Hank Hill (voiced by Mike Judge), trying to psych out the competition backstage at the 15th Annual Old Time Fiddle Festival in Branson, Missouri. See also **The A Men**; **Cane and the Stubborn Stains**; **The Dale Gribble Bluegrass Experience**; **4 Skore**; **The Harris Twins**; **John Redcorn and Big Mountain Fudge Cake**; **Pastor K**; **Pimp Franklin**.

BLUES BROTHERS, THE—*Saturday Night Live* cast members John Belushi and Dan Aykroyd were Joliet Jake and Elwood Blues. They first appeared on the show in giant bee costumes singing the blues oldie "King Bee" on 01/17/76, but had worked up the act earlier using it to warm up the crowd before the live broadcast. Subsequent performances on the show in their trademark black suits, skinny ties, fedoras, and shades featured them cutting loose on a number of soul and R&B classics, and they cut the album *Briefcase Full of Blues* in 1978. True soul/R&B fans may have snorted, but you can't accuse Belushi of not putting his heart and soul into his performances. Also, the duo were backed up by a veritable who's who of R&B session men: Murphy Dunne, Donald Dunn, Steve Cropper, Willie Hall, Tom Malone, Alan Rubin, Lou Marini, and Tom Scott.

They opened for comedian Steve Martin and even The Grateful Dead (12/31/78) before launching their own concert tour in 1979. Then they got an entire movie to themselves, the 1980 comedy *The Blues Brothers*, which featured Jake getting out of the slammer and trying to get the band back together to raise money to pay off the taxes on the Catholic orphanage where they had been raised. Many over-the-top hijinks ensue, leading to a car chase INSIDE a mall, and the amazing finale, featuring the most cars crashed in celluloid history.

The Blues Brothers
(Dan Akroyd and John Belushi)

They even find room to squeeze in soul queen Aretha Franklin, soul godfather James Brown, soul genius Ray Charles, and jumpin' 30s jivist Cab Calloway. A hit soundtrack album was released and the band had four top forty singles and another album, *Made in America* (1981), before John Belushi's premature death from drugs in 1982. If it had been left there, all would have been well. But no. The musicians cut a 1992 album under The Blues Brothers name, *Red, White & Blues*, which was ignorable. But then John Goodman appeared on *SNL* (03/25/95) in Blues Brother garb with Aykroyd and sang "Flip, Flop, and Fly." He became new Blues Brother Mighty Mack and starred with Aykroyd in the critically disdained and poorly received movie *Blues Brothers 2000* (1998). An ignominious end to a well-loved franchise. See also **The Good Ole Boys; Murph and the Magictones; Street Slim.**

BLUES REDUCTION—See **Stillwater.**

BLUESHAMMER—Headliners at a club who play a frat-boy, hard-rock version of "Pickin' Cotton Blues" that spits in the face of everything music collector Seymour (Steve Buscemi) loves in the 2001 movie *Ghost World*. He only went because authentic acoustic bluesman Fred Chatman was opening. Their song (on the soundtrack album) was cowritten by director Terry Zwigoff, and Steve Pierson and Guy Thomas. The band was played by Steve Pierson, Jake La Botz, Johnny Irion, and Nate Wood. See also **Alien Autopsy; Fred Chatman; Vanilla, Jade and Ebony.**

BOBBARINE AND THE WOOKIEE KOTTERS—See **Figrin D'an and the Modal Nodes.**

BOBBY FLEET AND HIS BAND WITH A BEAT—See **Jim Lindsey.**

BOBBY, JOHNNY—50s rock and roll singer of the "Jailhouse Rock" parody "Mental House Rock" in the "Take My Wife, Sleaze" episode (01/28/99) of long-running animated FOX sitcom *The Simpsons*. Marge and Homer win the motorcycle of Homer's dreams at a dance contest dancing to this song on the jukebox at the 50s-themed Greaser's Café. See also **The Beach Boys Experience; The Be Sharps; Johnny Calhoun; Captain Bart and the Tequila Mockingbirds; The Crazy Old Man Singers; Cyanide; Gulliver Dark; Ferl Dixon and His Second Helping Boys; Funky C Funky Do; Garfunkel, Messina, Oates, and Lisa; Hooray for Everything; Koveant; Krusty and the Krums; The Larry Davis Experience; Little Timmy and the Shebangs; Loggins and Oates; Lurleen Lumpkin; M. C. Safety and the Caution Crew; Melvin and the Squirrels; "Bleeding Gums" Murphy; The Party Posse; The Rappin' Rabbis; Red Breem and His Band of Some Esteem; The Satin Knights; The Steve Sax Trio; Testament; Blind Willie Witherspoon; The Ya-Hoo Recovering Alcoholic Jug Band; Yodelin' Zeke.**

BOCK—Dumb, washed-up rock star, played by Earl Ray Saathoff, who lets llama-lovin' psycho Dr. Albert (Kelley Swinney) experiment on him. He gets himself electrocuted in *Barn of the Blood Llama* (1997), a movie as bizarre as it is unwatchable. And we're complimenting it by calling it a "movie."

BODY BAG—This recently murdered metal band reaches from beyond the grave in the 1988 horror schlock movie *Slaughterhouse Rock*. They infest the dreams of high schooler Alex Gardner (Nicholas Celozzi), and his seriously screwed-up dreams turn real. It's all about some evil spirit buried under Alcatraz (?!) trying to take him over. Turns out the band—or, rather, their ghosts—are on his side; lead singer Sammi Mitchell (Toni Basil of one-hit-wonder fame "Micky" in 1982) does some kinda afterlife dance to help Gardner leave his body so he can fight the bad dead guy. The soundtrack has some embarrassingly bad tunes by real band Devo.

BOLTON CHORAL SOCIETY—From the "The All-England Summarize Proust Competition" episode (11/16/72) of legendary BBC sketch show *Monty Python's Flying Circus*. This group are finalists in the All-England Summarize Proust Competition, but, unfortunately, their contrapuntal madrigal stylings eat up the fifteen seconds allotted, so they never get past "Proust in his first book wrote about, wrote about." They're from Bingley! Played by The Fred Tomlinson singers, with Mr. Tomlinson himself as Superintendent McGough. See also **Arthur Ewing and His Musical Mice; Johann Gambolputty de von Ausfern-schplenden-schlitter-crasscrenbon-fried-digger-dingle-dangle-dongle-dungle-burstein-von-knacker-thrasher-apple-banger-horowitz-ticolensic-grander-knotty-spelltinkle-grandlich-grumblemeyer-spelterwasser-kurstlich-himbleeisen-bahnwagen-gutenabend-bitte-ein-nürnburger-bratwustle-gerspurten-mitz-weimache-luber-hundsfut-gumberaber-scöenedanker-kalbsfleisch-mittler-aucher von Hautkopft of Ulm; The Herman Rodriguez Four; The Hunlets; Jackie Charlton and the Tonettes; Arthur "Two Sheds" Jackson; Not Noel Coward; Not Tony Bennett; Rachel Toovey Bicycle Choir; Inspector Jean-Paul Zatapathique.**

BOPKAS, THE—In the hit Disney flick (1989) turned cruddier TV show *Honey, I Shrunk the Kids: The TV Show*, wacky inventor Wayne Szalinski (Peter Scolari, the perfect poor man's Rick Moranis) remembers this 60s band from an old TV show, but no one else does. So what does he do to see if they're real? He gets in his time machine and GOES BACK IN TIME. Why can't he just use the Internet like the rest of us?! Szalinski discovers this British Invasion band is really Russian spies, trying to turn American kids against their parents with their music. From the "Honey, Name That Tune" (11/25/99) episode.

The Bower Family Band

BOWER FAMILY BAND, THE—From the obscure 1968 Disney dog *The One and Only, Genuine, Original Family Band*. This period movie featured a brass band of Bower brats trying to get to the 1888 St. Louis Democratic National Convention to play their song, "Let's Put It Over with Grover," only by the end of the movie to end up in the Dakotas, changing their tune to "Oh Benjamin Harrison." Lineup: Grandpa Renssaeler Bower (Walter Brennan) on violin, Father Calvin Bower

(Buddy Ebsen) on banjo, Katie Bower (Janet Blair) on recorder, Alice Bower (Lesley Ann Warren) on coronet, Sidney Bower (Kurt Russell) on drum, and the rest of the massive family playing other stuff: Mayo Bower (Bobby Riha), Quinn Bower (Jon Walmsley), Nettie Bower (Smitty Wordes), Rose Bower (Heidi Rook), LuLu Bower (Debbie Smith), and Laura Bower (Pamelyn Ferdin). How could this movie fail? It had it all: Buddy Ebsen AND Walter Brennan AND John Davidson AND, of course, Disney-movie mainstay Kurt Russell. Goldie Hawn made her feature debut! Butch Patrick (Eddie Munster) was there! Plus music by perennial Disney songsters the Sherman brothers, Richard M. and Robert B. All that was missing was Dean Jones!

BOYDS, THE—The band of giant puppet birds that sings the blues-rock version of the show's theme during the end credits of the slightly insane 1969 Sid and Marty Krofft TV series *H. R. Pufnstuf*. Lady Boyd (Sharon Baird) was the Tina Turner–inspired lead singer.

BOYNEUDO—See **The Party Posse**.

BRADLEY AND THE BILLIONAIRES—Competition of band California Dreams in the "Battle of the Bands" episode (09/19/92) of lightweight TV show *California Dreams*. See also **California Dreams**; **Total Defiance**; **Zane Walker**.

BRADY KIDS, THE—In the completely unnecessary *Brady Bunch* spinoff, the animated *Brady Kids* (1972–74), the Brady children were stripped of their parents and housekeeper and given a dog named Moptop, a pair of pandas, and a magical talking mynah bird named Marlon. Marlon (voiced by *F Troop's* Larry Storch) wears a hat and does magic tricks. No, seriously! Too bad he couldn't magically make this show any better. The kids also

played in this family pop band, as trippy psychedelic backgrounds washed behind them. Most of the kids from the live series did their own voices here. From who else but the discount animation house of Filmation Associates! See also **The Banana Convention**; **The Brady Six**; **Johnny Bravo**; **Phlegm**; **The Silver Platters**.

BRADY SIX, THE—In the "Dough-Re-Mi" episode (1/14/72) of 70s über-sitcom *The Brady Bunch*, Greg Brady (Barry Williams) writes what he is sure is a hit song, "We Can Make the World a Whole Lot Brighter." But the recording studio will cost $150. Peter Brady (Christopher Knight), chums with Johnny Dimsdale, the recording engineer's son, hears Mr. Dimsdale (John Wheeler) talk about how family groups sell millions of albums (a veiled reference to *The Partridge Family*?). So all six Brady siblings throw in together to sing the song and split the recording costs. Then puberty grabs Peter by the throat, changing his voice right in the middle of recording. But this is TV land, so the happy ending comes when Greg whips up another song, "Time to Change," that actually utilizes Peter's, um, unique vocal qualities. See also **The Banana Convention**; **The Brady Kids**; **Johnny Bravo**; **Phlegm**; **The Silver Platters**.

IT'S A SUNSHINE DAY: THE BEST OF THE BRADY BUNCH
(1993, MCA RECORDS)

THIS ALBUM WAS a welcome, much-needed CD release of 1993. The Brady Bunch had a surprisingly large musical output, as detailed in the informative and engaging liner notes, and this compilation marked its first availability on CD. Fans of the sitcom should be delighted at the album inclusion of songs showcased in actual episodes: the twee "We Can

Make the World a Whole Lot Brighter" and the groovy jam of "Time to Change" from the "Dough-Re-Mi" episode, and the pure bubblegum rock of "It's a Sunshine Day" and "Keep On" from "Amateur Night." Alas, it does not have the songs from the "Johnny Bravo" or "Where There's Smoke" episodes, but those tunes were never released anyway. The album begins and ends with the short bonus spoken-word tracks "Promo Intro" and "Promo Outro," a nice touch. The Brady kids are obviously not professional singers, but sweet, slick productions and lots of echo hide it well. Almost all the tunes work surprisingly well, but the uptempo numbers like "Candy (Sugar Shoppe)" and "Sweet Sweetheart," with their groovy horns and funked up guitars, are much more enjoyable than the slower, more serious numbers with their acoustic guitars and strings—"Born to Say Goodbye" and "I Just Want to Be Your Friend," for example. The agreeably dizzy "Merry Go Round" is a standout tune with a surprisingly psychedelic feel. Cindy Brady's solo version of "Frosty the Snowman" is thankfully the only holiday-themed track, and a low point of cutesy schmaltz in The Bradys' recording career, and possibly the universe. The Bradys' version of Don McLean's classic-rock classic "American Pie" is the album's goofball, so-bad-it's-sublimely-ridiculous highlight. It's too bad the album omits their version of The Beatles' "Love Me Do," a similarly hilarious disaster that underscores the "bray" in "Brady."

BRAK—See **Zorak**.

BRAVO, JOHNNY—In the "Adios, Johnny Bravo" (09/14/73) episode of *The Brady Bunch*, a talent agent approaches the Bradys when they are auditioning for a TV amateur variety program. But the agent only wants Greg Brady (Barry Williams), not the rest of the family. Greg is offered the chance to be a rock star with this stage name, but he turns it down when he finds out he was only chosen because

he fit the costume. The episode features the Bradys singing "Good Time Music." *TRIVIA TIME!* On 09/28/99, Barry Williams released a CD called *The Return of Johnny Bravo*, featuring covers and the new song, "Johnny's Back." See also **The Banana Convention**; **The Brady Kids**; **The Brady Six**; **Phlegm**; **The Silver Platters**.

BREAD BROTHERS—Number five artist on the top-ten board in the record shop scene in the 1971 classic *A Clockwork Orange*. The song is "Dogs and Cats." See also **The Blow Goes**; **Comic Strips**; **Cyclops**; **Goggly Gogol**; **The Heaven Seventeen**; **The Humpers**; **The Legend**; **The Sharks**; **Johnny Zhivago**.

BREAKING GLASS—British punk/new wave band from the 1980 rags-to-riches-to-loony-bin movie of the same name. Lead singer Kate (Hazel O'Connor) gets slowly sucked into the machine, succumbing to record company pressures and getting hooked on drugs. In their final concert before Kate has a nervous breakdown, she sports an outfit that gets stolen by the *Tron* costume designers two years later. Band lineup: sax player Ken (Jonathan Pryce), bass player Dave (Gary Tibbs), guitar player Tony (Mark Wingett), and drummer Mick (Peter Hugo-Daly).

BRENDON POPPINS AND THE CHIMMINY SWEEPS—Yes, it's "chimminy"—how well do you expect a band of third-graders to spell? In the "Guitarmageddon" episode (10/27/02) of cartoon *Home Movies*, precocious tykes Brendon Small (voiced by Brendon Small), Jason Panopolis (voiced by H. Jon Benjamin) and Melissa (voiced by Melissa Bardin Galsky), take a break from filmmaking to give being a band a go. They don't let lack of ability get in the way of recording their cacophonous single, "Freaky Outie." They DO let their egos get in the way, and by the episode's end, the band has broken up. Also in the episode, metalhead mushmouth Duane of Scäb goes up against his rival Jimmy Monet in a guitar contest. See also **Alligator Shoes**; **Scäb**.

BREWSTER, LIVINGSTON — Unseen artist who sings 'n' strums the twee folk ballad "Thank You for the Ride," a song for the victims of The Devastator roller coaster, which goes underwater for two whole minutes. From a sketch in the "Heaven's Chimney" episode (09/12/97) of HBO's sketch comedy *Mr. Show*. See also **The Beetletown Players**; **Larry Black**; **Willips Brighton**; **Dickie Crickets**; **Indomitable Spirit**; **Kid Jersey**; **Kill or Be Killed**; **C. S. Lewis Jr.**; **Horace Loeb**; **Marilyn Monster**; **Norma Jean Monster**; **John Baptiste Philouza**; **Professor Murder**; **Puscifer**; **Salini**; **Smoosh**; **Old Swerdlow**; **Three Times One Minus One**; **Titannica**; **Sir Lloyd Wilson Webber**; **Wyckyd Sceptre**; **Daffy "Mal" Yinkleyankle**.

BREWSTER, RICK — Pop singer from "The Hottest Ticket in Town" episode (01/12/82) of *Simon and Simon*. The private-eye Simon brothers, Rick (Gerald McRaney) and A.J. (Jameson Parker), are scrambling to find tickets to his sold-out show for their cousin when they just happen to stumble onto a counterfeit ticket racket, which conveniently provides that week's plot. Played by Joey Travolta, brother of actor John Travolta.

BRIGHTON, WILLIPS — Parody of The Beach Boys' Brian Wilson from the "Sad Songs Are Nature's Onions" episode (12/29/98) of sketch comedy program *Mr. Show*. He (Bob Odenkirk) and Horace Loeb (David Cross) each get a Teardrop Award for saddest song. Brighton's is "Mouth Full of Sores." See also **The Beetletown Players**; **Larry Black**; **Livingston Brewster**; **Dickie Crickets**; **Indomitable Spirit**; **Kid Jersey**; **Kill or Be Killed**;

C. S. Lewis Jr.; **Horace Loeb**; **Marilyn Monster**; **Norma Jean Monster**; **John Baptiste Philouza**; **Professor Murder**; **Puscifer**; **Salini**; **Smoosh**; **Old Swerdlow**; **Three Times One Minus One**; **Titannica**; **Sir Lloyd Wilson Webber**; **Wyckyd Sceptre**; **Daffy "Mal" Yinkleyankle**.

BROCCOLI, LICK — See **The California Raisins**.

BROWN, TOMMY (I) — Country music legend Johnny Cash played this ex-con-turned-gospel-singer in the "Swan Song" episode (03/03/74) of *Columbo*. We first meet Tommy on a Bakersfield, California, stage in front of some stock crowd footage. He's singing the hell out of Hank Williams's "I Saw the Light," backed by a gospel group that looks like various failed Marcia Brady clones. Soon we see that Tommy is chafing under the thumb of his "sanctimonious hypocritical Bible-spouting blackmailer" wife Edna (Ida Lupino), who earmarks all of the money from Tommy's sold-out concerts for her Lost Soul Crusade's $5 million tabernacle. Edna keeps Tommy on a short leash by reminding him how she rescued him from an Arkansas prison farm and how she knows about his indiscretions with sixteen-year-old backup singer Maryann (Bonnie Van Dyke). Damn that Mann Act! So Tommy sneaks a parachute into his backpack, some pills in a thermos of coffee, and takes care of the Edna situation PERMANENTLY by drugging the gals and abandoning his post behind the wheel of their small plane. The perfect crime, except that Columbo was involved. See also **Marcy Edwards**.

BROWN, TOMMY (II) — African-American country singing star, à la Charley Pride, in Robert Altman's 1975 film *Nashville*. Tommy Brown (Timothy Brown) gets insulted by another African-American character for being too white. See also **Sueleen Gay**; **Haven Hamilton**; **Barbara Jean**; **Linnea**

Reese; The Smoky Mountain Laurels; Tom, Bill & Mary; Connie White.

Tommy Brown II (Timothy Brown) (I)

BROWNSVILLE BOYS, THE—See **The Five Heartbeats.**

BUCKAROO BANZAI AND THE HONG KONG CAVALIERS—Buckaroo Banzai's (Peter Weller) rock band from the cult, comic-booky, over-the-top movie *The Adventures of Buckaroo Banzai Across the Eighth Dimension* (1984). Brain surgeon, rocket scientist, rock musician—a true Renaissance man! He doesn't get much time to play though, as aliens are threatening to destroy the planet if he doesn't take care of some of their renegades. The rest of the band is guitarist Perfect Tommy (Lewis Smith), saxophonist Reno Nevada (Pepe Serna), keyboardist New Jersey (Jeff Goldblum) and guitarist Pinky Carruthers (Billy Vera of Billy Vera and the Beaters). The DVD rerelease of the movie gave the band a full five-album discography as a bonus feature: *Native Texan (But a Rising Son)*, *Your Place or Mayan?*, *Echo Location*, *Progress Over Protocol*, and *Live at Artie's Artery.*

BUDDAH STALIN—Marilyn Manson parody, played by Peter Benson, from the "Is Freedom Free?" episode (07/17/00) of Comedy Central's show *Strangers with Candy.* After getting an assignment to do a freedom-themed art project, forty-seven-year-old high-schooler Jerri Blank (Amy Sedaris) writhes naked to his music while taking photos of herself. Buddah Stalin's song and gothy music video "The United Hates of Ascaria" (off his album *Suck My Freedom*) is also played during the closing credits.

BUDDY RIGHTEOUS ORCHESTRA, THE—Swingin' six-man jazz combo that appeared in the "Jack and the Gangsters" episode (11/26/01) of Cartoon Network's *Samurai Jack.* The green-suited sextet—drums, bass, clarinet, sax, trumpet, and piano—backed up chanteuse Lala Lilywhite. Apparently, the drummer's initials are CW, because that's what's on his bass drum. And if the piano player's mother is reading, you really need to talk to your boy about his posture. See also **Lala Lilywhite.**

BUFFAY, PHOEBE—Ditzy, blond singer/songwriter who is a member of that must-see sextet of sitcom *Friends.* Phoebe (Lisa Kudrow) plays acoustic guitar and sings quirky songs for her friends and unfortunate patrons of the coffeehouse Central Perk. Some of her songs include "Tiny Tarzan," "Terry's a Jerk," and "Jingle Bitch." Her signature tune, though, is "Smelly Cat," about a feline with such a gastrointestinal problem that he is, as the song goes, "no friend to those with noses." A producer gets Phoebe to record "Smelly Cat" and release a video in "The One Where Eddie Moves In" episode (02/22/96), but things fall through when the producer overdubs Phoebe with another singer. Alas, Phoebe loses

"Smelly Cat" when her ex-partner Leslie sells the tune as a kitty-litter jingle, in "The One With Phoebe's Ex-Partner" (02/06/97). Buffay is also the #1 fan of Ross Gellar's keyboard stylings. See also **Ross Gellar; Leslie; Stephanie Schiffer.**

Phoebe Buffay
(Lisa Kudrow)

BUGALOOS, THE—From the downright wacky 1970–72 kids' show of the same name. Sid and Marty Krofft, the maniacs who held the color-saturated, puppet-inhabited childhoods of a gener-ation in their hands, created this fake band of British bugs who live in Tranquility Forest. They try to rock out, when evil rock-star-wannabe Benita Bizarre isn't trying to bite their style or harsh their mellow. The jealous and talentless Bizarre (a consistently over-the-top Martha Raye) and her bungling henchmen (Funky Rat, Woofer, and Tweeter), naturally always failed. Lineup: Joy, the singing butterfly (Caroline Ellis); Harmony, the bumblebee on keyboards (Wayne Laryea); IQ, a grasshopper guitarist (John McIndoe); and Courage, a drum-playing male ladybug (tee-hee!) (John Philpott). An album called, appropriately enough, *Bugaloos*, was released in 1970 on Capitol Records. *TRIVIA TIME!* Did you know that Phil Collins of Genesis was almost a Bugaloo?! True! He auditioned for the role of IQ but was turned down.

BURNED BEYOND RECOGNITION—Siblings Bud (David Faustino) and Kelly Bundy (Christina Applegate) spend the episode "Nooner or Later" (4/10/94) of the long-running lowbrow FOX sitcom *Married with Children* waiting in line for tickets for this never-seen, bad-tempered heavy-rock band (they pee on their audience and one member, Dung, is known for bashing people's teeth in). They keep losing their place in line and end up, in traditional sitcom fashion, with the guy in front of them getting the last ticket. In a further twist of irony, they return home empty-handed to find their parents off to the concert, having won tickets in a Rick Dees radio contest. See also **Jimmy Dick and the Night Sticks; Joanie and the Slashettes; Oozing Meat; Ottis Media; Shoes 'n' Socks; Tears and Vomit; The Tuxedos; The Wanker; The Why; Yodeling Andy.**

BURNEY, FLOYD—Jerk folk singer (played by Gary Crosby, Bing's son) roaming the boonies looking for songs to steal in the "Come Wander with Me" episode (05/22/64) of *The Twilight Zone*—only the song he finds keeps changing lyrics (even after it's taped!) to describe his caddish wooing of a girl and his killing of her brother. He offhandedly mentions another group, The Raytones, at one point.

BURTON, PEARL—From the "Brian Wallows and Peter's Swallows" episode (01/17/02) of FOX animated TV show *Family Guy*. Brian, the family dog, is depressed about his love life and hits the bottle. Pulled over for DUI (hey, it's a cartoon), he's sentenced to community service with the Outreach to the Elderly program. After doing thankless chore after chore for horrible reclusive ole hag Pearl, he finally quits and tells her to drop dead. Later he sees Pearl profiled on TV as the top advertising jingle singer of 1945–60. But when she tried to turn serious with a 1961 Carnegie Hall performance of "Habañera," from Georges Bizet's opera *Carmen*, the bored audience demanded Coppertone jingles. Crushed, she fled the stage, disappeared, and became a recluse. Brian, enchanted with her singing, rushes back just in time to prevent her suicide. Smitten, he urges her to finally go outside with him, where she is promptly hit by a truck. On her deathbed, she and Brian experience a lifetime of marital bliss, thanks to the miracle of virtual reality goggles. It's weird how the implied bestiality is undercut by the strange sentimentality. And vice versa. See also **Billy Bob and the Nocturnal Emissions; Stewie and the Cowtones.**

CAIN WAS ABLE—Rock band from the first half of the eighth season of *Beverly Hills, 90210*. They first appear in the "Coming Home" episode (10/01/97), where they are being managed by cast regular David Silver (Brian Austin Green). They're trouble! Rowdy and unprofessional, the band's leader Devin Taggart (Phil Buckman) is a racist! David negotiates them a record deal, but then their new song with ethnic slurs and white supremacist advocacy is revealed (not "Desperate Love," that's their other song). David tussles with the band, refusing to let them play an upcoming showcase in the band's last appearance, "Pride and Prejudice" (10/22/97). Rest of the band played by James Berg, David McCrea, and Jeff Van Atta. See also **Jasper's Law; Ray Pruit.**

CALHOUN, JOHNNY—TV Dad Homer Simpson (voiced by Dan Castellaneta) wins a radio contest by knowing the title of this 60/70s artist's second album, *These Things I Believe*, a spoken-word album of his right-wing political beliefs that kinda killed his career. From the animated FOX show *The Simpsons* "Homer the Heretic" episode, (10/8/92). His earlier hit song was "I'm Gonna Find Me a Genie With a Magic Bikini." See also **The Beach Boys Experience; The Be Sharps; Johnny Bobby; Captain Bart and the Tequila Mockingbirds; The Crazy Old Man Singers; Cyanide; Gulliver Dark; Ferl Dixon and His Second Helping Boys; Funky C Funky Do; Garfunkel, Messina, Oates, and Lisa; Hooray for Everything; Kovenant; Krusty and the Krums; The Larry Davis Experience; Little Timmy and the Shebangs; Loggins and Oates; Lurleen Lumpkin; M. C. Safety and the Caution Crew; Melvin and the Squirrels; "Bleeding Gums" Murphy; The Party Posse; The Rappin' Rabbis; Red Breem and His Band of Some Esteem; The Satin Knights; The Steve Sax Trio; Testament; Blind Willie Witherspoon; The Ya-Hoo Recovering Alcoholic Jug Band; Yodelin' Zeke.**

CALIFORNIA DREAMS—From the 1992–96 TV series of the same name. Pop/rock band of pretty California high schoolers in a lightweight show from the same people who gave us *Saved by the Bell*. Original lineup: Matt Garrison (Brent Gore), Tiffani Smith (Kelly Packard), Tony Wicks (William James Jones), Jenny Garrison (Heidi Lenhart), and the band's manager, Sylvester "Sly" Winkle (Michael Cade). Tough guy Jake Sommers (Jay Anthony Frake) joined the band in the "Jake's Song" episode (09/11/93). Jenny was replaced by Hong Kong exchange student Samantha Woo (Jennie Kwan) in the "Wooing Woo" episode (09/25/93). Matt was replaced by Sly's cousin Mark Winkle (Aaron Jackson) in "The Unforgiven" episode (09/10/94). In the "Dirty Dog Days" episode (01/29/94) the band played their songs on pirate radio under the name The Dirty Dogs. A soundtrack album for the show was released on MCA in 1992. See also **Bradley and the Billionaires**; **Total Defiance**; **Zane Walker.**

CALIFORNIA RAISINS, THE—Invented by Will Vinton Studios for a 1986 California Raisin Advisory Board commercial, their popularity inexplicably skyrocketed and they appeared in the CBS TV specials: *The Claymation Christmas Celebration* (1987), *Meet the Raisins* (1988), and *The Raisins: Sold Out* (1990). They actually also had a brief animated Saturday morning kids show in 1989, *California Raisins*. Not the Claymation of the ad and specials, but inexplicably regular cel animation. They also gained backup singers, The Raisinettes. The *Meet the Raisins* special actually defined the characters, giving them names, personalities, and distinguishing characteristics (they were mostly identical in the ad). They were now AC, Bebop, Red, and Stretch, and their manager's name was Rudy. In *The Raisins: Sold Out*, they tangle with metal-playing ax shredder Lick Broccoli, but end up dumping manager Rudy for Lick's sleazy manager Leonard Limabean.

He has them jump on a series of ridiculous musical fads (disco polka, country rap, demolition rock) before they come to their senses. Four albums were released to cash in on this fad franchise: *The California Raisins Sing the Hit Songs* (1987), *Meet the Raisins!* (1988), *Christmas with the California Raisins*, and *Sweet, Delicious and Marvelous* (1990). The California Raisins were accepted into the Smithsonian Institute in 1991, one of the biblical signs of the apocalypse. *TRIVIA TIME!* Real musician Buddy Miles provided the main singing voice for the band. Miles has a storied career, drumming for The Electric Flag, Jimi Hendrix, and Carlos Santana.

CANCER BOY—Inexplicably cheery wheelchair-bound kid (Bruce McCullough) with, duh, cancer from the 1996 Kids in the Hall movie *Brain Candy*. The video from his album *Whistle When You're Low* is nominated for best new rap, hip-hop, or folk act at the World Video Awards. He doesn't sing, he just whistles. See also **Armada**; **Death Lurks**; **Mississippi Gary**; **The Noodles**; **Tammy.**

CANDY BAND, THE—In the General Cinema pre-movie promo trailer, an animated popcorn-bag guy and his sexy Pepsi-cup date go see The Candy Band play. This group of talented anthropomorphized snacks is a five-piece combo. There's a yellow candy box with sunglasses playing the guitar and a Reese's Peanut Butter Cup on saxophone. They play a rockin' 50s-style version of the General Cinema theme music.

CANDY SLICE AND THE SLICERS—See **Candy Slice.**

CANE AND THE STUBBORN STAINS—Real hit punk rock trio Green Day play this horrible teenage garage band in "The Man Who Shot Cane Skretteberg" episode (11/16/97) of animated FOX show

King of the Hill. These four punks irritate the neighborhood kicking out extremely poor jams in their garage. When Hank (Mike Judge) goes to tell them to turn it down, the four teens (Cane, Zeus, Face, and a nameless guy) make fun of Hank and continue playing. Suddenly, Hank and his buddies are feeling old, and after the punks tear around the streets popping people in the foreheads with a paintball gun, they challenge the band to paintball duel. After Hank and his buddies get their asses kicked bad, they try again, this time relying on the cunning and deceit of old age instead of the physical prowess and energy of youth. Finally defeating the young snots, they win the band's amps, leaving Cane and his cohorts to thrash futilely and very, very quietly in their garage. Frank Wright (aka Tré Cool) played Cane Skretteberg, Michael Pritchard (aka Mike Dirnt) played Zeus, and Billie Joe Armstrong (aka Billy Joe) was Face. See also **The A Men; The Bluegrass Brothers; The Dale Gribble Bluegrass Experience; 4 Skore; The Harris Twins; John Redcorn and Big Mountain Fudge Cake; Pastor K; Pimp Franklin**.

CAP'N GEECH AND THE SHRIMP SHACK SHOOTERS— See **The Wonders**.

CAPTAIN BART AND THE TEQUILA MOCKINGBIRDS— In the "Bart to the Future" episode (3/19/00) of FOX cartoon *The Simpsons*, Bart Simpson (voiced by Nancy Cartwright) sees an extended vision of his future where he's a money-mooching loser trying to be a rock star with this "band." Meanwhile, his sister Lisa (voiced by Yeardley Smith) is our first straight female president. The band is Bart on lead guitar and vocals with Ralph Wiggum (also voiced by Nancy Cartwright) on tambourine. They would cover Jimmy Buffet, but since Mr. Buffet charges for that, they do a rip-off called "Wastin' Once More Again in Daiquiriville." The band breaks up after

their one and only gig at Nelson's Krab Shack. See also **The Beach Boys Experience; The Be Sharps; Johnny Bobby; Johnny Calhoun; The Crazy Old Man Singers; Cyanide; Gulliver Dark; Ferl Dixon and His Second Helping Boys; Funky C Funky Do; Garfunkel, Messina, Oates, and Lisa; Hooray for Everything; Kovenant; Krusty and the Krums, The Larry Davis Experience; Little Timmy and the Shebangs; Loggins and Oates; Lurleen Lumpkin; M. C. Safety and the Caution Crew; Melvin and the Squirrels; "Bleeding Gums" Murphy; The Party Posse; The Rappin' Rabbis; Red Breem and His Band of Some Esteem; The Satin Knights; The Steve Sax Trio; Testament; Blind Willie Witherspoon; The Ya-Hoo Recovering Alcoholic Jug Band; Yodelin' Zeke**.

CAPTAIN GUS AND HIS POLKA PIRATES— Swashbuckling oompah band that played the bar and sitcom *Cheers* during the "Unplanned Parenthood" episode (10/24/91). Carla (Rhea Perlman) and her daughter Serafina (Leah Rimini) hired the aging musicians to provide music for the latter's wedding. And even though their polka version of "Hava Nagila" "managed to insult two cultures" (according to Frasier), their duet with an eye-patched Loretta Tortelli (Jean Kasem) wasn't half bad. See also **Eddie Barnett and the Eddie Barnetters; Nancy Gee; The Grinning Americans**.

CARL BENSON'S WILDCATS— Mild-mannered quartet (drums, stand-up bass, sax, and accordion) playing the Class of '45 high school reunion in the "Class Reunion" episode (02/04/63) of *The Andy Griffith Show*. They shuffle through "Chattanooga Choo Choo" and several other numbers. They're so sedate, the accordion player sits down, and the sax player is Carl Benson's mom! See also **The Darlings; Keevy Hazelton; Jim Lindsey; The Sound Committee**.

CARLOS O'CONNER AND THE CELESTIALS—See **Carlos O'Conner**.

CARPENTER, ROSS—See **Robin Gantner**.

CARRIE NATIONS, THE—Innocence-losing all-female rock trio from the insane 1970 movie *Beyond the Valley of the Dolls*. Originally known as The Kelly Affair, after lead singer Kelly MacNamara (former *Playboy* playmate Dolly Read), they move to Hollywood and are rechristened with this moniker by bizarre rock impresario Ronnie "Z-Man" Barzell (John Lazar). They quickly get sucked into a morass of decadence, mainly of the sex-and-drugs variety. Their star rises as the bottom falls out from under them and they lose their moral compass in the labyrinthine plot that's just way too complicated. The other band members are Casey Anderson (Cynthia Myers, also a former *Playboy* playmate) and Petronella Danforth (Marcia McBroom). Musically, the band is in danger of being overshadowed by the cameo performance of psychedelic lightweights The Strawberry Alarm Clock. Songs by The Carrie Nations include "Come With the Gen-

tle People," "Look on Up at the Bottom," and "Sweet Talkin' Candy Man." *TRIVIA TIME!* This ridiculous Russ Meyer–directed movie was penned by none other than film critic Roger Ebert!

CB4—Hardcore gangsta rap trio from the 1993 comedy of the same name. Their name stands for Cell Block 4. But really their attitude, toughness, and jail time is all a front. Comedian Chris Rock plays leader MC Gusto, who's really ordinary non-felon Albert Brown. The other members are Stab Master Arson, really Brown's pal Otis (rapper Deezer D), and Dead Mike, really Brown's other pal Euripides (Allen Payne).

CELESTIALS, THE—From the "On the Flip Side" episode (12/07/66) of wildly uneven ABC anthology show *ABC Stage 67*. This quite literally heavenly quartet descends from the skies to help the ailing career of pop singer Carlos O'Conner (Ricky Nelson). Their divine mandate is to watch over the stars, but, "star-struck" leader Angie (Joanie Sommers), cheats a bit to include her fave singers—they helped Sinatra in 1953, dontcha know. Are they really from heaven? Angie sez, "We're not exactly from Big Pearly, we're sort of in the suburbs." These painfully earnest day trippin' hippies (played by Tyrone Cooper, Steve Perry, and Jeff Siggins) take twenty-four hours off to resurrect Carlos O'Conner's career. The Celestials ambush O'Conner in his hotel room, lengthen his hair, trade his button-down plastic-fantastic threads for sequined pants and a flowery-powery shirt. But stubborn O'Conner refuses their free

The Carrie Nations

makeover, 'cause he's a loner, Dottie. Not even their prancing around in matching powder-blue gear with Plexiglas instruments and singing the unlikely Bacharach/David tune "Fender Mender" can convince him. Their next attempt at helping, trying to get Carlos moved to top billing at Greenwich Village's Way Out Inn, ends with his show being canceled. Guess only the pope is infallible. Third time's the charm though, as they turn Juanita's Place, the clothing shop next door, into a club, to the tune of, um, "Juanita's Place." There, as Carlos O'Conner and the Celestials, they are seen by reviewers from *Cashbox, Billboard, Newsweek*, and, best of all, a spy for Don Prospect, head of Vertigo Records. Prospect (Anthony Holland) signs 'em immediately, records 'em immediately ("Take a Broken Heart"), and rush-releases the single immediately to the hottest DJs. Immediately. Alas, it turns out that, like vampires, the supernatural Celestials don't show up in photographs or on magnetic tape. The record is just O'Conner singing! It becomes a hit anyway, and the Celestials split back for Limbo Heights, mission accomplished. But it really just proves the point—angels should stick to helping sports teams. Also, someone ask God why the black angel has to be the drummer. See also **Bernice and Her Mammals; Chuck Roast and the Rares; The Harpoons; Heinrich and the West Berlin Nine; The Hors D'Oeuvres; Carlos O'Conner.**

CHABLIS, THE—This band had the 1968 song "Riff With It" that was sampled some thirty years later by another artist, Scratch. This led to trouble. From *The Sopranos* "A Hit Is a Hit" episode (03/14/99). See also **Massive Genius; Scratch; Visiting Day; Little Jimmy Willis.**

CHAM—Popular female j-pop (j for Japanese) trio from the psychothriller anime flick *Perfect Blue*. Lead singer Mima Kirigoe (voiced by Junko Iwao in the Japanese version, Ruby Marlowe in the English dub) pisses everyone off by leaving the band to start an acting career, only then to be threatened by an obsessed fan and haunted by her own past cutesy image.

CHAN CLAN, THE—That Hanna-Barbera, always thinking. In this case, they were thinking, "What if the Scooby-Doo gang were also a band? And had a magical van? And ripped off an old movie character?" Thus, the 1972–74 animated Saturday morning show *The Amazing Chan and the Chan Clan*. They solve some mysteries, play some music, and if that wasn't enough, their van could change form to look like any type of car or truck. Take that, Mystery Machine! The older kids had the band, and their pet dog, Chu-Chu, played tambourine. He was Simon to their Garfunkels, really. *TRIVIA TIME!* Actress Jodie Foster was the voice of Anne Chan! Poppa Charlie was voiced by Keye Luke, who used to play Number One Son in the old 40s Charlie Chan movies. And Ron Dante, who also sang for The Archies, provided lead vocals.

CHANTRELLINES, THE—Early 60s black female Motownish trio à la The Supremes/Shirelles/Ronettes from *That Thing You Do* (1996). They're on the same 1964 Playtone Galaxy of Stars package tour as The Wonders. The girls sing "Hold My Hand, Hold My Heart." The Wonders' bass wuss (Ethan Embry) really likes them. He has a crush! Aww! Played by Kennya J. Ramsey, Julie L. Harkness, and Darlene Dillinger. See also **Elizabeth Anne; Blue Spot Trio; Diane Dane; The Echoes; Freddy Fredrickson; The G Men; The Heardsmen; The Hollyhocks; Jon D and the Walkers; Legends of Brass; Marilyn Lovell and the Geminis; The Norm Wooster Singers; Del Paxton; The Saturn 5; The Tempos; The Trends; Two Eriks; The Vicksburgs; The Wonders.**

CHARLES, DAVY—The 1973 low-budget film *Super-chick* is pure blaxploitation, er, that is, if you replace "black" with "white woman." Cough. Tara B. True (Joyce Jillson) is a mousy, brown-haired stewardess by day, and a blond-tressed superwoman by later in the day. She has a boyfriend in every (air)port, and in Los Angeles, it's this pop superstar (Timothy Wayne-Brown) with two records in the charts and his own top TV show. But at the ripe old age of twenty-one, he feels threatened and worried—you gotta stay on top! He's desperate for a new sound. Inspiration hits him at club Filthy McNasty's while mulleted goon McNasty brays some off-tune garbage. His new sound? Davy and Tara record themselves having sex inside a piano! Um . . . ow!? Alas, their relationship doesn't last. Davy: "We literally made music last night." Tara: "I don't want to have to worry about screwing off-key the rest of my life." *TRIVIA TIME!* The club Filthy McNasty's was a real Hollywood club at the time of the movie, and later became the infamous Viper Room, in front of which River Phoenix OD'd.

CHATMAN, FRED—Old authentic old African-American old acoustic old-school bluesman from the 2001 movie *Ghost World*. Seymour (Steve Buscemi) and Enid (Thora Birch) go see him play. Seymour has one of his 78s—only one of two known copies! Fred Chatman (J.J. "Bad Boy" Jones) has the misfortune to open for all-white "authentic" blooze rockers, Blueshammer. Seymour mentions other real period artists throughout the film (Skip James, Memphis Minnie, Geeshie Wiley, Lionel Belasco), but this one is fake. See also **Alien Autopsy**; **Blueshammer**; **Vanilla, Jade and Ebony**.

CHEAP GIRLS, THE—Musical group of unknown style, composed of hideous transvestites. Actually that's an insult to transvestites. These are just big burly bearded men in discount summer frocks and

hats. That's always gotta be good for a laugh, right? Okay, maybe not. Their lawyer is the protagonist of *The Money Pit* (1986), Walter Fielding (Tom Hanks). At one point the band wants to change their name to Meryl Streep, until Fielding talks some sense into their big, burly, bearded, behatted heads. They show up at the end as the bridesmaids at Fielding's wedding. Wacky, wacky, wack . . . whatever. Played by real blues band The Fabulous Heavyweights: Tom Filiault, Doug Plavin, Chris Tuttle, and Ed Vadas. The movie also featured real cheese metal band White Lion as another nameless client of Fielding's. See also **Benny**.

TOP TEN REAL BANDS THAT SHOULD BE FAKE
BY GALEN BLACK

1. **MC Hammer**—He was invented straight from a sitcom writer's notebook—a WHITE sitcom writer's notebook. He dressed and talked just like a TV version of a rock and roll star. He might as well have been a character from a *Diff'rent Strokes* episode.

2. **Journey**—The fact that Journey is a real band ruins a perfectly good video game. *Journey's Escape* would be considered a classic of the arcade video game genre, if it hadn't been just another way for a rock band to make a quick buck.

3. **The Cure**—Imagine how much better all those John Hughes movies from the 80s would have been if The Cure had been the fake band playing the high school dances.

4. Milli Vanilli—If only they had just been a real fake band instead of a fake real band no one would have cared that they didn't sing their own material, were exposed as frauds, had their Grammy repossessed, and, more importantly, no one would still be making stupid Milli Vanilli jokes.

5. Pat Boone—The whole Pat Boone thing would have made a lot more sense if he had been what Hollywood THOUGHT America wanted to hear in the 50s. But, sadly, he was exactly what mainstream America WANTED to hear back in the 50s.

6. The Rolling Stones—Now this band would make for one kick-ass TV show! Too bad it would quickly be canceled due to their outrageous, unpredictable behavior.

7. Unpronounceable Symbol—It's in at least one episode of every family sitcom since the 1960s: a kid changes his or her name to something that makes the parents roll their eyes. By the end of the episode the teenager realizes what a special name he or she already have and changes it back. So this chapter of The Artist Formerly Known As Prince's life would have come off much, much better in TV land instead of being a sad and ludicrous episode in such a talented man's life.

8. The Grateful Dead—If The Grateful Dead were a fake band instead of a real one, there would be no net change in the fabric of the universe. Instead of concert venue parking lots, Deadheads would gather in convention centers around the world, seeking autographs and trading video tapes of the TV show and the subsequent movies, while dressed in crude, homemade approximations of Grateful Dead costumes.

9. Warrant—Warrant wasn't a heavy metal band, they were a parody of a heavy metal band. If there was any justice in the world, they would be fake and Spiñal Tap would be real.

10. Bruce Willis (and the rest of his ilk)—There should be more sitcoms about TV/movie stars and every one should have an episode where the star decides to change careers and become a rock star. By the end of the episode the star should learn his/her lesson and return to his life as an actor. And Bruce Willis should star in every one of these sitcoms. Blue-collar people have plenty of role models on TV, teaching the valuable lessons of life. But rich, famous actors don't have those heroes to look to for guidance, and so the world ends up with *The Return of Bruno*.

CHERRY BOMB—Bomb, indeed. This all-female "punk" band was in the 1986 bomb *Howard the Duck*. They were the mid-80s, Hollywood/TV version of punk, that is to say, a terrible pop/rock band with dyed hair. Lead singer and guitarist Beverly Switzler (Lea Thompson) becomes disturbingly enamored of Howard (hello?! different species!) and he ends up managing the band. The movie ends with a rousing guitar duel (on "Howard the Duck"—cowritten by Thomas Dolby and George Clinton!!!) between Beverly and Howard. Rest of the lineup: Ronette (Liz Sagal), Cal (Dominique

Beverly Switzler (Lea Thompson) of Cherry Bomb

Davalos), and K. C. (Holly Robinson). *TRIVIA TIME!* You know how respected actor Tim Robbins has never been in a really awful movie? Wrong! He was in this mess of a movie that has anthropomorphic duck Howard sucked from his alternate anthropomorphic duck planet into ours, and then has to help this punk band fight off a demon . . . oh, never mind. It all worked better in the comic book series the movie was based on.

CHESTERFIELDS, THE—One of the artifacts of the 70s fad for 50s nostalgia was the 1978 flick *American Hot Wax*, which dramatized real-life Cleveland DJ Alan Freed's championing of rock and roll. Real rockers Jerry Lee Lewis, Chuck Berry, and Screamin' Jay Hawkins appeared as themselves, but for some reason, fictionalized versions of other real groups were created, like this Frankie Lyman and the Teenagers stand-in, played by Carl Weaver, Al Chalk, Sam Harkness, and Arnold McCuller. See also **The Delights**; **Clark Otis**; **Professor La Plano and the Planotones**; **Timmy and the Tulips**.

CHIP DOUGLAS AND THE DYNAMITERS—In the "Liverpool Saga" episode (12/23/67) of classic sitcom *My Three Sons*, son Chip (Stanley Livingston) has this band. He gets some help from one half of British Invasion group Chad and Jeremy. The Jeremy half, specifically—Jeremy Clyde, playing visiting Liverpool folkie Paul Drayton. Together they perform a rocking version of the traditional tune "Greensleeves" and win a local teen battle-of-the-bands contest. See also **Susan Duvall**; **Claudia Farrell**; **The Greefs**.

CHIPETTES, THE—During the second coming of The Chipmunks, in the form of their 1983–91 animated show *Alvin and the Chipmunks*, the boys were given female counterparts. Alvin, Simon, and Theodore—meet the Miller sisters: Brittany, Jeanette, and

Eleanor. Ha ha! They have last names and you don't! Oh, wait. It's Seville, isn't it? Never mind. The three girls were all voiced by Janice Karman, the wife of Ross Bagdasarian Jr., who voiced Alvin and Simon and was the son of the Chipmunks' creator, Ross Bagdasarian Sr. The gals also sang and appeared with the boys in their 1987 full-length movie, *The Chipmunk Adventure*. See also **The Chipmunks**.

CHIPMUNKS, THE—Popular hits sung in high, squeaky voices must just never get old. This trio of high-pitched rodents was invented by songwriter Ross Bagdasarian (aka Dave Seville) way back in 1958. The members are Alvin, the roguish egotistical leader; Simon, the bespectacled smart one; and Theodore, the fat one who likes to eat. And, of course, their manager and father figure, Dave Seville, who's always about to pop with apoplexy from Alvin's antics with the familiar yell of "ALVVV-I-I-I-I-N!!" Actually, the sped-up voices predated the precocious vermin. Bagdasarian came up with the idea of singing slowly into a tape recorder at half-speed, then playing it back at full speed for his 1957 hit novelty single "Witch Doctor" for Liberty Records. The next year, he used the same trick to invent The Chipmunks, with the Christmas single "The Chipmunk Song," also a smash hit. Bagdasarian did all the voices himself! He named his creations after his bosses, Liberty Records heads Al Bennet and Si Waronker, and Ted Keep, Liberty recording engineer. Wow, what a suck-up move. The original pictures of The Chipmunks on this early single look pretty much like real chipmunks, with some extra cuteness thrown in. When CBS came knocking to turn them into an animated show, they got a complete makeover, becoming simpler, easier-to-draw, and most important of all, clothed. The prime-time animated show ran only from 1961 to 1962, but did much better in syndication on Saturday mornings. Several albums were released with children's songs, novelty tunes, and more and more covers of popular hits, as with *The Chipmunks Sing The Beatles Hits* (1964), for example. All in all, they had EIGHT top forty hits from December 1958 to December 1962. Granted, three of those were the same recording of their Christmas novelty, "The Chipmunk Song." Even more bizarrely, they once covered that tune in a surreal collaboration with 60s blues rock band Canned Heat (1968)! They even earned three Grammy Awards, in the comedy (1958) and children's recording categories (1958 and 1960). Plus, their harmonies on "Mr. Tambourine Man" can shatter glass. Bagdasarian retired the group circa 1968 and died in 1972, leaving the group understandably quiet for thirteen years. But they came back with the 1980 album *Chipmunk Punk* (1980), thanks to the efforts of Bagdasarian's son, Ross Bagdasarian Jr., who took over voicing his father's creations. The revival was sparked by the old TV show once more being run in syndication, and radio DJs doing comedy bits by playing 33 rpm records at 45 and passing off the results as The Chipmunks. *Chipmunk Punk* did surprisingly well, even if it was all New Wave covers and nothing to do with punk rock. Junior took the trio country on their next album, *Urban Chipmunk* (1981). He put out a couple more albums, *A Chipmunk Christmas* (1981), and *Chipmunk Rock* (1982), before scoring the boys a new animated series, *Alvin and the Chipmunks*, which ran from 1983 to 1991. The show added their female counterparts, The Chipettes. Both trios appeared in the full-length movie, *The Chipmunk Adventure* (1987). The 90s saw a slew of albums churn forth, as well as a couple of straight-to-video movies, *Alvin and the Chipmunks Meet Frankenstein* (1999) and *Alvin and the Chipmunks Meet the Wolfman* (2000). The Chipmunks have been around longer than the Rolling Stones, which ain't bad for what amounts to a glorified cover band. ***TRIVIA TIME!*** Ross

Bagdasarian Sr. had a small role in Hitchcock's classic *Rear Window* (1954). He also cowrote the Rosemary Clooney hit "Come On-a My House" with his cousin, playwright William Saroyan. See also **The Chipettes**; **The Nutty Squirrels**.

ALVIN AND THE CHIPMUNKS GREATEST HITS: STILL SQUEAKY AFTER ALL THESE YEARS
(1999, CAPITOL)

WITH ANY GREATEST hits collection, it's all about the song selection. This 1999 CD is a good appetizer but leaves you hungry for more. It covers mostly originals from The Chipmunks' early years, but has zero from the group's 80s revival or beyond. The Chipmunks exist for two reasons, musically speaking—to entertain kids and record high, squeaky versions of popular hits to be laughed at. This album severely lacks the latter. Where's their version of Tom Jones's "What's New, Pussycat?" or Bob Dylan's "Mr. Tambourine Man?" All you get is "Please Please Me" and "She Loves You" from *The Chipmunks Sing The Beatles Hits*, and The Chipmunks' rendition of "Supercalifragilisticexpialidocious" from the movie *Mary Poppins*. And while we're picking nits, if this is supposed to be a greatest hits collection, where's the infectious "Ragtime Cowboy Joe" and trend-jumping "The Alvin Twist," both top-forty charting singles for The Chipmunks in 1959 and 1962, respectively?! Of course there're obviously going to be problems encapsulating a band with a more than FORTY-YEAR history in a single disc. The inclusion of the original opening and closing music for *The Alvin Show* is great, and it's nice to see The Chipmunks give America a big patriotic shout-out with their seldom-heard version of "America the Beautiful." The album's closer, a faux interview between Alvin and Ross Bagdasarian Jr. at the end is a nice touch. But really, The Chipmunks should rate a box set or a two-CD set, minimum.

CHOCK FULL O' NOTES — From the "Chock" episode (01/13/98) of NBC sitcom *NewsRadio*. This was station manager Dave Nelson's (Dave Foley) college a cappella (NOT barbershop) group. (They played BadgerJam '88). Guest stars David Cross, Bob Odenkirk, and Brian Posehn (all of HBO's sublime *Mr. Show*) played David, Bob, and Brian, the other members. They all talk about getting the band back together, but it turns out that no one really wants to except Bob, so he kicks everyone else out of the group and goes it alone. The name is a play on the Chock Full o' Nuts brand of coffee.

CHOMSKY, IRENE — From the "Find the Monkees" episode (01/23/67) of *The Monkees*. She's the long-suffering secretary (Bobo Lewis) of eccentric TV producer Hubbell Benson (Carl Ballantine), who has put invitations out to all the local bands, except, it would seem, The Monkees. When Benson finally tracks down The Monkees to sign them to do the theme of his new show, he asks the adequate Miss Chomsky to sing it to them. Suddenly entranced, Benson hires HER to sing the theme, leaving the other disappointed bands to mope back to the "extras" window to pick up their paltry checks. See also **Fern Badderly; The Foreign Agents; The Four Martians; The Four Swine; Honey and the Bear; The Jolly Green Giants (I); Lester Crabtree and the Three Crabs; Sven Helstrom and the Swedish Rhythm Kings; The Swinging Android; The West Minstrel Abbies**.

CHRIS WAITES AND THE CAROLLERS — See **John Smith and the Common Men**.

CHROME — Eurotrash antiwar singer against the U.S. invasion of Iraq (the second one) in the "Club Traxx" sketch (02/08/03) on *Saturday Night Live*. Played by that week's guest star Matthew Mc-Conaughey.

CHROMIUM SKATEBOARDS, THE — In the "Glitter with a Bullet" episode (11/18/75) of 70s cop drama *Police Woman*, the titular (hee hee hee) Sgt. Pepper Anderson (Angie Dickinson) used her two enormous talents to fight crime, in this case investigating the suspicious, drug-related death of the bass player of this band. You just gotta bet it was their evil manager, David Griffin (Frank Gorshin), c'mon, he played the Riddler on *Batman*— evil, people, evil! The band was played by real rockers Commander Cody and His Lost Planet Airman. Cody himself (George Frayne) had a small speaking role. There's a terrible pun lurking in Angie's Golden Globe nominations, but let's leave it be.

CHUCK ROAST AND THE RARES — Hideously fur-coated Chuck is trying to impress dandy Don Prospect (Anthony Holland), the manic teddy-boy head of Vertigo Records, with a recording of their song in the "On the Flip Side" episode (12/07/66) of anthology show *ABC Stage 67*. But alas, not only is Prospect NOT impressed with Murray's glockenspiel playing, but Prospect's mom/secretary (Evelyn Russell) thinks they're "the worst." Prospect tells him, "Come back when you're well done." Rimshot, please. See also **Bernice and Her Mammals; The Celestials; The Harpoons; Heinrich and the West Berlin Nine; The Hors D'Oeuvres; Carlos O'-Conner**.

CHUNKY A — Comedian/host Arsenio Hall invented this overweight rapper parody character back in the heyday of his late-night talk show, *The Arsenio Hall Show*. He released an entire 1991 album in character, *Large and In Charge*, on MCA.

CICERO, VERA — From the 1984 Francis Ford Coppola Depression-era film *The Cotton Club*. Played by Diane Lane, she's the teenage tail who's the property of mob boss Dutch Schultz, see? So hands off!

An aspiring singer, she's happy to sleep with the psycho so he'll buy her her own nightclub. Dutch (James Remar) hires cornet player Dixie Dwyer (Richard Gere) to escort her around while he's busy taking over the numbers racket. We don't actually get to hear her sing until three years later (or does it just feel like three years?) when she is hobnobbing with nattering nabobs in, yup, Vera's Club. Dixie, now a movie star, tries to woo her away, but she's Dutch's property . . . until new gangster-on-the-grow "Lucky" Luciano (Joe Dallesandro) does everyone a favor and offs the hothead, which leads into a ridiculous and enormous song-and-dance finale with Vera and Dixie on the train to Hollywood. See also **Dixie Dwyer**; **Lila Rose Oliver**.

CIRCUS MONKEY — Poppy indie/alternative-type band and star of the independent 1998 movie *Bandwagon*. Personnel: Tony Ridge (Lee Holmes) as lead singer and rhythm guitar, Charlie Flagg (Matthew Hennessey) on drums, Wyn Knapp (Kevin Corrigan) on lead guitar, and Eric Ellwood (Steve Parlavecchio) on bass. *TRIVIA TIME!* Their manager is played by Doug MacMillan of real band The Connells. See also **Spittle (II)**.

CITIZEN DICK — Hey, remember Seattle? And grunge? Hollywood managed to make the 1992 movie *Singles* about it before the trend winds blew elsewhere. The movie featured this local grunge band and their big song, "Touch Me, I'm Dick," (basically, Mudhoney's first big single, "Touch Me, I'm Sick," with slightly changed lyrics). Members were Cliff, Eddie, Stone, and Jeff, played by Matt Dillon and three members of Pearl Jam: Eddie Vedder, Stone Gossard, and Jeff Ament, respectively. Their CD was called *Smarter Than You* and included a track titled "Louder than Larry," a reference to Soundgarden's *Louder than Love* album.

Cliff Poucier (Matt Dillon) of Citizen Dick

CLARENCES, THE — See **Clarence Walker.**

CLASS ACTION — From the *Knight Rider* episode "Let It Be Me" (05/13/84). Michael Knight (David Hasselhoff) joins this band as lead singer to figure out the truth behind the previous singer's accidental death. Accidental, right. Hasselhoff sings! *TRIVIA TIME!* Hasselhoff had several hit songs in Europe, but not here in the U.S.A., thank goodness.

CLEAR FOG — At the end of the 01/20/99 episode of *The Sifl and Olly Show*, MTV's po-mo sock puppet powerhouses talk about how they're going to go see this band because they knew member Uncle Cleo when they were exchange students in Appalachia. They then are inspired to burst into the hillbilly tune "Hound-Dog," which goes "Uncle Cleo is a Leo and he's got a banjo trio called Clear Fog, Clear Fog!" The show is the brainchild of Matt Crocco and Liam Lynch, who do the voices and compose and record the music. See also **Kee Kee and The P.P. Gang; Sgt. Blind Kiwi Tarzan; Yeah; Zafo.**

CLICK BROTHERS, THE—String tie–wearing Everly Brothers clones from the 1996 period flick *Grace of My Heart*. They are recording "Heartbreak Kid" when pregnant main character and the song's writer Denise Waverly's (Illeana Douglas) water breaks and everybody freaks out and bolts. They are also shown singing "Love Doesn't Ever Fail Us." They were played by real singers The Williams Brothers. *TRIVIA TIME!* The Williams Brothers, David and Andy, are nephews of the famous crooner Andy Williams. See also **Little Tammy Lee; The Luminaries; Kelly Porter; The Riptides; The Stylettes; Denise Waverly.**

CLIFTON, TONY—Deceased comedian Andy Kaufman invented this schlocky, obnoxious, bad-attituded Vegas lounge singer character in a hideous 70s sky-blue tux. He only played him a few times before letting his pal Bob Zmuda take over the role. He made several guest appearances on various talk shows and also appeared on Muppet TV special *The Fantastic Miss Piggy Show* (1982), guest starring with Miss Piggy of the Muppets! See also **Miss Piggy.**

CLOWNS, THE—From the 1980 trashy horror flick *Terror on Tour*. This KISS-like group of a-holes wears matching face paint, goony afro wigs, and black body suits, and their onstage shtick involves threatening their audience. Some psycho, dressed as a member of the group, is running around killing

prostitutes/groupies. The cop investigating the case even gets offed, but the band's roadie stumbles into the truth: the killer is their screwed-up manager, Tim (Larry Thomas, as Larry Thomasof), who would later come to fame as the Soup Nazi on *Seinfeld*.

CLYDE—Unihandled rock sensation with a tattoo of a cactus (!?) on his tongue. His noisy music blares from Denise (Lisa Bonet)and Sondra's (Sabrina La Beauf) room, causing dad Cliff Huxtable (Bill Cosby) to storm in and turn it down. Later in the episode, widower Dr. Mike Newcomb (Robert King) is dating a new hot thang, Nicki Phillips (Terry Farrell), who's young enough to be his daughter. The Huxtables disapprove, but the couple seems happy, and she has even taken the old man to a couple of Clyde gigs and now he digs Clyde! *TRIVIA TIME!* Lisa Bonet would go on to star as fake singer Marie deSalle in *High Fidelity*. See also **JT Freeze; The Icicles; The Jazz Caravan; The Lipsticks; The Maniacs; Slim Claxton and His Trio; Walking Lemons; The Wretched.**

COCOZZA, TONI—Small-time Glasgow pub 'n' club crooner whose act is "Strictly Sinatra," which is also the title of this 2001 movie (aka *Cocozza's Way*). His piano accompanist is Bill (Alun Armstrong). He gets entangled with the local mob in the hopes of bettering his career. Played by Ian Hart, better known for his role as a young John Lennon in *Backbeat* (1993).

COHEN, MITCH—See **Mitch and Mickey.**

COLD SLITHER—Back before we had Al Qaeda to kick around, there was international terrorist group COBRA, dedicated to whatever evil plan the writers could think up that week. In the "Cold Slither" episode (12/02/85) of kids' cartoon show *G.I. Joe*,

COBRA finances this rock band to try and raise more funds . . . for evil! But really the band is just made up of disguised freelance mercenaries Zartan (voiced by Zack Hoffman) and His Dreadnoks, lip-synching to a bad rock song (also called "Cold Slither") with . . . bum BUM BUM . . . subliminal messages! People are helplessly hypnotized by the song, even some of the Joes! The faux/forced fans fill the stadium at the Cold Slither show, but the G.I. Joe team swings into action, kicks some CO-BRA ass, and frees the audience. See also **The Average Joe Band**.

COLT, JAMES — Rupert Everett played this hot rock star of the moment in the forgotten 1987 film *Hearts of Fire*, which starred . . . Bob Dylan?! See also **Molly McGuire**; **Billy Parker**.

COMIC STRIPS — Number ten artist on the top-ten board in the record shop scene in the 1971 classic *A Clockwork Orange*. The song title is "Art Nouveau." Anthony Burgess's original novel had even more bands in it. See also **The Blow Goes**; **Bread Brothers**; **Cyclops**; **Goggly Gogol**; **The Heaven Seventeen**; **The Humpers**; **The Legend**; **The Sharks**; **Johnny Zhivago**.

COMMITMENTS, THE — The 1991 movie *The Commitments* was a surprise hit, a reasonably simple story of working-class lad Jimmy Rabbitte's strange obsession with forming an old-school soul band in Dublin. Silver-tongued entrepreneur Rabbitte (Robert Arkins) starts with bassist Derek Scully (Kenneth McCluskey) and guitarist Outspan Foster (Glen Hansard), whom he recruits from their wed-

The Commitments

ding band. He adds various members, going through an amusing montage of failed applicants before finding his lead singer at a wedding: Deco Cuffe (Andrew Strong), who is a total ass but has amazing pipes. It's a big band, so hang on. There's Joey "The Lips" Fagan (Johnny Murphy), a washed-up trumpet player who claims to have played with the greats—or is just a big fat liar. He manages to sleep his way through all three of the band's backup singers—Bernie McGloughlin (Bronagh Gallagher), Imelda Quirke (Angeline Ball), and Natalie Murphy (Maria Doyle). He provides music-biz advice and tutors saxophonist Dean Fray (Felim Gormley), who starts soul and tragically turns jazz. Pianist Steven Clifford (Michael Aherne) steals his own grandmother's piano to be in the band. Drummer Billy Mooney (Dick Massey) has had enough of Cuffe's stuff and quits, to be replaced by scarred Mickah Wallace (Dave Finnegan), an ex-bouncer who isn't afraid to head-butt unruly audience members. Egos clash, Cuffe pisses off everybody, but they eventually turn into a top-notch soul band. But alas, it can't last, and the band's last hope holding it together is the promise of R&B legend Wilson Pickett coming to watch them play, but he never shows—or does he? The band rips itself apart with internal squabbling and goes its separate ways. One of the reasons the movie works so well is that their music actually sounds great. Director Alan Parker (who also directed *Pink Floyd The Wall*) hired actual musicians (mostly) to play the band. The soundtrack album sold so well, they released a second volume! *TRIVIA TIME!* Wimpy Irish band The Corrs all have bit roles in the movie. Kenneth McCluskey, Dick Massey, and Michael Aherne still perform as The Commitments (with a bunch of replacements)! See also **And And And**.

CONNOLLY, NIAMH—Sinead O'Connor–like, feminist (to put it mildly) rock star who visits the tiny Irish

isle of Craggy Island looking for a place to live, from the blasphemously funny Irish sitcom *Father Ted* (episode "Rock-a-hula Ted," 04/12/96). Played by Clare Grogan, who used to front 80s band Altered Images. Idiot priest Father Dougal McGuire (Ardal O'Hanlon) manages to give her the parochial house, and Father Ted Crilly (Dermot Morgan) has to convince her to give it back. Her beef with the Church is evident when she sings "Big men in frocks, telling us what to do, they can't get pregnant like I do." She also claimed the Catholic church secretly had lots of potatoes during the Great Potato Famine, and hid them in pillows. See also **Eoin McLove**.

COPY CATS, THE—Incompetent, bumbling henchmen of the evil record exec Master Blaster (voiced by Pete Renaday) in the animated show *Kidd Video* (1984–86). They were also his only act, and Master Blaster's evil schemes frequently centered on forcing people to listen to *The Copy Cats*, or kidnapping real artists and forcing them to perform music *The Copy Cats* would then take credit for. You'd think it would just be easier to find some other band, only with talent. Lineup: The vain and preening She Lion (voiced by Susan Silo), the gluttonous Fat Cat (voiced by Marshall Efron), and the slothful Cool Kitty (voiced by Robert Towers). See also **Kidd Video**.

COTTON CANDY—From the tepid 1978 NBC made-for-TV movie of the same name. Directed by Ron Howard, the plot concerns George Smalley (Charles Martin Smith) starting a high school band with a bubble-gum sound that goes up against the obligatory evil hard-rock band in the also obligatory "Battle of the Bands." Ron Howard's brother, Clint (who also cowrote the movie with Ron), plays Corky Macpherson, the band's manager. See also **Rapid Fire**.

COUNTRY BEARS, THE—The vast and powerful Disney Corporation works strangely backwards, taking their Country Bear Jamboree animatronic theme park attraction and turning it into the 2002 movie *The Country Bears*, instead of vice versa. The original animatronic bear show was introduced to the two Disney theme parks in 1971 and 1972, and ripped off by lots of pizza restaurants in the 80s. Ironically, Disneyland closed this attraction in 2001, before the movie came out—Disney giveth and Disney taketh away. In the movie, little Beary Barrington (voiced by Haley Joel Osment) discovers he's adopted. Duh, he's an actual bear and his parents and brother are humans! He runs away from home to the Country Bear Hall, where legendary all-bear country rock band The Country Bears played. At least until 1991, when they broke up. When Beary discovers the hall is set for demolition, he reunites the ursine group to raise the money to save the hall. Lineup: Zeb Zoober (voiced by Stephen Root) on fiddle, Fred Bedderhead (voiced by Brad Garrett) on harmonica, Ted Bedderhead (voiced by Diedrich Bader, John Hiatt singing voice) on lead guitar and vocals, and Tennessee O'Neal (voiced by Toby Huss, singing voice Don Henley of The Eagles) on one-strang thang. **TRIVIA TIME!** This movie was the harbinger of a terrifying new Disney trend: movies based on Disneyland attractions. In 2003, Disney released two more ride-based movies: *Pirates of the Caribbean: The Curse of the Black Pearl*, and *The Haunted Mansion*. Can't wait for the Tiki Tiki Room Birds movie!

COX, RON—See **Jem and the Holograms**.

CRACKERS, THE—A roving band of Wild West outlaws slash electric rock and rollers played by hippie band Country Joe and the Fish in the odd, electric Western *Zachariah* (1971). Our protagonist Zachariah, a young one-horse-town yokel, buys himself a mail-order six-shooter, dreaming of being a gunslinger. When The Crackers crash the local saloon and play "We're the Crackers," Zach is trying to groove to the tunes, when he is forced into a confrontation with an a-hole who snorts "Music?! You call this dumb stupid noise music?" Zach (John Rubinstein) beats him on the draw, killing him, and runs off to join The Crackers with his blacksmith buddy Matthew (Don Johnson). After passing the job interview (Zach: "I learned to draw at home in my spare time"), he joins the group in various amusing capers. But after slowly realizing that "These guys sure play better than they rob . . . ," he and Matt ditch the small-time bearded bunch to try their luck joining up with legendary gunslinger Job Cain (played by John Coltrane's jazz drummer Elvin Jones) and his backup band, played by The James Gang. The movie also features performances by The New York Rock Ensemble (who play naked) and bluegrass duo White Lightnin'.

CRASH PAPAYAS—From the "MTV4" sketch of *Saturday Night Live* (04/06/02). MTV4 is the MTV channel that actually has music on it, featuring this oddball underground Japanese band. They sing a song in very, very bad English. Played by that week's guest host Cameron Diaz (lead singer), and Rachel Dratch, Maya Rudolph, Tina Fey, and Amy Poehler.

CRAZY OLD MAN SINGERS, THE—When Krusty the Klown (voiced by Dan Castellaneta) is forced out of the children's show-host biz by rival Gabbo in the "Krusty Gets Kancelled" episode (05/13/93) of *The Simpsons*, he falls so low that he is even outshone by a crazy old man on the sidewalk, who manages to get his own TV show, complete with this unseen group. They sing that public-domain fave rave "The Old Gray Mare." See also **The Beach Boys Experience**; **The Be Sharps**; **Johnny Bobby**; **Johnny**

Calhoun; **Captain Bart and the Tequila Mockingbirds; Cyanide; Gulliver Dark; Ferl Dixon and His Second Helping Boys; Funky C Funky Do; Garfunkel, Messina, Oates, and Lisa; Hooray for Everything; Kovenant; Krusty and the Krums; The Larry Davis Experience; Little Timmy and the Shebangs; Loggins and Oates; Lurleen Lumpkin; M. C. Safety and the Caution Crew; Melvin and the Squirrels; "Bleeding Gums" Murphy; The Party Posse; The Rappin' Rabbis; Red Breem and His Band of Some Esteem; The Satin Knights; The Steve Sax Trio; Testament; Blind Willie Witherspoon; The Ya-Hoo Recovering Alcoholic Jug Band; Yodelin' Zeke.**

CREIGHTON, MARCY—See **Marcy Edwards**.

CRENSHAW, OTIS LEE—Comedian Rich Hall (of sniglet fame . . . hmm . . . is fame the right word? Never mind) plays this Tennessee-born country singer with seven ex-wives and a dozen jail terms. His songs include the prison rape ballad "He Almost Looks Like You"—"When he sneaks off with other men/He almost looks like you." From the straight-to-video *Otis Lee Crenshaw: Live* (2001). There's also a CD, and Hall toured in character with an entire Otis Lee show. Backup band: The Black Liars, bassist Rev. Alvy Ronson (Damian Coldwell) and guitarist Orson Carson (Christian Reilly). The Black Liars also have their own solo CD, *The Black Album*.

CREVICE—From the two-parter "Music in My Veins" episode (09/13/95 and 09/20/95) of HBO's series *Dream On*, starring the irrepressibly repugnant Brian Benben as Martin Tupper. He manages to hook up with rock star Katrina Banks (Shannon Kenny), the heroin-addicted frontwoman of this parody of real artists Courtney Love and Hole, to the approving astonishment of his teenage son, Jeremy (Chris Demetral), who's a fan. Yeah, hot rock stars can't get enough of them middle-aged, divorced Jews. Martin tries to get her off heroin, and exposes her to his old college poetry, which may be why she soon starts taking heroin again. Martin's influence on her doesn't sit well with the other members of the band and they break up. Katrina's manager bans Martin from hanging around the band and is able to get the band back together. Katrina says she and Martin will get back together, sure . . . after the album and an eighteen-month tour. *TRIVIA TIME!* Real rocker Warren Zevon appears as himself ripping Martin a new one in the buffet line. Composer Paul Williams also appears as himself.

CRICKETS, DICKIE—The 1920s "king of megaphone crooning" (Bob Odenkirk) is the subject of a frightfully good *Mr. Show* sketch in "The Velveteen Touch of a Dandy Fop" episode (12/20/96). He had three #1 hits in 1923: "Automobile," "Elevator," and "Aeroplane." Nobody could touch him . . . until Kid Jersey (David Cross) came along with the hit "Penicillin" in 1925. Dickie hit back hard with "Time Machine," to discover the public only wanted songs about NEW inventions, not things that hadn't been invented yet. In 1929, Dickie and the Kid teamed up for the Monsters of Megaphone tour, where they took turns inventing things on stage and then singing a song about them, like "Sports Bra" and "Electric Sports Bra." See also **The Beetletown Players; Larry Black; Livingston Brewster; Willips Brighton; Indomitable Spirit; Kid Jersey; Kill or Be Killed; C. S. Lewis Jr.; Horace Loeb; Marilyn Monster; Norma Jean Monster; John Baptiste Philouza; Professor Murder; Puscifer; Salini; Smoosh; Old Swerdlow; Three Times One Minus One; Titannica; Sir Lloyd Wilson Webber; Wyckyd Sceptre; Daffy "Mal" Yinkleyankle.**

Crucial Taunt

CRUCIAL TAUNT—Generic-y hard rock/metal band fronted by Wayne Campbell's (Mike Myers) totally babe-alicious, bass-playing, Asian-American girl-friend Cassandra Wong (Tia Carrere), in the movies *Wayne's World* (1992) and *Wayne's World 2* (1993). These movies are in a very rare category of *Saturday Night Live* spinoff movies that don't suck (Julia Sweeney should be indicted for crimes against humanity for *It's Pat*). The band covered Sweet's "Ballroom Blitz." The rest of the band was played by George Foster (guitar), Anthony Focx (drums), and Marc Ferrari (guitar). See also **Jolly Green Giants (II)**.

CHART BUSTERS!

Who are the fake bands that charted in the real top forty? Sure, it's easy to write a script where the band is a worldwide million jillion selling super-ultra-mega hit, but can they hack it in the real world? Most don't even try. Let's break down the numbers of the ones who had the chutzpah to go for the gold and platinum:

1. **The Monkees**—With eleven top-forty hits—including three, count 'em, three #1 hits ("Last Train to Clarksville," "I'm a Believer," and "Daydream Believer")—during their September 1966 to June 1968 heyday, The Monkees are way out in front here. They had a weekly TV show to push the songs, and the songs themselves were coming from the cream of the Brill Building crop, like Neil Diamond, Boyce and Hart, Carole King, and Gerry Goffin. Prefab ain't built to last, but it was a damn catchy, toe-tapping two years for The Beatles of fake bands.

2. **The Partridge Family**—They only scored one #1 ("I Think I Love You"), but they managed to garner another six top-forty hits between late 1970 and early 1973. Like their predecessors, The Monkees, The P-Fam were a Screen Gems production. They might have got farther if David Cassidy, aka Keith Partridge, hadn't gotten too big for his britches. He went solo for four top-forty hits himself.

3. **The Chipmunks**—Yep, them squeaky-voiced rodents were a real pip in the charts when they were shiny and new. Xmas marked the spot as they managed to get their Christmas novelty tune "The Chipmunk Song" into the top

(continued)

forty THREE times between the 1958 and 1962 holiday seasons. In between, they managed another five top-forty hits, which helped them get their 1961 TV show on CBS. On a completely different note, it apparently took America FOUR YEARS to get tired of "The Chipmunk Song." For most people, it's four BARS.

4. **The Archies**—These cheery cartoon Riverdalians had one big ole #1 ("Sugar, Sugar") in the summer of 1969 and three more top-forty hits before the decade was out. Respectable. Especially when you can't exactly tour, what with being an animated cartoon and all.

5. **The Blues Brothers**—Music snobs gagged, but comedians Dan Aykroyd and John Belushi turned a vanity project into highly listenable fun. Having the cream of the Memphis session-player crop behind them didn't hurt. They squeaked four songs into the top forty, with their cover of Sam and Dave's "Soul Man" going the highest, charting at #14 in January of 1979.

6. **O-Town**—Thanks to a collision between the fake-band show genre and the newly born reality show genre, viewers of *Making the Band* got to watch this band actually being assembled from scratch. "All or Nothing" went to #1 in 2001. They got "Liquid Dreams" up to #25 later that year and that was it. Four rejects from the show came to even less when they teamed up to form their own band, LMNT.

7. **The Heights**—The short, short-lived show of the same name went a mere twelve episodes (not even a full season!) from August to November of 1992 before low ratings took their toll. The bittersweet irony: the show was canceled a week after the band's song "How Do You Talk to an Angel?" hit #1. Maybe band members Stan, Dizzy, Rita, Hope, J.T., Lenny, and Alex should have sung "How Do I Talk to My Agent?" instead.

8. **The Nutty Squirrels**—You didn't think ole David Seville and his Chipmunks could keep their tape-speed trickery secret for long, did ya? Since you can't patent speeding up your voice, the world was introduced to The Nutty Squirrels, a beatnikified Chipmunks knockoff. Their song "Uh! Oh! Part 2" went to #14 on November 30, 1959; a year after The Chipmunks first topped the charts. They did manage to beat The Chipmunks into cartoons by a year, starring in a hundred syndicated five-minute shorts in 1960. Maybe one of them explains what happened to "Uh! Oh! Part 1."

9. **Ernie**—*Sesame Street* Muppet Ernie rode his signature tune "Rubber Ducky" all the way to #16 in August of 1970. And he did it without any help from that nattering nabob of negativism, Bert.

10. **Kermit**—As in, ". . . the Frog." Another artfully sculpted lump of felt and foam rubber cracks the flesh-and-blood charts with the single from *The Muppet Movie* (1979), "Rainbow Connection." Jim Henson's strangled croon put this one at #25 in October of 1979.

CRY-BABY COMBO, THE—Rocking 50s backup band and best friends of hunky dreamboat Wade "Cry-Baby" Walker (Johnny Depp) in the 1990 movie *Cry-Baby*. What puts Wade over the top in the hearts of the ladies is his trademark: he sheds a single tear. He's a leather-jacketed rebel who also sings like an angel and dances like the devil. His band is tough, too, but they have a heart of gold, and man, can they jam! Cry-Baby's sister Pepper Walker (Ricki Lake) hits the skins for the combo, while Milton Hackett (Darren E. Burrows) slaps the bass and Wanda Woodward (Traci Lords) plays the triangle. On saxophone is Mona "Hatchet-Face" Malrovawski, played by Kim McGuire in the finest female albino Buddy Hackett impersonation you will ever see. The combo is led, of course, by Cry-Baby on vocals and guitar, and even singer Allison Vernon-Williams (Amy Locane) gets to join in the fun. Fun, that is, until the riot starts. Isn't that always the way? Cry-Baby gets sent to the big house after the riot, originated by square band The Whiffles, led by Allison's ex, Baldwin, but that just adds to his cutesy rebel charm. He's released (naturally) and gets the girl back (naturally) and the squares and rebels live in harmony (unnaturally). See also **Allison Vernon-Williams**; **The Whiffles**.

Wade "Cry-Baby" Walker (Johnny Depp) of the Cry Baby Combo

CUBE SQUARED—Swedish pop band who need a music video shot in one day, in the 1988 movie *Tapeheads*. They get doused in paint and covered with glitter and feathers. Their song was the Devo song "Baby Doll," sung in Swedish. The band was played by Dan Blom, Billy Ferrick, and Thomas Persson. See also **The Blender Children**; **Ranchbone**; **The Swanky Modes**.

CUBENUDO—Rubik's Cube–mania strikes in the "Cube Wars" episode (07/26/02) of the Cartoon Network's *Whatever Happened to Robot Jones?* It hits so hard there's even this Rubik's Cube–themed

singing group singing "Got to Keep on Cubin'." See also **The Lavender Fudge Experience.**

CULPS, THE—Every generation of *Saturday Night Live* must have its own lounge act, it seems. The 90s belonged to the middle-aged, middling-talented, middle-school music teachers Bobbi Mohan-Culp (Ana Gasteyer) and Marty Culp (Will Ferrell). A sort of sub-lounge act, this husband-wife music-teacher duo tortures folks wherever they can find them with white-bread cheesy-synth medleys. They first appeared on the 11/02/96 episode and made a dozen or so appearances through 2002. See also **Nick the Lounge Singer**; **The Sweeney Sisters.**

CURR, SAMMI—Dead heavy metal singer who attempts to come back from the dead by taking over misfit metal-lovin' teen Eddie Weinbauer (Marc Price, better known as Skippy from *Family Ties*). *Trick or Treat* (1986) is the cream of the metal-sploitation horror movie subgenre, but that still doesn't mean much. KISS frontman Gene Simmons plays radio DJ Nuke, who gives Weinbauer a tape of Curr's last, unreleased material. When he plays it backwards, messages and instructions from the music give Weinbauer some payback on the jocks who torment him. But when things go too far and people start getting hurt, Weinbauer has to decide between listening to the insane, demonic spirit of his psychotic heavy metal idol and, uh, NOT listening to the insane, demonic spirit of his psychotic heavy metal idol. *TRIVIA TIME!* Metalmeister Ozzy Osbourne plays anti–rock music evangelist Aaron Gilstrom, in a meant-to-be-ironic cameo. The movie's music was done by English metal band Fastway.

CYANIDE—From the "It's a Mad, Mad, Mad, Mad Marge" episode (05/14/00) of the FOX hit animated series *The Simpsons*. This "loving tribute to

Poison" were the special musical guests at Otto and Becky's wedding. How great is that—a fake tribute band! Anyhoo, Cyanide played for a grand total of a couple of seconds before Becky (voiced by Parker Posey) yanked the plug on them. She didn't like heavy metal, and Otto (voiced by Harry Shearer) did, which counts as "irreconcilable differences" in eighteen states. Hence, the marriage got canceled. See also **The Beach Boys Experience; The Be Sharps; Johnny Bobby; Johnny Calhoun; Captain Bart and the Tequila Mockingbirds; The Crazy Old Man Singers; Gulliver Dark; Ferl Dixon and His Second Helping Boys; Funky C Funky Do; Garfunkel, Messina, Oates, and Lisa; Hooray for Everything; Kovenant; Krusty and the Krums; The Larry Davis Experience; Little Timmy and the Shebangs; Loggins and Oates; Lurleen Lumpkin; M. C. Safety and the Caution Crew; Melvin and the Squirrels; "Bleeding Gums" Murphy; The Party Posse; The Rappin' Rabbis; Red Breem and His Band of Some Esteem; The Satin Knights; The Steve Sax Trio; Testament; Blind Willie Witherspoon; The Ya-Hoo Recovering Alcoholic Jug Band; Yodelin' Zeke.**

CYCLOPS—Number nine artist on the top-ten board in the record shop scene in the 1971 classic *A Clockwork Orange*. The song title is "Black Christmas." See also **The Blow Goes; Bread Brothers; Comic Strips; Goggly Gogol; The Heaven Seventeen; The Humpers; The Legend; The Sharks; Johnny Zhivago.**

CYLON AND GARFUNKEL—From the "Bendin' in the Wind" episode (04/22/01) of the only animated FOX comedy set in the year 3000, *Futurama*. Robot Bender (voiced by John Di Maggio) hooks up with the preserved severed head of singer Beck (voiced by himself), becomes his washboard player, and goes on tour with him. The Bend-Aid benefit con-

cert the two arrange opens with this oddball folk-duo parody of Simon and Garfunkel, featuring a Cylon robot from the 1978–79 sci-fi *Battlestar Galactica* show and the great-great-great-etc.-grandson of original duo member Art Garfunkel. They sing Simon and Garfunkel's "Scarborough Fair." See also **Leaf Seven; Wailing Fungus.**

DALE GRIBBLE BLUEGRASS EXPERIENCE, THE—From "The Bluegrass Is Always Greener" episode (02/24/02) of FOX animated show *King of the Hill*. Pre-teen violin prodigy Kahn "Kahnie" Souphanousinphone (voiced by Lauren Tom) takes a break from her tedious classical exercises to jam in the alley with Hank Hill's (voiced by Mike Judge) acoustic guitar playing on some bluegrass tunes. It's so fun, Hank's beer-swilling buddies join up and they form a garage bluegrass band. Mush-mouthed Boomhauer (voiced by Mike Judge) reveals a previously hidden ability to play the banjo and actually sing (singing voice done by country star Vince Gill) on the Bill Monroe classic "Blue Moon of Kentucky." Dale Gribble (voiced by Johnny Hardwick) plays bass on his electronic keyboard, and Bill Dauterive (voiced by Stephen Root) chips in on washboard. Hank thinks they're pretty good—Branson-good, even—and enters them to compete in the 15th Annual Old Time Fiddle Festival. Kahnie ditches her Fort Worth audition for the boring ole Van Cliburn Summer Orchestra to hit the road with Hank and Co. In Branson, Hank turns into as demanding a taskmaster as Kahnie's dad Kahn and sucks all the fun out of the outing, so Kahnie and Hank's son, Bobby (voiced by Pamela Segall), bolt before the contest. Hank has to go after her, leaving the band two members short. Dale tricks country legend Charlie Daniels (playing himself) into replacing Kahnie on fiddle. Hank and Kahn (voiced by Toby Huss) find their kids busking for bus fare to Appalachia, and reconcile. See also **The A Men; The Bluegrass Brothers; Cane and the Stubborn Stains; 4 Skore; The Harris Twins; John Redcorn and Big Mountain Fudge Cake; Pastor K; Pimp Franklin.**

DANCING SCHUBERTS, THE — In the "Deviated Tonsils" episode (2001) of the animated WB kidvid show *Generation O!*, the titular band has a brief clash backstage at the TV dance program Dance Jam with the irritating, goody-two-shoes, insincere, phony-baloney, brother-sister duo The Dancing Schuberts. Generation O! has to suffer through their song "Mom and Dad Know Best" before they can take the stage. Later in the episode, Molly's bratty brother Buzz torments her by playing a Dancing Schuberts CD. Tragically, "Deviated Tonsils" turns out to be Molly's medical condition and not the name of any band. See also **Generation O!**

DANDI AND PANDI — Whew. Where to begin. Okay, this interracial singing duo comes from the jaw-droppingly, mind-numbingly bad 1980 movie *The Apple*, a sort of train wreck combo of *Rocky Horror Picture Show, The Phantom of the Paradise*, and The Book of Revelations, set in futuristic 1994. Dandi (Alan Love) is exactly half Roger Daltrey and half Davy Jones. Pandi (Grace Kennedy) is your standard-issue hot black chick. They are the super-huge, sequin-spangled, singing sensation of the BIM company (Boogalow International Music), controlled by satanic fop Mr. Boogalow (Vladek Sheybal). He uses them to seduce the fresh-faced innocent folk duo Alphie and Bibi. See also **Alphie and Bibi.**

DANE, DIANE — One of the headliners of the 1964 Playtone Galaxy of Stars package tour that main characters The Wonders join in the bandtastic 1996 movie *That Thing You Do*. Diane (Chaille Percival) sings the ballad "My World Is Over." Wonders' lead singer Jimmy (Johnathon Schaech) inadvertently pisses her off when he points out that The Wonders' song is going up the charts, because hers is going DOWN the charts. Jimmy chums up to her for some inexplicable reason, despite the fact that she's the type of gal who doesn't want to have much to do with guys like The Wonders. She tells Jimmy to "never trust a label," advice he takes to heart, carefully stowing it next to the bug up his butt. See also **Elizabeth Anne; Blue Spot Trio; The Chantrellines; The Echoes; Freddy Fredrickson; The G Men; The Heardsmen; The Hollyhocks; Jon D and the Walkers; Legends of Brass; Marilyn Lovell and the Geminis; The Norm Wooster Singers; Del Paxton; The Saturn 5; The Tempos; The Trends; Two Eriks; The Vicksburgs; The Wonders.**

DARK, DEACON — Real pop star and former U.S. Representative (R-CA from 1994 till his untimely death in a 1998 skiing accident) Sonny Bono portrayed this Alice-Cooper-slash-KISS-style rocker in the 08/11/79 episode of that guest star–studded series *The Love Boat*. As Captain Stubing (Gavin MacLeod) says, "He's no Jerry Vale!" Out of his face paint, he falls in love with a deaf girl and sings her a sappy love song. Sellout! Boo! Hiss!

DARK, GULLIVER — Recurring male-vocalist lounge act with inexplicable sex appeal to the ladies—a sort of low-budget Tom Jones—he (Sam MacMurray) first appeared in the "Kay's Adventure" sketch (12/13/87) on *The Tracy Ullman Show*. Interestingly, his character also made a crossover appearance on animated show *The Simpsons*, singing at a Vegas-style girlie show at Springfield's Sapphire Lounge in the "Homer's Night Out" episode (03/25/90). It's only fair, as *The Simpsons* got their start as animated shorts on *The Tracy Ullman Show*. See also **Ariel; Kristy Muldoon; The Nice Neighbors.**

DARK, LUNA—See **Jem and the Holograms.**

DARLINGS, THE—The stone-faced sons of the hill-billy Darling clan on *The Andy Griffith Show*, were played by real-life bluegrass group The Dillards. They made many appearances during the run of the show, being especially featured in the episodes "The Darlings Are Coming" (3/18/63), "Briscoe Declares for Aunt Bea" (10/28/63), and "Divorce Mountain-Style" (3/30/64). They also appeared in the 1986 reunion TV movie *Return to Mayberry*. Lineup: Rodney Dillard on guitar, dobro, and vocals; Doug Dillard on banjo and baritone vocals; Dean Webb on mandolin and tenor vocals; and Mitch Jayne on bass. Father of the clan (but not a member of The Dillards), Briscoe Darling Jr. (Denver Pyle) would occasionally chip in on jug. See also **Carl Benson's Wildcats; Keevy Hazelton; Jim Lindsey; The Sound Committee.**

DARROCK, JIMMY—Flintstonified version of singer and teen idol James Darren in the "Surfin' Fred" episode (03/25/65) of prime-time cartoon *The Flintstones*. The Flintstone and Rubble families go to the beach, but their vacation plans coincide with the national surf championships AND spring break. Bad planning! But they meet this surf music idol. In reality, James Darren was pop, not surf. See also **Ann-Margrock; The Beau Brummelstones; The Flintstone Canaries; "Hot Lips" Hannigan; Hi-Fye; Pebbles and Bamm-Bamm; Rock Roll.**

DARRYL AND THE CHAOS—Darryl McPherson's high school band in the "Hurtin' Inside" episode (04/08/00) of animated series *Baby Blues*. The four-some (guitar, bass, drums, keyboards) was in a battle of the bands against such notables as the punky Steve and the Apocalypse and the Jim Morrison-meets-Dylan-meets-bad-Nick-Cave-esque Flack and the Calamity. D and the C's planned entry was "Becky Won't You Read My Heart," an attempt to woo back a gal who'd thrown over Darryl for tortured jerk Flack. But Darryl quits the show because Flack's band performed first. In a classic sitcom crossing of paths, Darryl (voiced by Mike O'Malley) later discovers that Flack grew up to be a high school janitor. See also **Roadkill Hoagie; Scissor Bitch.**

DAVY AND FERN— See **Fern Badderly.**

DEACON, JOHNNY—See **Jem and the Holograms.**

DEAD GIRLS, THE—Late, cheap entry in the horror-flick metalsploitation-subgenre sweepstakes. This all-girl group find themselves being stalked and murdered at the mandatory secluded cabin in the 1990 flick *Dead Girls*. The obligatory twist? The victims are dispatched using methods from the group's own lyrics. Lead singer Gina (Diana Karanikas) has ESP and dreams of the future—so why the hell didn't she see this coming? Some of the band's songs are "You've Got to Kill Yourself" and "Angel of Death."

DEAN, RICKY—Former 80s pop star Huey Lewis stars in the 2000 flick *Duets* as Ricky Dean, a lowlife professional karaoke hustler. Uh, excuse me, professional karaoke hustler? Yeah, they really ruin it for the rest of us. Anyway, his modus operandi is to go to karaoke bars, act like an ignorant jerk, dare to belittle the art form that is karaoke to its fans, then challenge the local karaoke cock-of-the-walk to a heavily wagered-upon singing contest. At which point he whips out his own custom karaoke CD

Ricky Dean (Huey Lewis)

(warning sign!) and blows the chump off the stage. In the plot, he is reunited with his long-abandoned daughter Liv (Gwyneth Paltrow) at her mother's funeral and has to learn to like, love her and stuff. The soundtrack album has his versions of "Feeling Alright" and Jackie Wilson's "Lonely Teardrops." *TRIVIA TIME!* This karaoke-themed movie had all its stars doing their own singing.

DEATH LURKS — Anger 'n' angst-filled metal band fronted by long-haired metal dude Grivo (Bruce McCullough) who sings "Some Days It's Dark" at the Suicide Club in the 1996 Kids in the Hall movie *Brain Candy*. After taking Gleemonex, the miracle antidepressant drug of the title, Grivo becomes a happy-go-lucky popster with a sunshiny new song ("Happiness Pie") that wins the World Video Award for best new contemporary song. Both

songs are on the soundtrack album. *TRIVIA TIME!* Bruce did his own singing, backed by real Canadian band The Odds. Several Kids in the Hall members appeared in The Odds music video for "Heterosexual Man" and Odds' member Craig Northey scored the film. See also **Armada; Cancer Boy; Mississippi Gary; The Noodles; Tammy**.

DEF ZEPPLIN — From the "Toon TV" episode (11/09/92) of cartoon *Tiny Toon Adventures*. Warner Bros. needs to send its animators back to school, because they can't spell "zeppelin." In a music video for The Contours' oldie "Do You Love Me," Babs Bunny (voiced by Tress MacNeille) puts on a Walkman to ignore Buster Bunny (voiced by Charlie Adler), so Buster drops in this band's CD (*Live at Folsom Prison*) into her Walkman, causing her head to swell and explode. Now if only someone would name a band "Led Leppard." See also **Fuddonna; Skinhead O'Connell; Ruffee; Vanilla Lice**.

DEFCON ONE — From the "G Thang" sketch on the 11/20/99 episode of *Mad TV*. This African-American rapper (Phil Lamarr) comes out of the closet on a talk show (hosted by Michael McDonald), then raps a gay rap. See also **Dr. Dazzle; The Eracists; Hoppy Potty; Darlene McBride; Michael McLoud and Jasmine Wayne-Wayne; Savante; Shaunda; Little Hassan Taylor; Willow**.

DEFILER — See **Visiting Day**.

DELIGHTS, THE — One of the artifacts of the 70s fad for 50s nostalgia was the 1978 flick *American Hot Wax*, which dramatized real-life Cleveland DJ Alan Freed's championing of rock and roll. Real rockers Jerry Lee Lewis, Chuck Berry, and Screamin' Jay Hawkins appeared as themselves, but for some reason, fictionalized versions of other real groups were created, like this Chantels/Shirelles stand-in. The band was played by Stephanie Spruill, Joyce King, Yolande Howard, and Brenda Russell. See also **The Chesterfields; Clark Otis; Professor La Plano and the Planotones; Timmy and the Tulips**.

DELORIS AND THE RONELLES — See **Deloris Van Cartier**.

DEMON, MAXWELL — See **Brian Slade**.

DENNY AND BRIAN — Born-again surfer duo that sang "Surfin' to Heaven" on the 06/07/78 episode of talkshow spoof *America 2-Night*, hosted by Barth Gimble (Martin Mull) and Jerry Hubbard (Fred Willard). See also **Pharoah Fawcett; The Friedkin Family Singers; Happy Kyne and the Mirth Makers; Buck and Harriet Pine; The Punk Monks; Tony Roletti**.

DERO, BILLY — From the "Amazon Hot Wax" episode (02/16/79) of TV show *Wonder Woman*. He is a successful folk singer on the Phoenix Records label, and his disappearance drives the whole episode's plot. Turns out he faked his own death so his memorial album, *Farewell to the Master*, would go through the roof. But he left clues hidden in the songs and on the cover of his album *What's My Moniker, Veronica* (which resembles The Beatles' *Sgt. Pepper* cover). Phoenix label-mates AntiMatter figure them out and discover Billy (Martin Speer) hiding out at his boarded-up Santa Monica house. Hey, doofus! You can't cash royalty checks if you're supposed to be dead! See also **AntiMatter; Jeff and Barbi Gordon; Lane Kinkaid; Kathy Meadows; Hamlin Rule**.

DESALLE, MARIE — Ex-*Cosby* kid Lisa Bonet has an extended cameo as this über-sexy, dreadlocked, nose-studded singer playing Chicago's Lounge Axe club in the movie *High Fidelity* (2000). She sings, sells her CD, and has a meaningless one-night stand with Championship Vinyl store owner Rob Gordon (John Cusack), because she believes sex is one of the "basic human rights." She sings an acoustic version of Peter Frampton's "Baby I Love Your Way" in a way that makes it not suck (alas, not on the soundtrack album) and mentions a song she wrote called "Eartha Kitt Times Two." See also **Barry Jive and the Uptown Five; The Kinky Wizards; Licorice Comfits**.

Marie deSalle (Lisa Bonet)

DESIRE — See **Ebony; Scrooge**.

DESMOND, RONNY — Never-seen teen pop idol who sings the hit song "Puberty Love" in the wacky 1978 cult classic *Attack of the Killer Tomatoes*. The horrible song is the only thing that can stop the killer tomatoes, a gimmick lifted completely by Tim Burton for his crapfest *Mars Attacks!* The song's title and singer's name are parodies of real 70s hit "Puppy Love" (composed by Paul Anka) and its real singer,

Donny Osmond. *TRIVIA TIME!* This high-pitched ditty was sung by then fifteen- or sixteen-year-old Matt Cameron, future Soundgarden drummer!

DIAMONDS IN THE ROUGH—From the 2001 flick *Saving Silverman*. Main characters J.D. (Jack Black), Wayne (Steve Zahn), and Darren Silverman (Jason Biggs) like to occasionally don wigs and shiny duds and perform on street corners as this band, probably the only all–Neil Diamond cover band in fake-band land.

DICKIE AND DINO—Rat Pack–esque duo (played by Rik Mayall and Nigel Planer) who appear in the "Bomb" episode (11/30/82) of insane, surreal, and delightfully violent BBC comedy *The Young Ones*. They apparently star in some sort of painfully unfunny vaudeville show much beloved by the workers at the DHSS office. Sample lyrics: "I'm tying my dog to the railroad track / That choo-choo train's gonna break his back. / We used to call him Spot / but now he's called 'Splat.' / That's the kind of per-

son we are! / Oh baby, wontcha come home with me?" See also **Il Duce; Radical Posture**.

DIGGLER, DIRK—In the 1997 movie *Boogie Nights*, Burt Reynolds fails once again in sustaining a comeback attempt, but more importantly, the former Marky Mark of Marky Mark and the Funky Bunch, Mark Wahlberg, draws critical praise as fictional large-genitaled 70s and 80s porn star Dirk Diggler. You'd think that would be enough for any man, but no, the former Eddie Adams also wants to be a singing star and cuts an album, but runs out of money to pay the recording studio. *TRIVIA TIME!* One of the songs he performs, "The Touch," is from the soundtrack to *The Transformers: The Movie* (1986). I Guess if the drugs couldn't kill him, the embarrassment couldn't either.

DILL SCALLION AND THE DILLIONAIRES—School-bus-driver-turned-country-music-star (Billy Burke) in the 1999 indie flick *Dill Scallion*. A country-fried

Diamonds in the Rough

This Is Spiñal Tap, mockumentary cameras follow Scallion's rise after losing a local talent contest to his journey to Nashville and stardom. He meets a bevy of parodies of country artists on his way to the top, such as The Statlin Brothers, The Juggs, Bubba Pearl (David Koechner), and Joe Joe Hicks (Jason Priestley). Even several real country stars—such as Willie Nelson, Travis Tritt, and LeAnn Rimes—are captured on film fooled into thinking Scallion is the real McCoy. Real singer Sheryl Crow helped pen the parody songs.

DIMENSION—In the "I'm With the Band" (11/20/99) episode of short-lived/critically acclaimed TV show *Freaks and Geeks*, freak Nick (Jason Segel) bails out of his friends' as yet unnamed band (they kick around the names Creation and Mission Control) to try out for this band. His drumming is not up to snuff, and he fails the audition. Dimension was played by various members of the show's production team, including the creator, Paul Feig, on bass. See also **Feedback**.

DINGBATS, THE—Popular British Invasion group that arrives in town to crowds of screaming fans in the "Ring-a-Ding-Dingbat" episode (02/24/66) of sitcom *Gidget*. Gidget (Sally Field) isn't sure if she likes them for their music or just because adults DON'T like them. She tries to get in to see the band in some nincompoop plan. See also **The Gories**; **The Horribles**.

DINGOES ATE MY BABY—Alternative rock band from the TV show *Buffy the Vampire Slayer*. The lead guitarist, Daniel "Oz" Osbourne (Seth Green), is a werewolf. They play occasionally at a club called the Bronze. Osbourne's character left the show in the "Wild at Heart" episode (11/09/99), presumably taking his band with him. The band's music is done by real band Four Star Mary, but they don't play the band in the show. See also **Shy**.

DIPLOMATS, THE—Jesse (John Stamos) gets turned down by yet another record company and needs a little extra scratch, so he takes a job with this band that plays an airport lounge in the "Play It Again, Jess" episode (01/07/92) of *Full House*. He feels weird that Becky (Lori Loughlin) is the breadwinner, and not he. See also **The Funky Tongues**; **Hot Daddy and the Monkey Puppets**; **Human Pudding**; **Jesse and the Rippers**; **R.E.M.**

DIRTY DOGS, THE—See **California Dreams**.

DISASTER AREA—Fans agree, the best sound balance for a Disaster Area show is in large concrete bunkers some thirty-seven miles from the stage. Douglas Adams created this louder-than-loud, mega-rich rock band in the book *The Restaurant at the End of the Universe* (1980), a sequel to his 1979 novel *The Hitchhiker's Guide to the Galaxy*. Both started life as a 1978 BBC radio series, but the band was not originally in it. When the series was rerecorded as an album (1980), parts of the show were rewritten, most noticeably the insertion of this band. Then, when everything was reredone as the 1981, six-episode BBC TV series, the band sequence was used a second time. It's all too complicated to even mention the 1984 Infocom text-based computer-game version of the books. Oops, too late! Group member Hotblack Desiato (Barry Frank Warren) is spending a year dead for tax reasons when his former pal Ford Prefect (David Dixon) tries to strike up a conversation with him at Milliways, the aforementioned restaurant at the end of the universe. Rebuffed, Ford and Co. go off and unwittingly steal the band's stunt ship, which is preprogrammed to crash into a sun as part of the band's stage show. *TRIVIA TIME!* Douglas Adams got the name from London real estate firm Hotblack, Desiato and Co. He saw one of their signs and became so enamored of the name he got their permission to use it.

DISCO EXPRESS — This band can teach us all the value of never burning bridges, thanks to the good, good people behind the 1990 flop *The Adventures of Ford Fairlane*. In the waning days of disco, Disco Express came out with the single "Booty Time," with such insightful lyrics as "Booty time, booty time / Across the U.S.A. / Booty time, booty time / Hey hey hey!" Ford Fairlane (Andrew Dice Clay), at the time a publicist in the music industry, passed on Disco Express, and the band broke up. How does this teach us about never burning bridges? Well, the lead singer of Disco Express became police lieutenant Amos (Ed O'Neill), Fairlane's hard-nosed archnemesis, always busting the detective's chops when it comes to solving crimes. See also **Black Plague; F. F. & Captain John; The Pussycats; Slim; Kyle Troy**.

DR. DAZZLE — From the "Helpful Hand Gangsta" sketch on the 05/10/97 episode of sketch comedy show *Mad TV*. This African-American rap star (Phil Lamarr) shills for rap star life insurance—a comment on the Tupac Shakur and Notorious B.I.G. murders (09/13/96 and 03/09/97, respectively). See also **Defcon One; The Eracists; Hoppy Potty; Darlene McBride; Michael McLoud and Jasmine Wayne-Wayne; Savante; Shaunda; Little Hassan Taylor; Willow**.

DR. SNATCHCATCHER — Damon Wayans plays this controversial rapper who has to be reined in by rich Jewish-American princess Marci Feld (*Friends'* star Lisa Kudrow). She is forced to take over her dad's record label after he has a heart attack. She tries to tone him down before conservative Senator Spinkle (Christine Baranski) comes down on him and the label. Believe it or not, Dr. S and Marci actually fall

for each other! From the unlikely and unloved comedy *Marci X* (2003).

DR. TEETH AND THE ELECTRIC MAYHEM — Extremely groovy puppet rock band from *The Muppet Show* (1976–81), various Muppet movies, and random Muppet TV specials. The band started as full-blown hippie rockers, and, thank goodness, no Henson employee ever saw fit to try to update their look or style to fit the latest musical trends. They proudly let their freak flag fly. Lineup: Laid-back Dr. Teeth (keyboards), Valley girl Janice (guitar), man of few words Zoot (tenor sax), the comically violent Animal (drums), and scruffy Floyd Pepper (bass). Bet you didn't know Floyd had a last name, did you? Animal is a sharp contrast to his mellow

Animal (voiced by Frank Oz) of Dr. Teeth and the Electric Mayhem

counterparts, part Tasmanian Devil and part Keith Moon, he is pure rock and roll id, and has to be frequently chained to his own drum kit. The band was created for the 1975 *Muppet Show* pilot, "Sex and Violence." Jim Henson based Dr. Teeth on New Orleans ivory-tickler Dr. John, and also did his voice. The rest of the band were designed by muppeteer Michael Frith. Floyd was voiced by Jerry Nelson, Janice by Richard Hunt, Zoot by Dave Goelz, and Animal by Frank Oz. *TRIVIA TIME!* Bet you didn't know that both Janet and Floyd play left-handed, didja? Didja didja didja? See also **The Amazing Marvin Suggs and His Muppaphone**; **Mahna Mahna and the Two Snowths**; **Miss Piggy**; **Rowlf the Dog**; **Wayne and Wanda**.

DO RE MI—Warning! Before reading any further, you are hereby warned that the cloying, cheery title song of the 1963 British musical *Summer Holiday* will stick in your head like an unwrapped toffee in your pants pocket on a hot day. Duly warned, you may proceed. Do Re Mi is a trio of English lasses on their way to their first singing gig in Athens, attempting to cross the continent in a broken-down jalopy straight out of *Archie* comics. Naturally, there's one of each hair color: brown-haired Angie (Pamela Hart), black-haired Sandy (Una Stubbs), and blond-haired Mimsie (Jacqueline Daryl). In France they meet up with four English mechanics and their refurbished red doubledecker bus on their vacation trip to Paris. Don (Cliff Richard), Steve (Teddy Green), Cyril (Melvyn Hayes), and Edwin (Jeremy Bulloch) generously insist on giving the birds a ride after their car implodes. Since this just isn't quite enough plot for a lightweight musical, the boys also pick up a runaway who's really a famous American singer, a French mime, his surprisingly large entourage, and a dog. What, no cowboy or robot? Throw in several brushes with the law and everyone bursting into song every bloody five min-

utes and prancing around like a pack of Prozac-ed prats and that'll about do it. Sadly, when the gals finally do make it to Athens, they miss their gig due to all their legal troubles. Massive English pop star Cliff Richard is little known in the U.S.A. but has had approximately nine billion hit singles in the U.K. Give or take a few. Cliff's real backing band, The Shadows, put in numerous cameos and also appear as themselves playing a Paris club, injecting some much-needed rock and roll into the proceedings. *TRIVIA TIME!* Jeremy Bulloch would later play Boba Fett in *The Empire Strikes Back* and *Return of the Jedi*! See also **Barbara Winters**.

DOGS IN SPACE—INXS front man and autoerotic asphyxiation aficionado Michael Hutchence starred as Sam, the lead singer of the band Dogs in Space, also the title of this 1987 film set in 1978 Melbourne, Australia. They played punk rock, and had a song with the same name as the band, a warning sign of likely crappy bands everywhere.

DRAYTON, PAUL—See **Chip Douglas and the Dynamiters**.

DREGS OF HUMANITY, THE—In the depths of the 1980s, before Parker Lewis couldn't lose, before Ferris Bueller had his day off, there was the scheming, conniving kid Matthew Burton of the short-lived sitcom *It's Your Move*, played by Jason Bateman. In a two-part episode ("The Dregs of Humanity Part I" 01/02/85 and "The Dregs of Humanity Part II" 01/09/85), Matthew's idiot buddy Eli (Adam Jay Sadowsky) loses the money he was supposed to use to hire the band Morning Breath for a school dance. Out of cash and bandless, they resort to a brilliant piece of chicanery: they dress up some science-class skeletons in rock finery and manipulate them marionette-style as prerecorded heavy metal blares through the sound system, and smoke-machine fog and lighting obscure the truth. Not only do they get away with it, but the band is an instant hit! Too big of a hit, actually. Matthew pays the price for overexercising his promotional skills as new fans demand to know more. Matthew, in WAY over his head, agrees to an interview—conducted by his mom's reporter boyfriend, Norman Lamb (David Garrison, better known as Marcie's first hubby on *Married with Children*). Matthew sets up his skeletons again, Norman gets suspicious, and, as tension mounts, it's all to be continued next week! Except . . . next week's show was preempted by a speech from then President Reagan! Fans had to wait for summer reruns to learn the results: The Dregs are no-shows at a sold-out concert, Norman gets wise, Matthew gets sued and, in a second stroke of brilliance, kills off The Dregs by having them drive off a cliff into the sea. In a later episode, a newspaper shows The Dregs being posthumously inducted into the Rock and Roll Hall of Fame. *TRIVIA TIME!* The Grateful Dead used a similar puppet-skeleton band concept for its 1987 "Touch of Grey" video. Were The Dead Jason Bateman fans!? See also **Morning Breath**.

DUCE, IL—In the "Cash" episode (05/15/84) of batcrap-loony BBC series *The Young Ones*, British comedian Alexei Sayles finally capitalizes on his uncanny resemblance to Mussolini by playing a police recruiter who moonlights as this Eurovision Song Contest candidate from the Scumbag College area. See also **Dicky and Dino**; **Radical Posture**.

DUJOUR—Parody number one boy band from the beginning of the 2001 *Josie and the Pussycats* movie. They sing the songs "Backdoor Lover" and "DuJour Round the World" (both on the soundtrack album). Their evil manager Wyatt Frame (Alan Cumming) deliberately crashes their plane when they get too close to THE HORRIFYING TRUTH! Naturally,

he has to find a new band—cue Josie and the Pussycats! Lineup: D.J. (Donald Faison), Travis (Seth Green), Marco (Breckin Meyer), and Les (Alexander Martin). See also **Josie and the Pussycats**; **Alan M.**

DUKE FAME AND THE FAME THROWERS—See **Duke Fame**.

DUPRE, EDDIE—In "The Blues Brother" (01/24/88) episode of one of the biggest sitcoms of the 80s, *Family Ties*, Alex P. Keaton (Michael J. Fox) plays a blues song by the late Eddie Dupre (Brownie McGhee) on his college radio show only to have Eddie call in and complain he's not dead! He is a bitter, has-been pauper who has forsworn ever performing again, and Alex tries to convince him to return to the stage. Eventually he does, as Eddie is forced to obey the ironclad sitcom law that the more you resist something initially, the more likely you are to end up doing it. Brownie McGhee also played fake musician Toots Sweet in the movie *Angel Heart*. See also **The Permanent Waves**; **The Polka Boys**.

DUVALL, SUSAN—Nightclub singer played by real singer Jaye P. Morgan in the "Second Chorus" episode (01/09/64) of classic sitcom *My Three Sons*. Dad Steve Douglas (Fred MacMurray) starts to fall for her, but the boys suspect and intervene. Jaye P. Morgan also played another singer (Claudia Farrell) in a later episode of *My Three Sons*. See also **Chip Douglas and the Dynamiters**; **Claudia Farrell**; **The Greefs**.

DWYER, DIXIE—Swinging hepcat cornet player (Richard Gere) in 1928 Harlem in the overblown movie *The Cotton Club* (1984). He saves mob boss, psychopath, and jazz lover Dutch Schultz (James Remar) from gettin' blowed up. Dutch takes a shine to Dixie and introduces him to Vera Cicero (Diane Lane), a singer and Dutch's latest flame. Dutch makes Dix an offer he can't refuse: a job, a salary, and escorting lovely Vera all over town. Alas, she treats him like dirt, so he has to slap her around, which naturally makes her fall in love with him. Forbidden fruit is the sweetest! Amazingly, they both manage to keep it in their pants so Dutch doesn't have to kill either of them. At the club, Dix runs into (almost literally) movie star Gloria Swanson (Diane Venora) who tells him he's got star quality and to pop down to the studio for a screen test the next day. Then, for no reason, it's two years later and Dixie is now the star of the hit movie *Mob Boss*, but he ain't so big he can't sit in and play some hot cornet licks while Vera sings "Am I Blue" at her club, Vera's Club. All's well that ends well as Dutch dies in a hail of bullets, which frees Vera to run off with Dixie. *TRIVIA TIME!* Richard Gere did his own cornet solos! Also, real singer Tom Waits had a small role as Irving Stark, the Cotton Club stage manager. No singing for him, although he does get to shout through a megaphone. Finally, if you're a racist, you'll love this movie, because almost every major star (Nicolas Cage included) says the n-word. See also **Vera Cicero; Lila Rose Oliver**.

DYNAMITERS, THE — See **Chip Douglas and the Dynamiters**.

EAGLE, BUD — This rock and roller (played by Arch Hall Jr.) travels to Hollywood to try the road to stardom in the low-budget 1962 cult film *Wild Guitar*. He sings "Vicki" and "Twist Fever," which in ac-

tuality were performed by the actor and his band, Arch Hall and the Archers. The presence of Arch Hall Jr. is your reliable warning sign for "ridiculously bad movie ahead!" See also **Britt Hunter; Tom Nelson**.

EBONY BLACKBIRDS, THE — In Whoopi Goldberg's sitcom *Whoopi*, she plays Mavis Rae, a member of this one-hit-wonder band ("Don't Hide Love" in 1986) who took her money and bought a hotel. In the "She Ain't Heavy, She's My Partner" episode (10/21/03), she attends the funeral of one of the trio's members; the other member is Florence (Sheryl Lee Ralph). Her character is the TV version of "sassy"—insufferably annoying with a seemingly bottomless supply of hack insults and one-liners.

ECHOES, THE — Some anonymous mid-60s band from the 1996 Tom Hanks–produced movie *That Thing You Do*. During the scene where the future Wonders kick band names around, they were going to go with the name The Echoes, but there was already a band in Buffalo by that name. See also **Elizabeth Anne; Blue Spot Trio; The Chantrellines; Diane Dane; Freddy Fredrickson; The G Men; The Heardsmen; The Hollyhocks; Jon D and the Walkers; Legends of Brass; Marilyn Lovell and the Geminis; The Norm Wooster Singers; Del Paxton; The Saturn 5; The Tempos; The Trends; Two Eriks; The Vicksburgs; The Wonders**.

EDDIE AND THE CRUISERS — From the 1983 movie of the same name. This band of small-time Jersey goombah toughs are still sporting greaser looks when it's already 1962, for crying out loud. Then they come to a tour date at Tony Mart's, where shy poetry lover Frank Ridgeway (Tom Berenger) works. Eddie Wilson (Michael Paré) likes the kid, and he ends up in the group as pianist. He writes a fruity ballad for the group that Eddie turns into rock and roll ("On the Dark Side"). It becomes a smash #1 hit in the summer of 1963, and Eddie and Frank collaborate on their most ambitious work ever, the album *Season in Hell*. Way, way ahead of its time; the record company hates it and refuses to release it. Furious, Eddie storms off and his car goes off a bridge on March 15, 1964. But . . . no body. No master tapes, either—those went missing, too. Twenty years after Eddie is presumed dead, the movie picks up with Frank teaching English, and reporter Maggie Foley (Ellen Barkin) interviewing him for a story on Eddie's "death." This leads to Frank going to see the band's manager Doc Robbins (Joe Pantoliano), their old bassist Sal Amato (Matthew Laurance), and former backup singer Joann Carlino (Helen Schneider). Someone trashes Frank's and Doc's places, looking for the lost master tapes. Joann swears she's been getting calls from Eddie. Is he alive? What's the deal? Turns out it's all a scam by Doc to get the master tapes so he can make some money. Joann had them all the time. Joann and Frank have a heart-to-heart and let Doc have the tapes, to make money for all of them. In the ill-advised sequel, *Eddie and the Cruisers II: Eddie Lives!* (1989), they couldn't get most of the principals from the first movie, so the story concentrates on Eddie (now Joe West) trying to form a band in Montreal and restart a music career in disguise at the same time as public interest in his old stuff is skyrocketing. How he never gets spotted can only be chalked up to the same movie magic that lets a pair of glasses impenetrably conceal Superman as Clark Kent: bad writing. Eventually he confesses the truth of his identity to his tacked-on-romantic-subplot, Diane (Marina Orsini). Both movies featured the music of the John Cafferty and the Beaver Brown Band. The song "On the Dark Side" actually hit #7 on 09/15/84. See also **Eddie and the Cruisers Featuring Sal Amato**.

Eddie and the Cruisers

EDDIE AND THE CRUISERS FEATURING SAL AMATO—
From the 1983 movie *Eddie and the Cruisers*, and not to be confused with the 50s rock and roll legend Eddie and the Cruisers. This is a modern-day Holiday Inn oldies act featuring the original bassist, Sal Amato (Matthew Laurance), and a whole bunch of new people running through pablum like "Betty Lou's Got a New Pair of Shoes," but also the Cruisers' oldies. Played by Joey Balin, Howard Johnson, Robin Karfo, Louis D'Esposito, Michael Toland, and Bob Garrett.

EDDIE BARNETT AND THE EDDIE BARNETTERS—
Unimaginatively named Dixieland-esque quintet that plays bar and sitcom *Cheers* during Norm's ill-fated office toga party in the "Friends, Romans, Accountants" episode (11/11/82). See also **Captain Gus and His Polka Pirates**; **Nanny Gee**; **The Grinning Americans**.

EDMONDS, EVIL—See **Paul Kerr**.

EDMONDS-KERR, OLIVIA—See **Paul Kerr**.

EDWARDS, MARCY—Has-been female rock star with a half dozen gold records (such as *Rainstorms*, on Topaz Records), oh, and a Grammy. She then slacked off to become the mistress of super lawyer Hugh Creighton (Dabney Coleman) for four years—people even called her Mrs. Creighton when they weren't even married. When he finds out she's been seeing some young stud at their beach house, he tries to kick her out of the house. Marcy (Cheryl Paris) bitchily blackmails him into half his fortune with her knowledge of bought-off cops and witnesses. So, naturally, he engineers her murder (hence the title of this 1991 ABC Monday Night Movie: *Columbo and the Murder of a Rock Star*). She was strangled; cause of death is a broken neck, and Creighton pins the blame on her lover Neddy Mal-

colm (Julian Stone), her old drummer who has five assault charges, an attempted rape charge, and a crappy, crappy fake English accent. Even though you're shown Dabney Coleman planning the murder in the beginning, you still know he did it, regardless, because it's Dabney Coleman. If Dabney Coleman's in it, you know he did it! Also, please ignore the plot hole that has Creighton's suspicious partner Trish Fairbanks (Shera Danese) browbeating the truth out of him early on, and then it turning out later that she was a direct accomplice. The rest of the movie is just how Columbo (Peter Falk) figgers it all out (tree berries in Fairbanks's windshield-wiper well). Columbo is pretty sure his nephew was a big fan of Marcy and her hit "Closer, Closer, Your Lips to Mine" (played over the opening and ending credits). *TRIVIA TIME!* There's a gratuitous cameo by 50s rocker Little Richard as himself. He says Neddy's a good drummer. See also **Tommy Brown (I)**.

EGG ROLLS, THE—Susan Doyle (Renée Zellweger) is an average 50s high schooler with an amateur rock and roll band with her friends, which has never played a show. But one day her friend, the band's drummer, Tony Fazio (Max Perlich), gets the idea to turn an old Chinese restaurant his uncle bought and said he could use temporarily into a rehearsal space/club for their shows. Then rock and roll destroys young Susan's life, in the Showtime channel movie *Shake, Rattle & Rock* (1994), featuring a jukeboxful of B-listers: *Saturday Night Live*'s Nora Dunn and *St. Elsewhere*'s Stephen Furst as Susan's concerned parents, Mary Woronov as the evil rock-hating bitch, MTV VJ Rikki Rachtman in a cameo as Eddie Cochran, former punk rocker John Doe of X as the 50s type of punk, and comedian Howie Mandel. Mandel gives a surprisingly tasteful, textured performance as hepcat Danny Klay, aka Danny the K, host of Danny Klay's *3 O'Clock Hop* on TV station KORP. He MC's The Egg Rolls' first show until well-organized bitch Joyce Togar (Mary Woronov) shows up with the concerned-mothers brigade and an official noise-complaint form. She makes the cops shut the show down, and it turns into a teenage riot, with Joyce demanding Klay's arrest as the scapegoat instigator. There's a ridiculous finale that literally puts rock and roll on trial, but the less said about it the better. After that, Susan apparently has no choice but to run off with the disgusting greaser/biker/perv who's been stalking her, Lucky (John Doe), painting on her bedroom wall her final testament: "Awop Boopa loo Bopawop bam boom." As true today as it was then. Pretty much everything in this grab-bag mess of a movie was done first and better in John Waters's *Hairspray*. See also **Sireena and the Sirens.**

ELDRICH, CASSANDRA—In the 1986 comedy *One Crazy Summer*, Demi Moore plays this wandering singer-songwriter trying to save her family's house from unscrupulous developers. It's a lot funnier than it sounds. She sings "Don't Look Back." *TRIVIA TIME!* Director/writer Savage Steve Holland later worked on the series *Shasta McNasty*.

ELECTRIC SHOES, THE—Preteen garage band that Kevin Arnold (Fred Savage) joins in the "Rock and Roll" episode (01/02/90) of *The Wonder Years*, inspired by The Beatles' appearance on *The Ed Sullivan Show*. They play Amy Ermin's (Stefanie Scott) birthday party and then break up a week later. The rest of the band: Larry Beeman (Joshua Miller) on guitar, Mark Bernstein (Casey Ellison) on drums, and Neal Rhodes (Dana Young) on bass.

ELLEN AIM AND THE ATTACKERS—Diane Lane plays Ellen Aim, a female rock star kidnapped by a motorcycle gang in the 1984 "rock 'n' roll fable" *Streets of Fire*. The movie takes place in a strange, timeless world where everybody is just as surly and pissy as can be, all the time. She gets rescued by Tom Cody (Michael Paré, Eddie in *Eddie and the Cruisers*), the cops apparently not interested in a minor crime like kidnapping. The band performs "Nowhere Fast," "Never Be You," "Sorcerer," and "Tonight Is What It Means to Be Young." Ellen Aim's singing voice was Laurie Sargent and Holly Sherwood of Fire Inc. The music is horrible, 50s-influenced New Wave. Her manager/lover is the money-grubbing jerk Billy Fish (Rick Moranis). The Attackers were played by William Beard II, Stuart Kimball, Angelo, and John Ryder. *TRIVIA TIME!* The movie features Lee Ving of punk band Fear as a motorcycle hoodlum, and real band The Blasters playing at Torchie's, the motorcycle gang hangout. Ellen Aim and the Attackers is also listed on a computer (in a big list of fake bands) in the 1990 Andrew Dice Clay vehicle *The Adventures of Ford Fairlane*. See also **The Sorels**.

EMICA—Teenybopper pop star voiced by *Bold and the Beautiful* regular Adrienne Frantz in the "All Growed Up" hourlong special (07/21/01) of Nickelodeon cartoon *Rugrats*, which flashes forward ten years to check on its infant stars in the future. Emica wears a "retro" Scorpio medallion similar to one owned by Stu Pickles (voiced by Jack Riley), who views it as a good-luck charm for disco-dancing contests. At the end of the episode, Emica brings Tommy (voiced by E. G. Daily) and Angelica (voiced by Cheryl Chase) onstage for a singalong/flashback. *TRIVIA TIME!* Devo member Mark Mothersbaugh composed and performed the show's theme and incidental music.

ENTRY NUMBER FIVE—Not to be confused with the mambo of the same number. In the appropriately titled "The Band Episode" (02/27/98) of sitcom *Sabrina the Teenage Witch*, title character Sabrina Spellman (Melissa Joan Hart) can't stand to see her high school rival Libby Chessler (Jenna Leigh Green) win the school talent show. So she conjures up a six-pack of bottled talent and feeds it to her friends Harvey Kinkle (Nate Richert, drums), and Valerie Birkhead (Lindsay Sloane, guitar), and immediately they are rocking out a note-perfect rendition of Blondie's "One Way or Another" to win the show. But because they forgot to come up with a name, the host intros them as "entry number five" and they are stuck with it as a name. Contest judge Dwayne Kraft (John Ducey) wants them to perform on his local-cable local-band showcase, *Rock in a Hard Place*. Everybody in the band naturally and immediately suffers from sitcom success's evil twin: big heads. Harvey dreams up some especially stupid ideas for the band and wants to add his new brainless flame, Sunset, on tambourine. Sabrina restores them all to normality, but it's too late, they still have to perform on Kraft's show. So Sabrina swallows her pride, gets Libby to sing, and the band just mimes to a tape of Libby's song. However one bottle of talent goes missing, and is later drunk by five basketballers in the gym. They spontaneously break into the Backstreet Boys' "As Long as You Love Me," 'cause they are the Backstreet Boys! See also **The Flavor Babes**; **The Libby Chessler Generation**.

ERACISTS, THE — Quartet of upbeat teens who sing about the evils of racism in painfully earnest, high-school-assembly style, in at least six sketches on *Mad TV*. Ya see, they're here to "erase racism," hence the name. Lineup: Leader Debbie (Nicole Sullivan), handicapped Ann (Alex Borstein), African-American Steve (Phil Lamarr), and another member (Will Sasso). In the "Eracists—Middle East" skit, Steve has been replaced with the gay Reggie (Aries Spears). Appearances: "Eracism" (11/08/97), "Eracists: Stand Off" (sent into a white supremacist compound) (01/31/98), "Eracists Go to Jail" (last-

minute replacements at a Johnny Cash prison concert) (03/28/98), "Eracists—Middle East" (burst into Israeli/Palestinian peace talks) (12/05/98), "Eracists—St. Patrick's Day" (put themselves between gays and the Irish) (03/19/99), and "Eracists—Behind the Music" (parody of the VH1 show; explains Steve's replacement by Reggie) (05/01/99). See also **Defcon One**; **Dr. Dazzle**; **Hoppy Potty**; **Darlene McBride**; **Michael McLoud and Jasmine Wayne-Wayne**; **Savante**; **Shaunda**; **Little Hassan Taylor**; **Willow**.

ESQUIRES, THE — See **The Five Heartbeats**.

EVAR ORBUS AND HIS GALACTIC JIZZ-WAILERS — See **The Max Rebo Band**.

EVERETT, VINCE — In *Jailhouse Rock* (1957), ur-rocker Elvis Presley plays this ex-con who makes good. In prison for accidentally killing a guy in a bar fight (just one of the many, many bar fights Elvis would have in his movies), Everett is befriended by cellmate Hunk Houghton (Mickey Shaughnessy), a former country singer. Houghton is impressed by his voice and helps him learn guitar and otherwise mentors the callow lad. Thanks to some crappy writing, Houghton gets to run a prison variety show to be broadcast on TV! Sorry, but unless Johnny Cash is involved, no network is going to put on a prison show. Or maybe this is just a VERY talented prison. Naturally, Houghton features his boy Everett. Everett gets a satchel of fan mail, but Houghton keeps it from him, the better to get him to sign a fifty-fifty partnership deal. Now out of the joint, Everett uses a contact from Houghton to get a job at the Club La Florita. Unfortunately, it's a job as bar boy. But there Everett runs into recording-industry worker Peggy Van Alden (Judy Tyler). Inexplicably taken with his surly charm, she gets him a recording session. He gets them interested when he cuts slightly loose on "Don't Leave Me Now," but the record company steals his arrangement for another artist. Everett decides to start his own damn record company, and Van Alden comes with him. They cut "Treat Me Nice" and, thanks to Van Alden's legwork, he's soon a hit, buying a Cadillac and throwing parties. Soon the selfish SOB gets a TV-special appearance, the movie's famous show-stopper number "Jailhouse Rock," where Elvis

Vince Everett (Elvis Presley)

swivels his famous pelvis like there's no tomorrow. But uh-oh! Houghton's out of the pokey and in Everett's face, waving the "contract" they signed. Houghton wants to sing on the special, too, and Everett reluctantly uses his muscle to get him on the show. But Houghton gets cut at the last minute, his sound is too outdated. Houghton's contract isn't legally binding, but Everett pities him enough to give him a job as his flunky. That soon wears thin, and they get in a fistfight. A punch to the throat threatens to take away Everett's voice and hence his livelihood. Gee, will he ever be able to sing again?! As if that's even an issue. The real question is how much last-minute schmaltz you can take before the movie ends. See also **Hunk Houghton.**

EVIL CLOWNS, THE — The 1983 Sony "video LP," *We're All Devo* (a compilation of Devo music videos and short films), uses the framing device of having cheesy Big Entertainment exec Rod Rooter (Michael Schwartz) watching (and rejecting) Devo's stuff. He prefers his company's mega-metal group and its lead singer, Numero Uno. His daughter Donut (*Saturday Night Live*'s Laraine Newman) thinks they're "el vomito." The band also gets mentioned in Devo's 1996 CD-ROM game, *Adventures of the Smart Patrol.* **TRIVIA TIME!** The poster of Numero Uno shown is actually a poster of David Lee Roth from Van Halen, with the face replaced!

EVIL EDMONDS AND THE BEELZEBOPS — See **Paul Kerr.**

EXITS, THE — Kids Cory Matthews (Ben Savage) and Shawn Hunter (Rider Strong) claim membership in this bogus band they just made up to impress the chicks. They try to sing "The Name Game." They get outed when Mr. Feeny (William Daniels) wants them to play a school dance, all in the "Band on the Run" episode (11/11/94) of sitcom *Boy Meets World.* The episode also featured real rockers Micky

Dolenz of The Monkees, Billy Vera, and Rick Nielsen of Cheap Trick. (It should be pointed out that "Rider Strong" would make an excellent pseudonym for a porn actor.)

EYE, BILLY — See **Head Mistress.**

FABULOUS STAINS, THE — See **The Stains.**

FAIRIES, THE — Rock band that fairy godfather Cosmo (voiced by Daran Norris) led back in the day. In the "Boys in the Band" episode of cartoon *The Fairly OddParents*, the foursome opened for teen sensation Chip Skylark (voiced by *NSYNC's Chris Kirkpatrick). They got a lot of tomatoes in the face. Lineup: Pan on pan flute, Santa Claus on drums, Ludwig van Beethoven on organ, and Cosmo on the electric triangle. See also **Chip Skylark.**

FAIRY, JACK — Cutting-edge androgynous glam rocker in *Velvet Goldmine* (1998), an interesting experiment in how flamingly gay you can make a movie and still get a general release. At the beginning of the movie, Osheen Jones plays Fairy at age seven. Why he's shown isn't really explained, because his character is barely in the rest of the movie. When he is, he's the pioneering 70s glam-rock fashion template, wearing girl's clothes all the way back in 1969. One character puts it best: "The first of his kind . . . everybody stole from him." Fairy (Micko Westmoreland) gets a little bit of payback by snagging rocker Curt Wild from glam-star plagiarist Brian Slade after their tempestuous falling out. See also **The Flaming Creatures; Curt Wild; Brian Slade; Tommy Stone.**

FAITH + 1 — It's hard to be evil and sell a million Christian rock albums. Unless, of course, your name is Eric Cartman (voiced by Trey Parker). In the "Christian Rock Hard" episode (10/29/03), the four kids from crudely animated delight *South Park* form a band named MOOP, but they can't decide on MOOP's sound. Cartman suggests they play Christian rock, an idea so crazy he gets kicked out of the band. Before he leaves, though, Cartman bets Kyle $10 that his new Christian rock band will get a platinum album before MOOP. Cartman enlists the help of Butters (voiced by Matt Stone) on drums and Token (also voiced by Matt Stone) on bass to create Faith + 1. Their secret to success is to take popular songs and replace "baby" and "darling" with "Jesus." The album sells only okay at first, but after their performance at South Park's Christfest 2003 (where they replace the punk-metal Christian band Sanctified after locking them in a closet) sales go through the roof, selling over a million copies. Cartman spends all of Faith + 1's profits on a party celebrating the album and the winning of the $10 bet. When he finds out that Christian rock albums go myrrh instead of platinum, he lets forth with a string of profanity and blasphemy so over-the-top that Faith + 1 is ruined. See also **The Avenue Street Ghetto Boys; Fingerbang; Getting Gay with Kids; The Ghetto Avenue Boys; Jerome "Chef" McElroy; MOOP; Raging Pussies; Reach for the Skyler; Sanctified; Sisters of Mercy Hold No Pain Against the Dark Lord; Timmy! and the Lords of the Underworld.**

FAME, DUKE — Lead singer of Duke Fame and the Fame Throwers, this is the big, cheesy, more-famous rock star Spïnal Tap runs into in a Memphis hotel lobby in *This Is Spïnal Tap* (1984). The nonoffensive cover of his 1982 album shows Duke tied up and surrounded by bullwhip-wielding naked women, prompting Tap's classic comment: "[there is] ... such a fine line between stupid and ... clever." Duke Fame was portrayed by Paul Shortino. His manager is Terry Ladd (*WKRP in Cincinnati*'s Howard Hesseman). See also **Lambsblood; Meconium; The Regulars; Spiñal**.

FAREAL, CAMILLE—Real African-American female rapper MC Lyte guest-stars as this old-school rap diva with a real attitude problem in the "Loyalty" episode (04/29/03) of the gritty UPN drama series *Platinum*, created by Sofia Coppola. See also **Lady Bryce; Mace; VersIs**.

FARRELL, CLAUDIA—Former singing star of some twenty years ago, playing at The Indigo Room in the "Falling Star" episode (12/15/66) of *My Three Sons*. Her career is pretty much over, 'cause she's not with it no more. Dad Steve Douglas (Fred MacMurray) helps her get with it by having her sing with his son Robbie's rock and roll band, The Greefs. Played by singer/entertainer Jaye P. Morgan, who did have a career in the 50s that waned in the 60s. She also played a different singer (Susan Duvall) in an earlier episode of *My Three Sons*. See also **Chip Douglas and the Dynamiters; Susan Duvall; The Greefs**.

FAWCETT, PHAROAH—Singer played by Sherri Spillane on the 04/27/78 episode of talk-show parody *America 2-Night*. Or the answer to the joke "What do you call an Egyptian plumber?" See also **Denny and Brian; The Friedkin Family Singers; Happy Kyne and the Mirth Makers; Buck and Harriet Pine; The Punk Monks; Tony Roletti**.

FEEDBACK—Guidance counselor Mr. Rosso's (Dave Allen) cover/bar band from the "Carded and Dis-

carded" (1/10/00) episode of *Freaks and Geeks*. They perform Alice Cooper's "Eighteen" and Grand Funk Railroad's "We're an American Band" at the bar The Rusty Nail. See also **Dimension**.

FELLOW'S FELLOWS—See **Stillwater**.

FERL DIXON AND HIS SECOND HELPING BOYS—Traditional country-and-western band playing at the Springfield Chili Cook-off in the "El Viaje Misterioso de Nuestro Homer (The Mysterious Voyage of Our Homer)" episode (01/05/97) of *The Simpsons*. That's the one where he eats the Guatemalan insanity peppers and hallucinates. *TRIVIA TIME!* Ferl Dixon's name is later glimpsed on a marquee in Branson, Missouri, in the "Bart on the Road" episode (03/31/96). See also **The Beach Boys Experience; The Be Sharps; Johnny Bobby; Johnny Calhoun; Captain Bart and the Tequila Mockingbirds; The Crazy Old Man Singers; Cyanide; Gulliver Dark; Funky C Funky Do; Garfunkel, Messina, Oates, and Lisa; Hooray for Everything; Kovenant; Krusty and the Krums; The Larry Davis Experience; Little Timmy and the Shebangs; Loggins and Oates; Lurleen Lumpkin; M. C. Safety and the Caution Crew; Melvin and the Squirrels; "Bleeding Gums" Murphy; The Party Posse; The Rappin' Rabbis; Red Breem and His Band of Some Esteem; The Satin Knights; The Steve Sax Trio; Testament; Blind Willie Witherspoon; The Ya-Hoo Recovering Alcoholic Jug Band; Yodelin' Zeke**.

FERN AND DAVY—See **Fern Badderly**.

F. F. & CAPTAIN JOHN—This singing duo consisted of Ford Fairlane (comedian Andrew Dice Clay) and Johnny Tinenbalm (comedian Gilbert Gottfried) in the 1990 movie *The Adventures of Ford Fairlane*. The band got the boys from Brooklyn to L.A., but when the singing gigs failed to pan out, they went their separate ways: Fairlane becoming the rock and roll detective, and Tinenbalm becoming Johnny Crunch, L.A.'s favorite shock jock. That is, until his "accidental" electrocution. See also **Black Plague; Disco Express; The Pussycats; Slam; Kyle Troy.**

FIGRIN D'AN AND THE MODAL NODES — Did you know that the *Star Wars* (1977) alien cantina band had a name? No? Then you have severely underestimated geeks, my friend. Do not let it happen again. A plethora of info is available on this band of Bith "jizz" musicians from Clak'Dor VII, such as how the Bith method of respiration makes them excellent wind-instrument players, capable of holding a note practically indefinitely. Shortly after arriving on Tatooine, the band was contracted to play exclusively for crimelord Jabba the Hutt. Unfortunately, they accepted a huge sum to secretly play rival crimelord Lady Valerian's wedding reception, figuring the money sufficient to get off Tatooine. However, after fleeing a Jabba-arranged imperial raid of the reception, the band lost their instruments gambling and ended up having to play at the Mos Eisley Cantina, to cover debts (this is where you see them in the movie). The bar owner hid them from Jabba, but eventually he found out, and as soon as the band heard, they fled the planet. While on the lam from Jabba the Hutt, they performed under the alias Bobbarine and the Wookiee Kotters until Jabba's death in *The Empire Strikes Back* (1980), which freed them to go back to their original name. They were later joined by Figrin's brother, Barquin, a kloo horn player of no small talent himself. Apparently, the soundtrack cut "Cantina Band #1" is really called "Mad About Me" and "Cantina Band #2" is really called "If I Only Could Let Go and Cry." Lineup: Ickabel G'ont (fanfar), Lirin Car'n (kloo horn), Nalan Cheel (bandfill), Tech Mo'r (Omnibox), Tedn Dahai (fanfar), Doikk Na'ts (fizzz/Doren-

ian Beshniquel), and of course band leader Figrin D'an (kloo horn, gasan string drum). He is the group's leader and negotiator, but has a bad habit of losing all the group's earnings in sabacc games. He's nicknamed "Fiery Figrin" for his hot, wailing style of kloo horn playing. His brother, Barquin D'an, played briefly with The Max Rebo Band. If you're really a geek, you recall that only six aliens were playing in the cantina scene, while seven are listed here. Well sir, Lirin Car'n is the Bith seated at a table in the bar scene, he only fills in on kloo horn when Figrin switches to gasan string drum. So there. In reality, the musicians were portrayed in the movie by Rick Baker, Phil Tippett, Jon Berg, Laine Liska, Doug Bestwick, and Tom St. Amand. The minute details come from the short story "We Don't Do Weddings: The Band's Tale" by Kathy Tyers, in the book *Tales from the Mos Eisley Cantina*. See also **The Max Rebo Band.**

FINAL WARNING — See **Robert J. "Robbie" Hart.**

FINGERBANG — From the "Something You Can Do with Your Finger" episode (07/12/00) of animated Comedy Central show *South Park*. Fat-ass kid Eric Cartman (voiced by Trey Parker) has a dream that he and his pals are in a boy band called Fingerbang and make ten million dollars. He figures it's a message from God and attempts to make it real. Since he only has three friends—Stan Marsh (voiced by Trey Parker), Kyle Broslofski (voiced by Matt Stone), and Kenny McCormick (also voiced by Matt Stone)—and all boy bands have five members, they hold auditions and accept Wendy Testaberger (voiced by Mary Kay Bergman), who is not a boy. None of the kids really know what the band's name means. Stan's dad, Randy (voiced by Trey Parker), forbids Stan to be in the group, because he was once in a boy band himself, The Ghetto Avenue Boys. He hit the heights, but then quickly crashed and burned. As the rest of the band waits for Stan at their gig at the mall (they can't go on with only four members, they'll look like idiots), Mr. Marsh has a change of heart and drives his son to the show. But then Kenny is killed, as usual, and they're a foursome again. Then Mr. Marsh steps up to replace him. Delusional after performing in front of a sparse, indifferent crowd, Cartman and Co. reject the imagined pressures of fame and dissolve the band. See also **The Avenue Street Ghetto Boys; Faith + 1; Getting Gay with Kids; The Ghetto Avenue Boys; Jerome "Chef" McElroy; MOOP; Raging Pussies; Reach for the Skyler; Sanctified; Sisters of Mercy Hold No Pain Against the Dark Lord; Timmy! and the Lords of the Underworld**.

FINN, DEWEY — See **No Vacancy; Maggot Death; School of Rock**.

FIRST MATES, THE — See **The Bird Brains**.

FISHER, DANNY — Elvis Presley portrayed this New Orleans club singer caught between a crime boss and his girlfriend in *King Creole* (1958). This is the Elvis movie with the best pedigree: it stars Walter Matthau, Vic Morrow, Carolyn Jones (the future Mrs. Morticia Addams); has a script based on a Harold Robbins book; and was directed by Michael Curtiz, who also directed *Casablanca*! But will this dog hunt? Sure, why the hell not. A great opening scene with sellers' cries of "Crawfish" intros us to the Big Easy, where troubled youth Fisher quits high school to get a job, since his old man hasn't

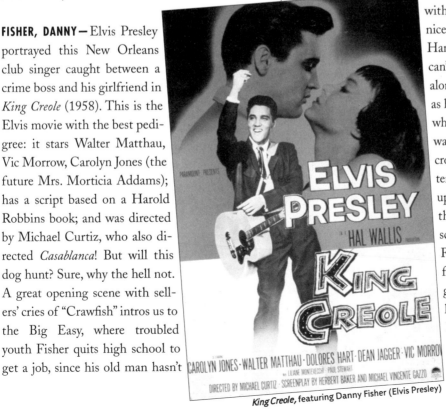

King Creole, featuring Danny Fisher (Elvis Presley)

done a damn thing since their mom died. He sweeps up at the Blue Shade, a nightclub owned by nasty mobster Maxie Fields (Walter Matthau). Fisher runs afoul of Fields's clingy, desperate, doomed trophy girlfriend, Ronnie (Carolyn Jones). He also runs afoul of a gang of street toughs, who get him involved in a scheme that's the best excuse for a song in an Elvis movie ever. Fisher croons "Lover Doll" on his acoustic guitar to distract a crowd at a five-and-dime while the rest of the gang goes on a five-finger-discount spree! Back at the Blue Shade, an unhappy accident has Fisher singing "Trouble" for Fields, to somehow prove he's not hitting on Ronnie. He wows the crowd and, to Fields's anger, ends up working for Charlie LeGrand (Paul Stewart), a smalltimer running the King Creole club down the street. There, Elvis has the audience in his palm by the first horn solo of "Dixieland Rock" (a total "Jailhouse Rock" rip-off—sorry, but it is). There's some subplot with Fisher's love interest, nice gal Nellie (Dolores Hart), but Ronnie just can't leave that Fisher boy alone. Neither can Fields, as he's one of those types who always gets what he wants, by hook or by crook. Typically the latter, as Fisher's dad ends up in the hospital, no thanks to a complicated scheme orchestrated by Fields. Fields springs for the expensive surgeon that can save his life, and now owns Fisher. Just to rub it in, Fields makes him sign a blank piece of paper to be filled in later. Then the plot gets more complicated until the simple beauty of Fields beating Fisher with a chair arrives to clear the palate. Fisher returns the favor by beating the bejesus out of Fields, and then Fisher is on the lam! It's "the big get even" as Fisher and Ronnie flee and enjoy a few fleeting moments of happiness before the final showdown that leaves Ronnie and Fields dead. But the show goes on, and Fisher returns to the King Creole for "As Long as I Have You." Elvis has some great moments in the movie, and it's bracing to watch him actually act instead of just singing and hitting on whatever female costar he's been teamed with. Just remember this handy Elvis-movie rule of thumb: black-and-white Elvis movie—good; color Elvis movie—bad.

FITCH, STAN—The first all-dead singer from "The Old Gay Whistle Test" sketch (06/02/75) on *Rutland Weekend Television*, Eric Idle's post-Python TV show. He "performs" his song "Even Further Beyond the Grave." He just lies there silently as the cameras pan and swoop around him and his acoustic guitar. See also **Mantra Robinson**; **The Rutles**; **Splint**; **Toad the Wet Sprocket**.

FITCHLY, STILES—The singer of "Hang Ten," an (apparently) instrumental tune played in the "Bye, Bye Birdie" episode (10/22/95) of Nickelodeon's cartoon *Rocko's Modern Life*. **TRIVIA TIME!** *Rocko's Modern Life* may be the first kids' cartoon to portray a character having an orgasm—Heffer has a run-in with a milking machine in "The Good, the Bad, and the Wallaby" (10/17/93), likely censored from subsequent reruns.

FIVE ACES, THE—In the "Slater's Sister" episode (10/31/92) of *Saved by the Bell*, the gang has a doo-wop group instead of their regular pop/rock band

(Zack Attack). FOR NO APPARENT REASON. They sing "Ginger, My Love" and "Come, Go With Me" at their high school sock hop. The band was the following combination of regulars: Screech Powers (Dustin Diamond), Zack Morris (Mark-Paul Gosselaar), Albert Clifford "A. C." Slater (Mario López), Lisa Turtle (Lark Voorhies), and newer character Tori Scott (Leanna Creel). See also **Hot Sundae**; **Bo Revere**; **Stevie**; **Zack Attack**.

FIVE HEARTBEATS, THE—Robert Townsend was the motor behind the eponymous 1991 film, writing, directing, and starring in *The Five Heartbeats*. This Motown/R&B African-American vocal quintet consisted of songwriter and pianist Duck Matthews (Robert Townsend), his brother J. T. Matthews (Leon), lead singer Eddie King Jr. (Michael Wright), Dresser Williams (Harry J. Lennix), and the uptight and upright Anthony "Choirboy" Stone (Tico Wells). They've been singing together since high school. The movie starts off in 1965 at a small-time amateur-night contest, with the band competing against Flash and the Ebony Sparks, and Baby Doll and the Crystals, fronted by Eddie's girlfriend Baby Doll (Troy Beyer). The Heartbeats don't win, but Jimmy Potter (Chuck Patterson) is impressed enough to manage them. He gets them a record deal, a tour, a #1 single, and on the covers of as many magazines as the movie's art department can mock up. However, Potter's wife initially didn't want him to do it, because he already managed at least three other groups (The Brownsville Boys, The Four Clovers, The Esquires) and when they hit the big time, they all dumped him as manager and it nearly destroyed him and their marriage. However, her objections never come up again, er, until Potter actually IS destroyed; killed several years later on orders of crooked record company chief Big Red Davis (Hawthorne James). Fortunately, the band

and another singer are able to give the testimony needed to convict Davis. Still, the blowback takes out Eddie, their lead singer, as he had cut a deal on the side with Davis to go solo, but never expected Potter to be killed. He is so riddled with guilt and cocaine that he can no longer perform, and the band replaces him with Michael "Flash" Turner (John Canada Terrell) of Flash and the Ebony Sparks. The band starts to change to a funkier sound as the 60s turn into the 70s. But on the same day that Eddie is shot by cops while holding up a liquor store, Duck mistakenly thinks he's discovered his fiancée cheating on him with his own brother. Then, to top it all off, Flash leaves to go solo. It's the end of the band. In the present day, Choirboy engineers a reunion of sorts, revealing that Eddie has found God and a good twelve-step program. This leads to Duck's reconciliation with J. T. and a big happy reunion picnic finale. See also **Bird and the Midnight Falcons**; **The Five Horsemen**; **Flash and the Ebony Sparks**.

FIVE HORSEMEN, THE—Briefly appearing mid-60s vocal group so blond and white it's scary, in the 1991 movie *The Five Heartbeats*. They have matching letter-sweaters and everything. When a big record label shows interest in The Five Heartbeats, it turns out they don't want to sign the Heartbeats, they just want their song for this act. The Heartbeats wisely turn them down to sign with Big Red Records instead. Later, in the present day, we catch a glimpse of the modern day version of the band in hideous high-top fades and MC Hammer–style gear, fronted by Michael "Flash" Turner (John Canada Terrell), as Flash and the Five Horsemen. Played by Brian Bradley, Michael Conn, Barry Diamond, Carl Edwards, and Joey Gaynor. See also **Bird and the Midnight Falcons**; **The Five Heartbeats**; **Flash and the Ebony Sparks**.

5 NEAT GUYS—Late 50s/early 60s Pat Boone-esque, goody-two-shoes vocal group all in pastel sweaters who appeared in a couple of commercials on the sketch comedy show *SCTV*. Lined up, their sweater letters spelled 5-N-E-A-T. They didn't have names, but 5 was John Candy; N Joe Flaherty; E Eugene Levy; A Dave Thomas; and T Rick Moranis. In the 05/22/81 episode, their *Neatest Hits* album featured "Who Made the Egg Salad Sandwiches," "Let's Have a Party in My Rec Room," "Patsy Has the Largest Breasts in Town," and "Don't Step on My Clip-on Tie." The 11/06/81 episode retreaded the concept with their *5 Neat Guys*

The Five Heartbeats

Gold album, which included "Mom Pressed the Crease in My Chinos," "Should We Double Date with Stan and Wendy," "Pimples and Pockmarks," and "I Got a Hickey." See also **Vic Arpeggio; Big Momma; Happiness Unlimited; The Happy Wanderers; Lola Heatherton; The Lemon Twins; Linsk Minyk; Tom Munroe; The Queenhaters; The Ramblers; The Recess Monkeys; Russ Riley; Jackie Rogers Jr.; Jackie Rogers Sr.; Speed of Light; Dusty Towne; The Wally Hung Trio.**

FIZZ MERCHANT — See **Stillwater.**

FLACK AND THE CALAMITY — See **Darryl and the Chaos.**

FLAMING CREATURES, THE — Played by real band Placebo in *Velvet Goldmine* (1998). They play a minor glam band in a 70s club performing a cover version of T. Rex's "20th Century Boy." See also **Jack Fairy; Brian Slade; Tommy Stone; Curt Wild.**

FLAMING SNOT — With a name as cartoony as this, it's no wonder the band ARE cartoons. In the "Snot Your Mother's Music" (10/25/97) episode of tween-oriented cartoon *Pepper Ann*, Pepper Ann Pearson (voiced by Kathleen Wilhoite) gets a shock. Her boring mom Lydia (voiced by April Winchell), who even has that annoyingly boring Midwestern-Scandinavian accent, knows rock idol Mick Snot from back when he was just plain old Harry Schnitzer! In "The Sellout" (02/13/00), Pepper Ann and her friends are one ticket short for the sold-out Flaming Snot concert. Tickets exchange hands but no one is satisfied until finally Pepper Ann and Nicky (voiced by Clea Lewis) give their tickets away and decide not to go.

FLASH AND THE EBONY SPARKS — This showy R&B vocal group wins the opening amateur contest scene (set in 1965) in the movie *The Five Heartbeats*

(1991), to the dismay of contestants The Five Heartbeats. They go on to sign with Big Red Records and tour with label-mates The Five Heartbeats, and Bird and the Midnight Falcons. Their leader, Michael "Flash" Turner (John Canada Terrell), later replaces Five Heartbeats' frontman Eddie King Jr. as the lead singer for several years. That is, until Flash quits the band at its gold-record award ceremony to announce his own solo album coming out in two weeks! Jerk. Later, in the present day, we see him fronting the trying-way-too-hard-to-be-hip band, Flash and the Five Horsemen. The Ebony Sparks were played by Ron Jaxon and Wayne "Crescendo" Ward. See also **Bird and the Midnight Falcons; The Five Heartbeats; The Five Horsemen.**

FLASH AND THE FIVE HORSEMEN — See **The Five Horsemen.**

FLAT-TOP TONY AND THE PURPLE CANOES — See **Indomitable Spirit.**

FLAVOR BABES, THE — Popular sitcom *Sabrina the Teenage Witch* spun off the short-lived cartoon/sort-of-prequel *Sabrina the Animated Series* (1999–2000). In the "Witchy Grrrls" episode (09/20/99), Sabrina (voiced by Emily Hart) and her two aunts (both voiced by Melissa Joan Hart) and pal Chloe (voiced by Cree Summer) form this rock band, whose name is a nod to The Spice Girls. Too bad they suck and lose the talent show to Sabrina's insufferable brat rival, Gem Stone (voiced by Chantal Strand), who wins with a Britney Spears–like number. Mad, they use their magic powers to make the group superpopular. So popular even that Weird Al Yankovic (playing himself) makes a parody of their hit song! See also **Entry Number Five; The Libby Chessler Generation.**

FLINTSTONE CANARIES, THE — Prehistoric cartoon

character Fred Flintstone (voiced by Alan Reed) puts together this barbershop quartet in "The Flintstone Canaries" episode (10/24/64) of cartoon *The Flintstones*. Fred forms the group to win a contest on the *Hum Along with Herman* TV show (a Mitch Miller parody), but they can't sing. They find Fred's pal Barney (voiced by Mel Blanc) turns out to be a natural tenor—but only when he's in the bath. They get him to join the group, and the group ends up on the show singing in a bathtub—not for the contest, but for the show's sponsor, Softsoap. See also **Ann-Margrock**; **The Beau Brummelstones**; **Jimmy Darrock**; **"Hot Lips" Hannigan**; **Hi-Fye**; **Pebbles and Bamm-Bamm**; **Rock Roll**.

FOLKSMEN, THE—This trio of Jerry Palter (Michael McKean), Mark Shubb (Harry Shearer), and Alan Barrows (Christopher Guest) are the early-60s folk cousins of Spiñal Tap. Not satisfied with having created the fake metal legends, McKean, Shearer, and Guest went on to invent this mild-mannered, Kingston Trio–esque acoustic threesome. They made their first appearance on *Saturday Night Live* (11/03/84), during Guest and Shearer's tenure on the show. A brief Tap-style mockumentary showing the band being reunited after twenty years prefaced their live performance of their "hit" "Old Joe's Place." They appeared briefly in *The Return of Spiñal Tap* (1992), where they are supposed to open for Spiñal Tap, but a roadie wisely tells them to go home. When Spiñal Tap did actual, real-live tour dates in 1993 and 2001, they would open the show as this fake band, and then rush backstage to change outfits and return to play as Spiñal Tap. In 2003, The Folksmen finally got a whole movie to themselves, the Guest-directed *Mighty Wind*. Well, a third of a movie. In it, the son of a 60s folk promoter gathers his dead dad's top three acts for a televised reunion/tribute concert. And . . . no, that's it. *A Mighty Wind* reveals more about the band's past,

including their origins as Barrow (tenor, guitar) and Shubb's (bass, bass) duo, The Twobadors. They need a midrange singer and team up with pretty-boy frontman Palter. They have a string of ever-declining-in-popularity albums: *Singin'*, *Pickin'*, *Ramblin'*, *Hitchin'*, *Wishin'*, and their late-60s gone-electric flop, *Saying Something*. Much off-the-cuff, improvised hilarity occurs, but the movie suffers in comparison to Guest's previous mockumentaries, *Waiting for Guffman* (1996) and *Best in Show* (2000), as he relies on an even more unmanageably sprawling ensemble cast, and a hokey, sitcom-level twist ending for The Folksmen, where Shubb decides he was born the wrong gender. Don't miss their hilarious folk-afied version of the Rolling Stones' "Start Me Up." A favorite of their live shows, it didn't get into the film, but they did manage to squeeze it onto the movie's soundtrack album. See also **Jack and Judy**; **Mitch and Mickey**; **The New Main Street Singers**; **Spiñal Tap**.

FONTAINE, VIC—Former 60s pop teen idol and *Time Tunnel* star James Darren played this recurring Rat Pack–era/Vegas-lounge-style singer in the sci-fi series *Star Trek: Deep Space Nine*. A mere holodeck character (created for the show by writer/producer Ira Stephen Behr), he was thus doubly fake! James Darren actually had a # 1 hit in 1961 with the Grammy-nominated song "Goodbye Cruel World." Riding the tenuous popularity of his *Star Trek* character, Darren released a 1999 comeback-esque album, *This One's from the Heart*, chock-full of Sinatra-era classics that mister Vic Fontaine would be right at home with. Ring-a-ding-ding, you bozos! See also **Harry Kim and the Kim Tones**.

FONTANE, JOHNNY—Greasy crooner and mob boss Don Corleone's (Marlon Brando) godson in the immortal 1972 film *The Godfather*. It's because of him we have the infamous horse head in the bed-scene and the "offer he can't refuse" line. Fontane (real crooner Al Martino) goes whining to the Don (Marlon Brando) to get him a part in a film that will save his career. The Don dispatches Tom Hagen (Robert Duvall) to persuade film producer Jack Woltz (John Marley) to see reason, by popping the severed head of Woltz's racehorse into his bed. But the Don and Fontane go way back; years ago, the Don and right-hand henchman Luca Brasi (Lenny Montana) held a gun to a bandleader's head to help Johnny get out of his contract. Later in the movie, after the Corleone family muscles their way into a Vegas casino, they ask Fontane to appear there five times a year and persuade his show-biz buddies to also appear. Fontane is happy to oblige. *TRIVIA TIME!* The Fontane character and events are allegedly based on Frank Sinatra and his, again allegedly, receiving mob assistance in landing his role in *From Here to Eternity*.

FOREIGN AGENTS, THE—From the "Find the Monkees" episode (01/23/67) of *The Monkees*. Black-trench-coated rock trio that sneaks around carrying their band's gimmick a bit too far. They, along with the Monkees are all desperate to audition for eccentric TV producer Hubbell Benson (Carl Ballantine), who has put invitations out to all the local bands, except, it would seem, The Monkees. See also **Fern Badderly**; **Irene Chomsky**; **The Four Martians**; **The Four Swine**; **Honey and the Bear**; **The Jolly Green Giants (I)**; **Lester Crabtree and the Three Crabs**; **Sven Helstrom and the Swedish Rhythm Kings**; **The Swinging Android**; **The West Minstrel Abbies**.

FOSTER, MARY ROSE—The hard-living, bluesy rock goddess played by Bette Midler in *The Rose* (1979), a thinly veiled biopic of Janis Joplin. Foster, known as The Rose, became a legend and an idol to mil-

Johnny Fontaine (Al Martino) (I)

lions of fans, but all she wanted was the love of a good man and the respect of her hometown. It was all coming together, too; Rose had met her love Huston Dyer (Frederic Forrest) on the way to her big reunion show back in the small Florida town of her youth. Alas, it was not to be. The locals who knew her "back when" either forgot her, remembered too much about her, or gave her a massive dose of heroin. Huston leaves her after a bad scene at a local watering hole, so Rose shoots up the smack, hits the stage for a rocking first song, then mumbles a second song before collapsing and literally dying on stage. It's just like that famous saying: "A rose by any other name can never go home again." Er, something like that. See also **Monty's Band**; **Billy Ray**; **The Rose Band**.

Mary Rose Foster,
aka "The Rose"
(Bette Midler)

FOUR CLOVERS, THE — See **The Five Heartbeats**.

FOUR MARTIANS, THE — Four nameless guys in goony red-and-gold "sci-fi" costumes with pantyhose over their heads. A "gimmick" band, ya see. They, along with The Monkees, are all desperate to audition for eccentric TV producer Hubbell Benson (Carl Ballantine), who has put invitations out to all the local bands, except, it would seem, The Monkees. From the "Find the Monkees" episode (01/23/67) of *The Monkees*. See also **Fern Badderly**; **Irene Chomsky**; **The Foreign Agents**; **The Four Swine**; **Honey and the Bear**; **The Jolly Green Giants (I)**; **Lester Crabtree and the Three Crabs**; **Sven Helstrom and the Swedish Rhythm Kings**; **The Swinging Android**; **The West Minstrel Abbies**.

4 SKORE — Chris, Calvin, Cool Chris, and Todd are a boy band featured in the 2002 season premiere of Fox show *King of the Hill* (11/03/02), "Get Your Freak Off." Family patriarch Hank Hill (voiced by Mike Judge) is censoring son Bobby's (voiced by Pamela Segall) CDs. But when he checks out this band at the record-store listening booth, he is pleasantly surprised that he likes them, finding them "kinda like doo-wop." Later, when father and son attend their Houston concert, Hank is appalled when the band strips down and starts dancing in a very non-doo-wop way. See also **The A Men**; **The Bluegrass Brothers**; **Cane and the Stubborn Stains**; **The Dale Gribble Bluegrass Experience**; **The Harris Twins**; **John Redcorn and Big Mountain Fudge Cake**; **Pastor K**; **Pimp Franklin**.

FOUR SWINE, THE — In the "Your Friendly Neighborhood Kidnappers" episode (10/3/66) of *The Monkees*, this band's evil manager, Nick Trump (Andre Philippe), buddies up to The Monkees and peppers them with bad advice in an attempt to keep them from beating his band at an upcoming battle of the bands. He even calls in a favor from his mob friends to kidnap The Monkees the evening of the contest. After much shenanigans of a zany nature, The Monkees escape and make it to the contest, only for both bands to lose to Lester Crabtree and the Three Crabs. The Four Swine themselves only briefly appear in the episode, looking like Hell's Angels rejects and playing an instrumental that sounds suspiciously like some of the show's incidental music. See also **Fern Badderly**; **Irene Chomsky**; **The Foreign Agents**; **The Four Martians**; **Honey and the Bear**; **The Jolly Green Giants (I)**; **Lester Crabtree and the Three Crabs**; **Sven Helstrom and the Swedish Rhythm Kings**; **The Swinging Android**; **The West Minstrel Abbies**.

FOX, NEAL—An up 'n' coming singer played by Jesse Spencer, who writes "Sheets of Egyptian Cotton" inspired by Molly Gunn (Brittany Murphy). From the 2003 eye-roller *Uptown Girls*. See also **Tommy Gunn**.

Neal Fox (Jesse Spencer)

MISCELLANEOUS MUSIC FROM MORE MEDIUMS

BY ALAN BENSON

From the beginning, *The Rocklopedia Fakebandica* has been about one thing: fake bands from TV shows and movies. Does that mean that TV and movies are the only sources of fake bands? Of course not. Does that mean the book should have an entry for every time some damn cereal mascot jams with a fake band in a thirty-second commercial? Of course not. But here are the highlights, spotlighting some of the most notable non–TV show, nonmovie fake bands.

Bach, P.D.Q.—This fictional twenty-first son of the legendary Johann Sebastian Bach is actually the brainchild of real composer Peter Schickele, who attended Juilliard with Glenn Gould. Schickele created this last and least son of the great composer to be the author of Schickele's parodies of classical music that Schickele only "discovered." The first album, *Peter Schickele Presents an Evening with P.D.Q. Bach*, came out in 1965, to be followed by more than a dozen others over the succeeding decades. Schickele held and holds frequent concerts of Bach's buffoonery, satirizing classical music with P.D.Q.'s plagiarized, drunken, ham-fisted compositions and Schickele's mock-serious introductions on the pieces' origins and discovery. Schickele even wrote *The Definitive Biography of P.D.Q. Bach*, published in 1976. Fake rockers are a dime a dozen, but how many faux classical composers can you name? Well, now that you read this, one!

Danger Kitty—This spandex-and-feathered-hair-sporting quartet hit it big in 1983 with "Love Rocket." With a #3 chart hit, the cover of *Rolling Stone,* and enough tight pants and hair gel to last for years, DK was set, right? Sadly, no; by 1984, it was all over, and at least one band member was reduced to slinging wieners at L.A.'s Tail of the Pup hot dog stand. Their last show was before a bemused crowd at the Smuckler bar mitzvah. Truly tragic. And it all could have been avoided if they'd used their Discover cards. Or something like that, as these perfect-seeming 80s-hair metal gods only existed in a thirty-second Discover card TV ad that ran from 1999 to 2000. *TRIVIA TIME!* Danger Kitty was played by Metal Shop, a real L.A. hair band. During the ad campaign, you could send away for a free Danger Kitty CD single of "Love Rocket."

Dazzler—Issue 130 of Marvel Comics *Uncanny X-Men* held a treat for fake-band aficionados. That issue introduced Alison Blair, a mutant with the ability to turn sound into light. And apparently make a living as a roller-skating disco diva in 1980. (Of the two, the latter is probably more amazing.) Apparently, people went for the light shows she produced. After clashing with some bad guys, Blair got inspired to be a hero, grabbed some spandex, and got her own comic book. Since her introduction, Dazzler has learned to focus her light shows into laser blasts capable of opening locks and removing stubborn jar lids. Oh, and zapping bad guys.

Deathtöngue/Billy and the Boingers—Berke Breathed, in his comic strip *Bloom County,* satirized the big mid-80s glam metal craze with this tongue/drum/tuba band of talking, rocking animals. While most people remember the onstage component of the band—feline "Wild" Bill Katt on lead tongue, rabbit Hodge-Podge on drums, and penguin Opus Croakus on rhythm tuba—the real power lay in the hands of band manager/songwriter Steve Dallas. The creator of the band, his was also the mind that birthed their tunes like "Clearasil Messiah," "Skateboarding to Satan," "Demon Drooler of the Sewer," the holiday song "I Saw Mommy Kissing Santa Claus So I Blew Him Away," and the Princely titled "U Stink but I Luv U." Alas, their song "Let's

Run Over Lionel Richie with a Tank" kept them from getting a record deal from Lionel-loving record execs. Worse, busybody politicians called Dallas to D.C. for hearings on porn rock in a parody of the then-current P.R.M.C. hearings. Under pressure, Dallas suddenly announced the combo had traded in their violent name and image and was doing business under the more wholesome monicker "Billy and the Boingers." While the name change irritated some band members, it let the combo net a corporate sponsor (Dr. Scholl's Odor Eaters) and a world tour (one show at the 49th Annual Moose Lodge Banquet in Albuquerque). The end came when Bill the Cat sold "U Stink but I Luv U" as a Wheat Thins jingle. The resulting success tore the band apart. The Bloom County collection *Billy and the Boingers Bootleg* included a flexidisc of "I'm a Boinger" b/w "U Stink but I Luv U." Real bands Mucky Pup and The Harry Pitts Band provided the music, chosen from a contest held by Breathed. *TRIVIA TIME!* Breathed's earlier attempt at fakebandsmithery was Tess Turbo, a skanky Joan Jett–esque hard rocker. Reaganite swinger Steve Dallas won an appearance in her new video, but his brief moment of stardom turned sour when onstage pyrotechnics ignited his chest hair (à la Michael Jackson's 1984 Pepsi commercial).

Masked Marauders, The—From the pages of *Rolling Stone*, rock journalism's holy grail, came this band from a joke pushed farther than expected. A joke review (10/18/69), by "T. M. Christian" (really Greil Marcus), described an album by this nonexistent supergroup, allegedly composed of rock giants Bob Dylan, Mick Jagger, John Lennon, and Paul McCartney. The album was supposedly a pseudonymous bootleg, a legal dodge to get around the fact that the members were all signed to different record companies. The review was spoofing the then-current trend of supergroups, and a previous *Rolling Stone* review of the Dylan bootleg *Great White Wonder*. But some people didn't get the joke, and, as interest grew, Marcus and another *Rolling Stone* writer, Langdon Winner, found a real band (apparently The Cleanliness and Godliness Skiffle

(continued)

Band) to imitate the voices of the celebrities supposedly involved and record the songs described in the review, and actually release the album! It came out on a Warner Bros. subsidiary in late 1969, a triumph of the cart preceding the horse.

Meaty Cheesy Boys—The stars of one of burger chain Jack in the Box's most inspired ad campaigns, the MCBs were a boy band parody with a love for big burgers. The quintet— EJ, TK, JT, TJ, and the other EJ—debuted in 1999 with the fake album *Meat, Cheese, and Love*, eleven songs about, well, meat, cheese, and love. Their songs included "Your Love's Melting Me, Baby," "Cheeseless Nights," and "It Just Isn't a Party Without Meat and Cheese." The five heartthrobs appeared in one more Jack in the Box TV ad, then went the way of all boy bands. Farewell MCBs, we hardly knew ye.

Rock-Afire Explosion, The—Between 1981 and 1991, a real live fake band was playing their mechanical hearts out in your neighborhood pizzeria. That is, if your neighborhood pizzeria was a ShowBiz Pizza Palace. The Explosion was an animatronic nightmare . . . er, celebration that featured bears on bass and guitar, a dog in a spacesuit on drums, the sun and the moon on backup vocals, and (after 1986) a singing Statue of Liberty. Sadly, changing pizza-buying habits resulted in a downsizing of the show to a single player (Chuck E. Cheese). But weep not for Billy Bob Brockali and Fatz Geronimo, they live on at www.show-bizpizza.com.

Sugar Bears, The—In 1972, the Quaalude-mellow cartoon mascot of Post's Golden Crisp (aka Sugar Crisp, Super Sugar Crisp, and Super Golden Crisp) took time off from pimping cereal to cash in on the bubblegum pop fad. He hooked up with three other ursine musicians and recorded *Presenting the Sugar Bears* for Big Tree. His bandmates were big-haired tambourinist Honey Bear (voiced by Kim Carnes!), drummer Shoobee Bear, and bassist Doobee Bear. Ahem.

FRANK, BILLIE—The main character from the not-so-successful 2001 Mariah Carey vehicle *Glitter*. It's a pseudo-autobiographical but still predictable rags-to-riches-type story set in the early 80s. Julian Dice (Max Beesley) is her manager/lover/producer/Svengali.

Billy Frank (Mariah Carey)

FRANKS, HAPPY—In the amusing bit of period retro 30s screwball comedy fluff that is *The Imposters* (1998), character actor Steve Buscemi plays this suicidally depressed cruise-ship singer. A guy named Happy who's sad! This is irony so cheap, the filmmakers should pay us! His agent, whom he loved like a brother, stole his wife, whom he loved like a mother and a hooker. Although his character starts off the movie breaking down midsong, he (and everyone else) ends up happy and paired off by the finale, in the grand tradition of screwball comedies.

FREDDIE AND THE RED HOTS—Fifties rock and roll band from the "Stolen Melodies" (02/02/79) episode of sitcom *Happy Days*. They steal the song "Moonlight Love" from the group Leather and the Suedes. Naturally, cool guy Fonzie (Henry Winkler) has to set things right, in this instance by pulling off Freddie's (Fred Fox Jr.) hairpiece on the live TV dance show *Sok Hop*. See also **Leather and the Suedes**.

FREDRICKSON, FREDDY — Tuxedoed and coiffed vocalist who coheadlines the 1964 Playtone Galaxy of Stars package tour in the frothy, fun 1996 movie *That Thing You Do*. His popularity may not be at the peak it once was in the 50s, as he gets annoyed when Guy (Tom Everett Scott) from The Wonders reminisces about how Freddy's song "Mr. Downtown," was the first record he ever bought. Ouch! That's gotta make you feel old. "Mr. Downtown" (cowritten by director Tom Hanks) is, of course, the theme song from the show of the same name. Freddy Fredrickson was played by Robert Torti. See also **Elizabeth Anne**; **Blue Spot Trio**; **The Chantrellines**; **Diane Dane**; **The Echoes**; **The G Men**; **The Heardsmen**; **The Hollyhocks**; **Jon D and the Walkers**; **Legends of Brass**; **Marilyn Lovell and the Geminis**; **The Norm Wooster Singers**; **Del Paxton**; **The Saturn 5**; **The Tempos**; **The Trends**; **Two Eriks**; **The Vicksburgs**; **The Wonders**.

FREE WORLD, THE — Also referred to as The Leaders of the Free World, these rappers are rich and successful, er, sorry, are pimpin' an' flossin' wit' da mad bling-bling fixin' ta blow up, word, in Eminem's semi-autobiographical movie *8 Mile* (2002). Of course, if they're so successful, what are they doing still hanging around scummy Detroit, participating in penny-ante rap contests? They get into several brawls with B-Rabbit (Eminem) and his posse, and give him the big beatdown before the final rap contest, where they totally get their asses kicked by his skinny white-boy self. He slams them as all Tupac wannabes, reveals that member Papa Doc (Anthony Mackie) went to private school (street rapper faux pas!) and that Papa Doc's real name is Clarence (double faux pas!), and slyly uses all their insults on himself, leaving Papa Doc literally speechless.

Lineup: Papa Doc, Lyckety-Splyt (Strike), Lotto (Nashawn "Ox" Breedlove), Moochie (Malik Barnhardt), Day (Day Golfin), and Omar (Allen Adams). See also **B-Rabbit**.

FREEZE, JT — Really lame rapper who appears at a sixteen-plus club in the Village on the late-period episode "Warning: A Double-lit Candle Can Cause a Meltdown" (10/17/91) of *The Cosby Show*. Freeze (real rapper Special Ed), who ends the episode by dancing with Pam (Erika Alexander), dresses sort of like a D.A.I.S.Y. Age rapper and drops such written-by-a-forty-five-year-old-white-guy rhymes as "Rudy, Danielle, and Susan so fine, I'll always remember this birthday of mine." See also **Clyde**; **The Icicles**; **The Jazz Caravan**; **The Lipsticks**; **The Maniacs**; **Slim Claxton and His Trio**; **Walking Lemons**; **The Wretched**.

FRESH STEP — A spoof of manufactured "boy bands" created by the writers on *The Late Show with David Letterman*, and named after a brand of kitty litter. They were supposedly from Orlando, Florida. They appeared twice on *Letterman* (first on 03/03/99) and once on MTV's *Total Request Live*. DJ, Jeremy, Corey, Jamie, and Brad performed "Ya Gotta Be Fresh" and "Talk to the Hand," allegedly from an upcoming movie of the same name starring Sarah Michelle Gellar and James Van Der Beek and not to be confused with their other song, "Don't Talk to the Hand (Girl, Talk to the Heart)." The band was actually played by dancers of the Broadway show *Footloose*.

FRIEDKIN FAMILY SINGERS, THE — From the 04/10/78 episode of spoof talk-show *America 2-Night*, hosted by Barth Gimble (Martin Mull) and Jerry Hubbard (Fred Willard). This singing group paid too much money to be on the show. See also **Denny and Brian**; **Pharoah Fawcett**; **Happy Kyne and the Mirth Makers**; **Buck and Harriet Pine**; **The Punk**

Monks; Tony Roletti.

FRIENDS INDEED, THE—A uniformed, Salvation Army–type oompah band that can take any beautiful melody and turn it into a march. From the "How Not to Manage a Rock Group" episode (04/28/68) of forgotten series *The Mothers-in-Law*. Led by a fiercely mugging Joe Besser, the fifth (possibly sixth) of the Three Stooges. The titular mothers hire them as their last-minute backup band to play "Some Enchanted Evening." The mothers already scared off scheduled rock group The Warts with their squareness and they don't want to waste the nonrefundable studio time. See also **The Mamas and Papas-in-Law; The Warts**.

FROG, MICHIGAN J.—From the classic Warner Bros. cartoon *One Froggy Evening* (1955), and recently resurrected as the mascot of the WB TV network. This memorable one-shot character (singing voice by Bill Roberts) lay hidden in a box in a cornerstone of a building being demolished. Discovered by a construction worker, the frog (complete with top hat and cane) bursts into toe-tapping, Roaring 20s–style song-and-dance numbers—but only when alone with the worker, frustrating the worker's attempts to get rich off him. He's only referred to in the cartoon as the Singing Frog; the "Michigan J. Frog" name came later.

FROGTOWN HOLLOW JUBILEE JUG-BAND, THE—From the 1977 Muppet TV special *Emmet Otter's Jug-Band Christmas*. Impoverished Emmet Otter (voiced by Jerry Nelson) formed this band with his pals to play Waterville's First Annual Christmas Talent Contest. They rehearse the song "Barbecue," but when that idiot Yancy Woodchuck does it in the competition before they do, they quickly rehearse up another song, "Brothers." They don't win the competition, but dammit they had heart! Worse,

Emmet ruined his mom's washtub (and livelihood) to make a washtub bass for the band. He was going to get her a new one with the prize money. Thank goodness they get a paying gig singing at the Riverside Rest restaurant owned by Doc Bullfrog (not Kermit, he just narrated), or this surprisingly sad tale would be even more depressing. This semi-otter band featured Emmet Otter on washtub bass, Harvey the Muskrat (voiced by Jim Henson) on kazoo and washboard, Wendel the Porcupine (voiced by Dave Goelz) on jug, and Charlie the Otter (voiced by Richard Hunt) on cigar box banjo. Emmet's mother, Alice Otter (voiced by Marilyn Sokol) also performed at the contest. Composer Paul Williams composed the songs. See also **The Nightmare**.

FROST, MAX—See **Max Frost and the Troopers**.

FRYE, DUSTY—In Woody Allen's 1986 flick *Hannah and Her Sisters*, Daniel Stern has a cameo as this rock star client of accountant Elliot (Michael Caine), who says Frye's a trillionaire and has, like, six gold records. The nouveau-riche, faux pas–ing gauchehole has come to moody artist Frederick (Max von Sydow) for some big, wall-fillin' art, since he just bought this place in Southampton with a lotta wall space, ya know? Preferably something in puce. An outraged Frederick gives 'im the bum's

Dusty Frye (Daniel Stern) (3rd from left)

rush, but not before a smitten Elliot manages to plant a serious smooch on Frederick's girlfriend, Lee (Barbara Hershey), who is also Elliot's sister-in-law! *TRIVIA TIME!* The movie also features a cameo by real band The 39 Steps.

FUDDONNA — Elmer Fudd in Madonna cone-bra drag. That's it. At least he/she doesn't sing. From the "Tiny Toon Music Television" episode (02/01/91) of cartoon *Tiny Toon Adventures*. See also **Def Zepplin**; **Skinhead O'Connell**; **Ruffee**; **Vanilla Lice**.

FUNKY C FUNKY DO — A briefly mentioned, shirtless, hip hop–looking duo whose song "I Do Believe We're Naked" knocks the celebrity benefit tune "We're Sending Our Love Down the Well" out of the #1 spot. From the classic episode "Radio Bart" (01/09/92) of *The Simpsons*. See also **The Beach Boys Experience**; **The Be Sharps**; **Johnny Bobby**; **Johnny Calhoun**; **Captain Bart and the Tequila Mockingbirds**; **The Crazy Old Man Singers**; **Cyanide**; **Gulliver Dark**; **Ferl Dixon and His Second Helping Boys**; **Garfunkel, Messina, Oates, and Lisa**; **Hooray for Everything**; **Kovenant**; **Krusty and the Krums**; **The Larry Davis Experience**; **Little Timmy and the Shebangs**; **Loggins and Oates**; **Lurleen Lumpkin**; **M. C. Safety and the Caution Crew**; **Melvin and the Squirrels**; **"Bleeding Gums" Murphy**; **The Party Posse**; **The Rappin' Rabbis**; **Red Breem and His Band of Some Esteem**; **The Satin Knights**; **The Steve Sax Trio**; **Testament**; **Blind Willie Witherspoon**; **The Ya-Hoo Recovering Alcoholic Jug Band**; **Yodelin' Zeke**.

FUNKY TONGUES, THE — Hot high school metal band that's using Jesse's recording studio in the "Five's a Crowd" episode of sitcom (term used loosely) *Full House*. Also, teen regular and regular teen D. J. Tanner (Candace Cameron Bure) is dating member Pete (Roger Floyd). When Jesse (John Stamos),

Joey Gladstone (Dave Coulier), and Danny Tanner (Bob Saget) find out Pete has the normal urges of a high school teenager, they panic and track them down and barge in on her date. She reads them the riot act. See also **The Diplomats**; **Hot Daddy and the Monkey Puppets**; **Human Pudding**; **Jesse and the Rippers**; **R.E.M.**

FUTURE VILLAIN BAND — Aerosmith (Steven Tyler, Tom Hamilton, Joey Kramer, Joe Perry, and Brad Whitford) plays the bad guys in the 1978 pile of crapola, *Sgt. Pepper's Lonely Hearts Club Band*. Their mantra is "We hate love, we hate joy, we love money." Martin Sunk, as Father Sun (Alice Cooper), brainwashes an army for them. Dr. Maxwell Edison (Steve Martin) also helps brainwash an army for them, but in a different way. In FVB's confrontation with Sgt. Pepper's Lonely Hearts Club Band, Peter Frampton and Steve Tyler wrestle on a tall thing and fall off and die. *TRIVIA TIME!* This choice role was originally offered to KISS, who turned it down to ruin their careers with *KISS Meets the Phantom of the Park* instead. See also **Lucy and the Diamonds**; **Sgt. Pepper's Lonely Hearts Club Band**.

G MEN, THE — Never seen nor heard band in *That Thing You Do* (1996). They play Boss Vic Koss the Mattress King's (Kevin Pollack) rock and roll show in Pittsburgh, which opens with a poor performance by The Wonders. But you never actually SEE the band or anything, their name is just briefly glimpsed on the marquee. See also **Elizabeth Anne**; **Blue Spot Trio**; **The Chantrellines**; **Diane Dane**;

The Echoes; Freddy Fredrickson; The Heardsmen; The Hollyhocks; Jon D and the Walkers; Legends of Brass; Marilyn Lovell and the Geminis; The Norm Wooster Singers; Del Paxton; The Saturn 5; The Tempos; The Trends; Two Eriks; The Vicksburgs; The Wonders.

G-DOG — Big black shirtless rapper (Tim Meadows) in a couple of *Saturday Night Live* sketches. In "G-Dog Does the Nasty" (12/02/95) G-Dog has a new song/dance ("Do the Nasty") that's gonna blow up big, but G hurts his back doing it. Manager Phil (guest star Anthony Edwards) sends him to the doctor who discovers it's psychosomatic! The real reason G-Dog can't do it is that he would rather be (and turns into) nice-guy crooner Gordon Jones singing a revamped version of his song "Do the Handshake." So he gets booed offstage. Then Tim Meadows wakes up, revealing the whole thing to be every *SNL*er's nightmare: a sketch with a good premise that went nowhere. In "The Princess and the Homeboy" sketch (04/20/96), G-Dog stars in a fake sitcom where he moves in with a white middle-class family and curses like a straight-up sailor, y'all. Word.

GALLAGHER, NEIL — In the 1978 film *Tilt*, this country-and-western musician (played by Ken Marshall) meets up with pinball wizard Tilt, played

Neil Gallagher (Ken Marshall) (r) and Brenda Louise "Tilt" Davenport (Brooke Shields) (l)

by . . . Brooke Shields? Needing money for a demo tape, he teams up with her to win a series of pinball competitions that eventually leads to a final confrontation with pinball master "The Whale" (Charles Durning) High concept, huh?

GAMBOLPUTTY DE VON AUSFERN-SCHPLENDEN-SCHLITTER-CRASSCRENBON-FRIED-DIGGER-DINGLE-DANGLE-DONGLE-DUNGLE-BURSTEIN-VON-KNACKER-THRASHER-APPLE-BANGER-HOROWITZ-TICOLENSIC-GRANDER-KNOTTY-SPELLTINKLE-GRANDLICH-GRUMBLEMEYER-SPELTERWASSER-KURSTLICH-HIM-BLEEISEN-BAHNWAGEN-GUTENABEND-BITTE-EIN-NÜRNBURGER-BRATWUSTLE-GERSPURTEN-MITZ-WEIMACHE-LUBER-HUNDSFUT-GUMBERABER-SHÖ-NENDANKER-KALBSFLEISCH-MITTLER-AUCHER VON HAUTKOPFT OF ULM, JOHANN — Undeservedly forgotten German Baroque composer in the "It's the Arts" sketch (11/23/69) of BBC comedy series *Monty Python's Flying Circus*. His wife was Sarah . . . Gambolputty de von Ausfern-schplenden-schlitter-crasscrenbon-fried-digger-dingle-dangle-dongle-dungle-burstein-von-knacker-thrasher-apple-banger-horowitz-ticolensic-grander-knotty-spelltinkle-grandlich-grumble-meyer-spelterwasser-kurstlich-himbleeisen-bahnwagen-gutenabend-bitte-ein-nürnburger-bratwustle-gerspurten-mitz-weimache-luber-hundsfut-gumberaber-shönendanker-kalbsfleisch-mittler-aucher von Hautkopft of Ulm. See also **Arthur Ewing and His Musical Mice; Bolton Choral Society; The Herman Rodriguez Four; The Hunlets; Jackie Charlton and the Tonettes; Arthur "Two Sheds" Jackson; Not Noel Coward; Not Tony Bennett; Rachel Toovey Bicycle Choir; Inspector Jean-Paul Zatapathique.**

GANTNER, ROBIN — In *Girls! Girls! Girls!* (1962), for once it seems Elvis Presley is NOT playing the singer in an Elvis movie, someone else is—insensitive club singer Robin Gantner (Stella Stevens). She appears nightly at nightclub the Pirates Den. Elvis is sailor Ross Carpenter, who's desperate to buy the boat (*The West Wind*) he built with his dead father off of jerk Wesley Johnson (Jeremy Slate). Carpenter can't get no sympathy from bitchy Gantner who says he needs to get that foolish dream out of his system. Gantner is awful jealous and possessive for a supposedly ex-girlfriend. She hisses and spits whenever Carpenter's new flame Laurel Dodge (Laurel Goodwin) shows up. Ross, you are better off without that harpy! Things don't improve when Carpenter, desperate for some boat-buying cash, gets the club's manager Sam (Robert Strauss) to give him a job there singing. Dang it, Elvis does play a singer after all! In the course of the movie, though, he only sings ONE song professionally ("Return to Sender"). He sang before (the twisty "I Don't Wanna Be Tied"), but that was just for fun. *TRIVIA TIME!* Stella Stevens did her own singing; you get to hear her on "The Nearness of You," "Never Let Me

Go," and "Baby, Baby, Baby."

GARÇONS DE LA PLAGE, LES—"The French Beach Boys" (literally!) who are mentioned in the 1978 TV documentary *All You Need Is Cash*. Les Garçons are one of the other musical groups managed by the Rutles' manager Leggy Mountbatten (Terence Bayler) during the 60s. A pic of their *California Boys* album can also be glimpsed on the sleeve of the original soundtrack LP. See also **Arthur Hodgeson and the Kneecaps; The Machismo Brothers; Ruttling Orange Peel; Punk Floyd; Blind Lemon Pye; The Rutles**.

GARFUNKEL, MESSINA, OATES, AND LISA—From the "Lisa's Rival" episode (09/11/94) of long-running cartoon *The Simpsons*. Smart saxophone player Lisa Simpson feels threatened by a new, smarter, better saxophone-playing girl at school, Allison Taylor (guest-voiced by Winona Ryder). In a brief fantasy sequence, wondering if it's that bad to be number two, she sees herself performing in concert with this not-so-supergroup of lesser lights (the crappier halves of Simon and Garfunkel, Loggins and Messina, Hall and Oates). They get ready to play their #2 hit, "Born to Runner-Up" before being booed off the stage. As Lisa snaps out of it, she astutely realizes, "Why would they come to our concert just to boo us?" See also **The Beach Boys Experience; The Be Sharps; Johnny Bobby; Johnny Calhoun; Captain Bart and the Tequila Mockingbirds; The Crazy Old Man Singers; Cyanide; Gulliver Dark; Ferl Dixon and His Second Helping Boys; Funky C Funky Do; Hooray for Everything; Kovenant; Krusty and the Krums; The Larry Davis Experience; Little Timmy and the Shebangs; Loggins and Oates; Lurleen Lumpkin; M. C. Safety and the Caution Crew; Melvin and the Squirrels; "Bleeding Gums" Murphy; The Party Posse; The Rappin' Rabbis; Red**

Robin Gantner (Stella Stevens) (l), Ross Carpenter (Elvis Presley), and Laurel Dodge (Laurel Goodwin) (r)

Breem and His Band of Some Esteem; The Satin Knights; The Steve Sax Trio; Testament; Blind Willie Witherspoon; The Ya-Hoo Recovering Alcoholic Jug Band; Yodelin' Zeke.

GAY, SUELEEN—Wildly self-deluded waitress who thinks she can be a country singer in Robert Altman's 1975 film *Nashville*. Truth is, Sueleen (Gwen Welles) can't sing a lick, despite her impressive chest, a fact highlighted in a disturbing scene where she is forced to strip at a party that thinks it hired her to strip and that she thinks she was hired to sing at. See also **Tommy Brown (II); Haven Hamilton; Barbara Jean; Linnea Reese; The Smoky Mountain Laurels; Tom, Bill & Mary; Connie White.**

GEE, NANNY—In the "One Hugs, the Other Doesn't" episode (01/30/92) of sitcom *Cheers*, cast regular Frasier Crane (Kelsey Grammer) runs into his first wife (played by Emma Thompson!) who is now a successful singer of kids' music. All much to the dismay of Frasier's icicle of a wife, Lilith Sternin-Crane (Bebe Neuwirth). See also **Captain Gus and His Polka Pirates; Eddie Barnett and the Eddie Barnetters; The Grinning Americans.**

GELLAR, ROSS—Ross (David Schwimmer) is the nerdy paleontologist and one-sixth of the reason behind the megasuccess of sitcom *Friends*, but in the episode "The One Where Chandler Crosses the Line" (11/13/97), he finally fulfills a lifelong fantasy of becoming a keyboardist. First, he only jams for his friends (if by "jams" you mean playing all the weird samples together, much as if a group of stoners stumbled upon a Casio for the first time). All the titular friends are repulsed by his "music," except for Phoebe, the musician of the group, who thinks he's so talented she encourages him to play in public. Ross takes his cacophony to a coffee house, Central Perk, where Phoebe gets so intimidated by his "tal-

ent" that she refuses to follow him. In the end, Ross purposely performs poorly, to get Phoebe back on stage. See also **Phoebe Buffay; Leslie; Stephanie Schiffer.**

GEMINI'S TWIN—All-female trio spoof of acts like TLC and Destiny's Child from *Saturday Night Live*. The group is composed of Joanette (Ana Gasteyer), Britannica (Maya Rudolph), and whatever female guest-host the show has that week, such as Charlize Theron (11/04/00), Lucy Liu (12/16/00), Jennifer Lopez (02/10/01), Gwyneth Paltrow (11/10/01), and Britney Spears (02/02/02).

GENERATION O!—Rock band from the animated WB network afternoon kids show (2000) of the same name, featuring Molly O, your average eight-year-old girl with a internationally renowned rock band and a purple kangaroo for a drummer. Lineup: Molly O (voiced by Chantal Strand) on lead vocals, Molly's female cousin Eddie (voiced by Tabitha St. Germain) on lead guitar, Brit space case Nub (voiced by Scott McNeil) on bass guitar, and mute purple Australian kangaroo Yo-Yo on drums. Yo-Yo's first band, with three other kangaroos, was Baby Joey. *TRIVIA TIME!* The band's music is actually done by the real band Letters to Cleo. Letters to Cleo singer Kay Hanley also was the singing voice of Josie in the *Josie and the Pussycats* movie. See also **The Dancing Schuberts.**

GEORGIE AND THE G-MEN—These swingin' cats back up singer Guy Lambert (Elvis Presley) in *Double Trouble* (1967). Georgie (Monty Landis), the bandleader and best friend of Lambert, plays the guitar and trombone during gigs, and mysteriously disappears from the second half of the movie, never to be heard from again. The G-Men are credited as "The G-Men" and may be a real band. See also **Guy Lambert.**

GERMAINE, JOHN — Sexually unadventurous yet still "spongeworthy" saxophonist played by Jeff Yagher in "The Rye" episode (01/04/96) of sitcom *Seinfeld*. Germaine's jazz combo, which also includes Kramer's pal Clyde (Leonard Lightfoot), has a regular gig at a joint called Bradley's. Germaine and Elaine (Julia Louis-Dreyfus) are hot and heavy, but her interest in a certain sexual maneuver causes him to flub his big showcase before a recording industry weasel (Steve Ireland).

GETTING GAY WITH KIDS — In the "Rainforest Schmainforest" episode (04/07/99) of gleefully tasteless Comedy Central animated show *South Park*, the kids (Cartman, Kyle, Stan, and Kenny) sassmouth choir teacher Miss Stevens (voiced by *Friends* star Jennifer Aniston) who's come to speak to their class about this kids choir with a horrible, horrible name. As punishment, school counselor Mr. Mackey (who's on the choir's board of directors) makes them join on the eve of the choir's trip to Costa Rica to sing a dorky song about the rain forest. The choir takes a trip into the rain forest, but when their guide is killed and eaten by a snake, the kids and Miss Stevens wander lost and suffer various horrors of the green hell. Fortunately, they are rescued by heroic construction workers and their bulldozers, just in time for their performance for the president of Costa Rica and his people. They change the lyrics of their cheesy, tape-backed, pro–rain forest song to an anti–rain forest song. See also **The Avenue Street Ghetto Boys; Faith + 1; Fingerbang; The Ghetto Avenue Boys; Jerome "Chef" McElroy; MOOP; Raging Pussies; Reach for the Skyler; Sanctified; Sisters of Mercy Hold No Pain Against the Dark Lord; Timmy! and the Lords of the Underworld.**

GHETTO AVENUE BOYS, THE — From the "Something You Can Do with Your Finger" episode (07/12/00)

of animated Comedy Central show *South Park*. Stan's dad, Randy Marsh, gets upset when his son wants to join a boy band, because he himself quit high school to be in this boy band. After a short time at the top (looks to be the early/mid 80s), he and the other four members he didn't even know got thrown over by their producer for a new group he'd put together, The Avenue Ghetto Street Boys. Randy (voiced by Trey Parker) quickly crashed and burned. Penniless, he comes crawling back home. See also **The Avenue Street Ghetto Boys; Faith + 1; Fingerbang; Getting Gay with Kids; Jerome "Chef" McElroy; MOOP; Raging Pussies; Reach for the Skyler; Sanctified; Sisters of Mercy Hold No Pain Against the Dark Lord; Timmy! and the Lords of the Underworld.**

GIDGET AND THE GORIES — See **The Gories**.

GLITTER ROCK — From the Sid and Marty Krofft show *Electra Woman and Dyna Girl*, a cheesoid *Batman* ripoff, down to a Batcave (Electracave) and an Alfred-helper (Norman Alden as Frank Heflin). But all the more insane and ridiculous for it. And oh those spandex and Lycra costumes! Grrrrowl! In this particular episode ("Glitter Rock" 09/25/76), the supervillain is a glam rock star in a green clown wig and Bootsy Collins sunglasses (John Mark Robinson), who incapacitates his enemies with psychedelic guitar shrieks. He's after King Alex's (Jeff David) gem, because whoever possesses it is rightful king. Wow, that's a hell of a governmental system. Glitter Rock, like Electra Woman, has a sidekick, too, the appropriately named Sideman (Michael Blodgett), whose evil superpower is, apperently, the ability to say "man." A lot. And people wonder why only eight episodes were made of this show. Deidre Hall played Electra Woman, and Judy Strangis played Dyna Girl. See also **Colorado Johnson**.

GLUCKMAN, BRAD—See **B-Rad**.

GNATS, THE—The men of *Gilligan's Island*—Gilligan (Bob Denver), Skipper (Alan Hale Jr.), Mr. Howell (Jim Backus), and the Professor (Russell Johnson)—form this band so that visiting Beatle-esque rock group The Mosquitoes will take them back with them as an opening act and they can escape the godforsaken island already. Unfortunately, they're so terrible The Mosquitoes want nothing to do with them. Gilligan was on drums, the rest on guitars. From the "Don't Bug the Mosquitoes" episode (12/09/65). See also **The Honeybees; The Mosquitoes**.

GNOSIS, TOMMY—Young, arena-filling, rock superstar played by Michael Pitt in the 2000 indie rock-musical *Hedwig and the Angry Inch*. His video for "Tear Me Down" is #1 on MTV, and *Rolling Stone* magazine has crowned him Artist of the Year. How did he do it? Well, his transsexual former lover/mentor Hedwig carefully groomed him from a classic rock–lovin' Jesus freak (real name Tommy Speck) into a moody alterna-rock hunk. In gratitude, he ditched Hedwig and stole her songs (such as "The Origin of Love"). See also **Hedwig and the Angry Inch**.

GOGOL, GOGGLY—Number one artist on the top-ten board in the record shop scene in the 1971 classic *A Clockwork Orange*. The song title is "Mass in G." Pretty teenybopper Marty (Barbara Scott) asks her pretty teenybopper friend Sonietta (Gillian Hills), "Who you gettin' bratty? Goggly Gogol? Johnny Zhivago? The Heaven Seventeen?" just before Alex (Malcolm McDowell) sweet-talks them back to his place for sex. See

also **The Blow Goes; Bread Brothers; Comic Strips; Cyclops; The Heaven Seventeen; The Humpers; The Legend; The Sharks; Johnny Zhivago**.

GOLDING, JERRY—In the 1952 remake of the famous 1927 talkie *The Jazz Singer*, Jerry Golding (Danny Thomas) defies his cantor father (Eduard Franz) to become a singer. He sings "I'll String Along with You." See also **Keith Lennox; Jack Robin; Jess Robin**.

GOO GIRLS—See **The Grungies**.

GOOD OLE BOYS, THE—The country-and-western band The Blues Brothers impersonate at Bob's Country Bunker from the 1980 *Blues Brothers* movie. Leader and driver of the Winnebago Tucker McElroy (Charles Napier) was the only member who actually got a name. The rest of the band (with matching uniforms) were played by Russ Bruzek, Blair Burrows, Jack Callahan, Gene Janson, and Gil Pearson. They have a little trouble after Elwood (Dan Aykroyd) glues their gas pedal down. See also **The Blues Brothers; Murph and the Magic Tones; Street Slim**.

Orvis Goodnight (Little Richard)

GOODNIGHT, ORVIS — Real 50s rock and roller Little Richard stars in *Down and Out in Beverly Hills* (1986), the movie that shows being a suicidal homeless man can be hilarious! He plays this easily outraged aging rock and roller neighbor of rich Dave Whiteman (Richard Dreyfus). Little Richard basically plays his own outrageous self. Seriously, whom the hell else could he play?!

GORDON, JEFF AND BARBI — Upright, wholesome, clean-cut, all-American singing duo played by Sarah Purcell and Judge Reinhold in the "Amazon Hot Wax" episode (02/16/79) of *Wonder Woman*. Wonder Woman goes undercover to investigate shenanigans at the Phoenix record label. These two turn out to be the skunks in the woodpile. See also **AntiMatter**; **Billy Dero**; **Lane Kinkaid**; **Kathy Meadows**; **Hamlin Rule**.

GORIES, THE — Gidget goes goth! No, seriously! In the "Gidget's Career" episode (01/20/66) of sitcom *Gidget*, Gidget (Sally Field) is trying to get her shy, ugly (sorry, but she clearly is) friend Larue (Lynette Winter) out in the world. Gidget forces her to take up an invite to join a little beach guitar jam with Paul (Jimmy Hawkins) and Doug (Murray McLeod) from her guitar class. Paul and Doug get the idea to form a band. They let Larue in but get cute Gidget to front it, banging a tambourine, the biggest crutch instrument in rock history. As the boys say, though: "Girls as cute as you don't have to do anything." The new nameless foursome play an uptempo folk number at the Noon Dance the next day. After getting asked to play another show, Gidget sees Rick Farmer (Sandy Kenyon) on TV announcing a band contest. She writes in about her band, getting them an on-air audition in ten days. The band buckles down to brass tacks, changing their Up With People image. Gidget announces in whiteface, heavy mascara, and a black wig. "We've

gone spooky!" Gidget looks like the cutest li'l Marilyn Manson ever! They change their sound, too, bringing on a drummer, Ringo Feinberg (Dennis Joel) and rocking out. But Larue's guitar-playing isn't up to snuff, so the boys want to dump her, and make Gidget the bearer of bad tidings. Meanwhile, Dad (Don Porter) visits Farmer and finds out that it was the band's fresh-faced, no-gimmick appeal he liked, Farmer complaining it's all "moaners, wailers, and funny jumpies" these days. Dad chortles they have "hoisted themselves by their own guitars," when it's finally time for their TV performance. However, Farmer likes the new look even better! But Gidget isn't on the show or in the band! She demanded they take Larue back or she'd quit. So the guys replaced her (and Larue), and changed the name from Gidget and the Gories to just The Gories. And generic valuable lesson about friendship inserted here! See also **The Dingbats; The Horribles**.

GOSPELODEONS, THE — An African-American gospel sextet playing Harlem's Apollo Theater in the finale of the entertaining 1970 blaxploitation pic, *Cotton Comes to Harlem*. The group is comprised of three young ladies and three boys. They're singing onstage when evangelist Deke O'Malley (Calvin Lockhart) reveals himself as the skunk he is when he hits and curses one of the boys in front of a capacity crowd, trying to wrest a mic away from him.

GOURMET SCUM — This band features most prominently in two third-season (1988–89) episodes of Canuck teen series (later seen in the USA on PBS) *Degrassi Junior High* (1986–91). In "Twenty Bucks," Melanie Brodie (Sara Ballingall) gets invited to a concert by Snake Simpson (Stefan Brogren), only she has to go dutch and doesn't have the titular moolah. Desperate, she steals from her mom's purse, gets caught, grounded, and sells her ticket to teen mom Spike Nelson (Amanda Stepto), for yep, twenty bucks. In the two-parter "Taking Off," druggie Luke Cassellis (Andy Chambers) gets irresponsible Shane McKay (Bill Parrot) to try LSD at a concert. In the manner of cautionary anti-LSD tales everywhere, someone must injure themselves thinking they can fly, so Shane jumps off a bridge, falls into a coma, and suffers irreversible brain damage. See also **The Savages; The Zits**.

GRASSHOPPERS, THE—Cartoon-insect rock band of, duh, grasshoppers from the 1970–72 NBC cartoon series *Doctor Dolittle*, loosely, LOOSELY based on the hit 1967 Rex Harrison movie of the same name. This would be like a real band calling themselves "The Humans." Some of the grasshopper voices were done by Annabell, Ronnie Fallon, and Colin Julian. An album was released in 1970, *Dr. Dolittle Presents The Grasshoppers*. The band's music and lyrics are by Doug Goodwin, a cartoon composer for decades.

GREAT FROG SOCIETY, THE—From the "Behind the Music: Rock and Roll Heaven" sketch of the 12/09/00 episode of *Saturday Night Live*. In a parody of the VH1 show, we are taken beyond this mortal veil to see the rise and fall of this supergroup, comprised of dead rockers Jim Morrison (guest host Val Kilmer), Janis Joplin (Molly Shannon), Jimi Hendrix (Jimmy Minor), Buddy Holly (Jimmy Fallon), Keith Moon (Horatio Sanz), and wildcard Louis Armstrong (Tracy Morgan) . . . what, no Elvis?! Their band is a big hit in Heaven, garnering the attention of Jesus Christ, the son of God and also a record producer. He signs them, but then the band falls apart when egos clash and Morrison wants to add his new girlfriend, Amelia Earhart. Then they tragically lose Buddy Holly when he's reincarnated as a sheep, and the band

breaks up and goes its separate ways, being reincarnated as various people and things.

GREEFS, THE—Robbie Douglas's rock and roll band on the sitcom giant *My Three Sons*. They are featured in the "Falling Star" episode (12/15/66), where they rehearse "A Good Man to Have Around the House," which was actually written by actor Don Grady, who played Robbie, and was released as a single under his name. The band teams up with faded has-been singer Claudia Farrell (Jaye P. Morgan) to rejuvenate her sound on another Grady-penned tune, "Gonna Getcha." *TRIVIA TIME!* Don Grady was in a real band called The Yellow Balloon. They managed a Top 40 hit in 1967. See also **Chip Douglas and the Dynamiters; Susan Duvall; Claudia Farrell**.

GREG AND PAUL—From the very, very short-lived show *A Year at the Top*, which ran from August to September of 1977. Greg (Greg Evigan of *BJ and the Bear*, *My Two Dads*) and Paul (Paul Shaffer, David Letterman's right-hand band man) play a naive pair of songwriting Boise, Idaho, bumpkins who come to the big city to try to put on their musical. But Frederick J. Hanover (Gabriel Dell), head of Paragon Records, has other plans. Turns out he's the Devil's son, and pop needs two more souls, posthaste. So rather than give the bumpkins and their uncle Mickey (a seriously slumming Mickey Rooney), their deserved bum's rush, Hanover has them step into his parlor. With his satanic powers, he has the talentless twosome both playing the piano and singing like a pair of less outrageous Elton Johns. He convinces them to make the unlikely jump from musical songwriters to pop stars. Hanover's modus operandi is to put them into the big leagues fast, then threaten to take it all away unless they sell their soul for one more year at the top (hence the show's name, duh). See also **Hogwash;**

Billy Worthy.

GRIMLEY COLLIERY BRASS BAND—The brass band of a British coal mine, both over 100 years old, from the 1996 indie film *Brassed Off*. They have a varied repertoire, including "Danny Boy" and Rossini's *William Tell Overture*. Members include bandleader Danny (Peter Postlethwaite), his son Phil (Stephen Tompkinson), and flugelhorn player Gloria (Tara Fitzgerald). You're probably wondering what the heck a colliery is. Well, it's where collies are mined.

Phil (Stephen Tompkinson) of
Grimley Colliery Brass Band

GRINNING AMERICANS, THE—Never-seen band from the "If Ever I Would Leave You" episode (02/28/85) of sitcom *Cheers*. After Nick Tortelli's wife, Loretta (Jean Kasem), leaves him to go on tour singing with this Up With People-esque group, Nick (Dan Hedaya) comes crawling back to the titular bar to woo his waitress ex-wife Carla (Rhea Perlman). *TRIVIA TIME!* Jean Kasem is the wife of radio announcer and voice artist Casey Kasem (he did Shaggy's voice in *Scooby-Doo*). See also **Captain Gus and His Polka Pirates; Eddie Barnett and the Eddie Barnetters; Nanny Gee**.

GRIVO—See **Death Lurks**.

GROOVIE GOOLIES, THE—From the animated 1970 Saturday morning TV cartoon *Sabrina and the Groovie Goolies*. They were a somewhat less successful spinoff of Filmation's *Archie Show*. The members were Drac (voiced by Larry Storch of *F Troop*), Wolfie (voiced by Howard Morris), and Frankie (also voiced by Howard Morris)—a vampire, a werewolf, and a Frankenstein monster, respectively. The show featured a lot of rapid, inane, *Laugh-In*-style jokes, and then the band would rock out. One album was released in 1970, *The Groovie Goolies*. Apparently, the monstrous threesome also appeared in, get ready for this, the 1972 TV movie, *Daffy Duck and Porky Pig Meet The Groovie Goolies*! Now THAT's scary! *TRIVIA TIME!* Howard Morris played crazy-ass hick Ernest T. Bass on *The Andy Griffith Show*. See also **The Archies**.

GRUNGIES, THE—Clever Monkees/grunge parody in a sketch (11/15/92) from the short-lived *The Ben Stiller Show*. Since they smashed all their instruments, they beg instruments from the riot grrrl–type trio, Goo Girls (played by Jeanne Tripplehorn, Janeane Garofalo, and an uncredited drummer), and smash them instead. Lineup: long-haired lead singer Jonsie (Ben Stiller), drummer Dolly (Andy Dick), bassist Stone (Bob Odenkirk), and silent guitarist stoner Tork (Jeff Kahn, who wrote the skit). Mr. Adult (Paul Dooley) was their manager, who admonished them not to misbehave in front of Pretentious Artists Records rep Josh Goldsilver (played by real Monkee Micky Dolenz!). They sing a parody of Nirvana's "Smells Like Teen Spirit" at Club Panties. See also **Ice Man McGee**.

GUMBIES, THE—Art Clokey created the original Claymation character Gumby and got him his own TV show, *The Gumby Show*, in 1957. When he brought his animated clay brainchild back to television a second time, with the 1987–88 series *Gumby Adventures*, newly minted episodes had Gumby living on a farm with his family and this rock band that practiced in the barn. It was made up of Gumby (guitar), and his pals Pokey, Prickle, and Goo. Later, they add Denali the Wooly Mammoth on French horn, and Tillie the Chicken on xylophone. Gumby always played lead guitar and his band only did instrumentals. In the "Band Contest" episode, they go up against perennial bad guys, the Blockheads, who form rival band The Block Rockers. There's also a third, unheard band called The Metro Gnomes. See also **Gumby and the Clayboys**.

GUMBY AND THE CLAYBOYS—Art Clokey's brainchild Gumby had a band with his pals (Pokey, Prickle, Goo) in the 1988 version of his TV Claymation cartoon series, called *The Gumbies*. But in weak, watered-down snoozer *Gumby: The Movie* (1995), he's apparently dumped them all for a bunch of personality-less ringers (Fatbuckle, Thinbuckle, and Nobuckle). What a jerk! That's the cutthroat, take-no-prisoners world of animated clay lumps for you. Gumby and his band try to play a benefit show for some farmers, while the always-mischievous Blockheads try to screw it up. If you have lovely childhood memories of the original 1957 *Gumby Show*, DON'T WATCH THIS MOVIE. See also **The Gumbies**.

GUNN, TOMMY—Molly Gunn (Brittany Murphy) is the daughter of this well-heeled, conveniently dead rock star, whose wealth allows her to grow up spoiled and completely unprepared for the life lessons the crappy, cutesy 2003 movie *Uptown Girls* throws at her when her dad's accountant absconds with all his money, leaving her broker than this emotionally bankrupt film. See also **Neal Fox**.

HAMILTON, HAVEN—Henry Gibson plays this nudie-suit-wearing, country-music-traditionalist oldtimer in Robert Altman's sprawling 1975 film *Nashville*. He has all the best songs: the superpatriotic "200 Years," the weepie "For the Sake of the Children," and his oldie "Keep A-Goin'." It's all the more impressive when you consider that the stars all wrote and performed their own songs in the movie. See also **Tommy Brown (II)**; **Sueleen Gay**; **Barbara Jean**; **Linnea Reese**; **The Smoky Mountain Laurels**; **Tom, Bill & Mary**; **Connie White**.

Haven Hamilton (Henry Gibson)

HANNIGAN, "HOT LIPS"—An old friend of Fred Flintstone's who now has a dance band in the "Hot Lips Hannigan" episode (10/07/60) of *The Flintstones*. His band played at the Bedrock club, The Rockland. Voiced by Jerry Mann. See also **Ann-Margrock**; **The Beau Brummelstones**; **Jimmy Darrock**; **The Flintstone Canaries**; **Hi-Fye**; **Pebbles and Bamm-Bamm**; **Rock Roll**.

HAPPINESS UNLIMITED—From the parody of teen dance shows and a recurring skit "Mel's Rock Pile," from comedy sketch series *SCTV*. In the 04/10/84 show, host Rockin' Mel Slirrup (Eugene Levy) shows a clip from 1969, where The Tangerine Conspiracy play and Mel freaks out after being slipped spiked water. In the present, he presents the band again, only now they're called Happiness Unlimited, and Mel has acid flashbacks as they play. Lineup: Vocalist Melissa Humphries (Catherine O'Hara), drummer Chuck Humphries (Martin Short), and the rest of the band played by unnamed extras. See also **Vic Arpeggio**; **Big Momma**; **5 Neat Guys**; **The Happy Wanderers**; **Lola Heatherton**; **The Lemon Twins**; **Linsk Minyk**; **Tom Munroe**; **The Queenhaters**; **The Ramblers**; **The Recess Monkeys**; **Russ Riley**; **Jackie Rogers Jr.**; **Jackie Rogers Sr.**; **Speed of Light**; **Dusty Towne**; **The Wally Hung Trio**.

HAPPY KYNE AND THE MIRTH MAKERS—The house band for the 1977 TV talk-show spoof *Fernwood 2Nite* and its renamed 1978 reincarnation *America 2-Night*. Real-life composer and bandleader Frank De Vol was Happy Kyne, leader of the quartet. His character also ran the Bun 'n' Run fast-food chain on the side. Tommy Tedesco played guitar. *TRIVIA TIME!* Frank De Vol wrote many, many themes for such TV shows as *The Brady Bunch*, *My Three Sons*, and *The Addams Family*. See also **Denny and Brian**; **Pharoah Fawcett**; **The Friedkin Family Singers**; **Buck and Harriet Pine**; **The Punk Monks**; **Tony Roletti**.

HAPPY WANDERERS, THE—Traditional polka band from the sketch comedy show *SCTV*. This band first appeared in the 05/21/82 episode hosting their own show within a show, also called *The Happy Wanderers*. Playing easy-listening polka in the Lawrence Welk mold, it was fronted by the Shmenge brothers, Yosh (John Candy) on clarinet and Stan (Eugene Levy) on accordion. The pair sported the thick Eastern European accents of their fictional home country, Leutonia. They made several appearances afterwards, playing polka tributes to John Williams and New Wave. After *SCTV* ended, the characters were showcased retiring in the 1984 HBO special *The Last Polka* (a spoof of *The Last Waltz*, Martin Scorsese's documentary of The Band). It delved into their history, showing clips from their first TV show, the 1952 *Strikes, Spares and Shmenges*, and their mid-60s TV show, *Polka Variety Hour*, where they launched (and were possibly romantically involved with) singing group The Lemon Twins. To promote the special, Candy and Levy appeared on *Late Night with David Letterman* in character and performed their signature tune, the "Cabbage Rolls and Coffee Polka." Their last appearance was on the 1986 *Best of Comic Relief* album. See also **Vic Arpeggio**; **Big Momma**; **5 Neat Guys**; **Happiness Unlimited**; **Lola Heatherton**; **The Lemon Twins**; **Linsk Minyk**; **Tom Munroe**; **The Queenhaters**; **The Ramblers**; **The Recess Monkeys**; **Russ Riley**; **Jackie Rogers Jr.**; **Jackie Rogers Sr.**; **Speed of Light**; **Dusty Towne**; **The Wally Hung Trio**.

HARD CORE LOGO—A Canadian punk band on its ill-

Joe Dick (Hugh Dillon) (l) and Billy Tallent (Callum Keith Rennie) (r) of Hard Core Logo

fated reunion tour in the 1996 film of the same name. The lead singer is Joe Dick (Hugh Dillon), the lead guitarist Billy Tallent (Callum Keith Rennie), the bassist John Oxenberger (John Pyper Ferguson), and the drummer Pipefitter (Bernie Coulson).

HARMONY CATS, THE—Small-time touring country-and-western band from the little-known 1993 movie *Harmony Cats*. Lineup: Former concert violinist Graham Braithwaite (Kim Coates), singer Debbie Hay (Lisa Brokop), her father and the band's leader Frank Hay (Jim Byrnes), and drummer Reg (Alex Willows). They sing "Honky Tonk Love Affair," "Embers," and "Hell Stays Open All Night Long."

HARPER, BILLY "EYE"—See **Head Mistress**.

HARPOONS, THE—Vertigo Records artists who just called label head Don Prospect to say that they are meeting the queen! Probably of England, possibly some other European country, it's not really made clear. Yes, one member is named Moby Dick. From the "On the Flip Side" episode (12/07/66) of short-lived anthology show *ABC Stage 67*. See also **Bernice and Her Mammals**; **The Celestials**; **Chuck Roast and the Rares**; **Heinrich and the West Berlin Nine**; **The Hors D'Oeuvres**; **Carlos O'Conner**.

HARRIS TWINS, THE—From "The Bluegrass is Always Greener" episode (02/24/02) of FOX animated show *King of the Hill*. Unseen pair competing in the 15th Annual Old Time Fiddle Festival in Branson, MO. One holds the fiddle, the other the bow. Tough act to follow. See also **The A Men**; **The Bluegrass Brothers**; **Cane and the Stubborn Stains**; **The Dale Gribble Bluegrass Experience**; **4 Skore**; **John Redcorn and Big Mountain Fudge Cake**; **Pastor K**; **Pimp Franklin**.

HARRY KIM AND THE KIM TONES—Instrumental jazz quartet fronted by Ensign Harry Kim (Garrett Wang) in the "Virtuoso" (01/26/00) episode of *Star Trek: Voyager*. Harry Kim plays clarinet. Other crew members played drums, standup bass, and keyboards. Their performance is not well received by an audience of short aliens (the Komar) who have never heard music. Their leader Koru, is played by composer Paul Williams! It turns out the aliens love the ship's opera-singing computer-generated hologram doctor (Robert Picardo), who almost leaves when his fame goes to his head, er, overwhelms his logic subroutines. See also **Vic Fontaine**.

HART, ROBERT J. "ROBBIE"—Adam Sandler forgoes his usual drillin' for crude in his tasteful 1998 attempt at romantic comedy, *The Wedding Singer*. In this movie, set deep in the mid 80s, he fronts a nameless wedding band playing the hits of the day. But when his own bride-to-be, Linda (Angela Featherstone), leaves him at the altar, he stops singing. He sinks into depression, only to fall for Ju-

Robbie Hart (Adam Sandler)

lia Sullivan (Drew Barrymore) as he helps her plan her wedding to cheatin' preppie scum Glen Gulia (Matthew Glave). Briefly mentioned is Robbie's former rock band Final Warning, which he fronted in spandex pants and silk shirt, "licking the microphone like David Lee Roth." Billy Idol, looking only slightly embalmed, makes a cameo as himself, encouraging Robbie to take his terrific songs to Los Angeles and to become a big star. Teddy Castellucci, Randy Razz, and John Vana played the rest of Robbie's band. See also **Jimmy Moore**; **David Veltri**.

HARTACHES, THE — Late 50s/early 60s pop rock band in the 1999 CBS miniseries *Shake, Rattle and Roll: An American Love Story*, which featured today's rock stars playing yesterday's rock stars, as the other way around just isn't feasible, dammit. They also inserted this fictional band composed of Tyler Hart (Brad Hawkins) and Lyne Danner (Bonnie Somerville). Too bad the intercapped name is way too 90s and sticks out like a sore thumb. They perform "One Bad Stud," "My Back Seat," Little Richard's classic "Slippin' and Slidin," "A Touch of Heaven," "Just One Dance With You," and "Detour."

HAWKINS, PURVIS — Comedienne Lily Tomlin created this character, a smooth-crooning, black male soul/R&B singer in the mold of oh, say, Marvin Gaye. She performed as him on an episode of *Saturday Night Live* she hosted (01/22/83), but he also appeared earlier in Tomlin's 1982 CBS TV special *Lily for President*? See also **Agnus Angst**; **Linnea Reese**.

HAZELTON, KEEVY — First off, what the heck kinda name is "Keevy"? Well, it's no weirder than "Elvis." In the "A Singer in Town" episode (04/11/66) of *The Andy Griffith Show*, this rock and roller (Jesse Pearson) drives into the hick town of Mayberry for some reason, maybe he was thinking of buying it.

Ole biddies Aunt Bee (Frances Bavier) and Clara (Hope Summers) pitch him a civic-minded li'l snoozer they've written called "My Hometown." For some reason, instead of siccing security goons on them like today's rock stars, Keevy plays the song on his TV show, but a crazy rock and roll version, dig? The biddies go ballistic and get him to perform it the way they and God intended. *TRIVIA TIME*! Jesse Pearson also played rocker Conrad Birdie in *Bye Bye Birdie*. See also **Carl Benson's Wildcats**; **The Darlings**; **Jim Lindsey**; **The Sound Committee**.

HEAD MISTRESS — Metal frontman Billy Eye (Tray Loren) goes bonkers one day for no reason and goes on a killing spree in the only movie with the word "rocktober" in the title, horror flick *Rocktober Blood* (1984). Billy's backup singer and occasional girlfriend Lynn Starling (Donna Scoggins) delivers the eyewitness testimony that gets him executed. Two years later, she's FRONTING the band, now named Head Mistress, as they launch their Rocktober Blood tour. But it seems Billy has returned from the grave to stalk her and go on a second killing spree. Naturally they have to go dig up his grave to check if he's still in there. He is. Well, that's a relief, it was all just some kinda crazy . . . wait a minute—plot twist! It's not Billy, it's his twin brother, John, who's behind the murders and who did all the original killing, too! John-boy takes over the concert, planning to kill Lynn onstage, but gets taken out by an electric guitar. *TRIVIA TIME*! The songs are by real metal band Sorcery, fronted by singer Nigel Benjamin, former lead singer of late-era Mott the Hoople. He also played Chris, Lynn's boyfriend /manager. Richie King (bass), Perry Morris (drums), and Richard Taylor (guitar) of Sorcery played the band.

HEARDSMEN, THE — From *That Thing You Do* (1996). The Wonders' lead singer James "Jimmy" Mattingly

II (Johnathon Schaech) forms the Heardsmen after acrimoniously quitting The Wonders when Play-Tone label rep Mr. White (Tom Hanks) informs him that he is to record what he's told instead of his own music. Somehow he comes back to the Play-Tone label with this band and cuts three gold albums for them. They have the song "She Knows It" on the soundtrack album. The liner notes for the soundtrack album continue the fictitious universe of the movie, claiming the band was merely Jimmy and a bunch of hired-gun sidemen, with Jimmy eventually becoming a producer. In the beginning of the movie, when the Wonders are trying to come up with a name, he pitches this one and is shot down. See also **Elizabeth Anne; Blue Spot Trio; The Chantrellines; Diane Dane; The Echoes; Freddy Fredrickson; The G Men; The Hollyhocks; Jon D and the Walkers; Legends of Brass; Marilyn Lovell and the Geminis; The Norm Wooster Singers; Del Paxton; The Saturn 5; The Tempos; The Trends; Two Eriks; The Vicksburgs; The Wonders**.

HEATHERTON, LOLA — This parody of 60s sexpots Joey Heatherton and Lola Falana first appeared on sketch comedy show *SCTV* in a 09/16/78 promo for her concert. Played by Catherine O'Hara, she was a ditzy, emotional car-wreck of a B-level celebrity, frequently appearing in talk and awards show parodies. Over the run of the show, she got more and more unstable, hitting the bottle and checking into the Betty Ford Clinic. Her name was given at least once on the show as Lola Heatherington. See also **Vic Arpeggio; Big Momma; 5 Neat**

Guys; **Happiness Unlimited; The Happy Wanderers; The Lemon Twins; Linsk Minyk; Tom Munroe; The Queenhaters; The Ramblers; The Recess Monkeys; Russ Riley; Jackie Rogers Jr.; Jackie Rogers Sr.; Speed of Light; Dusty Towne; The Wally Hung Trio**.

HEAVEN SEVENTEEN, THE — Number four artist on the top-ten board in the record shop scene in the 1971 classic *A Clockwork Orange*. The song title is "Inside." Pretty teenybopper Marty (Barbara Scott) asks her pretty teenybopper friend Sonietta (Gillian Hills), "Who you gettin' bratty? Goggly Gogol? Johnny Zhivago? The Heaven Seventeen?" just before Alex (Malcolm McDowell) sweet-talks them back to his place for sex. Real New Wavers Heaven 17 named themselves after this fictitious band. See also **The Blow Goes; Bread Brothers; Comic Strips; Cyclops; Goggly Gogol; The Humpers; The Legend; The Sharks; Johnny Zhivago**.

HEDWIG AND THE ANGRY INCH — The 2000 indie rock-opera *Hedwig and the Angry Inch*, based on the

Hedwig and the Angry Inch

way off-Broadway rock musical of the same name, features the transsexual Hedwig/Hansel (John Cameron Mitchell), who didn't quite become a woman after surgery (the "angry inch" of the title). But he/she does become an embittered rock star never-was, touring the Bilgewater's seafood restaurant chain with his/her band, which includes husband/wife Yitzhak (Miriam Shor). Hedwig taught young superstar/former lover Tommy Gnosis all he knows. See also **Tommy Gnosis**.

HEINRICH AND THE WEST BERLIN NINE — Once upon a time, there was a war that was not a war: the Cold War. Commie rats vs. capitalist pigs. They had half of Germany, we had the other half. We also had half of Berlin, the west half. They had East Berlin. Hence, we can deduce that Heinrich and the West Berlin Nine are fine, upstanding, democratic-tradition-upholding folks. Which is good, as little else of them is known, as they are barely mentioned in passing in the "On the Flip Side" episode (12/07/66) of anthology show *ABC Stage 67*. See also **Bernice and Her Mammals**; **The Celestials**; **Chuck Roast and the Rares**; **The Harpoons**; **The Hors D'Oeuvres**; **Carlos O'Conner**.

HERMAN RODRIGUEZ FOUR, THE — A four-piece Mexican rhythm combo (guitar, trumpet, maracas, and the leader) having an affair with Mrs. Vera Jackson (Terry Jones) in the "Strangers in the Night" skit from 12/21/69 episode of mostly legendary BBC sketch show *Monty Python's Flying Circus*. Unfortunately, they have to get in line behind Maurice, Roger, Biggles, and Algy. Mrs. Jackson must get around, as the band leader implies they met in Acapulco. See also **Arthur Ewing and His Musical Mice**; **Bolton Choral Society**; **Johann Gambolputty de von Ausfern-schplenden-schlitter-crasscrenbon-fried-digger-dingle-dangle-dongle-dungle-burstein-von-knacker-thrasher-apple-banger-horowitz-ticolensic-grander-knotty-spelltinkle-grandlich-grumblemeyer-spelter-wasser-kurstlich-himbleeisen-bahnwagen-gutenabend-bitte-ein-nürnburger-bratwustle-gerspurten-mitz-weimache-luber-hundsfut-gumberaber-shönendanker-kalbsfleisch-mittler-aucher von Hautkopft of Ulm**; **The Hunlets**; **Jackie Charlton and the Tonettes**; **Arthur "Two Sheds" Jackson**; **Not Noel Coward**; **Not Tony Bennett**; **Rachel Toovey Bicycle Choir**; **Inspector Jean-Paul Zatapathique**.

HEY, THAT'S MY BIKE — Troy Dyer's (Ethan Hawke) alterna-rock/borderline-grunge band in the 1994 blatantly Gen X–targeted flick *Reality Bites*. They cover the Violent Femmes' "Add It Up," but alleged tough guy Ethan Hawkes (lead singer) can't bring himself to say the f-word and censors himself. The band also sings "I'm Nuthin'." The rest of the band was played by Nathan December (guitar), Jack Irons, and Christopher Wagner.

HI-FYE — From "The Girls' Night Out" episode (01/06/61) of *The Flintstones*. Cartoon character Fred Flintstone is made over by "The Colonel" into this Buddy Holly–looking rocker after a do-it-yourself record Fred recorded at an amusement park becomes a radio hit. He sings "Rockin' Bird." His wife Wilma and her pal Betty soon tire of life on tour and deliberately ruin his career by starting a rumor that he's a square. See also **Ann-Margrock**; **The Beau Brummelstones**; **Jimmy Darrock**; **The Flintstone Canaries**; **"Hot Lips" Hannigan**; **Pebbles and Bamm-Bamm**; **Rock Roll**.

HICKS, JOE JOE — See **Dill Scallion and the Dillionaires**.

HIGH, RAY — Real name Raymond Highsmith (John Labanowski). Retired 60s rock star lured out of retirement in Pete Townshend's (of The Who) 1993 concept album/rock opera/concert film *Psychoderelict*. Nasty music journalist Ruth Streeting (Jan Ravens) tricks him by writing him pretending to be an aspiring artist, so he gives her the song "Flame" to record, which she performs under the name Rosalind "Roz" Nathan. When it becomes a big hit, Ruth twists his letters to Roz to make it seem all porno-ey and creates a big scandal on her show, which gets the public buying his albums again, and gets Ray out of his funk and back into the studio to finish up an old concept album he had. See also **Rosalind "Roz" Nathan**.

HIGHTOWER, STEVE — See **Steve Hightower and the Hi-Tops.**

HILLIARD, CLARENCE "GOD" — A rock star (Timothy Carey) who used to be a bored insurance salesman in the obscure 1962 film *The World's Greatest Sinner*. He later forms a new political party and runs for president. The film is also notable for having an original score by Frank Zappa, his first.

HOAGIE, ROADKILL — Dutch rock star who played Club Xerxes in the "Teddy Cam" episode (02/03/02) of animated show *Baby Blues*. Based on the comic strip of the same name, the show was originally on the WB network for all of two months (July–August 2000), before it was picked up in 2002 by the Cartoon Network as part of its "Adult Swim" lineup. New mom Wanda MacPherson (voiced by Julia Sweeney) purchases Roadkill Hoagie's latest album, which includes these lyrics: "Buried in the basement, starting to smell / buried in the basement, please don't tell / or you'll be buried in the basement . . ." etc. See also **Darryl and the Chaos; Scissor Bitch.**

HODSTETTER, BILLY ROY — See **Fern Badderly.**

HOGWASH — From the first episode of very, very short-lived show *A Year at the Top*, which ran from August to September of 1977. Frederick J. Hanover (Gabriel Dell), head of Paragon Records, makes some claim that elicits a cry of "Hogwash!" from Uncle Mickey (Mickey Rooney?!), enabling Hanover to make the weak, weak joke that that is the name of a band that sold eight million records last year. See also **Greg and Paul; Billy Worthy.**

HOLIDAY, SUNNY — In the 2001 flick *Jackpot*, would-be singer Sunny (Jon Gries) abandons his wife and kid to travel the karaoke circuit in the American West with his manager Lester Irving (*Saturday Night Live*'s Garrett Morris), trying to build up a fan base so Sunny will be poised to be a big pop hit.

HOLLYHOCKS, THE — Never-seen band in *That Thing You Do* (1996). They play Boss Vic Koss the Mattress King's (Kevin Pollack) rock and roll show in Pittsburgh, which opens with a disastrous performance by The Wonders. But you never actually SEE this band or anything. Hey, you're lucky they're even mentioned in the radio ad for the Orpheum show! See also **Elizabeth Anne; Blue Spot Trio; The Chantrellines; Diane Dane; The Echoes; Freddy Fredrickson; The G Men; The Heardsmen; Jon D and the Walkers; Legends of Brass; Marilyn Lovell and the Geminis; The Norm Wooster Singers; Del Paxton; The Saturn 5; The Tempos; The Trends; Two Eriks; The Vicksburgs: The Wonders.**

HOLY MOSES — From the bad movie *Hard Rock Zombies* (1984). This metal band is murdered on tour in the town of Grand Guignol (warning sign!) by a family of Nazis, whose leader turns out to be . . . Hitler?! That's the movie's high point, regretfully. Fortunately, band leader Jesse (E.J. Curcio), was fooling around with a riff he got out of some medieval book that has the power to raise the dead. He gives a tape of it to his new girlfriend Cassie (Jennifer Coe), in case anything happens. Which is super convenient, what with them then getting summarily murdered and all. By Hitler. Cassie uses the tape to summon the band back from the dead to wreak their revenge on the weirdo townsfolk, becoming the hard rock zombies of the title. The movie also has midgets. You be the judge.

HONEY AND THE BEAR—In "The Spy Who Came In from the Cool" episode (10/10/66) of *The Monkees*, a pair of Rooski spies are after microfilm hidden in a pair of red maracas that Davy Jones has mistakenly ended up with. The spies, femme fatale Madame Olinsky (Arlene Martel) and her beefy underling Boris (Jacques Aubuchon), dress up as hipsters to infiltrate the club where The Monkees are playing and pull a hidden gun on them after their song ends. Quick-thinking Mike Nesmith introduces them to the audience as the folk-protest duo Honey and the Bear. Faced with an expectant crowd, they sing "Blow Up the Senate" to a cavalcade of boos while The Monkees beat a hasty getaway. See also **Fern Badderly; Irene Chomsky; The Foreign Agents; The Four Martians; The Four Swine; The Jolly Green Giants (I); Lester Crabtree and the Three Crabs; Sven Helstrom and the Swedish Rhythm Kings; The Swinging Android; The West Minstrel Abbies**.

HONEYBEES, THE—The women of *Gilligan's Island*—Ginger (Tina Louise), Mary Ann (Dawn Wells), and Mrs. Howell (Natalie Schafer)—form this singing trio in the hopes that visiting rock band The Mosquitoes will take them back with them to be their opening act and they can get off the *verdammt* isle of the title. But they're TOO good, and The Mosquitoes, feeling threatened, sneak off the island

without taking anyone. The Honeybees sing the not-so-subtle song "You Need Us." From the 12/09/65 episode "Don't Bug the Mosquitoes." See also **The Gnats; The Mosquitoes**.

HOORAY FOR EVERYTHING—This relentlessly cheerful, mercilessly clean-cut, white-bread yet multiracial, at least eighteen-member vocal group first appeared in the "Bart vs. Thanksgiving" episode (11/22/90) of cartoon *The Simpsons*. They played the Superbowl halftime show at the Silverdome, with their tribute to "the greatest hemisphere on earth, the Western hemisphere! The dancingest hemisphere of all!" Then they go into a cover of the cheesy disco song "Get Dancin'" by Disco Tex and His Sex-o-lettes. Their second appearance on the long-running FOX animated series was the "Selma's Choice" episode (01/21/93), where they were featured in a commercial performing at amusement park Duff Gardens, ruining Lou Reed's "Walk on the Wild Side." Hooray for Everything is a parody of Up With People (who actually did four Superbowl halftime shows), Duff Gardens a parody of Busch Gardens, and *The Simpsons* a parody of reality. See also **The Beach Boys Experience; The Be Sharps; Johnny Bobby; Johnny Calhoun; Captain Bart and the Tequila Mockingbirds; The Crazy Old Man Singers; Cyanide; Gulliver Dark; Ferl Dixon and His Second Helping Boys; Funky C Funky Do; Garfunkel, Messina, Oates, and Lisa; Kovenant; Krusty and the Krums; The Larry Davis Experience; Little Timmy and the Shebangs; Loggins and Oates; Lurleen Lumpkin; M. C. Safety and the Caution Crew; Melvin and the Squirrels; "Bleeding Gums" Murphy; The Party Posse; The Rappin' Rabbis; Red Breem and His Band of Some Esteem; The Satin Knights; The Steve Sax Trio; Testament; Blind Willie Witherspoon; The Ya-Hoo Recovering Alcoholic Jug Band; Yodelin' Zeke**.

HOPPY POTTY—Swedish synth pop dance quintet from a couple of *Mad TV* sketches: "Meet Hoppy Potty" (10/16/99) and "Hoppy Potty Video" (10/30/99), which premieres their Halloween video, "Hoppy Potty Shpooky Potty," a parody of Michael Jackson's "Thriller." Lineup: Schtein (Pat Kilbane), Inga (Nicole Sullivan), Gunter (Will Sasso), Yarl (Michael McDonald), and some other one (Mo Collins). "Hoppy Potty" is how they pronounce "happy party" with their thick accents. See also **Defcon One**; **Dr. Dazzle**; **The Eracists**; **Darlene McBride**; **Michael McLoud and Jasmine Wayne-Wayne**; **Savante**; **Shaunda**; **Little Hassan Taylor**; **Willow**.

HORNDOGS, THE—In the "That Thing You Don't" (11/26/97) episode of *The Drew Carey Show*, Drew (Drew Carey), Oswald (Diedrich Bader), and Lewis (Ryan Stiles) decide to revive their high school band, The Horndogs, to compete in a battle of the bands at their favorite bar, the Warsaw. They lose to The Underprivileged, played by real band The Reverend Horton Heat. Normally, that would be it, but the band pops back up in the "Ramada Da Vida" episode (09/30/98). Drew and the gang, screwing around, take over for an airport Ramada Inn house band when the regulars take a break. The manager likes them better, and offers them a regular gig. Oswald and Lewis quit, so Drew holds auditions (with various real rock star cameos), and picks space cadet guitarist Ed (played by Joe Walsh of The Eagles). Drew's rhythm section are Jim Fox and Dale Peters of The James Gang. Drew enjoys playing the accordion and rocking so much, he loses interest in his job, but a workplace crisis convinces him to quit the band in the "Drew Between the Rock and a Hard Place" episode (10/14/98). So much for that tour of every Ramanda Inn in Ohio! *TRIVIA TIME!* The musicians who audition for Drew include Joey Ramone, Dave Mustaine, Slash, Matthew Sweet, and Rick Neilsen. See also **Satan's Penis**; **The Underprivileged**; **The Unreliables**.

HORRIBLES, THE—Unseen band that just finished playing, back-announced by squinty but hep TV host Rick Farmer (Sandy Kenyon) in the "Gidget's Career" episode (01/20/66) of sitcom *Gidget*. He then announces the KXIW Swinging Teens Group of the Year Contest, which inspires Gidget to submit her new band, The Gories. See also **The Dingbats**; **The Gories**.

HORS D'OEUVRES, THE—Popular band of "Nashville birds" with "six golden oldies" in the "On the Flip Side" episode (12/07/66) of anthology show *ABC Stage 67*. Fading singer Carlos O'Conner's half-dozen-strong fan club, waiting for him at the airport while apparently all suffering from severe DTs (probably supposed to be dancing), suddenly ditch him for this band, spotted at the airport restaurant. If bitchy, egomaniacal member Irene D'Oeuvre (Lada Edmund Jr.) is any indication, the emphasis is on the Hors. She throws a fit when angels (yes, angels) divinely intervene to change the billing at Greenwich Village's Way Out Inn club to give Carlos O'Conner (Ricky Nelson) top billing. Irene threatens to walk if her band doesn't get top billing. Club manager Mr. Zuckerman (James Coco!) caves in and cancels O'Conner's show completely. Ouch! Blowback! See also **Bernice and Her Mammals**; **The Celestials**; **Chuck Roast and the Rares**; **The Harpoons**; **Heinrich and the West Berlin Nine**; **Carlos O'Conner**.

HOT DADDY AND THE MONKEY PUPPETS—From sitcom *Full House*. In the "Comet's Excellent Adventure" episode (09/27/94), Jesse's band (Jesse and the Rippers) kick Jesse out because he's spending too much time running the Smash Club instead of focusing on the band. Jesse (John Stamos) decides to go on without them. In the "On the Road Again" episode (11/08/94), his new band is finally revealed, Hot Daddy and the Monkey Puppets. Lineup: Viper (David Lipper) on guitar, Mongo (Ted Andreadis) on keyboards, and Jocko (John Del Regno). See also **The Diplomats**; **The Funky Tongues**; **Human Pudding**; **Jesse and the Rippers**; **R.E.M.**

HOT SUNDAE — Girl pop trio of high schoolers Jessie Spano (Elizabeth Berkley), Kelly Kapowski (Tiffani-Amber Thiessen), and Lisa Turtle (Lark Voorhies) in the "Jessie's Song" episode (11/03/90) of *Saved by the Bell*. Jessie succumbs to the pressures of dealing with the band and midterms and gets addicted to caffeine pills, possibly the lamest drug you can still get technically "addicted" to. After various confrontations with her friends, she bows out of their show at The Max, and spaz Screech (Dustin Diamond) fills in for her. The songs sung in the episode are "Go for It" and "I'm So Excited," the former is on the *Saved by the Bell* soundtrack album. See also **The Five Aces**; **Bo Revere**; **Stevie**; **Zack Attack**.

HOUGHTON, HUNK — Vince Everett's (Elvis Presley) cellmate in *Jailhouse Rock* (1957), played by Mickey Shaughnessy. He's a washed-up, ex–country star who tries to make a comeback on Everett's coattails once out of the big house, but he gets shafted on Everett's road to success and ends up walking Everett's dogs for a living. No wonder Houghton punches Everett in the neck. Houghton sang "One More Day." See also **Vince Everett**.

HOWARD, COREY — Successful sitcom *That '70s Show* begat the spinoff *That '80s Show*. Not a spinoff proper, as there were no characters transplanted from one show to the other, but it was made by the same creators/writers/producers. But it failed after several months' run in 2002. It centered on record clerk and musician wannabe Corey Howard (Glenn Howerton), who lives at home with sis Katie (Tinsley Grimes) and dad R.T. (Geoffrey Pierson). In the "Corey's Remix" episode (02/13/02), he records a downbeat ballad, which his sister sneakily remixes into an uptempo club dance song. She gets a DJ at Club Berlin to play it, where Corey disparages it until he realizes it's his own damn song! Then he gets real mad at Katie. See also **Wray Thorn**.

Corey Howard
(Glenn Howerton)

HOWARD, JOHN NORMAN — Occasional country singer Kris Kristofferson played this failing, fading rock star in the 1976 re-remake of the classic 1937 film *A Star Is Born*. (The first remake was in 1954 with Judy Garland and James Mason.) Howard helps struggling young Esther Hoffman (Barbra Streisand) of The Oreos into becoming the next big thing, while he slides into the traditional gutter, lubed by booze. His big song is "Hellacious Acres," penned by Paul Williams. *TRIVIA TIME!* Streisand wanted Elvis Presley to play this role, but it didn't happen, probably because the script wasn't stupid enough to be an Elvis movie. See also **The Oreos**.

John Howard Norman
(Kris Kristofferson)

HUMAN PUDDING—From the "Is It True About Stephanie?" episode (01/04/94) of featherweight sitcom *Full House*. Young cast regular Stephanie Tanner (Jodie Sweetin) runs into a guitar-totin' Jamie (Eric Lively) who's in this band. They plan a date, but Gia (Marla Sokoloff) is jealous, and tells her to back off. Stephanie says no way, so Gia starts a rumor Stephanie paid Jamie to go out with her. The date gets called off. Steph demands vengeance and posts a blow-up of the not-so-studious Gia's report card at school. The date is back on. At new band night at the Smash Club, owned by Stephanie's uncle Jesse (John Stamos), Stephanie feels bad about what she did, learns one of those damned sitcom "lessons," and makes up with Gia, right before Jamie's band takes the stage to sing "Human pudding! Human pudding! We're human. We're pudding. Human pudding!" See also **The Diplomats**; **The Funky Tongues**; **Hot Daddy and the Monkey Puppets**; **Jesse and the Rippers**; **R.E.M.**

HUMPERS, THE—Number three artist on the top-ten board in the record shop scene in the 1971 Stanley Kubrick classic *A Clockwork Orange*. The song title is "Sweaty Club." See also **The Blow Goes**; **Bread Brothers**; **Comic Strips**; **Cyclops**; **Goggly Gogol**; **The Heaven Seventeen**; **The Legend**; **The Sharks**; **Johnny Zhivago**.

THE HUNLETS—From the "The Attila the Hun Show" skit on the twentieth episode (11/11/70) of now legendary BBC sketch show *Monty Python's Flying Circus*. Attila has his own inane sitcom. The faux credits list the music as being by this band, but Attila's theme is actually "With a Little Love," the theme to then-concurrent *The Debbie Reynolds Show*. See also **Arthur Ewing and His Musical Mice**; **Bolton Choral Society**; **Johann Gambolputty de von Ausfern-schlenden-schlitter-crasscrenbon-fried-digger-dingle-dangle-dongle-dungle-burstein-von-knacker-thrasher-apple-banger-horowitz-ticolensic-grander-knotty-spelltinkle-grandlich-grumblemeyer-spelterwasser-kurstlich-himbleeisen-bahnwagen-gutenabend-bitte-ein-nürnburger-bratwustle-gerspurten-mitz-weimache-luber-hundsfut-gumberaber-shönendanker-kalbsfleisch-mittler-aucher von Hautkopft of Ulm**; **The Herman Rodriguez Four**; **Jackie Charlton and the Tonettes**;

Arthur "Two Sheds" Jackson; Not Noel Coward; Not Tony Bennett; Rachel Toovey Bicycle Choir; Inspector Jean-Paul Zatapathique.

HUNTER, BRITT — Teen singing idol from the crap spy farce *The Nasty Rabbit* (1964). Played by Arch Hall Jr., a kid with a face only a father could love. And then try to turn into a teen idol—like all Hall's other movies, this movie was written and produced by Hall's dad, Arch Hall, Sr. The band was really played by junior's band, Arch Hall Jr. and The Archers. See also **Bud Eagle; Tom Nelson**.

HUNZZ, THE — See **The Barbusters**.

ICE MAN MCGEE — In the "Ben Stiller's Music News" sketch (01/17/93) of ahead-of-its-time sketch show *The Ben Stiller Show*, this white rapper has just released a controversial song/video titled "Kill Doug Szathkey." Szathkey (Andy Dick) happens to be his annoying next-door neighbor, and the song gives his address. Bob Odenkirk played Ice Man McGee; Janeane Garofalo played Tabitha Soren. See also **The Grungies**.

ICICLES, THE — Singing group featuring Breezy Brown, a chanteur with straightened hair, mentioned in the "Independence Day" (01/10/85) episode of *The Cosby Show*. Back in the day, dad Cliff (Bill Cosby) attempted to emulate Brown and straighten his own hair to impress future wife Clair (Phylicia Rashad). One sizzling scalp later, and he'd learned his lesson. Visiting Grandpa Russell Huxtable (Earle Hyman) relates the tale to his son's

embarrassment when Cliff's son Theo (Malcolm-Jamal Warner) gets his ear pierced to impress a girl. See also **Clyde; JT Freeze; The Jazz Caravan; The Lipsticks; The Maniacs; Slim Claxton and His Trio; Walking Lemons; The Wretched**.

IMPOSSIBLES, THE — This animated rock trio was really a cover for a team of superheroes: Coil Man (voiced by Hal Smith), Fluid Man (voiced by Paul Frees), and Multi-Man (voiced by Don Messick). Apparently, no one made the connection that the rock band and the superhero team had the same damn name. Cartoon people are so stupid. Anyway, they were part of the 1966–68 *Frankenstein Jr. and the Impossibles* Hanna-Barbera series.

INCARCERATION — Oh-so-ironically named faux band created by the Albuquerque Police Department as part of a prostitution sting featured in an episode of reality show *Cops*. Wow, can you believe it? A freaking fake band on *Cops*! The band drove around in a white limo trying to pick up and bust hookers. According to the pre-sting debriefing, the drummer is the lead singer. They looked to be of the Foghat /Eddie Money genre of mulleted older guys who were going to pot but still hit the stage every night.

INDOMITABLE SPIRIT — An inspirational band of people with seemingly insurmountable problems playing feel-good rock to high school assemblies during a sketch in the HBO comedy series *Mr. Show*. Terry (David Cross) is the drummer with no hands or forearms. Jimbo (John Ennis) is the completely armless guitar player (he uses his feet), Mickey (Jay Johnston) is the flutist who is just a head, and Fran (Sarah Silverman) is a woman. But they're all actually whole and healthy. They were trying to make a point. Then their old drummer Tommy (Bob Odenkirk), from when they were Flat-Top Tony and the Purple Canoes (also the name of the episode, 10/10/97), shows up. He actually has only one arm, and complains about being kicked out of the band for only having one arm, but he was really kicked out for being a crappy drummer. See also **The Beetletown Players; Larry Black; Livingston Brewster; Willips Brighton; Dickie Crickets; Kid Jersey; Kill or Be Killed; C. S. Lewis Jr.; Horace Loeb; Marilyn Monster; Norma Jean Monster; John Baptiste Philouza; Professor Murder; Puscifer; Salini; Smoosh; Old Swerdlow; Three Times One Minus One; Titannica; Sir Lloyd Wilson Webber; Wyckyd Sceptre; Daffy "Mal" Yinkleyankle**.

INTERNATIONAL SILVER STRING SUBMARINE BAND—In the 1934 Our Gang/Little Rascals short *Mike Fright*, the gang forms this band to compete in a radio station audition. They perform "The Man on the Flying Trapeze" on junkyard instruments.

IRINA—From the 1995 James Bond movie, *Golden-Eye*. She is the fetching Russian mistress (despite her lack of a surname) of Valentin Dmitrovich Zukovsky (Robbie Coltrane), ex-KGB man turned Russian mobster. She spends about thirty seconds massacring "Stand by Your Man" in a thick Russian accent in Zukovsky's club. Played by Minnie Driver?! Well, okay.

IVAN AND THE TERRIBLES—Marijuana smoking rock band who have the misfortune to run into really nice psycho farmer Vincent (Rory Calhoun). He puts a steel bear trap in the road that causes their van to crash, then gasses them, cuts their vocal cords, buries them up to their necks, force-feeds them, hypnotizes them, snaps their necks by tying ropes around them and then to his tractor and going for a very short drive, and, finally, smokes their corpses for jerky. Whew! All in the 1980 slasher

comedy *Motel Hell*. Lineup: Ivan (Michael Melvin in a terrible fake beard), the drummer (*Cheers'* John Ratzenberger in a terrible fake mustache), the guitarist (Marc Silver), and a female who may be in the band or just a groupie (Victoria Hartman).

JACK AND JUDY—The DVD of *A Mighty Wind* (2003) comes packed with bonus footage that did not make it into the final movie. Especially enjoyable is an interlude featuring fake folkies Mitch and Mickey (Eugene Levy and Catherine O'Hara) as the doubly fictitious hippie act Jack and Judy in a clip from fictitious 60s drama *Dick Beyman—Private Eye*, starring Patrick Warburton as Dick Beyman. Although if he's a private eye, why do they call him "lieutenant?" Must be one of those cops who solves crimes in his spare time. See also **The Folksmen; Mitch and Mickey; The New Main Street Singers**.

JACK FROST BAND, THE—In the 1998 movie *Jack Frost*, Michael Keaton plays the title character, a frontman for this band and negligent father for his child, Charlie (Joseph Cross). Frost is always on the road and never there for his son, and when he dies in a car wreck, it looks like he REALLY won't be there for Charlie. But you're wrong! One year later, Frost comes back as a hideous, computer-animated snowman and tries to make things right with his kid, while avoiding fireplaces, heating ducts, the sun, things like that. Frost's band is played by Mark Addy (piano), Scott Colomby (bass), Lili Haydn (violin), Louis Molino III (drums), and mid-period Yes guitarist Trevor Rabin (guitar). All the actors played their own instruments except for Addy. Keaton learned guitar from Rabin for the role, and they even cowrote two songs for the movie.

Jack Frost (Michael Keaton) of The Jack Frost Band

JACKIE CHARLTON AND THE TONETTES—From episode #24 (12/08/70) of rather legendary BBC sketch show *Monty Python's Flying Circus*. This band performs "Yummy Yummy Yummy" entirely concealed in large, wooden packing crates, as the camera pans and swoops like it was a regular live performance. Their performance is the crowning punchline of the "How Not to Be Seen" sketch. **See also Arthur Ewing and His Musical Mice; Bolton Choral Society; Johann Gambolputty de von Ausfern-schplenden-schlitter-crasscrenbon-fried-digger-dingle-dangle-dongle-dungle-burstein-von-knacker-thrasher-apple-banger-horowitz-ticolensic-grander-knotty-spelltinkle-grandlich-grumblemeyer-spelterwasser-kurstlich-himbleeisen-bahnwagen-gutenabend-bitte-ein-nürnburger-bratwustle-gerspurten-mitz-weimache-luber-hundsfut-gumberaber-shönendanker-kalbsfleisch-mittler-aucher von Hautkopft of Ulm; The Herman Rodriguez Four; The Hunlets; Arthur "Two Sheds" Jackson; Not Noel Coward; Not Tony Bennett; Rachel Toovey Bicycle Choir; Inspector Jean-Paul Zatapathique.**

JACKSON, ARTHUR "TWO SHEDS"—From the first episode ("Whither Canada" 10/12/69) of now legendary BBC sketch comedy show *Monty Python's Flying Circus*. He is one of England's foremost modern composers who can't escape his silly nickname, at least during his interview (interviewer played by Eric Idle) on a parody of cultural talk shows called *It's the Arts*. Jackson is played by Terry Jones. See also **Arthur Ewing and His Musical Mice; Bolton Choral Society; Johann Gambolputty de von Ausfern-schplenden-schlitter-crasscrenbon-fried-digger-dingle-dangle-dongle-dungle-burstein-von-knacker-thrasher-apple-banger-horowitz-ticolensic-grander-knotty-spelltinkle-grandlich-grumblemeyer-spelterwasser-kurstlich-himbleeisen-bahnwagen-gutenabend-bitte-ein-nürnburger-bratwustle-gerspurten-mitz-weimache-luber-hundsfut-gumberaber-shönendanker-kalbsfleisch-mittler-aucher von Hautkopft of Ulm; The Herman Rodriguez Four; The Hunlets; Jackie Charlton and the Tonettes; Not Noel Coward; Not Tony Bennett; Rachel Toovey Bicycle Choir; Inspector Jean-Paul Zatapathique.**

JACKSON DECKER BAND, THE—From the short-lived 2000 MTV series *Live Through This*. An 80s band with a Heart/Fleetwood Mac/Scandal sound, they reunite in the present thanks to the efforts of their grown children. Lineup: bassist Keith Rooney (David Nerman), singer Annie Baker (Jennifer Dale), drummer Rick Parsons (Bruce Dinsmore), and lead guitarist Drake Taylor (Ron Lea). Apparently, à la Pink Floyd, there is no actual "Jackson Decker."

JACKSON, MOULING—Hot Vietnamese Communist rock star in the bizarre 1979 comedy set in 1998, *Americathon*. Played by Zane Buzby, she sang "Don't You Ever Say No" (on the soundtrack album). Buzby also had a bit part in *This Is Spiñal Tap*. See also **Earl Manchester**.

JACKSON, TED—In *Easy Come, Easy Go* (1967), Elvis Presley doesn't play a singer. He plays a FORMER singer. Big distinction, right? Fresh out of a stint in the navy disarming mines AND spotting a likely-looking shipwreck, he turns treasure hunter. He goes to his former partner, trumpet player and owner of the Easy Go-Go club, Judd Whitman (Pat Harrington, later Schneider on *One Day at a Time*). They go in on the treasure-hunting deal together. There's some "subplot" (term used loosely) involving hippie-chick ditz Jo Symington (Dodie Marshall), who's a great dancer and . . . no that's it. She's into yoga, which leads to one of the dumbest Elvis movie numbers ever, "Yoga Is as Yoga Does." They bring her into the deal; she wants to use her cut to build an arts center for her ridiculous kook-hippie friends with names like Zoltan (Diki Lerner). When it turns out the treasure chest full of doubloons or quadroons or whatever isn't really all that valuable, Ted goes back to work for Judd. With the

Ted Jackson (Elvis Presley) (center)

nameless Easy Go-Go house band, they throw a big benefit bash ("I'll Take Love") for Jo's art center, and Elvis contents himself with HER treasure chest, nudge, nudge.

JADESTONE, MICK — See **Mick Jadestone and the Rolling Boulders**.

JAGGED, MICK — See **Mick Jagged and the Stones**.

JAM BOYS, THE — See **N.W.H.**

JAMMY J — Hip-hopper mentioned in the "Krunch Time/Substitute Creature" episode (11/15/02) of Nickelodeon cartoon *The Adventures of Jimmy Neutron: Boy Genius*. His album, *Stank Dis Bad Thing Up*, is found to encourage plant growth.

JASPER'S LAW — Up-and-coming band from the second half of the eighth season of *Beverly Hills, 90210*. Series regular David Silver (Brian Austin Green) sells them a love song he originally wrote about Donna (Tori Spelling), in the band's first appearance, in "The Elephant's Father" episode (01/21/98). The band's keyboard player Mark (Eddie Ebell) gets himself kicked out of the band after getting in a car wreck because he was high and then lying about it. He gets replaced by David! The band gets a record contract, thanks to David's song, and it receives some radio airplay. However, in "Law and Disorder" (03/04/98), a record company shakeup gives the band a new rep who forces out Jasper McQuade (Paul Popowich) and puts David in charge. Jasper blames David, and David quits the band in the next episode, "Making Amends" (03/11/98), where it turns out his song only got airplay because of payola. See also **Cain Was Able**; **Ray Pruit**.

JAZZ CARAVAN, THE — Star-studded jazz combo that shares its name with a remarkable array of real-life jazz combos, radio shows, and fund-raising festivals. This particular Jazz Caravan appeared in the "Play It Again, Russell" episode (02/13/86) of *The Cosby Show*. Cliff's father, trombonist Russell "Slide" Huxtable (Earle Hyman), was a founding member of the group, which has been off the road for years. After a member dies, the combo—which features real-life jazz superstars Art Blakey, Bootsie Barnes, Eric Gale, Tommy Flannagan, Jimmy Heath, Percy Heath, Jimmy "Badman" Oliver, Tito Puente, Carlos "Patato" Valdias, and Joseph B. Wilder—gets together for a jam session. See also **Clyde**; **JT Freeze**; **The Icicles**; **The Lipsticks**; **The Maniacs**; **Slim Claxton and His Trio**; **Walking Lemons**; **The Wretched**.

JAZZ TIMES TEN — These prepubescent hepcats provide the musical interludes for the recurring *Saturday Night Live* skit "Wake Up Wakefield," the morning announcement program for Wakefield Middle School in San Jose. In one skit, Elijah Wood plays a trumpeter named Greg that cohost Megan (Maya Rudolph) develops a crush on. Other members of the band include Tony Tedusco (tenor sax), Mike Dusette (also tenor sax), and Scott Abasion (all-district for trumpet).

JEAN, BARBARA — Waiflike country singing star married to her manipulative manager and suffering a nervous breakdown in Robert Altman's 1975 film *Nashville*. Barbara Jean (Ronee Blakley) comes to a bad end at the film's finale. See also **Tommy Brown (II)**; **Sueleen Gay**; **Haven Hamilton**; **Linnea Reese**; **The Smoky Mountain Laurels**; **Tom, Bill & Mary**; **Connie White**.

JEFF BEBE BAND, THE — See **Stillwater**.

JEFFERS, BILLY — In the "Harem" episode (10/25/73) of cop drama *The Streets of San Francisco*, real 50s rocker Ricky Nelson plays this once-famous rock star who now bosses a bunch of prostitutes. Damn, Ricky! Ricky be sho nuff pimpin', but not in the good way, more in the I'll-kill-you-bitch-where's-my-money way.

JELLY, BLIND MELLOW—Fred G. Sanford's favorite bluesman from the TV show *Sanford and Son*. Fred (Redd Foxx) had an extensive collection of his 78s, worth $500, until they got broken in the "The Blind Mellow Jelly Collection" (aka "The Chameleon") episode (11/16/73).

FAKE BANDS YOU MOST WANT TO PARTY WITH
BY JASON TORCHINSKY

Sex, drugs, and rock and roll. And even if the rock and roll is fake, the sex and drugs are still real. And really, isn't that what matters? The sex, the drugs, the parties, the wild times that make all this rocking and rolling about worth it? Of course it is. Even among fake bands, partying is a very real business. And here's the top fake bands you'd most like to party with on your next trip to the Partiers' Republic of Fakebandlandia:

1. **Dr. Teeth and the Electric Mayhem** *(The Muppet Show, et al)*—First of all, you've got to respect a band that's done every performance with hands wedged deep up their asses. More specifically, this all-Muppet band is a loud, rollicking good time cast in foam rubber. Dr. Teeth himself has the air of someone who could score pretty much any mind-altering agent you'd desire, and Floyd Pepper seems like he's taken them all. So does Zoot, for that matter. Janice has a dopily arousing quality that simply screams free-lovefest, and the final, gigantic, railroad spike–sized nail in the party coffin is Animal, the drum-

mer, and perhaps the highest concentration of pure rock and roll mayhem in the free world. Just think about what a party with the barely controlled Animal would mean: You'd probably wake up a month later in the back of a burned out microbus outside of Vegas with bright orange fur in your hair and a slew of exciting new tattoos and piercings.

2. **The Carrie Nations** *(Beyond the Valley of the Dolls)*—You've got to figure that severe mental instability and free and easy access to drugs make for great rock and roll parties, and this band has them in spades. Throw in a healthy dose of late 60s psychedelia, relaxed sexual mores, and a crazy transsexual manager who enjoys throwing orgies, and you've got yourself a hell of a time.

3. **Wyld Stallyns** *(Bill and Ted's Bogus Journey)*—While perhaps among the least-listenable of any fake band, Wyld Stallyns has the very distinct advantage of being the cornerstone of the society prophesized in the (perhaps) horrifyingly prescient *Bill and Ted* movies. Since Wyld Stallyns' music is the cornerstone of the predicted civilization, you know the parties would have to be amazing, being state-sanctioned, religiously motivated, and philosophically imperative for the entire population of the planet. That would make any Wyld Stallyns party like Mardi Gras, Christmas, and the 4th of July rolled into one massive orgy of bad heavy metal–inspired music, large futuristic boots, and wild times.

4. **The Misfits** *(rival band to Jem and the Holograms from Jem!)*—Any animated band is already going to have an advantage over their real-world brethren (impervious to hangover, injuries, or inconvenient pregnancies), so you know an animated band composed entirely of BAD girls is going to knock you so hard on your ass, party-wise, you'll never want to get back up.

5. **Josie and the Pussycats** *(animated series Josie and the Pussycats)*—For many of the same reasons as The Misfits

(#4), you'd be a fool to miss out on a Pussycats party. Long tails, ears for hats, animated legs that don't quit, and a creepily infectious, wildly positive outlook—that sounds like a pretty good animated time.

6. **Spiñal Tap** *(This Is Spiñal Tap)*—Come on, if you're going to Idaho, you're going to eat a potato. They're the kings of this whole fake-band genre, hands down. No matter what the party's actually like (my guess is good at first, rapidly degenerating into a drunken hotel-room smashup) you need to be able to say that you did your wild time with Tap.

7. **Lancelot Link and the Evolution Revolution** *(Lancelot Link/Secret Chimp)*—Chimps. Imagine partying with chimps. Then imagine partying with ROCK AND ROLL chimps! Talk about your party animal! It would be the wildest party you've ever been to, but even better, because you'd be the hottest one in the room, and if anything gets flung you can blame it on the band.

JEM AND THE HOLOGRAMS—Stars of the cartoon *Jem!* (1985–88). When Jerrica Benton's father dies, she inherits his half of Starlight Music and the Starlight House, a home for orphans. Unfortunately, the other half is owned by conniving Starlight exec Eric Raymond (voiced by Charles Adler). Raymond has just signed The Misfits (no, not the Glenn Danzig Misfits), whom he plans to make megabig, starting with their performance at an upcoming battle of the bands he's fixed. Meanwhile Benton gets a pair of earrings that lead her to Synergy (voiced by Marlene Aragon), a talking supercomputer built by her father that has the ability to project holograms, using the transmitters in the earrings. Jerrica, disguised by hologram, becomes Jem and forms a band with her little sister Kimber (voiced by Cathianne Blore) and friends Aja Leith (also voiced by Cathianne Blore) and Shana Elms-

ford (voiced by Cindy McGee). Jem and the Holograms show up univited to the battle of the bands and steal the show. Raymond foolishly makes a bet that whoever's group is more popular in six months wins control of Starlight Music. So, six months later, they have another battle of the bands, and who do you think wins? Hint: the show is called *JEM!*, not *THE MISFITS*. Jem and the Holograms and The Misfits have a rivalry just shy of the East Coast/West Coast rap wars. Granted, nobody busts a cap in anyone's ass, but everything else is fair game. The Misfits crash parties, steal instruments and master tapes, sabotage shows, and even impersonate Jem in their remarkably single-minded grudge against the group. Naturally they are thwarted in every attempt by the forces of saccharine-sweet goodness. Nicey-nice Jem/Jerrica manages to keep her dual identity hidden from everyone (except her band, of course). This leads to the occasional issue with Jerrica's boyfriend/stage manager Rio Pacheco (voiced by Michael Sheehan), who sometimes falls for Jem, not knowing they're the same person. In "The Jem Jam" two-part episode (02/08/87 and 02/15/87), Jem and the band invite a bunch of other singers to join them in a big all-star jam session ("Jam All Night Long"). Each singer is a thinly disguised version of a real singer: Luna Dark (Madonna), Lena Lerner (Tina Turner), her son Dominic (Michael Jackson), Ron Cox (Mick Jagger), Roland Owens (Stevie Wonder), and Johnny Deacon (Bruce Springsteen). Each show had two or three music video segments from Jem and the Holograms, The Misfits, or some rare third act. The success of this show and its tie-in line of dolls prompted the Mattel company to give their long-lived Barbie doll a band, Barbie and the Rockers. See also **Bobby Bailey**; **Barbie and the Rockers**; **The Ben Tiller Orchestra**; **The Limp Lizards**; **The Misfits**; **The Stingers**; **The Tapps Tucker Quartet**.

JEM!: THE COMPLETE FIRST AND SECOND SEASONS (RHINO, 2004)

Childhood memories always suffer when later compared to the cold facts of the adult present: grandma's huge house where you used to play has shrunk, the candy-colored amusement park turns garish and seedy, and your favorite cartoons are revealed as hackneyed, formulaic, and poorly animated. Alas, so it is with the *Jem!* DVD set. In the harsh, cold light of adulthood, this ostensibly rock-oriented drama reveals itself as a ridiculously unlikely soap opera cast from the exact same mold as its grown-up 80s prime-time cousins. Jerrica Benton/Jem leads the insane, up-and-down life of a poor little rich girl straight out of *Dallas* or *Dynasty*. Her rivals, the scenery-chewing Misfits, are more than a match for any *Falcon Crest* or *Knots Landing* bitch goddesses. Every episode downfalls are plotted, deadly accidents threaten, adversity strikes, and plot holes are conveniently ignored.

The audio and picture quality are excellent, even if they serve to underscore the cheap, cheap production values of the show. In one early episode, you can see Jem's mascara disappear and reappear several times in the same shot! The animation is so minimal, it makes *Huckleberry Hound* look like *Fantasia*. The quality did improve as the show went on, and the animators saved their best for the show's music video segments, which sparkle with creativity in comparison to the rest of the show. But for all its flaws, if you're a child of the 80s, this DVD set is a must-have. Well, if you're a FEMALE child of the 80s, that is. This show perfectly captures the era of the mid 80s, and sweet childhood memories conquer adult nitpicking any day of the week.

The four-disc set is a bit light on traditional DVD extras and commentary. Rhino could only round up writer/creator Christy Marx, who only comments on one episode per disc, and even then, there are some dead spots. She does begrudge a fair amount of trivia as she discusses what she was trying to do with the show, and admits the show was designed to be a total escapist fantasy for girls. Disc four has more stuff, including a short interview with Marx, as well as Samantha Newark, who voiced Jerrica/Jem during the show's run. There's also some Jem PSAs and stills from the show's production bible. The one really cool extra is the "Play All Songs" feature on each disc, which strings together all the music video segments from each show, turning your TV into a Jem jukebox. Showtime, Synergy!

JENKINS, DOC — Real country star Willie Nelson plays singer/songwriter Doc Jenkins in the 1984 movie *Songwriter*. Country-music hanger-on Kris Kristofferson plays his former partner Blackie Buck. Melinda Dillon plays Doc's singer wife, Honey Carder. Lesley Ann Warren plays rising up 'n' comer Gilda.

JESSE AND THE RIPPERS — Hermes "Jesse" Katsopolis (John Stamos) was guitarist and lead vocalist for this band from day one of sitcom *Full House*, when he moved in with his brother-in-law Danny Tanner (Bob Saget) after Danny's wife died, to help raise their kids. A dedicated performer, he tried his hand at jingle-writing, Elvis-impersonating, and even joining an airport cover band to make money for the family. He eventually got a radio show, *Rush Hour Renegades*, and inherited a local bar called the Smash Club. Despite his best efforts, rock-star success constantly eluded him and his band, although they got close a few times, especially when they got real-life Beach Boys Mike Love and Bruce Johnston to sing backup on Jesse's song "Forever," in the "Captain Video (part 1)" episode (05/05/92). It becomes a brief hit in Japan, and the band tours there for a few weeks. In the "Comet's Excellent Adventure" episode (09/27/94), Jesse has become so wrapped up in the club and other stuff that his own band kicks him out, so he forms a second band, Hot Daddy and the Monkey Puppets. See also **The Diplomats**; **The Funky Tongues**; **Hot Daddy and the Monkey Puppets**; **Human Pudding**; **R.E.M**.

JIMMY DICK AND THE NIGHT STICKS — From the "The Great Escape" episode (02/21/88) of *Married with Children*. Teen daughter Kelly Bundy (Christina Applegate) tries to escape her Dad's shoe store to go see this band. But she's been grounded and the whole family has to stay the night at the store while their house is fumigated. See also **Burned Beyond Recognition**; **Joanie and the Slashettes**; **Oozing Meat**; **Shoes 'n' Socks**; **Tears and Vomit**; **The Tuxedos**; **The Wanker Triplets**; **The Why**; **Yodeling Andy**.

JOANIE AND THE HEPCATS — see **Joanie and the Slashettes**.

JOANIE AND THE SLASHETTES — From the second of the two-part *Married with Children* episode, "Kelly Does Hollywood" (11/17/91). Airhead hottie Kelly Bundy (Christina Applegate) gets her Chicago trash-talking public-access discussion show, *Vital Social Issues 'n' Stuff with Kelly* picked up by a network. Her network show's house band is this trio of leather-clad, guitar-wielding rock chicks who sing a song whose only lyric is "Sex." Later, the network ruins the show by remaking it into 50s niceness, and the band is transformed into three besweatered, long-skirted accordionists, Joanie and the Hepcats, whose single-word song is now "Milk!" Then the show gets canceled. No, no, not lowbrow FOX sitcom *Married with Children*, but *Vital Social Issues 'n' Stuff with Kelly*. See also **Burned Beyond Recognition**; **Jimmy Dick and the Night Sticks**; **Oozing Meat**; **Otitis Media**; **Shoes 'n' Socks**; **Tears and Vomit**; **The Tuxedos**; **The Wanker Triplets**; **The Why**; **Yodeling Andy**:

JOEY MIDNIGHT AND DARK HIGHWAY — Band of rock star Joey Midnight (Adrian Zmed) in the "Best Friends" episode (04/09/81) of the best crossdressing-themed sitcom ever, *Bosom Buddies*. Amy Cassidy (Wendy Jo Sperber) has camped out for two tickets to his show at Madison Square Garden. But it turns out he's a childhood friend of Kip Wilson (Tom Hanks), who, with one phone call, has Joey eating breakfast with Kip and his starstruck friends the very next morn. Joey enters in the standard rock-star uniform: leather jacket, shades, black T-shirt, and tight, tight pants. He suggests they all have breakfast in his limo instead, but Kip's bud and roommate Henry Desmond (Peter Scolari) gets left behind in the shuffle. Kip makes it up to Henry with two backstage passes to his Garden concert—"better seats than Robert Stigwood." But Henry still feels left out when Kip ignores him for the band. Even though Henry gets ditched again, the episode ends in warm fuzzy apologies and hugs, but not before Kip gets Joey in drag to get him into his women-only apartment.

JOHN REDCORN AND BIG MOUNTAIN FUDGE CAKE — In the "Witches of East Arlen" episode (05/18/2003) of animated show *King of the Hill*, young Bobby Hill (voiced by Pamela Segall) runs afoul of hardcore-magic nerd Ward Rackley (voiced by David Cross). Bobby gets sucked into the witchcraft subculture, at least until he has to drink dog's blood at an upcoming ceremony. While researching how to get out of it at the New-Agey 9th Dimension bookstore, Bobby runs into Native American John Redcorn (voiced by Jonathan Joss) handing out flyers for his rock band. Knowledgeable about his tribe's ceremonies and rituals, he assures Bobby that drinking dog's blood is perfectly gross. See also **The A Men**; **The Bluegrass Brothers**; **Cane and the Stubborn Stains**; **The Dale Gribble Bluegrass Experience**; **4 Skore**; **The Harris Twins**; **Pastor K**; **Pimp Franklin**.

JOHN SMITH AND THE COMMON MEN—Early 60s British Merseybeat band that London Coal Hill School student Susan Foreman (Carole Ann Ford) briefly grooves to on her transistor radio in the first-ever episode—"An Unearthly Child," aka "100,000 BC" (11/23/63)—of long-running BBC sci-fi series and geeks' delight *Doctor Who*. Susan is the granddaughter of the mysterious titular character played by William Hartnell. The band's song (whatever it is) jumped from #19 to #2 on the charts. Susan's hip teacher, Ian Chesterton (William Russell) points out that "John Smith" is the stage name of the Hon. Aubrey Waites and that he started his career as Chris Waites and the Carollers. Presumably, Waites finds it amusing to call his band "The Common Men" when he's a son of a peer. The episode was written by Anthony Coburn. See also **The Lorells.**

JOHNNY AND THE DEER TICKS—Garage band featured in the "Johnny B. Badd" episode (09/01/00) of Cartoon Network's *Johnny Bravo* cartoon. Their big hit was "Funky Monkey." The band was Carl Chryniszzswics (voiced by Tom Kenny) on drums, Suzy the neighbor girl (voiced by Mae Whitman) on keys, Bunny Bravo (voiced by Brenda Vaccaro) on double-necked guitar, and Johnny Bravo (voiced by Jeff Bennett) on unplugged microphone. They were popular as long as no one could hear Johnny actually sing. See also **The Round Pound; Berry Vanderbolten.**

JOHNSON, COLORADO—Reporters Lori (Deidre Hall) and Judy (Judy Strangis), better known as superheroines *Electra Woman and Dyna Girl*, have been assigned to interview "Mr. Country Rock himself" in "The Sorcerer's Golden Trick" episode (09/11/76). Judy pulled a few strings to get this assignment, but the evil sorcerer's plan to steal all the gold from Ft. Knox gets in the way of them meeting Judy's idol. Colorado is only glimpsed on a poster hanging by the back door of the concert venue. On the poster he looks a lot like Gordon Lightfoot. See also **Glitter Rock.**

JOLLY GREEN GIANTS, THE (I)—From the "Find the Monkees" episode (01/23/67) of *The Monkees*. A rock quartet all dressed, yep, you guessed it, as the Jolly Green Giants. They are never shown playing, but with a gimmick like that, do you really need to? They, along with The Monkees, are all desperate to audition for eccentric TV producer Hubbell Benson (Carl Ballantine), who has put invitations out to all the local bands, except, it would seem, The Monkees. One member slags The Monkees as having "no gimmick." Which should be a lot funnier coming out of the mouth of a guy dressed as the Jolly Green Giant. See also **Fern Badderly; Irene Chomsky; The Foreign Agents; The Four Martians; The Four Swine; Honey and the Bear; Lester Crabtree and the Three Crabs; Sven Helstrom and the Swedish Rhythm Kings; The Swinging Android; The West Minstrel Abbies.**

JOLLY GREEN GIANTS (II)—From the 1992 comedy *Wayne's World*. This band is playing at the Gas House and is just mentioned in passing by bouncer Tiny (Meat Loaf). They are glimpsed later, in full Jolly Green Giant costumes, in the background when Cassandra Wong (Tia Carrere) kicks some guy's ass. See also **Crucial Taunt.**

JOLSON, OWL—The jazz-loving cartoon owl and son of serious classical music teacher Fritz Owl in the 1936 Warner Bros. cartoon *I Love to Singa*, a parody of Al Jolson's *The Jazz Singer*. His stern Germanic father kicks him out of the tree for singing jazz, but they later reconcile live on the radio station G-O-N-G program, *Jack Bunny and His Amateur*

Hour, where little Owl Jolson's jumping jazz singing wins first prize.

JON D AND THE WALKERS — One of the many mentioned but never-seen bands in *That Thing You Do* (1996). They play Boss Vic Koss the Mattress King's (Kevin Pollack) rock and roll show in Pittsburgh, which opens with a stinky performance by The Wonders. But you never actually SEE the band or anything, be glad they're even mentioned in the radio ad for it. And isn't that an unusual spelling of "John" for 1964? See also **Elizabeth Anne; Blue Spot Trio; The Chantrellines; Diane Dane; The Echoes; Freddy Fredrickson; The G Men; The Heardsmen; The Hollyhocks; Legends of Brass; Marilyn Lovell and the Geminis; The Norm Wooster Singers; Del Paxton; The Saturn 5; The Tempos; The Trends; Two Eriks; The Vicksburgs; The Wonders**.

JONES, GIOVANNI — Pompous, hot-headed Italian opera singer and Bugs Bunny nemesis in the 1949 Warner Bros. classic cartoon *Long-Haired Hare*. This was back when "long-hair music" meant classical, not classic rock. While he's trying to rehearse, Bugs ticks him off with his banjo playing, and Jones smashes it. So Bugs takes revenge later at the concert by various means, including impersonating a conductor (Leopold Stokowski) and making Jones jump through various vocal hoops. Both Bugs and Jones were voiced by cartoon legend Mel Blanc.

JONES, GORDON — See **G-Dog**.

JONES, RAY PAUL — Aging rock star (Ian Patrick Williams) who appears in the "Rock Star" episode (10/04/95) of sitcom *Unhappily Ever After*, a show best described as *Married with Children: The Sequel*. Wife Jennie Malloy (Stephanie Hodge) wrangles a date with this guy, her teenage crush.

JORDAN, RACHEL — See **Kovenant**.

JOSIE AND THE PUSSYCATS — This female pop rock trio were originally created as comic book characters by Dan DeCarlo. They were a spinoff from *Archie* comics, and introduced in their own comic book, *She's Josie* in February of 1963. It is therefore quite appropriate that the band was introduced to television as a spinoff of the successful cartoon *The Archie Show*. The Hanna-Barbera animated version of *Josie and the Pussycats* debuted in 1970, and was revamped in 1972 as *Josie and the Pussycats in Outer Space*. Band leader Josie McCoy (voiced by Janet Waldo) sang and played guitar, ditzy Melody Valentine (voiced by Jackie Joseph) played drums, and African-American Valerie Brown (voiced by Barbara Pariot) played tambourine and sang. They got a remarkably full sound from just drums, guitar, and tambourine. Their manager was cowardly Alexander Cabot III (voiced by Casey Kasem), and his evil sister Alexandra (voiced by Sherry Alberoni) constantly vied for the affection of Josie's clean-cut yet hunky boyfriend Alan M. Mayberry (voiced by Jerry Dexter). A 1970 album *Josie and the Pussycats* was released but the band had no luck duplicating the chart success of The Archies. A live-action movie version of the band came out in 2001. *Josie and the Pussycats* kept all the characters, updated the band to garage rock, and dropped them into a fun, reasonably clever plot. Originally just called The Pussycats, the band is renamed Josie and the Pussycats as part of evil manager Wyatt Frame's scheme to divide the band. He (Alan Cumming) quickly and easily makes them megapopular, since he is part of a vast conspiracy to keep teens hooked into buying fad after fad through subliminal messages. Josie (Rachel Lee Cook), Melody (Tara Reid), and Val (Rosario Dawson) have to thwart his schemes and keep the band together. Best scene? A bat-wielding Carson Daly (from MTV's *Total Request Live*) trying to beat Valerie and Melody to death after they know too much. Now that's entertainment! See also **The Archies; DuJour; Alan M.**

Josie and the Pussycats
(from the 2001 movie)

JUDDSON BROTHERS, THE — See **Stillwater**.

JUGGS, THE — See **Dill Scallion and the Dillionaires**.

JUICY FRUITS, THE — From the 1974 movie *Phantom of the Paradise*. They start off as a greaser/50s rock and roll band singing "Goodbye, Eddie, Goodbye" and evolve into an early Beach Boys–like surf group, The Beach Bums. Then they get blown up by the Phantom and die. The band was played by Archie Hahn, Jeffrey Commanor, and Harold Oblong. Archie Hahn sang lead on "Goodbye, Eddie, Goodbye," which tells the tale of metafake singer

Eddie Mitty, who kills himself to guarantee his final album will raise enough money to pay for his sister's operation. *TRIVIA TIME!* Archie Hahn would later land a bit part in *This Is Spĩnal Tap*. See also **The Beach Bums; Phoenix; The Undead**.

KAIMANA, LANI — Hawaiian hotel lounge singer in the 1966 Elvis movie *Paradise, Hawaiian Style*. Elvis does an awful lot of singing in this flick, considering he's only playing an airline pilot. She (Marianna Hill) sings at a lounge called (you gotta love this) The Piki Niki. She sings "Scratch My Back (Then I'll Scratch Yours)" in a duet with Elvis. Lani is one of Rick Richard's (Elvis Presley) old flames— he's got a bonfire's worth of them, apparently, as he hits up all the ones that work at hotels to recommend his new charter-plane service to guests. An incident chauffeuring around a helicopter full of frisky dogs for some damn ole haole rich bitch almost gets Rick killed, and definitely gets him in trouble with everyone. This movie is not high up in the Elvis canon: It has more damned helicopter landing shots than you can shake a lie at, and you get the same entertainment value if you mute the movie and just enjoy the fantastic Hawaiian scenery.

KAPTAIN KOOL AND THE KONGS — Is having a band name that abbreviates to KKK a good thing? Anyway, this group was created by the Krofft brothers to host the Saturday morning *Krofft Supershow* (1976–78). In the words of Sid Krofft, ". . . a group we just put together out of actors who could sort of sing." After two years, they were replaced by real band, The Bay City Rollers. That's showbiz!

Michael Lembeck was the Fonzie-esque Kaptain Kool, Debra Klinger was Superchick, Michael McMeel was Turkey, and Louise DuArt was Nashville. They had a 1978 album on Epic. There was a fifth member, Flatbush (Bert Sommer), but he was only in the first season and was replaced—like how Pete Best was kicked out of the Beatles for Ringo.

KATT, BONNIE—Former jiggle queen Suzanne Somers, at the height of her jiggle powers, took a break from the heavy, heavy demands of her series *Three's Company* to play this rock singer in the 1978 NBC TV movie *Zuma Beach*. Bonnie needs to get away from the pressure of fame and just chill on the beach . . . Zuma Beach! Duh! Somers did her own singing on "Don't Run Away." Rosanna Arquette also jiggles. Do not watch for the music but rather for the jiggling.

KEE KEE AND THE P. P. GANG—Sock puppets Sifl (voiced by Matt Crocco) and Olly (voiced by Liam Lynch) of MTV's po-mo *The Sifl and Olly Show*, hold their First Annual Sifl and Olly Show Battle of the Bands in the 01/12/99 episode. First up was this pop rock band of four tiny, irregular, roughly spherical objects, maybe rocks. Or possibly potatoes. They played a sped-up, high-energy li'l ditty about themselves. Which is amazing, considering they had no visible appendages of any kind. The show was the brainchild of Matt Crocco and Liam Lynch, who did the voices and composed and recorded the music. See also **Clear Fog**; **Sgt. Blind Kiwi Tarzan**; **Yeah**; **Zafo**.

KELLY AFFAIR, THE—See **The Carrie Nations**.

KENOSHA KICKERS, THE—Gus Polinski (John Candy) is the shuttle chief of this Midwest polka band from *Home Alone* (1990). He accidentally left his kid

alone overnight at a funeral parlor, so Kate McCallister (Catherine O'Hara) doesn't feel quite so bad about accidently leaving her kid Kevin (Macaulay Culkin) behind on a family Christmas trip, as she rides with the band to get back home. The rest of the band was played by real polka band Eddie Korosa and the Boys (Edward Bruzan, Frank Cernugel, Eddie Korosa, John Hardy, Robert Okrzesik, Leo Perion, and Vince Waidzulis). *TRIVIA TIME!* Those of you with long memories might remember John Candy's stint in another fictional polka band, *SCTV*'s **The Happy Wanderers**.

KERR, PAUL—Washed-up 80s Scottish pop star played by Craig Ferguson (perhaps best known as Drew Carey's casually cruel Brit boss on *The Drew Carey Show*) in the 2003 movie *I'll Be There*. After driving his dirt bike out of a second-floor window of his mansion, Kerr discovers that he has a daughter he never knew he fathered. His daughter, Olivia, was born from a one-night stand with Rebecca Edmonds (Jemma Redgrave) in 1987, when Kerr's hair

Paul Kerr (Craig Ferguson) (r) and Evil Edmonds (Joss Ackland) (l)

was at its poofiest. Ironically, Rebecca's father is ancient rockabilly rocker Evil Edmonds (Joss Ackland), of Evil Edmonds and the Beelzebops, who's still touring despite his age. Olivia, played by Welsh singer Charlotte Church (in her movie debut), has been taking voice lessons on the sly, since her mom doesn't want her to be a singer. Well, you can easily see where this is going. Kerr has to learn to love his daughter, support her desire to sing, and ditch the booze. He gets some help from his old drummer Digger McQuade (Ralph Brown). Ferguson wrote and directed the film.

KID, THE — Otherwise nameless protagonist from the 1984 movie *Purple Rain*. This Prince vehicle features him as an artistic, inscrutable, tormented genius. He's a rising up-and-comer in Minneapolis (Prince's real hometown). His rivals are hilariously outrageous Morris Day and his band, The Time, playing themselves. The Kid gets grief from his band members (Prince's real band, The Revolution, playing themselves). His parents are always fighting, and his dad tries to shoot himself! He survives though. It's all The Kid can do to get hottie singer-wannabe Apollonia (Apollonia Kotero) in the sack (you get to see her topless!). Day is tired of sharing the club with The Kid and wants to muscle him out, and also tries to steal his girl. The movie doesn't hold up as well today, but at the time, it and the soundtrack album were monster hits, propelling Prince into superstardom. Unfortunately, Prince tried

The Kid (Prince)

to follow up the success of this movie with a sequel, *Graffiti Bridge* (1990). Too little, too late. The Kid and Morris are still rivals, each with their own club. They make an idiotic bet to see who can write the best song, putting their clubs on the line.

KID JERSEY — From a sketch on the HBO comedy show *Mr. Show*, in the "Velveteen Touch of a Dandy Fop" episode (12/20/96). He's a rising young 20s megaphone-crooner star (David Cross) who bursts on the scene in 1925 with "Penicillin." He always said, "thank you" after every song, coining the term that's become so popular today. After vying for the public's affections versus rival megaphone king Dickie Crickets (Bob Odenkirk), the two joined forces for the 1929 Monsters of Megaphone tour, where the Kid got busted by The Man for singing his new song "Counterfeit Money Machine," which he had just invented. See also **The Beetletown Players; Larry Black; Livingston Brewster; Willips Brighton; Dickie Crickets; Indomitable Spirit; Kill or Be Killed; C. S. Lewis Jr.; Horace Loeb; Marilyn Monster; Norma Jean Monster; John Baptiste Philouza; Professor Murder; Puscifer; Salini; Smoosh; Old Swerdlow; Three Times One Minus One; Titannica; Sir Lloyd Wilson Webber; Wyckyd Sceptre; Daffy "Mal" Yinkleyankle.**

KIDD VIDEO — A man, a band, a show—Kidd Video was all three in one. This thrice-eponymous band was named after its leader (voiced by Bryan Scott) in the 1984–86 animated series *Kidd Video*. Rest of the lineup: dorky Ash (voiced by Steve Alterman), nerdy Whiz (Robbie Rist, *The Brady Bunch*'s Cousin Oliver), and hot Hispanic chick Carla (voiced by Gabriele Bennett). This live-action teen foursome was rehearsing in their storage space one day when they were zapped by the evil Master Blaster (voiced by Pete Renaday), turned into cartoons, and transported into his strange, music-based, animated universe called "Flipside." They spent their time there foiling Master Blaster's evil, convoluted schemes and tangling with his henchman, The Copy Cats. Each episode would end with a live-action music video by the band. **TRIVIA TIME!** An album of the band's music was released by CBS in 1986—but only in Israel! See also **The Copy Cats.**

KIDNEY ROCK—Viral rapper who rocks a germ bar (aka a big zit on Bill Murray's face) during *Osmosis Jones* (2001). Kidney Rock bears a striking resemblance to real rocker Kid Rock, mainly 'cause it IS him (even sidekick Joe C. is in it, too). See also **Metabolica.**

KILL OR BE KILLED—African-American rapper in a sketch about the East Coast–West Coast ventriloquist rivalry, which hilariously parodies the East Coast–West Coast rap rivalry. KOBK appears on a news program about the two rivalries, trying hard to still look cool while debating with a ventriloquist dummy. From the "Oh, You Men" episode of HBO's *Mr. Show* (10/03/97). See also **The Beetletown Players; Larry Black; Livingston Brewster; Willips Brighton; Dickie Crickets; Indomitable Spirit; Kid Jersey; C. S. Lewis Jr.; Horace Loeb; Marilyn Monster; Norma Jean Monster; John Baptiste Philouza; Professor Murder; Puscifer; Salini; Smoosh; Old Swerdlow; Three Times One Minus One; Titannica; Sir Lloyd Wilson Webber; Wyckyd Sceptre; Daffy "Mal" Yinkleyankle.**

KING BLUES—Standard old black bluesman in the B. B. King mold from the 1983 comedy *Get Crazy*. A running gag in the film has every band at the New Year's Eve concert playing a version of his hit, "Hootchie Cootchie Man." He takes a moment to eulogize a deceased fellow bluesman, Howling Blind Luther Washington, whose name is likely a parody of real bluesman Blind Lemon Jefferson. See also **Auden; Nada; Reggie Wanker.**

KING RING-A-DING—In the *Petticoat Junction* episode "Hooterville A-Go-Go" (11/09/65), the bevy of Bradley beauties want mom Kate (Bea Benaderet) to invite this rock and roll star to a benefit show. Ray Hemphill plays King Ring-a-Ding, whose real name is Herbie Willis. See also **The Ladybugs.**

KING THUNDER—In the "Glitter Rock" (04/10/91) episode of sci-fi series *Quantum Leap*, the time-traveling, body-jumping Sam Beckett (Scott Bakula) jumps back to 1974 and the body of Geoffrey "Tonic" Mole (Bruce Michael Paine), a member of this English KISS-esque (i.e., full-face makeup) hard rock/metal band. Sam has to figure out who's gonna stab him to death before it happens. Is it evil manager Dwayne, played by 60s pop star Peter Noone of Herman's Hermits? Jealous fellow band member Flash McGrath (Jon Gries)? Or crazed fan Philip Silbart (Christian Hoff) who might be the singer's illegitimate son? King Thunder played the songs "Rock the Redhead" and "Fate's Wide Wheel" (both on the TV soundtrack album); in the latter Scott Bakula did his own singing.

KINKAID, LANE—Real-life 70s teen heartthrob Leif Garrett played this pop star and his twin brother Michael in the "My Teenage Idol Is Missing" episode (09/22/78) of comic-book-turned-TV-adventure-drama, *Wonder Woman*. Lane gets kidnapped and is ransomed to his manager Ripley

(Michael Lerner) for a cool two mil. But his twin brother Michael (sorta working with the kidnappers), is sent to take his place so no one will suspect except the manager, who knows. But the money drop gets interrupted by Wonder Woman, and the kidnapper reneges, and a desperate Ripley puts Mike on stage to lip-synch. In a pre–Milli Vanilli moment, the crowd catches on and boos him! Then Mike ditches the lip-synching, sings on his own, and the crowd loves him! Too bad that didn't work for Milli Vanilli. Anyhoo, Wonder Woman frees Lane, and he and Michael (a mysteriously unindicted coconspirator) form an act together. See also **AntiMatter; Billy Dero; Jeff and Barbi Gordon; Kathy Meadows; Hamlin Rule**.

KINKY WIZARDS, THE — A pair of shoplifting, no-good teen skate punks, Vince (Chris Rehmann) and Justin (Ben Carr), who put together a surprisingly good demo tape, to the dismay of snobby record clerks Barry (Jack Black) and Dick (Todd Louiso) in *High Fidelity* (2000). Store owner Rob Gordon (John Cusack) is so impressed he offers to release the tape on his own, just-made-up record label, Top Five Records. Later, he DJs at the release party of their three-song EP, *I Sold My Mom's Wheelchair* (with title track of the same name). See also **Barry Jive and the Uptown Five; Marie deSalle; Licorice Comfits**.

KLAPPER FAMILY, THE — See **The New Main Street Singers**.

KOVENANT — Christian country-and-western/rock band playing the local Springfield church in the "Alone Again Natura-Diddily" episode (02/13/00) of animated comedy *The Simpsons*. This episode was somewhat controversial at the time, as the producers deliberately killed off the character of Ned Flanders's wife, Maude, because voice actress Maggie Roswell wanted more money. After the funeral,

lonely Ned (voiced by Harry Shearer) reluctantly returns to the dating scene, where, after a string of disappointments, he bumps into lovely Rachel Jordan, the lead singer of this band. The episode ends hinting that they may be perfect for each other. We also learn that the band's bass player was originally in Satanica, that the band lost their drummer to a Pentecostal ska band, and that they are heading out on the Monsters of Christian Rock tour. But alas, when the thread of this storyline is picked up again more than a year later, in "I'm Goin' to Praiseland" (05/06/01), we find that Ned totally dropped the ball. Only now returning to the dating scene, he finds all of Springfield's bachelorettes flawed. When he runs again into Jordan (whose band has now broken up), his obsessive devotion to his dead wife scares her off. Folk singer Shawn Colvin guest-starred as the singing and talking voice of Rachel Jordan. See also **The Beach Boys Experience; The Be Sharps; Johnny Bobby; Johnny Calhoun; Captain Bart and the Tequila Mockingbirds; The Crazy Old Man Singers; Cyanide; Gulliver Dark; Ferl Dixon and His Second Helping Boys; Funky C Funky Do; Garfunkel, Messina, Oates, and Lisa; Hooray for Everything; Krusty and the Krums; The Larry Davis Experience; Little Timmy and the Shebangs; Loggins and Oates; Lurleen Lumpkin; M. C. Safety and the Caution Crew; Melvin and the Squirrels; "Bleeding Gums" Murphy; The Party Posse; The Rappin' Rabbis; Red Breem and His Band of Some Esteem; The Satin Knights; The Steve Sax Trio; Testament; Blind Willie Witherspoon; The Ya-Hoo Recovering Alcoholic Jug Band; Yodelin' Zeke**.

KRAZEE-EYEZ KILLAH — HBO's series *Curb Your Enthusiasm* lets *Seinfeld* co-creator Larry David write, star, and curse in his own show where he plays himself. In the "Krazee-Eyez Killah" episode (11/03/02),

David runs into this fictional African-American gangsta rapper at Killah's engagement party to Wanda Sykes (herself). Killah (Christopher James Williams) takes an inexplicable shine to David after David helps him with some hard-core lyrics, and confides his love of oral sex. David later lets it accidentally slip to his wife that Killah's cheating on Sykes, and begs her not to tell Sykes, as David would like to keep his testicles. But alas, somehow Sykes finds out and breaks off the engagement. Killah blames David, but at least the latter gets to keep his testicles.

KREB ZEPPELIN — From the "35 Hours" episode, the first episode of the third season, of Nickelodeon's *Adventures of Pete and Pete* (1993–96). When the brothers' parents go away for the weekend, they go nuts and crank up some loud hard rock, courtesy of an eight-track of Kreb Zeppelin's *So-So* album. The word "Kreb" was a running gag in the series, as almost every product shown was made by the mysterious and ubiquitous KrebStar corporation (Kreben-Up soda, Krebgate toothpaste, etc.). Presumably the band had some connection to the company. See also **The Blowholes.**

KRUSTY AND THE KRUMS — House band of *The Krusty the Klown Show* in the "Like Father, Like Clown" episode (10/24/91) of *The Simpsons*. The episode, a parody of the movie *The Jazz Singer*, reveals that Krusty became a clown against the wishes of his long-estranged father, Rabbi Hyman Krustofsky (voiced by Jackie Mason). After Bart and Lisa engineer an on-air reconciliation, Krusty turns to this band and requests "Lenny, a little reconciliation music, if you please." The four-piece band (tuba, accordion, Lenny the bald conductor, and what looks to be the drummer from The Larry Davis Experience slumming) plays the old standard "Oh Mein Papa." The band's name is on the bass drum. See also **The**

Beach Boys Experience; The Be Sharps; Johnny Bobby; Johnny Calhoun; Captain Bart and the Tequila Mockingbirds; The Crazy Old Man Singers; Cyanide; Gulliver Dark; Ferl Dixon and His Second Helping Boys; Funky C Funky Do; Garfunkel, Messina, Oates, and Lisa; Hooray for Everything; Kovenant; The Larry Davis Experience; Little Timmy and the Shebangs; Loggins and Oates; Lurleen Lumpkin; M. C. Safety and the Caution Crew; Melvin and the Squirrels; "Bleeding Gums" Murphy; The Party Posse; The Rappin' Rabbis; Red Breem and His Band of Some Esteem; The Satin Knights; The Steve Sax Trio; Testament; Blind Willie Witherspoon; The Ya-Hoo Recovering Alcoholic Jug Band; Yodelin' Zeke.

LADY BRYCE — From the short-lived UPN drama series *Platinum* (2003). This African-American chanteuse (played by Kia Joy Goodwin) is a very promising new act whose debut album could save the Sweetback record label. Unfortunately, her clingy, neurotic husband/manager Devon (Lyric Bent), who's been edged out by the Sweetback promo team, commits suicide in front of her at her release party. She returns the favor by OD'ing on pills later that night. See also **Camille FaReal; Mace; VersIs.**

LADYBUGS, THE — This all-girl Beatles parody band came out only a month after the Beatles' famous Ed Sullivan appearance! In "The Ladybugs" episode (03/24/64) of *Petticoat Junction*, Uncle Joe (movin' kinda quick this time) throws his three hot nieces and the sheriff's daughter together into a beat combo to cash in on Beatlemania! In a master stroke of publicity, the band played *The Ed Sullivan Show* two days before the episode aired (03/22/64), performing a gender-reversed cover of the Beatles' "I Saw Him Standing There!" The band was Betty Jo Bradley Elliot (Linda Kaye Henning), Billie Jo Bradley (Jeannine Riley), Bobbie Jo Bradley (Pat Woodell), and Sally Ragsdale (Sheila James). We may have a winner for the first band in the insect invasion of TV land! See also **King Ring-a-Ding**.

LAGOON, SLEEPY — From the 1943 Warner Bros. classic cartoon *Yankee Doodle Daffy*. This, yes, sleepy-looking kid duck with a big lolly just sits there as his agent Daffy Duck (voiced by Mel Blanc) furiously pitches him to talent scout Porky Pig (also voiced by Mel Blanc). At the end, the kid finally lets loose with a deep operatic baritone (singing voice by Billy Bletcher). *TRIVIA TIME!* Sleepy Lagoon is an actual place in Southern California that made the news in 1942 as the scene of a nasty gang rumble that ended in murder. The resulting crackdown on Hispanic zoot-suiters led to the "Zoot Suit Riots" of June 1943.

LAMBERT, GUY — A club singer (Elvis Presley) from the 1967 film *Double Trouble*, who wants nothing more than to rock out Europe and score some tail. Yet his plans of rockin' and humpin' get interrupted by an underaged (at least for most of the movie) British heiress whose uncle is trying to kill her for her inheritance, some incompetent thieves who hide some stolen jewelry in his suitcase, and a seemingly

Double Trouble, featuring Guy Lambert (Elvis Presley)

unrelated couple of salty dogs who want to blow up their own ship. And you thought you had problems getting laid. See also **Georgie and the G-Men**.

LAMBSBLOOD — Christian metal band featuring bassist Derek Smalls (Harry Shearer), who joined in 1988 while on break from Spiñal Tap. They toured the States, playing the Monsters of Jesus Festival and are shown briefly playing "Whole Lotta Lord" on some 1989 camcorder footage in *The Return of Spiñal Tap* (1992). The rest of the band was played by Robert Bauer, John Carlyon, and James Harrah. In interviews, Smalls revealed how he got a Christian fish-symbol tattoo to prove he was down with the band, but then on rejoining Spiñal Tap for the "Break Like the Wind" album/tour, he got another tattoo of a devil's head EATING the fish, to show what side he was now on—the winning side! See also **Duke Fame**; **The Folksmen**; **Meconium**; **The Regulars**; **Spiñal Tap**.

LANCELOT LINK AND THE EVOLUTION REVOLUTION — Everyone loves monkeys. What better than an all-monkey band! From the 1970 *Lancelot Link/Secret Chimp* show. After a hard day spying and defeating evil organization C.H.U.M.P., secret agents Lancelot Link and Mata Hairi and the band would flail away on their instruments after being introduced by Ed Simian. Rapid cutting and wild camera movements attempted to mate the monkeys' actions to the dubbed-over bubblegum pop songs. They actually released a self-titled album in 1970. The liner notes tell us about the other members, drummer Bananas Marmoset and keyboardist Sweetwater Gibbons who's really the "creative genius" of the band. Guitarist Lance is just a pretty-boy celebrity frontman.

LARRY DAVIS DANCE KINGS, THE— See **The Larry Davis Experience**.

LARRY DAVIS EXPERIENCE, THE— From the early seasons of animated TV show *The Simpsons*. They initially appear in the first-season episode "Some Enchanted Evening" (05/13/90). Their next big appearance is in the flashback episode "The Way We Was" (1/31/91), where they play Elton John's "Goodbye Yellow Brick Road" at Homer's 1974 high school prom. In "Old Money" (03/28/91) they show up as an expanded swing band, under the name The Larry Davis Dance Kings. Somewhere in their unillustrious careers they received a gold record for something. See also **The Beach Boys Experience**; **The Be Sharps**; **Johnny Bobby**; **Johnny Calhoun**; **Captain Bart and the Tequila Mockingbirds**; **The Crazy Old Man Singers**; **Cyanide**; **Gulliver Dark**; **Ferl Dixon and His Second Helping Boys**; **Funky C Funky Do**; **Garfunkel, Messina, Oates, and Lisa**; **Hooray for Everything**; **Kovenant**; **Krusty and the Krums**; **Little Timmy and the Shebangs**; **Loggins and Oates**; **Lurleen Lumpkin**; **M. C. Safety and the Caution Crew**; **Melvin and the Squirrels**; **"Bleeding Gums" Murphy**; **The Party Posse**; **The Rappin' Rabbis**; **Red Breem and His Band of Some Esteem**; **The Satin Knights**; **The Steve Sax Trio**; **Testament**; **Blind Willie Witherspoon**; **The Ya-Hoo Recovering Alcoholic Jug Band**; **Yodelin' Zeke**.

LAVENDER FUDGE EXPERIENCE, THE— Psychedelic foursome who played TV show *The Groovesicle*, a thinly veiled *Soul Train* parody, in the "Groovesicle" episode (09/06/02) of Cartoon Network cartoon series *Whatever Happened to Robot Jones?* The quartet played their big hit, "The Nudist and Mr. Pendle-

ton," which recounts the travails of a dog (Mr. P) trying to keep the world from being shocked by the titular (hee hee) nudist. *FUN FACT:* Apparently, the sight of a naked, flying man was what caused the Sphinx's nose to fall off. See also **Cubenudo**.

LEAF SEVEN— From the "Luck of the Fryrish" episode (03/12/01) of animated FOX comedy *Futurama*. Twentieth-century man in the year 3000, Philip J. Fry (voiced by Billy West) researches what happened to his family only to discover that after his disappearance (into a cryogenic tube), his copycat brother Yancy (voiced by Tom Kenny) stole his name, identity, and worse, his lucky seven-leafed clover. With all this under his belt, former loser Yancy becomes a philanthropist, astronaut, the first man on Mars, and, more importantly, a 21st-century rock star with several top ten hits with this band. Then Fry finds out that Yancy didn't steal his name at all, Yancy had named his son Philip J. Fry in Fry's honor and it was his son who had all those accomplishments. Unfortunately, Fry only finds it out after a teensy-weensy bit of grave desecrating. See also **Cylon and Garfunkel**; **Wailing Fungus**.

LEAPING LIZARDS, THE— Lesser 60s sitcom *Hazel* featured teen Harold Baxter (Bobby Buntrock) forming this instrumental garage band in the "My Son, The Sheepdog" episode (02/14/66). They appear on a TV contest and win, despite the fact that Baxter plays the accordion.

LEATHER AND THE SUEDES— Oh those oh-so-tuff Tuscadero sisters from sitcom *Happy Days*! Grrrowl! Roz Kelly was Pinky Tuscadero, real-life rocker Suzi Quatro played her sister, reform-school graduate Leather Tuscadero, who fronted her own band. The Suedes were originally Bertie (Donna Fein) and Gertie (Kathy Richards) when they first appeared in the two-part "Fonzie: Rock Entrepreneur" episode (11/08/77 and 11/15/77), but in all later appearances were Millie and Jillie (Jan and Jill Bunker). Richie's little sister Joanie Cunningham (Erin Moran) temporarily becomes a Suede and threatens to run away from home to stay with the band. Fonzie (Henry Winkler) sets her straight. See also **Freddie and the Red Hots**.

LEATHERETTES, THE — See **The Limp Lizards**.

LEE, LITTLE TAMMY — An early-60s singer just mentioned in passing on the radio in the movie *Grace of My Heart*. Her song "Truth Is You Lied" was written by Denise Waverly (Illeana Douglas), the songwriting main character. It plays right before Denise hears the married DJ (with whom she's having an affair) announce he's moving to Chicago, and she realizes he's abandoning her. The song was really written by M. Fosson and Paul Marshall and sung by singer Jill Sobule ("I Kissed a Girl"), who also had a tiny part in the film. See also **The Click Brothers**; **The Luminaries**; **Kelly Porter**; **The Riptides**; **The Stylettes**; **Denise Waverly**.

LEEDS, SIMON — British rocker (Simon Templeman) who becomes almost a semiregular in the seventh season of *Just Shoot Me*. He first appears in the episode "Nina and the Rocker" (10/22/02). Later, they almost get married in "For the Last Time, I Do" (08/16/03). See also **2 Fine**.

LEGEND, THE — Number eight artist on the top-ten board in the record shop scene in the 1971 classic *A Clockwork Orange*. The song title is "Jelly Roll." Let's hear it for the freeze frame! See also **The Blow Goes**; **Bread Brothers**; **Comic Strips**; **Cyclops**; **Goggly Gogol**; **The Heaven Seventeen**; **The Humpers**; **The Sharks**; **Johnny Zhivago**.

LEGENDS OF BRASS, THE — Six horn-playing frat dorks

at the 1964 Mercyhurst College Talent Show with a hell of a name to live up to. They play some polka-sounding instrumental with a half-assed Latino beat right before The Wonders go on and wow the crowd with the title track of *That Thing You Do* (1996). Tragically, the LOB are the best group up until The Wonders—that's 1964 Midwestern America for you. It's called the breadbasket of America, but they never tell you it's all WHITE bread. Played by Steve Billington, Andy Duncan, Dave Ryan, Todd Simon, Mike Uhler, and Marco Villanova. See also **Elizabeth Anne**; **Blue Spot Trio**; **The Chantrellines**; **Diane Dane**; **The Echoes**; **Freddy Fredrickson**; **The G Men**; **The Heardsmen**; **The Hollyhocks**; **Jon D and the Walkers**; **Marilyn Lovell and the Geminis**; **The Norm Wooster Singers**; **Del Paxton**; **The Saturn 5**; **The Tempos**; **The Trends**; **Two Eriks**; **The Vicksburgs**; **The Wonders**.

LEMON TWINS, THE — Schmaltzy all-female pop-singing trio, yes a trio, played by Robin Duke, Catherine O'Hara, and her sister, Mary Margaret O'Hara, from the 1984 HBO mockumentary, *The Last Polka*. They were a parody of The Lennon Sisters, longtime *Lawrence Welk Show* regulars. The girls got their start with The Happy Wanderers and are seen performing in a 1964 clip of their show, *Polka Variety Hour*. There was a scandal when the girls were romantically linked to band leaders the Shmenge brothers. See also **Vic Arpeggio**; **Big Momma**; **5 Neat Guys**; **Happiness Unlimited**; **The Happy Wanderers**; **Lola Heatherton**; **Linsk Minyk**; **Tom Munroe**; **The Queenhaters**; **The Ramblers**; **The Recess Monkeys**; **Russ Riley**; **Jackie Rogers Jr.**; **Jackie Rogers Sr.**; **Speed of Light**; **Dusty Towne**; **The Wally Hung Trio**.

LENNOX, KEITH — Jerkwad millionaire blond Brit rocker in *The Jazz Singer* (1980) who hires 'n' fires singer/songwriter Jess Robin (Neil Diamond) all in the course of one day. In a great scene in a movie notable for not having any, Jess plays his slow tender ballad "Love on the Rocks" for Lennox, who turns it into a sneering rock song. Played by Paul Nicholas. See also **Jerry Golding**; **Jack Robin**; **Jess Robin**.

THE JAZZ SINGER
(1980, CAPITOL)

THE SONGS ON the soundtrack album of Neil Diamond's *Jazz Singer* are not the exact same versions that play in the film, these are re-recorded versions, so that no chance for studio polish is missed. The album opens with the lovely power-chord bombast of "America," which rivals Elvis's version of "An American Trilogy" for melodrama and dramatic scope. Diamond has an excellent rocker here, "Amazed and Confused," but the album is swollen with terrific ballads, exemplified by "Hello Again," "Love on the Rocks," and "Summerlove." Diamond even pulls off the ragtime-y little number "On the Robert E. Lee" that could have easily fallen flat in less capable hands. Toward the end, you start hitting filler like "Acapulco" and "Hey Louise," but the lush orchestration and arrangements mask it so well, you hardly realize it. Tragically, the album omits rocker character Keith Lennox's blasphemous, hard-rocking version of "Love on the Rocks" from the film, but its inclusion would have spoiled the mood. The album includes some unnecessary snippets of dialogue from the movie, because this album stands apart from the movie and is actually better if you DON'T see the movie, so you don't have the songs ruined by memories of Diamond's (and everybody else's) lackluster performances. You can hear Neil emoting all over the album, but he couldn't do it on film, dammit. This album was a huge hit for Diamond, and although he would continue to have later hits, this is the last time Neil Diamond mattered.

LENNY AND THE SQUIGTONES — Laverne and Shirley's annoying greaser neighbors, Lenny Kosnowski (Michael McKean) and Andrew "Squiggy" Squiggman (David L. Lander) formed this two-man band to play the annual Schotz brewery talent show, and appear in several episodes of classic sitcom *Laverne and Shirley*. In the "Suds to Stardom" episode (05/11/76), they sing "Starcrossed," and "I Believe." The boys sing "The Jolliest Fat Man" at a mental hospital show in the Christmas episode "Christmas at the Booby Hatch" (12/21/76). In "The Second Almost Annual Shotz Talent Show" episode (01/31/78) they perform "Night After Night." In "The Third Annual Shotz Talent Show" episode (01/30/79) they perform "Just a Couple of Lover Boys." In "The Fourth Annual Shotz Talent Show" episode (12/06/79) they sing "If Only I'd Have Listened to Mama." Even more interesting, Lander and McKean appeared on *American Bandstand* (07/09/79) in character as Lenny and the Squigtones, singing "King of the Cars." In 1979 they released a live album on the Casablanca label, *Lenny and Squiggy Present Lenny and the Squigtones*. Their songs on the album and from the show were written mostly by McKean and Landers themselves. *TRIVIA TIME!* Christopher Guest's guitar playing on the album is credited under the name "Nigel Tufnel," an early appearance of Guest's Spiñal Tap character. See also **Benny and the Beefeaters**; **London's Bridges**; **Spiñal Tap**.

LENNY STOKE BAND, THE — Just your standard washed-up rock-star-turned-supervillain in "The Wall of Sound" episode (09/25/94) of *Lois and Clark: The New Adventures of Superman*. After several well-reviewed but poor-selling albums and several financial setbacks, Stoke, instead of just telling all in a VH1 special, becomes a cartoonish supervillain. His snooty, upperclass English accent giving him a decided advantage in that department. Stoke (Michael

Des Barres) used Dr. Derek Camden (Scott Colomby), a mad scientist (sadly, the babbling, paranoid, homeless, street-person type of mad), to make the sound weapon Stoke uses to put crowds to sleep and create building-shattering sympathetic vibrations. He even has a Superman-defeating frequency! Which is handy when Superman shows up to stop him. Unfortunately, Stoke succeeds and destroys Metropolis. Just kidding! Seriously, when does that EVER happen? Superman discovers the trick to penetrate Stoke's literal "wall of sound"—flying fast enough to break the sound barrier! No, of course the science makes no sense—we're talking about a man who can shoot heat beams out of his eyes without his face melting off. Bonus points for having Lois Lane (played by the then-hot, pre–Radio Shack huckstering Teri Hatcher) dress up in rocker-slut chic to try and get close to Stoke. *TRIVIA TIME!* One of Stoke's hot bouncer goonettes at his Stoke Club is renowned bodybuilder and six-time Miss Olympia Cory Everson. Michael Des Barres also played a member of fake band Scum of the Earth. See also **Scum of the Earth.**

LERNER, DOMINIC—See **Jem and the Holograms.**

LERNER, LENA—See **Jem and the Holograms.**

LESLIE—Commercial jingle writer and ex-partner of Phoebe Buffay (Lisa Kudrow). Played by Elizabeth Daily, she appears in the *Friends* episode "The One With Phoebe's Ex-Partner" (02/6/97), where she first tries to reunite with Phoebe and later steals Phoebe's signature song, "Smelly Cat," for a kitty litter jingle. She's the subject of Phoebe's song "Jingle Bitch." See also **Phoebe Buffay; Ross Gellar; Stephanie Schiffer.**

LESTER CRABTREE AND THE THREE CRABS—In the "Your Friendly Neighborhood Kidnappers" episode (10/3/66) of *The Monkees*, this band pops up at the end to win the battle of the bands contest, making a mockery of all the efforts of The Monkees and their rivals, The Four Swine. The genesis of this band happens when The Monkees go to a restaurant where, on the deliberately bad advice of The Four Swine's manager, they've paid girls to run in and rip Davy Jones's clothes off. To create "buzz," dig? But the manager sabotages it, and the girls instead rip the clothes off of Lester Crabtree, a mild, middle-aged, visiting shoe salesmen. See also **Fern Badderly; Irene Chomsky; The Foreign Agents; The Four Martians; The Four Swine; Honey and the Bear; The Jolly Green Giants (I); Sven Helstrom and the Swedish Rhythm Kings; The Swinging Android; The West Minstrel Abbies.**

LEWIS JR., C. S.—Bearded country singer (Bob Odenkirk) who is so gung-ho about NASA's new plan to blow up the moon he releases a song/music video about it, "Blew Moon." When a space monkey asks "why" in sign language, ruining everyone's fun, he writes a new song, "Big Dumb Ape." From the "Goin' on a Holiday" episode (10/31/97) of the sketch comedy foolishness that is *Mr. Show*. See also **The Beetletown Players; Larry Black; Livingston Brewster; Willips Brighton; Dickie Crickets; Indomitable Spirit; Kid Jersey; Kill or Be Killed; Horace Loeb; Marilyn Monster; Norma Jean Monster; John Baptiste Philouza; Professor Murder; Puscifer; Salini; Smoosh; Old Swerdlow; Three Times One Minus One; Titannica; Sir Lloyd Wilson Webber; Wyckyd Sceptre; Daffy "Mal" Yinkleyankle.**

LEWIS, JIMMY—Cartoon rock star who invites his cartoon pals Fred (voiced by Frank Welker), Velma (voiced by Patricia Stevens), Daphne (voiced by Heather North), and Shaggy (voiced by Casey Kasem) to the recording studio where a KISS-looking phantom is causing trouble and after a missing man's song. Naturally the gang investigate and solve the case. From the "The Diabolical Disc Demon" episode (11/18/78) of *The Scooby-Doo /Dynomutt Hour*. **TRIVIA TIME!** Shaggy's real name is Norville Rogers. See also **Ace Decade**.

LIBBY CHESSLER GENERATION, THE—From "The Band Episode" (02/27/98) of sitcom *Sabrina the Teenage Witch*. Snotty, Little-Miss-Perfect Libby Chessler (Jenna Leigh Green) is a sure win at the Westbridge High School talent show, with this slick, four-piece vocal pop/R&B group with immaculate choreography (hey, she's a cheerleader). But her rival, Sabrina Spellman (Melissa Joan Hart) can't stand to see her win yet again. So she gifts her friends with magical musical talent to form a band to win the contest. But Sabrina has to come crawling back to Chessler later in the episode. See also **Entry Number Five**; **The Flavor Babes**.

LICORICE COMFITS—Possibly Liquorice Comfits. In the 2000 movie *High Fidelity*, based on Nick Hornby's 1995 novel of the same name, sneaky Nick works in this fake band in passing just to give music geeks a sleepless night or two. Annoying music nerd Dick (Todd Louiso) mentions to an irritated Rob (John Cusack) that he just found their first album over at Vintage Vinyl you know the Japanese import only? The one on Testament of Youth? Anyway he can tape it for you it's no problem really since you liked the second album (*Pop Girls, Etc.*) the one with Cheryl Ladd on the cover oh but you didn't see the cover 'cause you just had the tape that he made you so he'll just go ahead and make a tape of it for you. Arrgh! See also **Barry Jive and the Uptown Five**; **Marie deSalle**; **The Kinky Wizards**.

LILYWHITE, LALA—Sultry blond diva (voiced by Grey Delisle) who appears in the "Jack and the Gangsters"

episode (11/26/01) of *Samurai Jack*. She's a true professional—not even a gun/flamethrower/samurai sword battle can distract her from her performance. See also **The Buddy Righteous Orchestra**.

LIMP LIZARDS, THE—Loser all-girl trio from the battle of the bands in the first episode of *Jem!* They compete along with The Space Cadets and The Leatherettes, all bands picked by Starlight Music honcho Eric Raymond to make his band, The Misfits, sound good. The Limp Lizards had the song "Broken Glass." See also **Bobby Bailey**; **The Ben Tiller Orchestra**; **Jem and the Holograms**; **The Misfits**; **The Stingers**; **The Tapps Tucker Quartet**.

LINDSEY, JIM—In "The Guitar Player" episode (10/17/60) of sitcom staple *The Andy Griffith Show*, Sheriff Andy Taylor (Andy Griffith) uses his sly ways to help out this young guitar player played by James Best, who would later become a sheriff himself—Sheriff Rosco P. Coltrane on *The Dukes of Hazzard* (1979–85). Andy throws visiting band Bobby Fleet and His Band with a Beat in the slammer on a parking violation pretext and then has Lindsey brought in for "questioning," all just so the band can check out Lindsey's great guitar-playing. Andy's flagrant and egregious abuse of his authority works like a charm, and Bobby Fleet (Henry Slate) offers Lindsey a spot in the band. Lindsey returns to Mayberry a success in "The Guitar Player Returns" episode (05/15/61), such a success, in fact, that he's decided to quit the band and go solo. But really he just got big-head syndrome and quarreled with Fleet. Worse, Lindsey's run up a bunch of debts he can't pay off. Andy meddles some more, and gets Fleet and Lindsey to reconcile and Lindsey back in the band. See also **Carl Benson's Wildcats**; **The Darlings**; **Keevy Hazelton**; **The Sound Committee**.

LIPSTICKS, THE—In the "How Do You Get to Carnegie Hall" episode (12/01/88) of *The Cosby Show*, Vanessa Huxtable (Tempestt Bledsoe) and her two pals Janet (Pam Potillo) and Kara (Elizabeth Narvaez) form this quickie band to enter a music video contest at a local TV station. They want to redo oldie "The Loco-motion" and take vocal lessons from Mrs. Woods, who, in one of Bill Cosby's constant jazz-glorifying and rock-denigrating moves during the show, is played by real jazz singer Betty Carter. The girls think singing scales is boring, and slack off to work on suggestive, parent-horrifying dance moves and outfits. They figure that's all they really need anyway (dammit, Cosby!). Vanessa pads her bra! See also **Clyde; JT Freeze; The Icicles; The Jazz Caravan; The Maniacs; Slim Claxton and His Trio; Walking Lemons; The Wretched.**

LIQUORICE COMFITS—See **Licorice Comfits.**

LITTLE TIMMY AND THE SHEBANGS—News reporter Kent Brockman (voiced by Harry Shearer) is eulogizing the to-be-demolished Springfield casino in a news story, and mentions some of the bands that played there, such as ". . . Little Timmy and the Shebangs, The Shebangs, and The New Shebangs Featuring Big Timmy." Obviously a band with personnel problems. From the "Viva Ned Flanders" episode (01/10/99) of *The Simpsons*. See also **The Beach Boys Experience; The Be Sharps; Johnny Bobby; Johnny Calhoun; Captain Bart and the Tequila Mockingbirds; The Crazy Old Man Singers; Cyanide; Gulliver Dark; Ferl Dixon and His Second Helping Boys; Funky C Funky Do; Garfunkel, Messina, Oates, and Lisa; Hooray for Everything; Kovenant; Krusty and the Krums; The Larry Davis Experience; Loggins and Oates; Lurleen Lumpkin; M. C. Safety and the Caution Crew; Melvin and the Squirrels; "Bleeding

Gums" Murphy; The Party Posse; The Rappin' Rabbis; Red Breem and His Band of Some Esteem; The Satin Knights; The Steve Sax Trio; Testament; Blind Willie Witherspoon; The Ya-Hoo Recovering Alcoholic Jug Band; Yodelin' Zeke.**

LOEB, HORACE—Parody of Eric Clapton from the "Sad Songs Are Nature's Onions" episode (12/29/98) of sketch comedy program *Mr. Show*. He (David Cross) and Willips Brighton (Bob Odenkirk) each get a Teardrop Award for saddest song. Loeb's is "No More Room in Heaven," a parody of Clapton's "Tears in Heaven." See also **The Beetletown Players; Larry Black; Livingston Brewster; Willips Brighton; Dickie Crickets; Indomitable Spirit; Kid Jersey; Kill or Be Killed; C. S. Lewis Jr.; Marilyn Monster; Norma Jean Monster; John Baptiste Philouza; Professor Murder; Puscifer; Salini; Smoosh; Old Swerdlow; Three Times One Minus One; Titannica; Sir Lloyd Wilson Webber; Wyckyd Sceptre; Daffy "Mal" Yinkleyankle.**

LOGGINS AND OATES—Terrifying supergroup of the lesser halves of long-irrelevant bands Loggins and Messina, and Hall and Oates, in the "Viva Ned Flanders" episode (01/10/99) of *The Simpsons*. Mom Marge Simpson (voiced by Julie Kavner) is rummaging through the cassette bin at the car wash and finds this atrocity. What do they play? Bart says "crap rock" but Homer knows it's "wuss rock." See also **The Beach Boys Experience; The Be Sharps; Johnny Bobby; Johnny Calhoun; Captain Bart and the Tequila Mockingbirds; The Crazy Old Man Singers; Cyanide; Gulliver Dark; Ferl Dixon and His Second Helping Boys; Funky C Funky Do; Garfunkel, Messina, Oates, and Lisa; Hooray for Everything; Kovenant; Krusty and the Krums; The Larry Davis Experience; Little Timmy and**

the Shebangs; Lurleen Lumpkin; M. C. Safety and the Caution Crew; Melvin and the Squirrels; "Bleeding Gums" Murphy; The Party Posse; The Rappin' Rabbis; Red Breem and His Band of Some Esteem; The Satin Knights; The Steve Sax Trio; Testament; Blind Willie Witherspoon; The Ya-Hoo Recovering Alcoholic Jug Band; Yodelin' Zeke.

LONDON'S BRIDGES—If you ever wanted to see *Laverne and Shirley*'s Squiggy (David L. Lander) paranoid from pot, too bad! The "I Do, I Do" episode (02/24/81) doesn't appear in reruns anymore. Why? Read on. The mono-monikered leader of this band, London (Peter Noone of Herman's Hermits), and his "thick as a brush" guitarist Derek DeWoods (Monty Python member Eric Idle) drop in for lunch at Cowboy Bill's where Laverne DeFazio (Penny Marshall) and Shirley Feeney (Cindy Williams) waitress and invite them to a party they're having that night to kick off their American tour. At the party are the band, Lenny and Squiggy, and drugs! The gals eat pot brownies proffered by creepy band member Malcolm (composer Stephen Bishop)! That, plus other drug references, including Laverne dumping a pile of white powder off a hand mirror to check her hair, keep this episode on the shelf. Too bad, 'cause then you don't get to hear this mid-60s British Invasion group play their hit song "Love, Love, Love." Lyrics: "Your love, love, love fits me like a glove, glove, glove from heaven up above, above, above. I'm giving you a shove if you don't give me some love." Ah, the land of Shakespeare! After L and S get goofy enough to try to play the Rolling Stones' "(I Can't Get No) Satisfaction" on the band's instruments, one of the band thinks up the bright idea of getting the blitzed birds to marry them so they can become citizens and avoid 'er Majesty's ferocious tax bite. They must have had a few too many brownies them-selves. At a Vegas quickie wedding chapel, the girls are so giggly they can barely walk, and, alas, pass out before they can say "I do" to London and Derek, who tuck a few bob in their bosoms for bus fare home before ditching them. Ah, the land of chivalry! *TRIVIA TIME!* The band's sunny pap, er, pop song was written by Stephen Bishop and Eric Idle. See also **Benny and the Beefeaters; Lenny and the Squigtones**.

LOOTERS, THE—A British punk band that tours with bands The Stains and The Metal Corpses in the movie *Ladies and Gentlemen, The Fabulous Stains* (1981). The Looters start as the opening band for aging rockers The Metal Corpses, then become the headliners when the Corpses' bassist overdoses. The Stains open for a while, until their popularity takes off and The Looters turn into the openers for The Stains. Lead singer Billy (Ray Winstone) falls for Stains' singer Corinne Burns (Diane Lane), but when spurned by Corinne's ever-growing ego, he lashes out at the Stains and their fans, killing the Stains' career, at least momentarily. The Looters have a grand punk sound, and it's no wonder, since the rest of the band consists of bassist Johnny (Paul Simonon of The Clash), guitarist Steve (Steve Jones of The Sex Pistols) and drummer Danny (Paul Cook, also from The Sex Pistols). See also **The Metal Corpses; The Stains**.

LORD, LONNIE—Rockabilly/rock and roll singer who is secretly the nonsuper-superhero Rat Pfink, from the 1965 nutsy *Batman* parody and cult-fave flick, *Rat Pfink a Boo Boo*. Lonnie's pal and Rat Pfink's sidekick is Boo Boo, really Titus Twimbly (Titus Moede). Lord was played by real rocker Ron Haydock, who was a close friend of the filmmaker, Ray Dennis Steckler. Ron Haydock and The Boppers perform "You Is a Rat Pfink," "Running Wild," and "Big Boss a Go-Go Party."

LORELLS, THE—From the long, LONG, LONG-running BBC show *Doctor Who*. The Doctor (Sylvester McCoy) and his companion Bonnie Langford (Mel Bush) win a trip to the British Shangri-La Vacation Camp in the year 1959 in the three-part episode "Delta and the Bannermen" (11/02/87, 11/09/87, and 11/16/87). This band plays the music for the camp dances. *TRIVIA TIME!* This band's real reason for existing was to save the BBC a few quid by covering some 50s tunes to avoid paying for the original versions. It was made up of some studio musicians and singing duo The Wilson Sisters. The episode was written by Malcolm Kohll. See also **John Smith and the Common Men**.

LOUIS STEVENS EXPERIENCE, THE—See **The Alan Twitty Project**.

LUCY AND THE DIAMONDS—In the 1978 stinkfest *Sgt. Pepper's Lonely Hearts Club Band*, Dianne Steinberg and trio Starguard play this band that doesn't do so much singing as acting as personal assistants to Big Deal Records head B. D. Brockhurst/Hoffler (Donald Pleasence). Lucy basically serves whatever role her boss wants: chauffeur, photographer, hostess, etc. What the hell kind of contract did she sign? See also **Future Villain Band; Sgt. Pepper's Lonely Hearts Club Band**.

LUMINARIES, THE—Standard early-60s black female vocal group like, say, The Shirelles, from the 1996 movie *Grace of My Heart*. Doris Shelley (Jennifer Leigh Warren), Betty (Natalie Venetia Bel-con), and Sha Sha (Kathy Barbour) make up the trio. Main character songwriter Denise Waverly (Illeana Douglas) meets Doris at the Philadelphia 1958 McMartin Singing Competition. They run into each other eleven months later in New York where they're both trying to make it big. Denise gets a job at the famous Brill Building and gets her boss Joel Millner (John Turturro) interested in Doris's group. Denise writes "Born to Love That Boy" for them, and, with her goateed beatnik socialist songwriter boyfriend Howard Cazsatt (Eric Stoltz), pens the controversial unwed-pregnant-teen weepie "Unwanted Number" (really by Elvis Costello). They also write two or three other controversial tunes for the Luminaries, which get banned from radio, so Joel brings in another songwriting team, Cheryl Steed (Patsy Kensit) and husband Matthew Lewis (Chris Isaak). Ironically, this unhappily married couple brings in an upbeat wedding tune, "I Do," which becomes a big hit, going to #4. The Luminaries' singing was done by group For Real. See also **The Click Brothers; Little Tammy Lee; Kelly Porter; The Riptides; The Stylettes; Denise Waverly**.

The Luminaries

LUMPKIN, LURLEEN—In the "Colonel Homer" (3/26/92) episode of *The Simpsons*, Homer discovers and promotes this country singing star voiced by Beverly D'Angelo. Lurleen sings several songs, including "Your Wife Don't Understand You," "Bagged Me a Homer," and "Stand By Your Manager." She also mentions several other songs she's written: "I'm Basting a Turkey with My Tears," "Don't Look Up My Dress Unless You Mean It," and "I'm Sick of Your Lying Lips and False Teeth." She has a brief cameo in another episode ("Marge vs. the Monorail" 01/14/93) where she just came out of the Betty Ford Clinic. And her name is briefly glimpsed on a marquee in Branson, Missouri, in the "Bart on the Road" episode (03/31/96). See also **The Beach Boys Experience**; **The Be Sharps**; **Johnny Bobby**; **Johnny Calhoun**; **Captain Bart and the Tequila Mockingbirds**; **The Crazy Old Man Singers**; **Cyanide**; **Gulliver Dark**; **Ferl Dixon and His Second Helping Boys**; **Funky C Funky Do**; **Garfunkel, Messina, Oates, and Lisa**; **Hooray for Everything**; **Kovenant**; **Krusty and the Krums**; **The Larry Davis Experience**; **Little Timmy and the Shebangs**; **Loggins and Oates**; **M. C. Safety and the Caution Crew**; **Melvin and the Squirrels**; **"Bleeding Gums" Murphy**; **The Party Posse**; **The Rappin' Rabbis**; **Red Breem and His Band of Some Esteem**; **The Satin Knights**; **The Steve Sax Trio**; **Testament**; **Blind Willie Witherspoon**; **The Ya-Hoo Recovering Alcoholic Jug Band**; **Yodelin' Zeke**.

LURCH—In the "Lurch, the Teenage Idol" episode (05/14/65) of creeped-out sitcom *The Addams Family*, Lurch (Ted Cassidy), the family butler, records himself on his beloved harpsichord. Promoter Mizzy Bickie (Herbie Styles) gets his hands on the recording, and soon the Addams mansion is swarmed with fans. Monosyllabic Lurch forgets his butlering duties and is about to do a world tour, but when he gets mobbed by fans, he retreats to the safety of the Addams household and gives up showbiz. **TRIVIA TIME!** In real-life Ted Cassidy recorded a novelty dance song in character, "The Lurch." It was released before this episode, and he also appeared on dance show *Shindig* (10/30/65) in character to promote it for Halloween.

M, ALAN—Alan M is the singer/songwriter hunk and the "sexiest guy in Riverdale" from the live-action *Josie and the Pussycats* movie (2001) and Josie's best non-band-member friend. While she rockets to stardom, he plays some crappy open mic night. But Josie's meddling manager Wyatt Frame (Alan Cumming) lies to Josie to make her miss it. See also **DuJour**; **Josie and the Pussycats**.

MACE—Sleazy, middle-aged African-American R&B singer. His admirable propensity to recycle used videotapes leads to trouble when a six-year-old tape of his turns up at his record company with about twenty seconds of him raping or having seriously rough sex with some underage girl. Confronted by his label heads, he claims the latter. It was the former, but he paid off the girl, and she stays paid off, despite label lawyer Monica Rhames' (Lalanya Masters) attempt to get her to press charges. Trace was played by real R&B singer Brian McKnight. From the "Power" episode (05/06/03) of short-lived UPN series *Platinum*. See also **Camille FaReal**; **Lady Bryce**; **VersIs**.

MACHISMO BROTHERS, THE—One of the musical groups managed by the Rutles' manager Leggy

Mountbatten (Terence Bayler) in the 60s, according to the 1978 documentary *All You Need Is Cash*. They all have matching plaid jackets. The group originated on Eric Idle's post–Monty Python show, the BBC's *Rutland Weekend Television*, which also birthed The Rutles. See also **Arthur Hodgeson and the Kneecaps**; **Les Garçons de la Plage**; **Ruttling Orange Peel**; **Punk Floyd**; **Blind Lemon Pye**; **The Rutles**.

MAGGOT DEATH — Only shown in a snapshot, Dewey Finn (Jack Black) tries to rekindle Ned Schneebly's love of music with memories of this gothed-up, face-painted trio they were in together. Ned (Mike White) used to play bass, but now's he's given up on music and become a substitute teacher and an incredibly whipped wimp. Blame his ball-breaking girlfriend, Patty (Sarah Silverman). From *The School of Rock* (2003). See also **No Vacancy**; **School of Rock**.

MAHATMAMAS, THE — Dual-guitar, bass, and standup-drum combo that "rivals Ronnie James Dio in . . . rockability." During the "Splitsville" episode (11/23/03) of cartoon *Sealab 2021*, the quartet (Dr. Virjay on guitar/lead vocals, three random "feckless nincompoops" on the rest) played a sample of their surprisingly Creedence-y "Fishin' Hole," then took on longtime rivals the Ocean Bottom Nightmare Band in an undersea battle of the bands. Sadly for Dr. Virjay, the three nincompoops developed big heads (literally and figuratively) after being exposed to radiation and kicked him out of his own band. Rock and roll is a harsh mistress, Doc. See also **MC Chris**; **The Ocean Bottom Nightmare Band**.

MAHNA MAHNA AND THE TWO SNOWTHS — Mahna mahna. DOO dooo doo doodoo. Okay, you know the song. But why? Probably due to this group's odd appearance on the Juliet Prowse–hosted episode (04/25/77) of *The Muppet Show*. Goofy, catchy song, goofy Muppets, whatever, right? If only it were that simple. Let's dig a little deeper, shall we? The song "Máh-ná Mah-ná" was written by Italian composer Piero Umiliani for the 1968 movie *Sweden, Heaven and Hell* (*Svezia, inferno e paradiso*), which was, uh, a "Swedish documentary," i.e., PORNO movie! The song did okay in America, chartwise (peaked at #55 on 10/4/69). In 1970, Jim Henson performed the song with the Muppet character Mahna Mahna on *The Ed Sullivan Show*. So this was some seriously old shtick being recycled here. Anyhoo, perhaps due to *The Muppet Show* performance, or not (the song was also used frequently on *The Benny Hill Show*), on April 30, 1977, Umiliani's original version reentered the U.K. charts at #38, peaking at #8 on May 28, 1977. Then, the week of June 18, 1977, Kermit's nephew Robin's song "Halfway Down the Stairs," with the Muppet version of "Mahna Mahna" as the B-side, peaked at #7 on the U.K. charts. The Muppet version (rerecorded) was included on the 1977 Arista records *The Muppet Show* soundtrack album. The song is also on the 1993 *Muppet Hits* CD on Jim Henson Records/BMG Kidz. And finally, in the 1996 *Muppets Tonight* series, they brought back Mahna Mahna and the song for a skit where Kermit hears singing whenever he says the word "phenomena" (Show #7, U.S. airdate 6/23/96, U.K. airdate 9/20/96). So. Nonsensical pop tune composed by an Italian for Swedish porno, later coopted by the muppetmaster for a family-friendly kids' show. If you've seen Henson's 1965 avant-garde *Time Piece*, you'll realize that this odd performance is closer to the true Jim Henson than all the syrupy renditions of "It's Not Easy Being Green" put together. See also **The Amazing Marvin Suggs and His Muppaphone**; **Dr. Teeth and the Electric Mayhem**; **Mahna Mahna and the Two Snowths**; **Miss Piggy**; **Rowlf the Dog**; **Wayne and Wanda**.

MAIN STREET SINGERS, THE—See **The New Main Street Singers.**

MALCOLM, NEDDY—See **Mary Edwards.**

MAMAS AND PAPAS-IN-LAW, THE—From the "How Not to Manage a Rock Group" episode (04/28/68) of forgotten series *The Mothers-in-Law.* At the grand conclusion of this episode, the two sets of parents (after failing in managing rock group The Warts, played by The Seeds) join with oompah band The Friends Indeed to tramp around in Salvation Army–style uniforms to "Some Enchanted Evening," set to a stirring martial beat. See also **The Friends Indeed; The Warts.**

MANCHESTER XI, DESMOND WINSTON—From the 2001 Wes Anderson film *The Royal Tenenbaums.* This briefly glimpsed Jamaican reggae artist was married to Margot Tenenbaum (Gwyneth Paltrow) for a mere nine days, but somehow she still managed to make it onto one of his album covers. Played by an uncredited Alem Brhan Sapp.

MANCHESTER, EARL—Elvis Costello played this English rocker in the bizarre 1979 comedy set in 1998, *Americathon.* Actually, he technically played an American, as England is the 51st state in the movie. He sang "Crawling to the USA" on the monthlong telethon to raise money to save America (the Americathon of the title). See also **Mouling Jackson.**

MANIACS, THE—Guitar rock band mentioned in the "How Ugly Is He?" episode (11/15/84) of *The Cosby Show.* According to father Cliff (Bill Cosby), their video is "a nightmare put to music." But if he knew what The Maniacs were all about, he'd understand. At least, that's what his son Theo (Malcolm Jamal-Warner) says. Just another excuse for Cosby to slag rock music. See also **Clyde; JT Freeze; The**

Icicles; The Jazz Caravan; The Lipsticks; Slim Claxton and His Trio; Walking Lemons; The Wretched.

MANN, SONNY—The cheeseball piano player in a high-class restaurant atop a skyscraper, played by Paul Kreppel in both versions of the wonderfully mediocre sitcom *It's a Living,* (1980–82, 1985–89). *TRIVIA TIME!* Later, series star (as waitress Cassie Cranston) and double-mastectomy patient Ann Jillian cut an entire album of songs by comedian Steve Allen.

Sonny Mann (Paul Kreppel) (center)

MANNING, REX—A now has-been spoiled former teen idol pop star played by Maxwell Caulfield in the irritating lightweight 1995 flick *Empire Records.* He does an in-store appearance at the title establishment, promoting his comeback album *Back with More.* Store employee and jailbait Corey Mason (Liv Tyler) is all hot to lose her virginity to his smarmy, over-coiffed self, but she gets cold feet and he ends up doing store slut Gina (Renée Zellweger) instead. Caulfield did his own singing on Rex's song, "Say No More, Mon Amour," written by Ralph Schuckett and Chris Ward. See also **Berko.**

MARILYN LOVELL AND THE GEMINIS — Never-seen act in *That Thing You Do* (1996). They play Boss Vic Koss the Mattress King's (Kevin Pollack) rock and roll show in Pittsburgh, which opens with a glitch-filled performance by The Wonders. But you never actually SEE this band or anything, their name is just briefly glimpsed on the marquee. Get the DVD and use the freeze frame—you'll see. See also **Elizabeth Anne; Blue Spot Trio; The Chantrellines; Diane Dane; The Echoes; Freddy Fredrickson; The G Men; The Heardsmen; The Hollyhocks; Jon D and the Walkers; Legends of Brass; The Norm Wooster Singers; Del Paxton; The Saturn 5; The Tempos; The Trends; Two Eriks; The Vicksburgs; The Wonders.**

MARRON, RACHEL — Singing star Whitney Houston made her movie debut playing this fictional pop singer in *The Bodyguard* (1992). Threatening notes from a stalker lead to the hiring of the title character, Frank Farmer (Kevin Costner). They dislike each other at first, and he irritates everyone by clamping down on security. But eventually, they get around to having the affair that he knows he's not supposed to have. And then he has to get around to that stalker, leading to a finale at an Academy Awards ceremony. But more importantly, Houston's cover of Dolly Parton's "I Will Always Love You" from the soundtrack spent an incredible fourteen weeks at #1, a new record.

PERRY HENZELL   CARL BRADSHAW · JANET BARTLEY · RAS DANIEL HARTMAN
WINSTON STONE · BASIL KEANE · BOBBY CHARLTON

The Harder They Come, featuring Ivan Martin (Jimmy Cliff)

MARTIN, IVAN — Reggae singer Jimmy Cliff plays this main character in the 1972 reggaesploitation classic *The Harder They Come.* A simple Jamaican hick, he comes to the big city with hopes of being a singer/songwriter. When he gets shafted by the corrupt, payola-driven system personified by producer Mr. Hilton (Robert Charlton), Martin turns to dealing ganja, with some cop killing on the side. His criminal antics fire sales of his record, and it all leads to a big ole bloody cop killin' shootout. Cliff's character is based on real outlaw/folk hero Rhygin.

THE UR-FAKE BANDS

Before television, there were movies, and before that, myths and legends were people's entertainment, the antics of the ancient gods as gripping and twisted as any episode of *Beverly Hills, 90210,* and twice as believable. Here are some of the more musically inclined.

Muses, The—The Partridge Family of the ancient mythological world. These nine sisters (Calliope, Clio, Erato, Euterpe, Melpomene, Polyhymnia, Terpsichore, Thalia, and Urania) were the daughters of Zeus himself, the king of the gods with the morals of an alleycat in heat. They sang the praises of the gods, which kinda makes them suck-ups and sellouts. On the positive side, they were credited with the invention of the alphabet and writing and inspired various poets and musicians. They also taught the Sphinx his deadly riddle (oh thanks a LOT, ladies!). Each muse was associated with a different type of poetry (epic, historical, love, erotic, tragic, sacred, comic, etc.). They could be found at godly parties and feasts, but also weren't above playing the occasional wedding (Cadmus and Harmonia) or funeral gig (Achilles). The Muses were also contestants in the earliest recorded battles of the bands! They took all comers, defeated them all, and were NOT gracious winners. They turned the nine daughters of King Pierus into birds after defeating them. On defeating Thamyris, they blinded him, and took away his musical abilities. They even went up against The Sirens, and plucked them bald after trouncing them.

Sirens, The—This batch of baddies hung around on their island, luring passing sailors to their deaths with their magically enchanting singing. They are surrounded by the rotting bodies of men who sat and listened until they starved to death. Hell of a way to get your kicks, but there you are. Odysseus gets by them thanks to a warning from Circe, and he has his men plug up their ears with wax. Except Odysseus, who wants to have his cake and eat it too, just has his men lash him to the mast so he can enjoy the concert. Jason and the Argonauts get by The Sirens another way, as they luckily have music-master Orpheus on board, who can sing louder and drowns out The Sirens with his own music. The Sirens vary in ancient accounts in parentage, names, and even number, from only two in Homer's *Odyssey*, to up to four in another account. Sometimes described as half-bird, half–hot babe, they were convinced by Hera to go up against The Muses in a battle of the bands, but the winning Muses plucked out The Sirens' feathers to make victory crowns for themselves. Ouch!

Pan—The horned, goat-legged, woodland god of the ancient Greeks was credited with the invention of his trademark instrument that bears his name today, the pan flute, or pan pipes. One day Pan was chasing a mythological hottie named Syrinx, but she was so desperate to get away from his clutches that she had her river-god father transform her into a bunch of marsh reeds just as Pan was clos-

ing in. But did Pan despair? Nope, Pan noticed the sound the wind made blowing over the reeds, and cut and bound some together to make an instrument. Hey, when the gods give you lemons, make lemonade! When this original party half-animal wasn't playing or dancing, he was typically chasing the highly desirable Nymphs—sounds like Pan's the blueprint for all future rock stars! He even inspired a batch of wannabe look-alikes, the Satyrs. Pan also once challenged Apollo, god of music (among other things), to one of the original battles of the bands. The contest was judged by mountain god Tmolus, who found ax-master Apollo the winner, for his superior lyre-playing. Pan should have known better than to go up against a charismatic, pretty-boy frontman type like Apollo—they always win.

Orpheus—When your mom's one of the Muses (Calliope), it's no wonder you'd turn out musical, too. Orpheus's lyre-playing and singing could charm not only wild animals, but also trees and rocks. Rocks, people—ROCKS! When his wife, Eurydice, tragically died, he traveled to the underworld to get her back, and used his musical abilities to charm his way past Charon, Cerebus, and even The Furies. His music even eased the suffering of the damned (temporarily)! Even more amazingly, he then convinced the god of the underworld to let him and Eurydice leave, all thanks to his amazing playing. There are many myths about his death, but they're all pretty grisly. His dismembered head still sang afterwards!

Thamyris—Not as well known, but he was a mythical Greek singer-songwriter of such great talent—he had an amazing voice, as well as lyre-playing ability—that he suffered that classic sitcom disease, Big Head Syndrome (hubris, in Greek). He challenged The Muses themselves to a musical contest, betting that if he won, he would get to sleep with them all. If they won, they could take from him whatever they wanted. Cocky, wasn't he? Still, what a total rock-star bet, even if you lose. The only cure for BHS/hubris is getting taken down a peg or two, and alas,

(continued)

the ancient Greek gods tend to do this with extreme prejudice. After defeating him in the contest, The Muses struck Thamyris blind, took away his beautiful singing voice, and even caused him to forget how to play his lyre. Hades hath no fury . . . !

Linus—Another gifted singer/player whose mother was one of The Muses, depending on which version of the myth you read. He was the music teacher of Orpheus, Thamyris, and, unfortunately, Heracles. Linus tried to teach him the lyre, but frustrated by Heracles's unappreciativeness, Linus gave Heracles a little taste of the rod, and enraged, Heracles beat him to death with a lyre. Heracles got off scot-free claiming self-defense!

Pied Piper of Hamlin—This mythical medieval German flute player cut a deal with the city fathers of the rat-infested town of Hamlin. He used his magic playing to charm away the rats, luring them out of the city and into a nearby river, where they drowned. When he came back to collect his money, the mayor and his cronies didn't want to cough up, so the piper played hardball. He puffed out a new tune, and all the children of the town followed him out and into a cave which sealed itself up after they had all passed in. You gotta pay the piper! You can be sure many a garage band has wished they could pull a similar stunt after getting shortchanged by some creep club owner. Oh, and "pied" is an old word describing his crazy, garishly multicolored clothes.

MARTINELLI, NICK—Italian Stallion Sylvester Stallone cowrote and starred in the stinker *Rhinestone* (1984), as this New York cab driver whom Jake Ferris (Dolly Parton) tries to turn into a country music star on a bet, in some kinda horrible, nightmarish twist of *My Fair Lady*. Culture clash doesn't do justice to the trainwreck of Martinelli's Bronx mouthful of marbles trying to learn Tennessee twang and drawl.

MARVIN BERRY AND THE STARLIGHTERS—This is the all-black band that played the 1955 high school prom in the 1985 movie *Back to the Future* and 1989 sequel *Back to the Future II*. It must be a pretty damn progressive high school if it was letting Negroes play for white kids in 1955. Band leader and guitarist Marvin (Harry Waters Jr.) cuts his hand getting time-traveling Marty McFly (Michael J. Fox) out of the trunk of a car and can't play, so Marty has to fill in for him. Marty plays a few numbers straight, then plays "Johnny B. Goode," a song that hasn't been written yet. Excited, Marvin immediately phones his cousin Chuck Berry so he can hear this "new sound," thus insinuating that Marty was responsible for the invention of rock and roll. The Starlighters were played by Tommy Thomas, Granville "Danny" Young, David Harold Brown, and Lloyd L. Tolbert. The soundtrack album features them singing "Night Train" and The Penguins'

Nick Martinelli
(Sylvester Stallone)

Marty McFly (Michael J. Fox) with
Marvin Berry and the Starlighters

"Earth Angel," as well the Marty McFly version of "Johnny B. Goode." See also **The Pinheads**.

MARVIN SUGGS AND HIS ALL-FOOD GLEE CLUB — See **The Amazing Marvin Suggs and His Muppaphone**.

MASSIVE GENIUS — Gangsta rap star and head of his own record label from the "A Hit Is a Hit" episode (03/14/99) of mob-based HBO drama *The Sopranos*. Once upon a time, Hesh Rabkin (Jerry Adler) had a little mob-connected record label. He cheated

singer Little Jimmy Willis out of his rightful monies. Massive Genius (played by Bokeem Woodbine) wants to right this wrong on behalf of Willis's widow. He puts the screws to Rabkin, but Rabkin plays hardball right back at him. See also **The Chablis**; **Scratch**; **Visiting Day**; **Little Jimmy Willis**.

MASSIVE HEAD WOUND — Heavy metal band from the 1996 comedy *Great White Hype*. Terry Conklin (Peter Berg) is the socially conscious lead singer, but is dragged to Vegas to box the heavyweight champion. The band's drummer is Lee (Phil Buckman). *TRIVIA TIME!* Phil Buckman was also in fake band Cain Was Able from *Beverly Hills, 90210*.

MATTHEWS, RONNIE — This olive-skinned heartthrob of indeterminate national origin and wildly inconsistent accent was featured in the "Curly Snaps/Preteen Scream" episode (09/23/98) of Nickelodeon's cartoon *Hey Arnold!* Matthews, whose big hit is "I Saw Your Face and Wow," is an amalgam of Ricky Martin, Robbie Williams, and one or more members of Milli Vanilli. He travels with a large entourage (including a video game consultant, personal trainer, personal psychic, personal one-on-one basketball opponent, and idiot brother-in-law), and prefers that his fans ask simple yes-and-no questions. During the episode, token smart Asian kid Phoebe Heyerdahl (voiced by Anndi McAfee) and rude, opinionated, horribly monobrowed harridan-in-training Helga Pataki (voiced by Francesea Smith) go backstage during one of Matthews's concerts. After the show, they learn that Matthews, who is either "the voice of our generation" (Phoebe) or a "lame no-talent guitarist" (Helga), does not write his own songs, can't play guitar, and doesn't actually sing on much of his album. Bronson Pinchot was Matthews's speaking voice; his singing voice was done by Christian Mena. See also **Dino Spumoni**.

MAU MAUS, THE—From the movie *Bamboozled* (2000), director Spike Lee's ham-fisted attempt at combining Mel Brooks's *The Producers* and Paddy Chayefsky's *Network* with a whole lotta racial issues, a lot even for Spike Lee. Pierre Delacroix (a terrible Damon Wayans) is the whitest black guy ever, a bitter TV writer at the Continental Network System. To get out of his contract, he comes up with the most offensive show idea he can think of: a revival of nineteenth-century minstrel shows. But his *Mantan: The New Millennium Minstrel Show*, set in, get this, an Alabama watermelon plantation, is an instant hit. Delacroix's assistant's brother's rap group, The Mau Maus, are furious and kidnap the star, Mantan (Savion Glover), even though they originally auditioned for the show ("Blak Iz Blak")! Yep, a stereotyped, foul-mouthed, 40-oz-drinkin' rap group is mad about a stereotyped, watermelon-lovin', shuckin' 'n' jivin' tap dancer. So mad they make him dance while they shoot at his feet and then kill him while broadcasting it all on the Internet. Then The Mau Maus all get mow-mowed down by the cops, except (ironically) the white member, who demands he also be shot, because he's $1/16^{th}$ black. The band was played by real rappers. Lineup: Julius "Big Blak Afrika" Hopkins (Mos Def), $1/16^{th}$ Blak (M.C. Serch), Double Blak (Gano Grills), Mo Blak (Canibus), Jo Blak (DJ Scratch), Smooth Blak (Charli Baltimore), and Hard Blak (muMs). See also **The Alabama Porch Monkeys**.

MAX FROST AND THE TROOPERS—Hot rock star Max Frost, born Max Flatow (Christopher Jones) was a millionaire by nineteen, and at age twenty-four gets involved in politics in the nutty 1968 flick *Wild in the Streets*. He teams up with Senator Fergus (Hal Holbrook) and lobbies to lower the voting age to fourteen with his protest song "Fourteen or Fight" and anthem "Fifty-Two Percent" (youth being fifty-

Max Frost (Christopher Jones) of Max Frost and the Troopers

two percent of the population). After successfully doping Congress, he gets the bill passed and runs for and gets himself elected president! He puts everyone over thirty in camps where they're forcibly dosed with LSD all the time. Not quite as bad as *Logan's Run*. **TRIVIA TIME!** Max's drummer, Stanley X, is played by a very young-looking, clean-shaven Richard Pryor. Also, the band's song "Shape of Things to Come" hit #22 on the U.S. Billboard charts on 10/28/68. The music was performed by Davie Allan and the Arrows, with an otherwise unknown Paul Wybier on vocals. Loungemaster Les Baxter composed the movie's score.

FAKE BANDS, REAL WHEELS. WELL, UNREAL ONES, TOO.
BY JASON TORCHINSKY

One of the best parts of being in a fake band is that, being fake, the cruel realities of the all-too-real world can be happily ignored. Such as how your band of unemployed teenagers can afford a customized van. In grim reality, a rusty Ford Econoline is by far the most common band transport. In the beautiful world of falsehood, band vehicles are far more varied and extraordinary. Here's seven of the best:

1. **The Monkees: The MonkeeMobile (1966 Pontiac GTO, heavily customized)**—In many ways, this is the iconic fake band car: a wild caricature of the real thing. When *The Monkees* TV show was being produced, they knew they wanted some kind of custom car. Via people knowing people, Pontiac signed on to provide the vehicles, and noted Hollywood car customizer Dean Jeffries (who, among many other things, turned a VW chassis into the Coyote X from TV's *Hardcastle and McCormick*) created a wonderfully stylized variation on that most muscular of muscle cars, the Pontiac GTO. He stretched the distinctive nose, added a third row of seats, an unusual convertible top, and a drag chute. To give this goat some serious go, he installed a massive supercharger on the already brawny engine and mounted weights in the back so that it was capable of doing wheelies with minimal effort. The supercharger was later removed when everybody found the damn thing just too scary to drive. Like all good stars, the MonkeeMobile had a strange later life: it was somehow left in Australia, ended up as a hotel courtesy car in Puerto Rico, and finally made it back to the U.S. via an auction in 1992. It's now been restored and lives in New York.

2. **The Blues Brothers: The Bluesmobile (1974 Dodge Monaco, with police package)**—The Bluesmobile, a former Mount Prospect police car, is actually the second Bluesmobile; the first one, a Cadillac, was apparently traded for a microphone. The Bluesmobile also has to earn its title from Jake, the Blues brother just out of prison who is understandably miffed at being picked up in a former cop car. It earns the title by jumping over a drawbridge. Elwood, the other Blues brother, gives a good description of the car in the movie: "It's got a cop motor, a four hundred and forty cubic inch plant. It's got cop tires, cop suspension, cop shocks; it was a model made before catalytic converters, so it'll run good on regular gas." But what makes the Bluesmobile unique is not what it is physically, but rather what it is spiritually. As the Blues Brothers are on a "mission from God," their chariot, the Bluesmobile, seems to be blessed as well. It is capable of incredible feats of speed, staggeringly long jumps that seem very deity-enhanced, and is never caught by Nazi or Chicago cop alike. And, as final proof of its holy nature, as soon as its mission is accomplished, it crumbles to rubble, a visceral reaction to the holy spirit releasing its grasp on this loyal American steel.

3. **The Amazing Chan and the Chan Clan: Transforming Van**—Charlie Chan's brood of ten musically inclined, mystery-solving cartoon children tooled around in a largeish van (there were ten of them, after all) that could somehow transform itself to resemble any other car or truck. Damn, that's handy! This is one of those situations where a limitation of the vehicle's incredible powers (can change appearance, but only to other road vehicles) somehow seems to mitigate the ludicrous nature of the very same power. Anyway, no matter what it turned into, it could still somehow seat ten Chan kids, otherwise there'd be gruesome scenes of crushed Asian children after their van compressed down to the size of a VW Beetle.

4. **The Banana Splits: Banana Buggies**—If you're in a fake band that requires you to wear hot, bulky fur suits, one of the smartest things you can do is to work in some gimmicky way to keep you from having to haul your heavy ass around all the time. That's just what the Banana Splits did,

(continued)

and the results were their small, six-wheeled vehicles, looking something like a cross between a golf cart and a dune buggy. These buggies were Amphicats, an early amphibious all-terrain vehicle, done up in custom wacky paint jobs to match each character. Amphicats are technically very interesting, and extremely capable ATVs, with a 16 hp, two-stroke, air-cooled engine powering all six axles. They steered tank-style, utilizing separate clutches for each band of three wheels to allow for turns. They even sported colored tires, which should have been available to the general public for years already, dammit. The upshot of all this is that if a rogue Banana Split decides to rampage off into the woods, the beach, or through a stream, you'd better damn well have a Hummer at your disposal if you even want to think about catching them.

5. **Kidd Video: The Kiddmobile**—In the same goofballification process that turned the members of Kidd Video into cartoons during their journey to the Flipside, band member Whiz's early-80s yellow-and-red Subaru Brat was transformed into the roomier, bulbous Kiddmobile: an amphibious, flying craft that also served as the band's home. In addition to such fine amenities as an autopilot, the Kiddmobile also featured a robotic trashcan. A remarkable vehicle, indeed, but so painfully dorky-looking it almost just doesn't matter.

6. **The Partridge Family: 1957 Chevrolet School Bus, with custom paint job**—This otherwise conventional school bus is notable for its Mondrian/De Stijl–style paintjob, which, according to the show, was painted by the Partridge family themselves (read: PA's from the props department). This icon of fake bandom sported the warning "Careful Nervous Mother Driving" and, despite its cult status, ended up junked in the 90s in the parking lot of Lucy's Tacos in East Los Angeles.

7. **The Commitments: Red Volkswagen Type 2 Pickup (1978?)**—Of all the fake vehicles on this list, this one is perhaps the most real. Well, it is real. But, in light of its role as

the vehicle to convey Jimmy Rabbitte and his often-drunk bandmates to gigs throughout Dublin, the VW does its job commendably, and with a working-class dignity that fits its environment wonderfully. Plus, as a rear-engined pickup, it has an interesting technical appeal, and, perhaps most important for its job of hauling The Commitments around, vomit washes easily off its all-metal pickup bed.

MAX REBO BAND, THE—The band of aliens entertaining crimelord/giant slug Jabba the Hutt in *Return of the Jedi* (1980). Originally Evar Orbus and His Galactic Jizz-Wailers, led by Evar Orbus, Max Rebo took over after Evar Orbus died under a cloud of

Sy Snootles (voiced by Annie Arbogast) of The Max Rebo Band

suspicion. Losing their gig and low on funds, they auditioned for crimelord Jabba the Hutt and got a lifetime contract. Barquin D'an, brother of Figrin D'an, joined up with the band and helped beef up The Max Rebo Band sound with additional members until it became The Rebo Twelve. Barquin later left, disgusted with Jabba's cruelty. After Jabba's death and the collapse of his criminal empire, the band eventually broke up and went their separate ways. In reality, the band was originally a mere trio: Max Rebo (Simon Williamson) on Red Ball Jett Organ, singer Sy Snootles (Annie Arbogast), and Droopy McCool (Deep Roy) on some wind instrument. When George Lucas rereleased his "Special Editions" of the *Star Wars* trilogy, he digitally inserted extra effects and aliens, including the following additional musicians: Barquin D'an, Doda Bodanawieedo, Joh Yowza, Greeata, Lyn Me, Rappertunie, Rystáll, Ak-rev, and Umpass-stay. The minute details come from the short story "We Don't Do Weddings: The Band's Tale" by Kathy Tyers, in the book *Tales From the Mos Eisley Cantina*. See also **Figrin D'an and the Modal Nodes.**

MAXWELL DEMON AND THE VENUS IN FURS — See **Brian Slade.**

MAYHEM — The punk band from the legendary 12/02/82 "punk rock episode" (actual title: "Next Stop Nowhere") of *Quincy*. They play "Get Up (I Wanna See You Choke)" at the club Ground Zero. Their lead singer is named Fly.

MC CHRIS — Rock star popular with the staff of cartoon *Sealab 2021*—and, coincidentally, the name of one of the writers (who also does the voice of Hesh) of the aforementioned show. He appears in the "All That Jazz" episode (10/28/01), where the staff takes off to see him perform in China, leaving Captain Murphy (voiced by Harry Goz) to get trapped un-

der a soda machine. MC Chris is apparently the leader of a quartet. After Debbie DuPree (Kate Miller) flashes the band, the Sealab staff becomes his roadies for a year. Debbie comes back pregnant! MC Chris's song "Fett's Vette" plays at the end. MC Chris also played MC Pee Pants on *Aqua Teen Hunger Force*. MC Chris's real name is Chris Ward. See also **The Mahatmamas; MC Pee Pants; The Ocean Bottom Nightmare Band.**

MC PEE PANTS — An eleven-year-old rapper whose prepubescent rhymes really connected with cartoon meatball Meatwad (voiced by Dave Willis), member of the not-so-super superhero group (and animated show) *Aqua Teen Hunger Force*. The latest MC Pee Pants single "I Want Candy" features such dynamite lyrics as "I'm her Hume Cronyn she's my Jessica Tandy." Later, we discover that MC Pee Pants is simply trying to get kids whacked out on candy so that he can use their elevated blood sugar to power a drill into Hell that will loose demons to run his worldwide diet-pill pyramid scheme. Even later, we discover he's really a crazed eight-foot spider wearing a disposable diaper. MC Pee Pants is voiced by MC Chris, who also wrote the songs and who works on the Cartoon Network Adult Swim's sister show *Sealab 2021*, where he plays, uh, MC Chris. From the "MC P Pants" episode (05/19/02). See also **MC Chris.**

M.C. SAFETY AND THE CAUTION CREW — From the "Bart vs. Lisa vs. the 3rd Grade" episode (11/17/02) of *The Simpsons*. He's an old-school-style rapper so lame that not only does he rap about crosswalks and juice at grade-school assemblies, AND only gets about thirty seconds to perform, but he still puts a period after the "M" and the "C" in "MC." Amazingly, he's an African-American, though the other three members of his crew are white. See also **The Beach Boys Experience; The Be Sharps; Johnny**

Bobby; Johnny Calhoun; Captain Bart and the Tequila Mockingbirds; The Crazy Old Man Singers; Cyanide; Gulliver Dark; Ferl Dixon and His Second Helping Boys; Funky C Funky Do; Garfunkel, Messina, Oates, and Lisa; Hooray for Everything; Kovenant; Krusty and the Krums; The Larry Davis Experience; Little Timmy and the Shebangs; Loggins and Oates; Lurleen Lumpkin; Melvin and the Squirrels; "Bleeding Gums" Murphy; The Party Posse; The Rappin' Rabbis; Red Breem and His Band of Some Esteem; The Satin Knights; The Steve Sax Trio; Testament; Blind Willie Witherspoon; The Ya-Hoo Recovering Alcoholic Jug Band; Yodelin' Zeke.

MC SKAT KAT — Animated cartoon cat who initially appeared in a 1989 Paula Abdul video duetting with her on "Opposites Attract." What could be more opposite than a flesh-and-blood person and an animated, anthropomorphic cat? Well, maybe if one was RE-ALLY talented and the other a mere artificial record-company construct. Much too later (1991) MC Skat Kat (voice of Derrick "Delite" Stevens) released an entire album, *The Adventures of MC Skat Kat*, featuring his overinflated and undeserved posse of other cartoon cats, some of whom also got to rap and sing: Leo, Silk, Fatz (voice of Squeak of The College Boyz), Taboo (voice of Rom of The College Boyz), Katleen (voice of Talanda Shorter), and cartoon mouse Micetro. *TRIVIA TIME!* This album had the dubious distinction of being named THE Least Essential Album of the 90s by *The Onion*'s AV Club!

IT'S **ELVIS** WITH HIS FOOT ON THE GAS AND NO BRAKES ON THE FUN !!!

Spinout, featuring Mike McCoy (Elvis Presley)

MCBRIDE, DARLENE — Rabidly right-wing and hideously over-made-up female country singer and recurring character from sketch comedy program *Mad TV*, played by Nicole Sullivan. She has appeared in at least seven sketches: "Darlene McBride" (10/04/97); "Darlene McBride Tour" (11/22/97), in which she launches her "Take Back America Tour"; "Darlene McBride Valentine's Album" (02/07/98); "Darlene McBride's Mother's Day Special" (05/09/98); "Darlene McBride's Thanksgiving" (11/21/98); "Darlene McBride's X-mas Album" (11/20/99); and "Marshall McBride LP" (04/14/01) which is her tribute to fellow hatemonger and rapper Eminem, complete with a parody of his song "Stan." See also **Defcon One; Dr. Dazzle; The Eracists; Hoppy Potty; Michael McLoud and Jasmine Wayne-Wayne; Savante; Shaunda; Little Hassan Taylor; Willow.**

MCCOY, MIKE — A club singer (Elvis Presley) who likes his cars fast and his women faster, in *Spinout* (1966). McCoy is a full-time singer and part-time race-car driver, and he needs all the speed he can get to avoid the three women wanting to marry him. One is the spoiled daughter (Shelley Fabares) of a millionaire car designer, who wants McCoy to drive his new model. The second is a world-famous anthropologist (Diane McBain) writing a book on the perfect American male, who desires to marry the most perfect male . . . yep, McCoy. The third is Les (Deborah Walley), the drummer for his backup band, 1 Plus 2 + $\frac{1}{2}$. All these women want to marry him, he makes out with all of them, then marries them all off to other men, and even makes out with the chicks at their weddings! That's what makes him The King, baby! See also **1 Plus 2 + ¹/₂**.

MCELROY, JEROME "CHEF" — Former singer who now works as an elementary school cafeteria cook on Comedy Central's animated show *South Park*. Although frequently the voice of reason, he does have a tendency to burst into hot funk/soul numbers at least once a show. The show's kids organized the benefit concert Chef Aid when Chef got sued by his old record company, in the "Chef Aid" episode (10/07/98). Voiced by 70s soulster Issac Hayes. See also **The Avenue Street Ghetto Boys; Faith + 1; Fingerbang; Getting Gay with Kids; The Ghetto Avenue Boys; MOOP; Raging Pussies; Reach for the Skyler; Sanctified; Sisters of Mercy Hold No Pain Against the Dark Lord; Timmy! and the Lords of the Underworld**.

MCGUIRE, MOLLY — Fiona (no last name) played this female rock star from *Hearts of Fire* (1987), which starred . . . Bob Dylan?! Go figure. See also **James Colt; Billy Parker**.

MCLOUD, MICHAEL AND JASMINE WAYNE-WAYNE — From at least five sketches on comedy show *Mad TV*. This bland adult contemporary singing duo (Will Sasso and Alex Borstein) has hit movie songs that all sound EXACTLY THE SAME. Appearances: "Love of My Life" (11/14/98), "You Are the One That I Love" (11/20/99), "One That I Love" (3/18/00), "This Is the Land That I Love" (01/20/01), and "Behind the Music" (04/06/02). This appearance was actually three separate skits in that episode and featured them duetting with real rappers Master P, Insane Clown Posse, and also the Bee Gees' Barry Gibb (played by Michael McDonald). See also **Defcon One; Dr. Dazzle; The Eracists; Hoppy Potty; Darlene McBride; Sa-**

vante; **Shaunda; Little Hassan Taylor; Willow**.

MCLOVE, EOIN — A namby-pamby, sweater-and-bow-tie-wearing pop star/TV host who appeared in the "Night of the Nearly Dead" (04/24/98) episode of the Irish sitcom *Father Ted*. Eoin (Patrick McDonnell) hosts a Lawrence Welk-y TV show and records albums like *Eoin McLovenotes*, featuring a cover shot of him dressed as a baby. Housekeeper Joan Doyle (Pauline McLynn) enters his weekly poetry contest and wins a chance to have tea with him. That's when she discovers he's a spoiled brat who compulsively swipes things, eats jam from the jar, thinks of his fans as a "big pile of dirty old biddies," is totally dependent upon his handler Patsy (former Commitments backup singer Maria Doyle Kennedy), and "has no willie." When word gets out about his visit, it inspires all the little old ladies of Craggy Island to converge on the rectory in a kind of Beatlemania-meets-*Night-of-the-Living-Dead* mob scene and inspires Eoin to shriek "Go away, I don't want to catch the menopause." See also **Niamh Connolly**.

MCQUADE, DIGGER — See **Paul Kerr**.

MEADOWS, KATHY — Lovely, lustable Lynda Carter playing superheroine Wonder Woman (disguised as Diana Prince), goes undercover as pop singer Kathy Meadows (ow! brain hurt!) to investigate a blackmailing at Phoenix Records in *Wonder Woman*'s "Amazon Hot Wax" episode (02/16/79). Lynda Carter had actually released an album, *Portrait*, several months previously, and two of the songs were used as Kathy Meadows's demos: "Want to Get Beside You" and "Toto (Don't It Feel Like Paradise)." In the plot, label head Eric Landau (Curtis Credel) is being blackmailed by crooks who stole the valuable master tapes of dead folkie Billy Dero's last album. Turns out Dero's really still alive and that another Phoenix label act, Jeff and Barbi Gordon, swiped the tapes for the blackmailers in the first place. Oh, and Wonder Woman saves the day, duh. The episode's title is a play on the 1978 movie title *American Hot Wax*. See also **AntiMatter; Billy Dero; Jeff and Barbi Gordon; Lane Kinkaid; Hamlin Rule**.

MECONIUM—Pomona, California, garage metal trio managed by David St. Hubbins (Michael McKean), while he's on break from Spiñal Tap. They are glimpsed in the 1992 special *The Return of Spiñal Tap*. The band was played by Ryan Datry, Colin McKean (Mike's kid!), and Dan Sloyan. Look up the band's name in the dictionary for bonus fun! See also **Duke Fame; Lambsblood; The Regulars; Spiñal Tap**.

MEDUSA—Comedienne/actress/singer Julie Brown (of the 1987 novelty hit "The Homecoming Queen's Got a Gun") starred, wrote, directed, produced, and penned the music for *Medusa: Dare to Be Truthful* (1992), a made-for-TV direct parody of the 1991 documentary *Madonna: Truth or Dare*. Egocentric pop diva Medusa is documented on her "The Blonde Leading The Blonde" tour, singing a number of direct Madonna parodies like "Vague" ("Vogue") and "Expose Yourself" ("Express Yourself"). *TRIVIA TIME!* Smith "Smitty" Wordes of The Bower Family Band shows up here as a character named Angel. Game-show host Wink Martindale appears as himself!

MELVIN AND THE SQUIRRELS—Quick parody of The Chipmunks in the "Homer's Barbershop Quartet" (09/30/93) episode of long-running animated FOX show *The Simpsons*. At a swap meet, Bart (voiced by Nancy Cartwright) pulls one of their albums out of the Comic Book Guy's (voiced by Hank Azaria) box. He explains they were ". . . part of the Rodent

Invasion of the early 60s." A quick burst of squeaky voices singing "Yankee Doodle" is played. MEL-VIIIIN! See also **The Beach Boys Experience; The Be Sharps; Johnny Bobby; Johnny Calhoun; Captain Bart and the Tequila Mockingbirds; The Crazy Old Man Singers; Cyanide; Gulliver Dark; Ferl Dixon and his Second Helping Boys; Funky C Funky Do; Garfunkel, Messina, Oates, and Lisa; Hooray for Everything; Kovenant; Krusty and the Krums; The Larry Davis Experience; Little Timmy and the Shebangs; Loggins and Oates; Lurleen Lumpkin; M. C. Safety and the Caution Crew; "Bleeding Gums" Murphy; The Party Posse; The Rappin' Rabbis; Red Breem and His Band of Some Esteem; The Satin Knights; The Steve Sax Trio; Testament; Blind Willie Witherspoon; The Ya-Hoo Recovering Alcoholic Jug Band; Yodelin' Zeke**.

MERYL STREEP—See **The Cheap Girls**.

METABOLICA—A garage band actually composed of microscopic germs, instead of just scum, in the 2002 *Ozzy and Drix* cartoon, a spinoff of the movie *Osmosis Jones* (2001). One could say their music is infectious! But that would be stupid. Having yet to be discovered, they spend most of their days performing their tunes on street corners and at smalltime events. Sometimes acting like a Greek chorus, this group of young rockers never fails to remind Ozzy (voiced by Phil Lamarr) that he's in the body of a thirteen-year-old, Hector (voiced by Justin Cowden). See also **Kidney Rock**.

METAL CORPSES, THE—True dinosaurs of rock, this aging metal band was used to playing sold-out arenas but are now doomed to unenthusiastic fans in small clubs in the movie *Ladies and Gentlemen, The Fabulous Stains* (1981). The Metal Corpses headline a tour with The Stains and The Looters, until bass player Jerry Jervey (Vince Welnick) dies of a drug overdose minutes before a show. The Metal Corpses, crushed by his death, quit the tour. Welnick and Fee Waybill, who plays lead singer Lou Corpse, are from real New Wave band The Tubes. See also **The Looters; The Stains**.

METRO GNOMES, THE — See **The Gumbies**.

MICK JADESTONE AND THE ROLLING BOULDERS — Rolling Stones parody from the "Pebbles' Big Boast" (10/23/71) episode of Hanna-Barbera cartoon *The Pebbles and Bamm-Bamm Show*. Pebbles Flintstone (voiced by *All in the Family's* Sally Struthers) lies that she knows this band, in an attempt to impress snobby "friend" Cindy Curbstone (voiced by Gay Hartweg). Pebbles then tries to crash all their appearances in an attempt to get them to play Cindy's party. Not to be confused with Mick Jagged and the Stones from the 2000 live-action movie *The Flintstones in Viva Rock Vegas*. See also **The Bedrock Rockers**.

MICK JAGGED AND THE STONES — Prehistoric Rolling Stones parody from the 2000 movie *The Flintstones in Viva Rock Vegas*. A prequel to *The Flintstones*, (1994) it shows how Fred (Mark Addy) and Wilma (Kristen Johnston) and Barney (Stephen Baldwin) and Betty (Jane Krakowski) met and paired up. The band is headlining at the Tardust casino, owned by scheming Chip Rockefeller (Thomas Gibson). Betty gets mad when she sees Barney with a show-girl and runs off with this (sigh) "rock band." Nice gag. Alan Cumming played Mick Jagged and also the alien Gazoo. Keith Rockhard was played by John Taylor, bassist for 80s bands Duran Duran and The Power Station. Other Stone-Age parody head-liners at various Rock Vegas venues are shown only on signs, such as: Frank Stoneatra, Stony Bennett, and Slime and the Family Stone. Not to be con-

fused with Mick Jadestone and the Rolling Boulders. See also **The BC-52s**.

MICROBE — From the Disney Channel live-action movies *Zenon: Girl of the 21st Century* (1999) and *Zenon: The Zequel* (2001). In the first movie, set in the year 2049, Microbe is the first band in space! They are to play the space station where title character Zenon Kar (Kirsten Storms) lives and has won a contest to meet hunky, spike-haired lead singer, Proto Zoa (Phillip Rhys). But after witnessing the station being sabotaged, she gets into trouble and gets sent to Earth. She sneaks onto the rocket carrying Microbe into space and saves the day, without even missing the concert (they sing "Super Nova Girl"). In the second movie, Zenon saves the space station AGAIN, in addition to finding the now-missing Proto Zoa and making first contact with aliens, who were using one of the band's songs as a distress call. At the end, the band sings the ominously titled "The Galaxy Is Ours." The rest of the band was played by Paul Reid, Kane Lawton, Craig Terris, and John Corker.

MIDNIGHT, JOEY — See **Joey Midnight and Dark Highway**.

MINYK, LINSK — Rick Moranis played this polka-singing native of the fictional Eastern European country of Leutonia with Ambrose Burnside facial hair. A former member of The Happy Wanderers, he struck out on his own, but remained on good terms with the band, as he returned to perform "Stairway to Heaven" with them on *The Happy Wanderers* TV show, really a sketch on the 05/21/82 episode of *SCTV*. He also appears in the 1984 HBO mockumentary, *The Last Polka*, performing with and reminiscing about The Happy Wanderers. Rick Moranis released the comedy album *You, Me, the Music and Me*, on IRS in 1989, which features a

Linsk-afied version of The Doors' "Light My Fire." See also **Vic Arpeggio**; **Big Momma**; **5 Neat Guys**; **Happiness Unlimited**; **The Happy Wanderers**; **Lola Heatherton**; **The Lemon Twins**; **Tom Munroe**; **The Queenhaters**; **The Ramblers**; **The Recess Monkeys**; **Russ Riley**; **Jackie Rogers Jr.**; **Jackie Rogers Sr.**; **Speed of Light**; **Dusty Towne**; **The Wally Hung Trio**.

MISFITS, THE — Not to be confused with the Danzig-fronted punk/hard-core band of the same name. This band was an all-girl band of brats who feuded constantly with nice-girl rivals Jem and the Holograms in the *Jem!* cartoon (1985–88). These trashy bimbos were originally signed by Starlight Music honcho Eric Raymond (voiced by Charlie Adler) but when he lost a bet with half-owner Jerrica Benton, he lost his half of the company, and he and The Misfits were out on their asses. The Misfits' leader Pizzazz (real name Phyllis Gabor) got her rich dad Harvey Gabor (voiced by Wally Burr) to buy them their own damn record company, Misfits Music. They had songs with titles like "Gimme Gimme Gimme," "Outta My Way," and "Let's Blow This Town." Get the idea? This band was obnoxious, rude, crass, and just downright mean. They were so engrossed in trying to screw over Jem and the Holograms, how they found time to record, play shows, or do any band stuff is a downright mystery. Seriously though, which band would you rather party with? The band was Pizzazz (voiced by Patricia Alice Albrecht), Roxy (voiced by Bobbie Block), Stormer (voiced by Susan Blu), and latecomer Jetta (voiced by Louise Dorsey). Pizzazz's singing voice was done by Ellen Bernfield. See also **Bobby Bailey**; **The Ben Tiller Orchestra**; **Jem and the Holograms**; **The Limp Lizards**; **The Stingers**; **The Tapps Tucker Quartet**.

MISSISSIPPI GARY — Standard clichéd old black bluesman played by Mark McKinney in several *The Kids in the Hall* (1989–94) skits. He played the harmonica. In one sketch he had the blues about his relationship with office worker Kathy (Bruce McCullough in drag). See also **Armada**; **Cancer Boy**; **Death Lurks**; **The Noodles**; **Tammy**.

MITCH AND MICKEY — Early 60s folkie duo from the charming faux folkumentary *A Mighty Wind*, the 2003 movie whose title song is one of the most hummable fart jokes ever written. This act provides some unexpected dramatic tension to the fluffy fun, as Mitch Cohen (Eugene Levy) went off his nut shortly after their acrimonious breakup and his series of ever-blacker solo albums: *Songs From a Dark Place*, *Cry for Help*, and *Calling It Quits*. His unexpected reunion with former partner/lover Mickey (Catherine O'Hara), now measuring out her life in coffee spoons and married to a boring medical equipment salesman (Jim Piddock), gives the movie some emotional heft. The big question is if they will re-create the shtick of their old hit "A Kiss at the End of the Rainbow" where they actually kiss during the song, on the big televised reunion concert. *TRIVIA TIME!* Interestingly, Levy appeared in an *SCTV* sketch (03/27/84) that could easily be the genesis of the entire movie: a short 'n' sweet commercial for a best-of album of fake folkies The Ramblers—a bunch of agitprop, over-educated whites singing twee pap deluded into thinking it's changing the world. *A Mighty Wind* seems similarly determined to knock the early 60s folk music boom as an inauthentic product created entirely by middle-class Jews. See also **The Folksmen**; **Jack and Judy**; **The New Main Street Singers**; **The Ramblers**.

MITCHELL, SAMMI — See **Body Bag**.

MOK — In the post-apocalyptic "Nuke York" of the

animated film *Rock and Rule* (1983), Mok, an extreme caricature of Mick Jagger, is up to no damn good. His popularity slipping, he's convinced he needs a live-concert show stopper. Lasers? Pah. Fireworks? Piffle. Giant inflatable pig? Puh-lease. Nope, only a real, genuine, horrible demon spawn from the utmost reaches of the netherworld will do. So, he abducts Angel from a nameless band in Ohmtown to summon the demon with her singing. Her bandmates Omar (hero), Stretch and Dizzy (comic relief bumblers), follow in hot pursuit. But Mok sends them packing with a little trickery and a ton of drugs. Mok then accidentally blows up Carnegie Hall because there wasn't enough juice in Nuke York to power the summoning. Demons require SO much electricity, you wouldn't believe it. So the concert is moved to Ohmtown with its convenient power plant. The beast is summoned, eats a few people, has a few laughs, then Omar frees Angel, who sings it back into whatever hell it came from and Mok gets thrown in the hole. The end! From Nelvana, your one-stop oddball cut-rate animated fare shop. *TRIVIA TIME!* Lou Reed was the singing voice of Mok. Deborah Harry of Blondie was singing voice of Angel. See also **Omar and the Daycares**.

MOLOCH — A KISS-like rock star, complete with full-face makeup, in the "Rock Devil Rock" episode (10/31/82) of *CHiPs*. Played by Ralph Malph (Donny Most) from *Happy Days!* A real hoot, it must be seen to be believed. Even deals with hidden messages in rock records! Ooo! His manager tries to engineer his accidental death to sell more records, which is like cutting open the goose that lays the golden eggs to get all the eggs out. See also **Pain**; **Snow Pink**.

MONET, JIMMY — See **Brendon Poppins and the Chimminy Sweeps**.

THE MONKEES
(1966, COLGEMS)

THE MONKEES' SELF-TITLED first album, released 10/10/66, earned them derision for playing nary a note of its music, which was performed by studio musicians, including Tommy Boyce and Bobby Hart, the composers of half of the album's songs. It produced a single hit, "Last Train to Clarksville," and no wonder. A lot of the other tracks are lacking one way or another, especially "I Wanna Be Free," a maudlin, women-hating, commitment-phobic weepie of the kind that doesn't get written anymore, and for good reason. It wants to be evocative and lyrical, but it really paints a picture of the singer as a self-involved jerk who just heard about "free love" and doesn't want to miss out. No one could have pulled this clunker off. "Let's Dance On" rocks, but in a forced, teeth-gritting, derivative way, sounding too much like a pale wash of The Rascals' "Good Lovin'." It's sadly followed by the completely forgettable "I'll Be True to You" which would have been corny and outdated a decade earlier. Closing the album is the fun time-waster "Gonna Buy Me a Dog," a wisely chosen take of Davy Jones and Micky Dolenz goofing and joking their way through this piece of filler—a "serious" take of its inane lyrics would have been insufferable! The three standout tracks of this album are undoubtedly "(Theme from) The Monkees," "Last Train to Clarksville," and "Sweet Young Thing," a lesser-known acid-country collaboration between Nesmith and the Goffin/King songwriting team. These gems shine out, mostly because the rest of the album slouches so low, feeling flaccid and weak in comparison. The problem with the whole album is it's not bad, but it's not so good either. The Monkees got BETTER—way, way better on later albums. Better songs, better arrangements, better Ne-

(continued)

smith tunesmithery. Their first album, ironically, is one of the worst introductions to the band. Try any one of their next three albums instead: *More of the Monkees, Headquarters,* or *Pisces, Aquarius, Capricorn & Jones Ltd.*

MONKEES, THE — The Beatles' *Hard Day's Night* (U.S. premiere 08/11/64) was a smash success. It was no longer possible to ignore the youth pop culture phenomenon. "The Man," personified by minor TV producers Bert Schneider and Bob Rafelson, set out to basically make *A Hard Day's Night: The Series.* Presumably The Beatles weren't available for a weekly series themselves, so Rafelson and Schneider placed an ad in *Variety* in September of 1965. It was as simple as that! They wanted four hep, hip, funny youngsters who could sing and improvise, and picked Micky Dolenz, Davy Jones, Mike Nesmith, and Peter Tork. Composers Tommy Boyce and Bobby Hart, who also auditioned, provided the music. They created a pilot, which originally tested terribly, so they successfully recut it and sold the series to NBC. The show debuted 09/12/66, and their first album the next month. Both were hits; the single "Last Train to Clarksville" shot to #1 two weeks after the show debuted. Music mogul Don Kirshner, brought in to produce the albums, actively discouraged musical input from the band. Sure, The Monkees didn't play their own instruments—they weren't allowed to! This led to a feud that resulted in Kirshner's ouster and the band securing creative control over subsequent albums. Over the course of the show's two-year run, they racked up eleven top forty hits and saw their first four albums all go to #1. They even toured, bringing then little-known Jimi Hendrix to open for them. That worked about as well as it sounds.

How did this granddaddy of fake bands pull it off? Kirshner/Screen Gems gave them access to great songs and top-notch composers. They also gave the teenyboppers something to bob their heads and tap their toes to after The Beatles and other groups had started dropping acid and making weirdo, undanceable concept albums. That is, at least until The Monkees started going psychedelic themselves, straining against their own inauthenticity. After the show was canceled for falling ratings, they made the cult classic feature film *Head* (premiered 11/06/68), which kicked The Monkees' surreal shenanigans into the psychedelic stratosphere. The movie played with the image of their own phoniness, summed up by the movie's "Ditty Diego" song—"Hey hey we are The Monkees, you know we love to please, a manufactured image with no philosophies." It did little business. The Monkees then topped themselves with the TV special *33⅓ Revolutions Per Monkee* (04/14/69), a bizarre head trip whose plot has The Monkees brainwashed into being, er, The Monkees. Only more so. Then the "plot" breaks down along with the fourth wall, taking The Monkees' careers with it. Tork left the group after taping the special. The remaining trio cut two more albums, *Instant Replay* (Feb. 1969) and *The Monkees Present* (Oct. 1969). Finally Nesmith left the band, and the once-hot group screeched to a halt as a mere duo with the contractually obligated album *Changes* (May 1970). In 1975, Davy Jones and Mickey Dolenz teamed up with Tommy Boyce and Bobby Hart to tour playing Monkees hits, but aside from the occasional syndicated run of the series, things were quiet until the mid 1980s. In 1986, the band's twentieth anniversary saw a mini-explosion of all things Monkee. They regrouped (minus Nesmith) to tour again, got a marathon on MTV, and managed to get a newly recorded single "That Was Then, This Is Now" on the charts. Arista Records released a double LP greatest hits collection, *Then & Now . . . The Best of the Monkees,* and Rhino Records started rereleasing the back catalog. Alas, 1986 also saw them release a new album, *Pool It*, and a year later there was the sad, strange, short-lived attempt to reinvent the show, *The New Monkees*. In 1996, the band reunited again for a thirtieth anniversary tour, and released another completely unnecessary new album, *Justus*. Their other evils include having their birth mark the day "The Man" tried to hijack the revolution, brothers! The squares learned to defang, bottle, market, and sell revolution back to the kids. But they would have figured that out anyway. On the positive side, The Monkees midwifed the music video, schooled a whole generation of clueless TV execs on the possibilities of "synergy," and made some damn catchy three-minute pop songs. What else do you want from a TV band? *TRIVIA TIME!* Michael Nesmith's mother invented Liquid Paper. See also **Fern Badderly; Irene Chomsky; The Foreign Agents; The Four Martians; The Four Swine; Honey and the Bear; The Jolly Green Giants; Lester Crabtree and the Three Crabs; The New Monkees; Sven Helstrom and the Swedish Rhythm Kings; The Swinging Android; The West Minstrel Abbies**.

MONSTER, MARILYN — In the last episode ("Patriotism, Pepper, and Professionalism," 12/18/98) of HBO's *Mr. Show*, this depraved Marilyn Manson parody has his own chain of pizza restaurants. He (David Cross) even appears in the training video for new employees, exhorting them to break the rules, but not any of his rules. Not to be confused with Norma Jean Monster from a different episode of the same show. See also **The Beetletown Players; Larry Black; Livingston Brewster; Willips Brighton; Dickie Crickets; Indomitable Spirit; Kid Jersey; Kill or Be Killed; C. S. Lewis Jr.; Horace Loeb; Norma Jean Monster; John Baptiste Philouza; Professor Murder; Puscifer; Salini; Smoosh; Old Swerdlow; Three Times**

One Minus One; Titannica; Sir Lloyd Wilson Webber; Wyckyd Sceptre; Daffy "Mal" Yinkleyankle.

MONTY'S BAND — The house band at dive bar Monty's in the 1979 movie *The Rose*. Singer Mary Rose Foster (Bette Midler), on her way to her sold-out homecoming concert, stops and sings at this watering hole, one of the first places she ever played. Things aren't so rosy for Rose, however, and her brief stint singing with this group is one of the last things she ever does. The band was played by Greg Prestopino, Bill Elliot, Jon Sholle, Scott Chambers, and Harry Stinson. See also **Mary Rose Foster; Billy Ray; The Rose Band**.

MOOP — All the boys from Comedy Central's animated show *South Park* want to do is rock, is that so wrong? The problem is, they just don't know how they want to rock. In the episode "Christian Rock Hard" (10/29/2003), the guys can't figure out the sound they want. Cartman suggests a Christian rock band, but he gets kicked out of the band and forms his own band, Faith + 1. Kyle, Stan, and Kenny (voiced by Matt Stone, Trey Parker, and Matt Stone, respectively) download music from the Internet to find their style, but the FBI breaks in and stops their piracy. After they are shown celebrities living in only semi-luxury due to Internet song piracy, the boys in MOOP decide not to play until everyone quits illegally downloading songs. Soon, other bands join their strike: Metallica, Britney Spears, and Timmy! and the Lords of the Underworld, to name but three. Kyle soon realizes that they were so caught up in protecting their music from piracy, they forgot to make any music to protect. See also **The Avenue Street Ghetto Boys; Faith + 1; Fingerbang; Getting Gay with Kids; The Ghetto Avenue Boys; Jerome "Chef" McElroy; Raging Pussies; Reach for the Skyler; Sancti-**

fied; **Sisters of Mercy Hold No Pain Against the Dark Lord**; **Timmy! and the Lords of the Underworld**.

MOORE, JIMMY—In Adam Sandler's 1998 romantic comedy *The Wedding Singer*, an uncredited Jon Lovitz has a brief cameo as a wedding singer, er, that is, not the one of the title. Another one. In his precious few minutes onscreen, he manages to create a character that's sleazy, arrogant, unpleasant, pathetic, full of himself, AND a bad singer. Bravo, Mr. Lovitz! He doesn't get the job. The members of Jimmy Moore's band were played by Mike Thompson, Michael Jay, John Sawaski, Christopher Alan, Kimberly Schwartz, and Sanetta Y. Gipson. See also **Robbie Hart**; **David Veltri**.

MORNING BREATH—Band that idiot Eli (Adam Jay Sadowsky) loses the money to hire for a school dance in the "Dregs of Humanity Part I" episode (01/02/85) of short-lived 1984–85 sitcom *It's Your Move*. This event kicks off the whole plot of the two-part episode. See also **The Dregs of Humanity**.

MOSQUITOES, THE—Beatle-esque quartet who visited Gilligan's Island in the "Don't Bug the Mosquitoes" episode (12/09/65). Gilligan (Bob Denver) is a huge fan, so huge he's driving the others nuts cranking Mosquitoes tunes on the radio. Then the real McCoy actually show up on the island, looking for a nice, quiet, monthlong vacation. The castaways want to leave now! So they pester The Mosquitoes, hoping to get them to leave early. But that just drives the band to the other side of the island and makes them so stressed that now they want to stay for TWO months. To make sure the band won't leave without them, the cast form their own band, hoping The Mosquitoes will take them along as an opening act. Naturally, it doesn't work, and The Mosquitoes callously leave them behind on the island, just like every other guest star. Lineup: Bingo (Les Brown Jr.), Bango (George Patterson), Bongo (Ed Wade), and Irving (Kirby Johnson). The band was played by The Wellingtons, who actually performed the show's theme song. See also **The Gnats**; **The Honeybees**.

MULDOON, KRISTY—Scottish rock star trying to get through customs with her band during the "Customs" skit in the 12/13/87 episode of *The Tracey Ullman Show*. Played by Tracey Ullman herself. See also **Ariel**; **Gulliver Dark**; **The Nice Neighbors**.

MUMBLIN' JIM—Hippie psychedelic band in the 1968 movie *Psych-Out* (is hippiesploitation a word?).

Mumblin' Jim

Future big star Jack Nicholson in a phoneytail plays the band's leader and lead guitarist, Stoney. A self-absorbed heel, he makes it with a deaf chick in search of her brother in the movie's plot. Stoney says they want to be "famous like the Airplane." African-American druggie drummer Elwood (Max Julien) and guitarist Ben (Adam Roarke) and uh, this other guy, fill out the rest of the band. There's an oh-so-60s scene where the band plays a complete "Purple Haze" ripoff instrumental, (really "Asbury Wednesday" by The Boeznee Cryque) as trippy lights wash over the band and go-go-booted dancers . . . uh . . . dance.

MUNROE, TOM — Smooth, soulless tune crooner in music videos on a couple of "The Gerry Todd Show" sketches from sketch comedy classic *SCTV*. Rick Moranis plays both Munroe and Gerry Todd. On the 05/22/81 episode, he ruins the New Wave hits "Turning Japanese" (by The Vapors) and "De Do Do Do De Da Da Da" (by The Police), both from his videodisc *On a New Wavelength*. On the 07/10/81 episode, Gerry shows Tom's video for "Downtown," from his *Tom Munroe Sings Petula Clark* album. *TRIVIA TIME! SCTV* was doing music video parodies before MTV went on the air, on 08/01/81! See also **Vic Arpeggio; Big Momma; 5 Neat Guys; Happiness Unlimited; The Happy Wanderers; Lola Heatherton; The Lemon Twins; Linsk Minyk; The Queenhaters; The Ramblers; The Recess Monkeys; Russ Riley; Jackie Rogers Jr.; Jackie Rogers Sr.; Speed of Light; Dusty Towne; The Wally Hung Trio.**

MURDOCH, EMMA — Jennifer Connelly plays this sultry 40s-esque noir lounge singer in the unsung weirdo sci-fi flick, *Dark City* (1998). At the end of the movie she's implanted with new memories and becomes Anna, who isn't a singer. Actually, technically, she's not really Emma either. No one is who they are, because the entire weird city of the title is all part of an experiment where aliens constantly change people's memories. Murdoch's singing voice was Anita Kelsey.

MURPH AND THE MAGIC TONES — Lounge act shown cheesing it up Latin-style in the Holiday Inn Armada Room in the 1980 *Blues Brothers* movie, before they are talked into rejoining the Blues Brothers band. Lineup: Murphy Dunne (keyboards), Donald "Duck" Dunn (bass), Steve "The Colonel" Cropper (guitar), Willie "Too Big" Hall (drums), and Tom "Bones" Malone (trombonist). The entire band are all seasoned professional musicians and veteran session men who did all their own playing. *TRIVIA TIME!* Murphy Dunne also did keyboards on the *Lenny and the Squigtones* album. See also **The Blues Brothers; The Good Ole Boys; Lenny and the Squigtones; Street Slim.**

MURPHY, "BLEEDING GUMS" — African-American blues saxophonist and running character from the hit FOX animated TV show *The Simpsons*. His character (voiced by Ron Taylor) was introduced in the first season episode "Moaning Lisa" (02/11/90), where he became an inspiration and mentor to little saxophonist Lisa Simpson (voiced by Yeardley Smith). Which is good, because she doesn't get any support from her music teacher Mr. Largo, who doesn't approve of Lisa's outbursts of jazz improvisation. Murphy penned the "I Never Had an Italian Suit Blues" and could be found at the Springfield club, The Jazz Hole. He had one album in the late 50s–early 60s, *Sax on the Beach*, tragically the same title as a John Tesh release. His character was killed off in the particularly maudlin "Round Springfield" episode (04/30/95), probably because they had nothing better to do with him by then. See also **The Beach Boys Experience; The Be Sharps; Johnny Bobby; Johnny Calhoun; Captain Bart and the**

Tequila Mockingbirds; The Crazy Old Man Singers; Cyanide; Gulliver Dark; Ferl Dixon and His Second Helping Boys; Funky C Funky Do; Garfunkel, Messina, Oates, and Lisa; Hooray for Everything; Kovenant; Krusty and the Krums; The Larry Davis Experience; Little Timmy and the Shebangs; Loggins and Oates; Lurleen Lumpkin; M. C. Safety and the Caution Crew; Melvin and the Squirrels; The Party Posse; The Rappin' Rabbis; Red Breem and His Band of Some Esteem; The Satin Knights; The Steve Sax Trio; Testament; Blind Willie Witherspoon; The Ya-Hoo Recovering Alcoholic Jug Band; Yodelin' Zeke.

MUSICIANS FOR FREE-RANGE CHICKENS — Funniest *Saturday Night Live* musical benefit parody since "Rock Against Yeast." A bunch of celebrities sing to protest er, NON-free-range chickens. That week's (04/20/91) musical guest Michael Bolton joins the fun, hamming it up singing "Brothers and sisters, let the chickens be." The big, big roster of stars includes Casey Kasem (Dana Carvey), Whoopi Goldberg (Chris Rock), Lenny Kravitz (Tim Meadows), Kenny Rogers (Phil Hartman), Diana Ross (Jan Hooks), Mick Jagger (Mike Myers), Axl Rose (Adam Sandler), Cyndi Lauper (Victoria Jackson), Carnie Wilson (Chris Farley), Tom Petty (David Spade), and Bob Dylan (Dana Carvey).

MYSTIK SPIRAL — Cartoon alternative-rock quartet from MTV's *Beavis and Butt-head* spinoff, *Daria.* The band first appeared in the "Road Worrier" episode (07/07/97), composed of just Jane Lane's slacker brother Trent (voiced by Alvaro J. Gonzalez), and hunky airhead Jesse Moreno (voiced by Willy Schwenz) rehearsing "Icebox Girl" in the basement. The other band members (voiced by Nick Campbell, bass, and Max Tyler, drums) didn't appear until the "Ill" episode (07/06/98), after which the band appeared in various other episodes, playing real gigs and everything.

NADA — A punk band from the 1983 movie *Get Crazy* (aka *Flip Out*). Real-life punk rocker Lee Ving of real punk band Fear played animalistic singer Piggy. Lori Eastside played the band's leader, Nada. See also **Auden**; **King Blues**; **Reggie Wanker**.

NATHAN, ROSALIND "ROZ" — From Pete Townshend's (of The Who) 1993 concept album/rock opera/concert film, *Psychoderelict.* She's really the manipulative, deceitful rock journalist Ruth Streeting (Jan Ravens). She hates rock star Ray High, and blasts him on her radio show, *Streeting's Street,* but cuts a secret deal with his frustrated manager, betting that she can get him to record again. She pretends to be this aspiring artist and starts a correspondence with him. Suckered hook, line, and sinker, he opens up to her and even sends her a demo of his song "Flame," which she records and sends back to him. Ruth goes back on her show to blast Ray some more, twisting all his letters to "Roz" to make Ray look bad, and uses the controversy to sell the album by her pseudonym! "Flame" goes to number one. Plus, she has a fling with his manager, Rastus Knight (Linal Haft). See also **Ray High**.

NELLY — Singing cartoon giraffe from the 1961 Warner Bros. cartoon short *Nelly's Folly.* An African safari expedition discovers her and brings her to America and fame. She rises to the top, only to fall back to the bottom over her scandalous affair with a married giraffe. And how often do you hear that phrase?! So she goes back home to Africa. Gloria Wood was the speaking and singing voice of Nelly.

NELSON, TOM—Arch Hall Jr. is the boy with the unfortunate face and the dad who won't stop putting his son in movies. His face is too small for his head. It's all mushed up there in the center. Also, he won't stop singing. In the wonderfully titled *Eegah* (1962), he plays this teen with his own band. He sings the songs "Vickie" and "Valerie." Fortunately, he runs out of girls' names that start with "V" just before his gal Roxy Miller (Marilyn Manning) is kidnapped by throwback caveguy Eegah (Richard Kiel). The film's one redeeming moment has Nelson trying his level teen best to gut-punch Eegah into submission. Eegah stares at him puzzled, then, with one mighty bitch slap, sends Nelson flying into all-too-brief unconsciousness. It's a real battle of the uglies. No wonder Roxy seems conflicted: Richard Kiel in caveman getup is better looking than boyfriend Tom, with his insane frosted pompadour. Nelson's unnamed drums/guitar/bass/sax combo (played by Arch Hall Jr. and the Archers) plays the hotel pool party just before Eegah attacks. Come to think of it, maybe that's why he attacks! Then, tragically, Eegah is gunned down, and not Tom Nelson. Be sure not to miss the scene where Roxy's dad (Arch Hall Sr.) has to coach his daughter on how not to get raped by a giant caveman. *TRIVIA TIME!* This film was also done up by *Mystery Science Theater 3000* (08/28/93). See also **Bud Eagle; Britt Hunter.**

NEPTUNES, THE—This cartoon band is from the gawd-awful 1976 Hanna-Barbera cartoons series *Jabberjaw*, featuring the second most annoying cartoon character ever, after Scrappy Doo. Jabberjaw (Frank Welker) is the great white shark drummer of the band who speaks in a bad imitation of Stooge Curly

Howard and Rodney Dangerfield. The band played in the underwater cities of the future—you know, remember in the 70s we were all going to live in underwater cities in the future? The other members were bassist Clamhead (voiced by Barry Gordon), keyboardist Bubbles (voiced by Julie McWhirter), guitarist Biff (voiced by Tommy Cook), and Shelly (voiced by Patricia Parris) on vocals/tambourine.

NERDS, THE—From a *Saturday Night Live* sketch (01/28/78) featuring the original appearance of recurring nerd characters Lisa Loopner (Gilda Radner) and Todd DiLaMuca (Bill Murray). Only, in this early incarnation, they're a band called The Nerds along with that week's guest host Robert Klein, playing "nerd rock" and pushing their album, *Trying Desperately to Be Liked*, to the radio DJ (Dan Aykroyd). The songs mentioned include: "I'll Give You My Lunch Money," "I Can't Help It If I Have Egg Salad on My Retainer," and "Let My Head Up Out of the John and I'll Give You Tomorrow's Lunch Money." The sketch's writer was inspired by Elvis Costello and how nerdy a rock star he was.

NEW KIDS IN A DITCH—See **The Party Posse.**

NEW MAIN STREET SINGERS, THE—The 2003 comedy *A Mighty Wind* gives you three fake bands for the price of one. The death of legendary 60s folk promoter Irving Steinbloom (Stuart Luce) kicks into action a tribute concert orchestrated by his uptight son Jonathan (Bob Balaban). He brings together three of his father's biggest acts: The Folksmen, Mitch and Mickey, and these guys. The original band, The Main Street Singers, was created in 1960, when quartet The Klapper Family united with quintet The Village Folk Ensemble after jamming together at a hootenanny. VFE leader George Menschell (Brian Riley) became entranced, hearing the big harmonies he'd been dreaming of, and combined the two groups into a "neuftet." The VFE lineup: George Menschell, Fred Knox (Todd Leiberman), Chuck Wiseman (Jared Nelson Smith), Ramblin' Sandy Pitnik (Marty Belafsky), and Bill Weyburn (Ryan Raddatz). The Klapper Family were a genuine family act composed of Ma Klapper (*Saturday Night Live*'s Mary Gross), Pa Klapper (Michael Baser), and their children, played by Matthew Joy and Laura Harris. In 1961, The Main Street Singers released their first album, *Strolling Down Main Street*, the start of a series of thirty albums that would be released before the group finally broke up in 1971. Some of their other albums are *Sunny Side Up*, *Songs of Good Cheer*, and a Christmas album *The Main Street Singers in Bethlehem*. In 1980, Menschell ran into manager Mike LaFontaine (Fred Willard), who got Menschell (Paul Dooley) to resurrect the group as The New Main Street Singers, with eight new members, to play amusement parks and cruise ships. Forged in the same hell that gave us Up With People and The New Christy Minstrels, they have all the musical soul of a white-bread sandwich with a slice of white-bread in the middle. If possible, the new version of the band is even more irritatingly wholesome and toothpaste-commercial nice. New members include married couple Terry and Laurie Bohner (titter!) (John Michael Higgins and Jane Lynch) and Sissy Knox (Parker Posey), a daughter of original member Fred Knox and a former teen runaway. After the reunion concert, LaFontaine gets the whole band its own TV show, *Supreme Folk*, where they play the members of the U.S. Supreme Court who like to kick back with some folk tunes after a hard day of constitutional law! ***TRIVIA TIME!*** Bill Cobbs, who played jazzman Del Paxton in *That Thing You Do*, has a bit role in the movie as an unnamed blues musician. See also **The Folksmen**; **Jack and Judy**; **Mitch and Mickey**.

A MIGHTY WIND
(2002, SONY)

THE MIGHTY WIND soundtrack is a true delight, even if you hate folk music. Maybe especially if you hate folk music. The Folksmen's hokey, dippy novelty "hit" "Old Joe's Place" and the ethnically insulting "Loco Man" help underscore everything that was wrong with the early 60s folk revival in the first place. The tracks by The New Main Street Singers underscore everything that then WENT wrong with the folk revival, when whatever loose, rough-hewn charm the genre might have had got burnished down into mindless cheery tripe by acoustic guitar-wielding, tightly harmonized clone armies like The Serendipity Singers and The New Christy Minstrels. For a perfect example, compare The Folksmen's "original" version of "Never Did No Wanderin'" on the album with the Mitch-Millerized version by The New Main Street Singers. This group can give even the most brain-dead of songs a lobotomy. The NMSS also have the second funniest track on the album, "The Good Book Song," which, for being such a funny song, strangely only appeared in the movie under the end credits. The flat-out funniest song on the album is one that never appeared anywhere in the movie, but has been a staple of The Folksmen's scant live performances: their folk-a-fied version of The Rolling Stones "Start Me Up." It's an absolute scream, and the cream of this album's rich, creamy crop. The Mitch and Mickey tunes represent a kinder, gentler folk music, and are the ones that are hardest to tell are parody, especially the obligatory Civil War tune "The Ballad of Bobby and June." With its martial beat, bittersweet melody, and oddly affecting lyrics, it seems out of place here, too much like the real McCoy. This difference in tone is partially due to the different artists' songs being penned by different writers; Eugene Levy (with occasional help by Catherine

O'Hara) created the M&M songs, while McKean, Shearer, and Guest composed The Folksmen's material. Also, The Folksmen's, songs have had a more than a decade of road-testing under their belt that the other tunes lack. The album closes appropriately with all three bands uniting to perform the title track, which sounds like retarded, third-rate Dylan crossed with a sniggering twelve-year-old's fart jokes. It works beautifully; a summation of the movie's entire theme—the answers, my friend, were "Blowin' in the Wind," because artists like those parodied were generating so much of it themselves.

NEW MONKEES, THE — In 1986, the twentieth anniversary of the original Monkees debut sparked a second life for the band. Bert Schneider and Bob Rafelson, the guys who invented The Monkees, thought: why not reinvent the wheel? So, in 1987, they came out with four new kids, a new album, and a new thirteen-episode, syndication-only show, *The New Monkees*. It bombed hard, critically and commercially. Fans of the old show didn't want NEW Monkees, they wanted the OLD Monkees. Heck, they should have given THEM a show. Jared Chandler (guitar), Dino Kovas (drums), Marty Ross (bass), and Larry Saltis (guitar)—were the big-haired chumps chosen for this thankless job. They all lived in a big, crazy, computer-controlled mansion and got into speeded-up shenanigans bordering on shrill. See also **The Monkees**.

NEW ROD TORFULSON'S ARMADA FEATURING HERMAN MENDERCHUCK, THE — See **Armada**.

NEW SHEBANGS FEATURING BIG TIMMY, THE — See **Little Timmy and the Shebangs**.

NICE NEIGHBORS, THE — Carmel Pinkum is an impossibly nice lady singer in the "Vive La Differ-

ence" sketch (05/17/87) of *The Tracey Ullman Show*. She is inexplicably auditioning for a bunch of big-haired metal heads whose band didn't get a name. She mentions this band, her old act, with their slogan "People for Positivity," which sounds like an Up With People–esque nightmare. When the audition goes poorly (duh!) she breaks into a show tune about being different. Wait, she breaks into song during a singing audition?! Say what? Pinkum was played by Tracey Ullman. The band was played by John Snyder, Tom Dugan, and Michael Cerveris. See also **Ariel**; **Gulliver Dark**; **Kristy Muldoon**.

NICK THE LOUNGE SINGER — Bill Murray played this cheeseball character to the hilt in eleven sketches during his tenure on *Saturday Night Live*, starting in 1977. Wherever people needed a song or two, there he would be. The character's last name changed from venue to venue, but he never traveled without accompanist Paul (Paul Schaffer) on keyboards. See also **The Culps**; **The Sweeney Sisters**.

WHAT IS NICK THE UNGE SINGER HIDING?
BY CHARLES REMPEL

On the surface, Bill Murray's long-running recurring *Saturday Night Live* character Nick the Lounge Singer seems to be a great guy. He's singing the songs and cracking the jokes that bring cheer to the otherwise cheerless, as well as adding now-classic lyrics to the *Star Wars* theme. However, Nick never had a consistent home base for his gigs, or even a consistent last name. Consider these places he's been, along with his aliases (which conveniently allude to his locations):

(continued)

Lake Minnehonka's Breezy Point Lodge: Nick Summers

Meatloaf Mountain's Powder Room: Nick Winters

Pocomount's Honeymoon Room: Nick Springs

Sands Strip North Oasis: Nick Sands

Auto Train (headed for Orlando): Nick Rails

TransEastern Airlines VIP Lounge: Nick Wings

Cape Farval (an early-warning base): Nick Borealis

Greg Lieberman's Bar Mitzvah: Nick Collins

Trader Nick's (a Buffalo-area Polynesian bar): Nick Lava

Riverboat Queen's Paddlewheel Lounge: Nick Rivers

Crestwood Minimum Security Prison Detention Center and Warehouse: Nick Slammer

Always moving around, always changing his name. Sounds like a man with a secret. What's Nick hiding? After consulting with finest fake criminologists and profilers, here are the five most logical possibilities:

1. *He committed a crime*—He's been in hundreds of bars, so he's probably seen hundreds of bar fights. The smart money says he tried to break up one fight, but in doing so he accidentally killed a man, and so did the only thing he could think of: he ran. He's still running to this day.

2. *He's accused of a crime he didn't commit*—Just like Dr. Richard Kimble from *The Fugitive*, Nick is being framed, and he's on the lam to clear his name, find the real perpetrator, and lift people's spirits through song. Okay, maybe not JUST like Dr. Kimble, but that's only because the good doctor never sang.

3. *He's about to commit a crime*—Oh, he hasn't done anything wrong yet, but it's coming. The best bet is he's stalking a victim across the country, waiting to strike.

4. *He works for organized crime*—This theory makes a lot of sense. He's got a cool nickname (Nick the Lounge Singer), he has a long list of aliases, and he's never in one spot long enough to be hassled by The Man. Plus his ownership roles with the Sands Strip North Oasis and Trader

Nick's throws in the possibility of money-laundering operations.

5. *He is Keyser Soze*—If you've seen *The Usual Suspects*, you know that Verbal Kint (Kevin Spacey) is crimelord supreme Keyser Soze, but have you ever considered on whose life the movie is based? Nick was seen on the lounge circuit in the late 1970s, then disappeared. He appeared once in the mid-1980s in a prison, supposedly to entertain the incarcerated. But didn't Keyser Soze go to jail to recruit criminals for his scheme? It makes you think, doesn't it?

NIGHTINGALE, NICK—Pianist and medical school dropout played by Todd Field in Stanley Kubrick's final film, *Eyes Wide Shut* (1999). He runs into former med-school classmate Dr. William "Bill" Harford (Tom Cruise) at a holiday party. This Seattleite was hired for the party because, in his words, "I know my Cole Porter and I work cheap." Later, the two meet again as Nick is finishing up a gig at Greenwich Village's Café Sonata. Over a scotch and soda, Nick mentions to Bill that he's got another gig that night—a weird late-night gig where he plays classical music blindfolded. Bill whines at Nick until Nick tells him enough about the party to waken Bill's gate-crashing instincts. For his trouble, Nick may be killed (we never really find out for sure). The moral: Never tell secrets to Tom Cruise. Dominic Harlan was the real fingers on the piano.

NIGHTMARE, THE—This AC/DC-inspired badass hard rock band is from the 1977 Muppet TV special *Emmet Otter's Jug-Band Christmas*. Arrogant, rude city folk, they come up to Waterville's First Annual Christmas Talent Contest to blow the rubes away with their slick, professional performance of their song "River Bottom Nightmare Band." They totally win the talent show, crushing competitors Emmet

Otter and his mom. This band of puppets could outrock many a human band. According to their lyrics, they're so badass they don't even brush their teeth! The band featured a bear on keyboards, a rat on guitar, a snake on bass (which is really impressive, since he has no hands), a frog on drums, and a spitting-fish dancer. You can't get much more ethnically diverse than that! See also **The Frogtown Hollow Jubilee Jug-Band.**

NO REFUND—Real boy band *NSYNC shows they either have a marvelous sense of humor or are totally clueless chumps when they participate in a sketch spoofing boy bands during their appearance (03/11/00) on *Saturday Night Live* as that week's musical guests. They portray the opening act for 7 Degrees Celsius, another spoof boy band made up of cast members. No Refund sings "Supersize It." ***TRIVIA TIME!*** *NSYNC member Lance Bass sprained his ankle during rehearsal for the show! Okay, okay, so it's not GOOD trivia. See also **7 Degrees Celsius.**

NO VACANCY—Guitarist Dewey Finn (Jack Black) lives to rock. He doesn't even care if there's an audience—until he tries to stage-dive. Unfortunately, the rest of his band considers him an "embarrassment," what with his twenty-minute solos and all, and votes him out of the group. Oh the humanity! Kicked out of a rock band for rocking TOO hard! And all in the first fifteen minutes of *The School of Rock* (2003). Band member Theo (Adam Pascal) replaces Dewey with tattooed pretty boy Spider (Lucas Babin). Dewey has his revenge when he takes his new band School of Rock up against them at the WROK Battle of the Bands concert. No Vacancy wins the big check (with "Heal Me, I'm Heartsick"), but School of Rock wins the audience's hearts. Aww! ***TRIVIA TIME!*** The band's song "Fight" was written by Warren Fitzgerald, a member of real punk act The Vandals. See also **Maggot Death;**

School of Rock.

NOODLES, THE—Bauer/Bower (Scott Thompson) is a stoner looking for pot in the "In Search of Pot Skit" of sketch show *The Kids in the Hall* (1989–94). He meets the Devil (Mark McKinney), who doesn't want his soul, as he has plenty already. But he will make him eternally high if Bauer/Bower gives him his jean jacket, 'cause he's starting this band, with like early T. Rex influences and stuff like that? See also **Armada; Cancer Boy; Death Lurks; Mississippi Gary; Tammy.**

NORM WOOSTER SINGERS, THE—White-bread 50s Ray Coniff–type pablum. They're never actually shown or mentioned in *That Thing You Do* (1996), but their hit, "Lovin' You Lots and Lots," plays over the opening credits, helping set the tone of Midwest America in 1964. Their song (composed by Tom Hanks himself) and a fictitious bio can be found in the soundtrack album's liner notes. See also **Elizabeth Anne; Blue Spot Trio; The Chantrellines; Diane Dane; The Echoes; Freddy Fredrickson; The G Men; The Heardsmen; The Hollyhocks; Jon D and the Walkers; Legends of Brass; Marilyn Lovell and the Geminis; Del Paxton; The Saturn 5; The Tempos; The Trends; Two Eriks; The Vicksburgs; The Wonders.**

NORMA JEAN MONSTER—This duo was a Marilyn Manson parody (complete with face paint) that went to a New Age relationship camp in a sketch from HBO's *Mr. Show.* They had a blast! Dave Cross was Norma Jean Monster, Bob Odenkirk was Adolph Hepburn. (Also in the sketch was Smoosh.) From the "Flat-Top Tony and the Purple Canoes" episode (10/10/97). See also **The Beetletown Players; Larry Black; Livingston Brewster; Willips Brighton; Dickie Crickets; Indomitable Spirit; Kid Jersey; Kill or Be Killed; C. S. Lewis Jr.; Ho-**

race Loeb; **Marilyn Monster; John Baptiste Philouza; Professor Murder; Puscifer; Salini; Smoosh; Old Swerdlow; Three Times One Minus One; Titannica; Sir Lloyd Wilson Webber; Wyckyd Sceptre; Daffy "Mal" Yinkleyankle.**

NORTH AMERICA — See **Veneer.**

NOT NOEL COWARD — In Monty Python's final and greatest sketch film, *Monty Python's The Meaning of Life* (1983), Eric Idle portrays this terribly, terribly witty pianist with the slicked-back hair at the ritzy restaurant where Mr. Creosote (Terry Jones) explodes. He sings "The Not Noel Coward Song," which is all about penises. So despite what you might think, he is clearly not Noel Coward. See also **Arthur Ewing and His Musical Mice; Bolton Choral Society; Johann Gambolputty de von Ausfern-schplenden-schlitter-crasscrenbon-fried-digger-dingle-dangle-dongle-dungle-burstein-von-knacker-thrasher-apple-banger-horowitz-ticolensic-grander-knotty-spelltinkle-grandlich-grumblemeyer-spelterwasser-kurstlich-himbleeisen-bahnwagen-gutenabend-bitte-ein-nürnburger-bratwustle-gerspurten-mitz-weimache-luber-hundsfut-gumberaber-shönendanker-kalbsfleisch-mittler-aucher von Hautkopft of Ulm; The Herman Rodriguez Four; The Hunlets; Jackie Charlton and the Tonettes; Arthur "Two Sheds" Jackson; Not Tony Bennett; Rachel Toovey Bicycle Choir; Inspector Jean-Paul Zatapathique.**

NOT TONY BENNETT — From legendary sketch comedy troupe Monty Python's final and greatest sketch film, *Monty Python's The Meaning of Life* (1983). Newly arrived denizens of Heaven are serenaded by this gent with a white-guy-afro (Graham Chapman), who, despite what you might think, is clearly listed in the credits as Not Tony Bennett. He sings "Christmas in Heaven," a rich Vegas-y show-stopper production number with all the hot topless angels in Santa-type costumes you can could ever want. See also **Arthur Ewing and His Musical Mice; Bolton Choral Society; Johann Gambolputty de von Ausfern-schplenden-schlitter-crasscrenbon-fried-digger-dingle-dangle-dongle-dungle-burstein-von-knacker-thrasher-apple-banger-horowitz-ticolensic-grander-knotty-spelltinkle-grandlich-grumblemeyer-spelter-wasser-kurstlich-himbleeisen-bahnwagen-gutenabend-bitte-ein-nürnburger-bratwustle-gerspurten-mitz-weimache-luber-hundsfut-gumberaber-shönendanker-kalbsfleisch-mittler-aucher von Hautkopft of Ulm; The Herman Rodriquez Four; The Hunlets; Jackie Charlton and the Tonettes; Arthur "Two Sheds" Jackson; Not Noel Coward; Rachel Toovey Bicycle Choir; Inspector Jean-Paul Zatapathique.**

NOTORIOUS FLUFFY G — Brak's favorite rapper in the "Gimme a Brak: War Next Door" (09/09/01) episode of the Cartoon Network's *Brak Show*, a spinoff of *Space Ghost: Coast to Coast*. Carmine (voiced by C. Martin Croker), a hideous pink lump that has been lodged in Zorak's throat for years, helped Fluffy G rise from "a ball of lint in a fat man's pocket" to a star with the biggest mansion in mansionland.

NOVA, EDDIE — See **The Skye Band.**

NUNS IN A BLENDER — During the "Song for Margo" (3/26/95) episode of animated show *The Critic*, Margo Sherman (voiced by Nancy Cartwright), younger sister of the titular critic (John Lovitz), falls in love with Johnny Wrath (voiced by Todd Louiso), the lead singer of "the most relevant band on the grunge-rock scene today." See also **Cyrus Tompkins.**

NUTTY SQUIRRELS, THE—Beatnikified *Chipmunks* knockoff put together by hipsters Don Elliot and Sascha Burland. They employed the same squeaky voices-via-tape-speed trickery, but these tricks weren't for kids. This duo was way cool, Daddy-o. They sported suits, berets, scat-singing, and they did no kowtowing to any damn David Seville, that's for sure. Their album *The Nutty Squirrels* (1960) even featured top jazzmen like saxophonist Cannonball Adderly. The single "Uh! Oh! Part 2" went to # 14 on November 30, 1959, a year after The Chipmunks first topped the charts. The next year, a hundred syndicated five-minute cartoon shorts were rush-released by Transfilm-Wilde in a deliberate, successful attempt to beat the Chipmunks show (suffering production delays) to the airwaves. Alas, too out there for most markets, the cartoons quickly faded from TV, and after two more albums—*Bird Watching* (1960) and *The Nutty Squirrels Sing A Hard Day's Night and Other Smashes* (1964)—The Nutty Squirrels faded as well. See also **The Chipmunks**.

N.W.H. (NIGGAZ WITH HATS)— Rap trio and focus of the bawdy, profanity-laden 1993 comedy *Fear of a Black Hat*, referred to by some as "Spiñal Rap," for its similarity to *This Is Spiñal Tap*. The mockumentary (is "rapumentary" a word?) showcased the group's trials and tribulations with rivals The Jam Boys, spoofed the conventions of rap, and detailed the band's breakup into solo acts. Lineup: laid-back Tone Def (Mark Christopher Lawrence), violent Tasty Taste (Larry B. Scott), and egotistic Ice Cold

(Rusty Cundieff). There were plenty of other spoof rap artists in the movie, mainly as one-joke ponies: lame white rapper Vanilla Sherbet (Devin Kamienny); Salt 'n' Pepa spoof Parsley, Sage, Rosemary and Thyme (K. Front, LaVerne Anderson, and Deborah Swisher), and a plethora of "Ice"-named variants too minor to mention.

OCEAN BOTTOM NIGHTMARE BAND, THE—Band of animatronic weasels that has won the undersea Battle of the Groups for the past ten years. Unfortunately, their eleventh try for the gold (using "Fishin' Hole," stolen from the Mahatmamas) during the "Splitsville" episode (11/23/03) of *Sealab 2021* was interrupted by a three-way girl fight and a Sealab explosion. The name is a spoof of "River Bottom Nightmare Band," the song sung

N.W.H. (Niggaz With Hats)

by The Nightmare in the Muppet special, *Emmet Otter's Jug-Band Christmas*. See also **The Mahatmamas**; **MC Chris**; **The Nightmare**.

O'CONNELL, SKINHEAD—From the "Toon TV" episode (11/09/92) of cartoon *Tiny Toon Adventures*. Shirley the Loon (voiced by Gail Matthius) with a shaved head sings the quickie Sinead O'Connor parody "Nothing Comes Close to Yul," a tribute to Yul Brynner and his baldness. See also **Def Zepplin**; **Fuddonna**; **Ruffee**; **Vanilla Lice**.

O'CONNER, CARLOS—Pop singer whose career is cooling in the "On the Flip Side" episode (12/07/66) of anthology show *ABC Stage 67*. Carlos (real singer Ricky Nelson) and his self-pitying manager Jerome (Will Mackenzie) are flying back from London, bemoaning the lackluster state of his career. Where once he had two singles in the top ten and chartered a private jet from London to New York City, now his latest record *Beck and Call* is played only in supermarkets and airplane headphones, and he has to fly back tourist-class, like an animal! A filthy, filthy animal! It doesn't look like Starspun Records will renew his contract, and Carlos refuses to get a group; it's all about groups these days, it seems. On top of that, he's twenty-five years old! Ancient, in pop terms. Even the bellhop pities him and gives him change back from his tip. Carlos prays for a miracle, and unlike, say, cancer patients and orphans, he gets it. An angelic pop group called The Celestials makes it their twenty-four-hour mission to remake his career. Sure, they screw it up once, but idiot Carlos keeps rejecting their help, even after HE DISCOVERS THEY'RE ANGELS! Now that's stubborn! Naturally his mind has to be changed via song, in this case, "Try to See It My Way." The Celestials beef up his sound to be more "now," and after a heavily publicized gig at Juanita's Place, Vertigo Records signs them. Nutsy

Vertigo head Don Prospect (Anthony Holland) records them singing "Take a Broken Heart" and rushes the single out, only to discover, to his horror, that The Celestials didn't record onto the tape (what with them all supernatural and all). Prospect—"It's rotten! Just a singer and a song—it's medieval!" Panicky, he tries to recall the record, but it's too late . . . it's a hit! Prospect knew it all along. The single tops the pops for ten weeks and soon Carlos is opening the London Palladium. All's well that ends well . . . except for those cancer patients and orphans. Now, why a character named "Carlos" is being played by Ricky Nelson, who helped put the white in white bread, is a mystery you'll have to ask writer Robert Emmett. *TRIVIA TIME!* All the songs in the show were written by the legendary songwriting team of Burt Bacharach and Hal David, doing some less than legendary work. A soundtrack album was released, but good luck finding it. See also **Bernice and Her Mammals**; **The Celestials**; **Chuck Roast and the Rares**; **The Harpoons**; **Heinrich and the West Berlin Nine**; **The Hors D'Oeuvres**.

OCTO RAYMOND AND HIS ALL-MOLLUSK ORCHESTRA—Octopus-themed bit-player supervillain with an all-octopus orchestra in the "Armless but Not Harmless" episode (09/25/95) of FOX animated superhero spoof *The Tick*. They play the 45th Annual Enemy Awards, a supervillain awards show.

OLIVER, LILA ROSE—Mixed-race singer (Lonette McKee) at the hottest nightspot in 1928 Harlem, The Cotton Club, in Francis Ford Coppola's 1984 gangsters-meet-musicals crossbreed movie of the same name. Club tap dancer Sandman Williams (Gregory Hines) won't leave her alone, proposing marriage after her every breath, but she keeps him at arm's length. Since they're just a subplot, they get dropped for a while while mob stuff happens and a montage shows us the Great Depression hitting, which then affects no character in the movie in any way whatsoever. If anything, they're all BETTER off after it! Then, several years later, we see that Lila's passing for white and singing under the name Angelina at mob-owned Vera's Club, where, we learn, she used to be with Ruth Edding and the Bluebells. Sandman tracks her down though, and they reconcile—so much so they need a hotel room for an hour, nudge, nudge. Lonette did her own singing on "Ill Wind." See also **Vera Cicero; Dixie Dwyer.**

OMAR AND THE DAYCARES—From the 1983 animated feature film *Rock and Rule.* Hero Omar (voiced by Paul Le Mat) and comic-relief bumblers Stretch and Dizzy, after being tricked by evil super-rocker Mok (voiced by Don Francks) into giving up the search for their lead singer Angel, are drugged up six ways to Sunday, and booted outta Nuke York by Mok. Omar, Stretch (voiced by Greg Duffell), and Dizzy (voiced by Dan Hennessey) go back to Ohmtown and form this crappier, happier band while still tripping. Club owner and rat man (or is that redundant?) Mylar (voiced by Martin Lavut) is not happy; the girl Angel (voiced by Susan Roman) was the big draw. They eventually snap out of it in time to save the day. See also **Mok.**

1 PLUS 2 + ½—The backup band for Mike McCoy (Elvis Presley) in *Spinout* (1966). The band consists of guitarist Larry (Jimmy Hawkins), bassist Curly (Jack Mullaney), and drummer Les (Deborah Walley). Les has the hots for McCoy, just like every other woman in the movie, but ends up with a Santa Barbara cop who shares her passion for gourmet cooking. The best thing about this group is that they're almost the Three Stooges: there's a Larry and a Curly, but instead of Moe there's Les. Guess sometimes Les is Moe! See also **Mike McCoy.**

ONEDERS, THE—See **The Wonders.**

OOZING MEAT—Rock band Kelly Bundy (Christina Applegate) wants to see bad, in the "Buck Saves the Day" episode (09/24/89) of sitcom *Married with Children.* We never see or hear the band, but they must be damn good—tickets for their Chicagoland show run $175! Damn! See also **Burned Beyond Recognition; Jimmy Dick and the Night Sticks; Joanie and the Slashettes; Otitis Media; Shoes 'n' Socks; Tears and Vomit; The Tuxedos; The Wanker Triplets; The Why; Yodeling Andy.**

OREOS, THE—In the 1976 remake of the classic 1927 film *A Star Is Born,* the milieu is changed from acting to music. Barbra Streisand plays young singer Esther Hoffman. She performs in this singing group with two African-American women (played by Venetta Fields and Clydie King), hence the name. Get it? She falls for falling rock star John Norman Howard (Kris Kristofferson), for some unfathomable reason. She rises, he continues to fall. *TRIVIA TIME!* The soundtrack album and Streisand's single "Evergreen" from the movie both topped the charts in 1977. See also **John Norman Howard.**

ORIGINALS, THE—See **The Regulars.**

OTIS, CLARK—One of the artifacts of the 70s fad for 50s nostalgia was the 1978 flick *American Hot Wax,* which dramatized real-life Cleveland DJ Alan Freed's championing of rock and roll. Real rockers Jerry Lee Lewis, Chuck Berry, and Screamin' Jay Hawkins appeared as themselves, but, for some reason, fictionalized versions of other real groups and artists were created, like this one, played by Charles Greene. See also **The Chesterfields; The Delights; Professor La Plano and the Planotones; Timmy and the Tulips.**

OTIS DAY AND THE KNIGHTS—All-black late-50s/early-60s rock-and-roll/R&B band from the 1978 comedy *Animal House*. They played "Shout" at the fraternity toga party and "Shama Lama Ding Dong" at the all-black Dexter Lakes Club (both on the soundtrack album). Actor DeWayne Jessie played Otis Day (lip-synching to the singing of Lloyd Williams). After the movie, DeWayne kept a version of the band alive, touring, releasing albums and a 1986 concert video, *Otis, My Man!* **TRIVIA TIME!** The onscreen band included blues/jazz guitarist Robert Cray as the bass player, believe it or not. The rest of the band was Robert Bailey, Sonny King, Tommy Smith, and Juan Steen.

OTITIS MEDIA — Band mentioned in the "Naughty but Niece" episode (09/25/94) of *Married with Children*. Also the name of a type of ear infection! See also **Burned Beyond Recognition; Jimmy Dick and the Night Sticks; Joanie and the Slashettes; Oozing Meat; Shoes 'n' Socks; Tears and Vomit; The Tuxedos; The Wanker Triplets; The Why; Yodeling Andy**.

OTTER, ALICE — See **The Frogtown Hollow Jubilee Jug-Band**.

OWENS, ROLAND — See **Jem and the Holograms**.

PAIN — Rotten, no-goodnik punk band in the "Battle of the Bands" (01/31/82) episode of 70s cop show *CHiPs*. They steal guitars from another artist's van (Snow Pink) and let it roll down a hill, trash a club bathroom, threaten the owner with a knife, tie him up, and start a riot at the club, all of which would be admirable in a punk band if it wasn't just to win some lame-ass battle of the bands. See also **Moloch; Snow Pink**.

THE BATTLE OF THE BANDS

A "battle of the bands" is a plot device typical of lazy, lazy television writers attempting to artificially generate conflict in a musical setting, where none previously existed. At all. You didn't see The Beatles pushing The Dave Clark Five into a wall, or The Rolling Stones stealing Freddie and the Dreamers' amps, did you? The writers ludicrously posit the protagonists' band against an "evil" band, as if such a thing existed. The evil band, invented out of whole cloth, will be "cooler" than the protagonists (evil always is, isn't it?) and play more "evil" music: harder rock, rap, metal, punk, etc. And, of course, they will single-mindedly stop at nothing to win the totally unrealistic high stakes at, er, stake: large cash prizes, recording contracts, opening slot for a national act, trip to another planet, what have you.

In reality, "battles of the bands" are contests typically held by small, crappy clubs looking to boost attendance on slow nights. Participation is usually disdained by artists of any real talent or caliber. Face it, when's the last time you saw *NSYNC competing against those dirty cheaters in Nine Inch Nails? Contestant bands are typically poor-quality high school/college/local bands grinding their way through painful cover versions of hit songs while a sparse audience of girlfriends (possibly augmented with relatives and/or coworkers) cheer. Winners usually receive only a small cash prize and bragging rights; competing bands do not find this worth the trouble to attempt to sabotage each other with wacky complicated schemes, not to mention their lacking the wit and will to make the attempt.

But hey, in the end, it's not about who kicks the hardest jams, or who busts the dopest rhymes, it's about coming together under the same roof, trying your best, and helping the club owner sell more beer!

PARKER, BILLY — Bob Dylan played this reclusive rocker who reemerges to help other rocker, Molly McGuire, to fame in the movie *Hearts of Fire*. (1987). Waitaminute. Bob Dylan?! See also **James Colt**; **Molly McGuire**.

PARLOW, JIMMY — Pop-singing pop star in the 1959 movie *Girls' Town*, played by real singer Paul Anka. He comes to do a charity show at the titular institution, where a crazed fan thinks he's in love with her. This movie was also given the business but good as an episode of *Mystery Science Theater 3000* (07/16/94). *TRIVIA TIME!* Other real singer Mel Tormé plays a hot-roddin' no-goodnik in the film.

PARSLEY, SAGE, ROSEMARY AND THYME — See **N.W.H.**

PARTRIDGE FAMILY, THE — From the extremely popular 1970–74 TV show of the same name. This singing TV family was loosely based on real-life singing family The Cowsills ("Indian Lake"). Apparently they were originally set to star in the series, but the network insisted on Shirley Jones as mom, so the Cowsills bailed rather than not have their real mom involved. Could you honestly tell YOUR mom you're replacing her with Shirley Jones? But later we all got to see Susan Dey naked in various B-movies, so it all

works out. Shirley Partridge (Shirley Jones) was the singing/keyboard-playing single mom, who sang in real life (*Oklahoma!*), but ended up taking a vocal back-seat to feather-haired, feather-talented, teen-heartthrob son Keith Partridge (David Cassidy). As a rock star, he was given lead guitar duties. Any real mom would have demanded he cut his hair and get a real job. Older sister Laurie Partridge (Susan Dey) mimed playing the keyboards for the band. Middle brother Danny Partridge (Danny Bonaduce) was the band's wisecracking, scheming bass player. Little drummer boy Christopher Partridge was played by Jeremy Gelbwaks from 1970 to 1971, until his parents got spooked by the series' enormous popularity

The Partridge Family

and pulled him from the show. He was replaced by Brian Forster for the rest of the show's run. Little Tracy Partridge (Suzanne Crough) was the little girl who played tambourine. Reuben Kincaid (Dave Madden) was their incompetent yet creepy manager. And the lineup would not be complete without the band's iconic, Mondrian-inspired school bus. Of the show's cast, only Shirley Jones's and David Cassidy's voices ever made it onto the Partridges' more than half a dozen albums, all other voices and all of the instruments being done by faceless session players. The band had seven top forty hits during the run of the show, most notably their first, "I Think I Love You," which spent three weeks at # 1 in 1970. After four years, Cassidy tired of the show, yearning to break free to pursue his burgeoning solo career. But even his posing in the buff in *Rolling Stone* magazine couldn't sink the über-wholesome show's ratings. Eventually, Cassidy got too big for his britches, and quit the show despite its high ratings, killing it. He went on to a brief, successful solo career, before crashing and burning in true VH1 *Behind the Music* style. ***TRIVIA TIME!*** There was also a short-lived 1974 Saturday-morning animated cartoon, *The Partridge Family, 2200* A.D.

PARTY POSSE, THE—After taking on rock, country, and barbershop, *The Simpsons* finally get around to manufactured boy bands in the 02/25/01 episode, "New Kids on the Blecch." Classified Records producer L. T. Smash (voiced by Hank Azaria) who put together Boyneudo and New Kids in a Ditch, turns Milhouse Van Houten (voiced by Pamela Hayden), Bart Simpson, Nelson Muntz, and Ralph Wiggum (all three voiced by Nancy Cartwright) into a quartet of preteen crooners, thanks to studio magic and songs like "You're My Special Girl" and "I Gotta Spell Out What I Mean." Unfortunately, as Lisa Simpson (voiced by Yeardley Smith) discovers, the band is really part of the U.S. Navy's Project Boy

Band, and has subliminal messages and backward masking (Yvan Eht Nioj) in their songs ("Drop Da Bomb" and "Let's Re-Up Tonight") to brainwash the youth of America to join the navy. The band ends when the navy tries to stop the project before a planned *Mad Magazine* spoofing, only to have L. T. Smash (really navy Lieutenant L. T. Smash) go nuts and kidnap the band and destroy the *Mad* offices. ***TRIVIA TIME!*** Real boy band *NSYNC guest-starred in the episode as themselves. See also **The Beach Boys Experience; The Be Sharps; Johnny Bobby; Johnny Calhoun; Captain Bart and the Tequila Mockingbirds; The Crazy Old Man Singers; Cyanide; Gulliver Dark; Ferl Dixon and His Second Helping Boys; Funky C Funky Do; Garfunkel, Messina, Oates, and Lisa; Hooray for Everything; Kovenant; Krusty and the Krums; The Larry Davis Experience; Little Timmy and the Shebangs; Loggins and Oates; Lurleen Lumpkin; M. C. Safety and the Caution Crew; Melvin and the Squirrels; "Bleeding Gums" Murphy; The Rappin' Rabbis; Red Breem and His Band of Some Esteem; The Satin Knights; The Steve Sax Trio; Testament; Blind Willie Witherspoon; The Ya-Hoo Recovering Alcoholic Jug Band; Yodelin' Zeke.**

PASTOR K—In the "Reborn to Be Wild" episode (11/09/03) of cartoon *King of the Hill*, preteen Bobby Hill (voiced by Pamela Segall), gets involved with a church youth group. But this ain't your father's church youth group! It's a bunch of hard-core skate punks for Jesus (played by band Sum 41), run by the tattooed badass Pastor K (voiced by David Herman), who's like a Christian Danzig. He's written a twenty-two-minute song about the disciples and plans to play it at the Messiah Fest, if he can remember all the words. Bobby's dad, Hank, is freaked out, especially when Bobby gets a cross earring and wants a Jesus tattoo. He grounds Bobby so he can't attend the Messiah Fest, but Bobby sneaks out and goes anyway. This leads to a confrontation between Pastor K and Hank, but Pastor K's dad, Jessie (voiced by KISS singer Gene Simmons!), intervenes to remind his son Kevin that he's forgetting the fifth commandment: Honor thy mother and father. Hank gives the best summation of Christian rock ever: "Can't you see you're not making Christianity better, you're just making rock and roll worse." See also **The A Men; The Bluegrass Brothers; Cane and the Stubborn Stains; The Dale Gribble Bluegrass Experience; 4 Skore; The Harris Twins; John Redcorn and Big Mountain Fudge Cake; Pimp Franklin.**

PAXTON, DEL — 60s African-American jazz pianist from *That Thing You Do* (1996), the idol of The Wonders' drummer Guy Patterson (Tom Everett Scott). You see Guy playing drums along to Del's album *Time to Blow* (on Capitol) in an opening scene. Later, when The Wonders become actual chart wonders and fly out to Los Angeles, Guy goes to the jazzy Blue Spot Club, actually runs into Del (Bill Cobbs) and drummer Bobby Washington (Robert Wisdom) there, and works up the nerve to buy him a drink and talk to him. That would have been enough for Guy, but no, he runs into him AGAIN at the recording studio and gets to JAM with him, with the tape rolling, on a number Guy calls "Spartacus" (composed by director Tom Hanks). Guy probably should have been hit by a bus immediately afterwards, as this was the highlight of his life. Del also had at least one other album, *Live at the Philadelphia Jazz Junction*, with Bobby Washington on drums. See also **Elizabeth Anne; Blue Spot Trio; The Chantrellines; Diane Dane; The Echoes; Freddy Fredrickson; The G Men; The Heardsmen; The Hollyhocks; Jon D and the Walkers; Legends of Brass; Marilyn Lovell and the Geminis; The Norm Wooster Singers; The**

Saturn 5; The Tempos; The Trends; Two Eriks; The Vicksburgs; The Wonders.

Dell Paxton (Bill Cobbs)

PEARL, BUBBA — See **Dill Scallion and the Dillionaires.**

PEBBLES AND BAMM-BAMM — In the "No Biz Like Show Biz" episode (09/17/65) of prehistoric cartoon The Flintstones, tiny infant tots Pebbles Flintstone (voiced by Jean Vander Pyl) and Bamm-Bamm Rubble (voiced by Don Messick) reveal hitherto unseen musical abilities and are discovered by supermanager Eppy Brianstone (voiced by Bernard Fox), manager of rock group The Termites. He takes over the kids' career and soon the dads are left in the dust. They resort to kidnapping their own children, until it's all revealed to be a dream Fred (voiced by Alan Reed) is having. *TRIVIA TIME!* Rejigger Eppy's name and it should be obvious that it's a nod to the Beatles' manager, Brian Epstein. See also **Ann-Margrock**; **The Beau Brummelstones**; **Jimmy Darrock**; **The Flintstone Canaries**; **"Hot Lips" Hannigan**; **Hi-Fye**; **Rock Roll**.

PEE-WEE RUNT AND HIS ALL-FLEA DIXIELAND BAND — Cartoon flea band in the 1954 Tex Avery cartoon short *Dixieland Droopy*. Pooch John Irving Pettybone (Droopy) lures this circus sideshow attraction into his fur, where, completely hidden, they play hot Dixieland jazz, to the bafflement of onlookers. The "Dog of Mystery" as he becomes known, eventually performs at the Hollywood Bowl. The fleas (rather generously) let Pettybone take all the credit. Pee-Wee, the band's leader, plays trumpet. The other four members play piano, stand-up bass, drums and trombone, albeit very tiny ones. See also **John Irving Pettybone**.

PEEL, RUTTLING ORANGE — African-American Mississippi Delta blues singer from whom The Rutles, The Everly Brothers, Frank Sinatra, and Lawrence Welk all stole their material and style. Or just a big pathological liar. From the 1978 documentary *All You Need Is Cash*. Wonderfully played by Bob Gibson. See also **Arthur Hodgeson and the Kneecaps**; **Les Garçons de la Plage**; **The Machismo Brothers**; **Punk Floyd**; **Blind Lemon Pye**; **The Rutles**.

PELL, SCOTT "WOLFMAN" — See **The Wonders**.

PERMANENT WAVES, THE — From the "Band on the Run" episode (02/26/87) of hit 80s sitcom *Family Ties*. Sibling Jennifer Keaton (Tina Yothers) has this all-girl rock band that auditions for the Leland College 10th reunion dance, where her brother Alex (Michael J. Fox) is on the entertainment committee.

After they wow the committee and win the audition, Alex talks himself into becoming the band's manager. He changes the band's name to The Swinging Corporate Raiders and makes the girls dress up and sing golden oldies. Midway through their now-boring set, they rebel and play their original stuff to the crowd's delight. Band members were keyboard player Kitten (a pre–*Married with Children* Christina Applegate), Ashley Berkhart (Rainbow Phoenix), Brooke Bowman (Yael Nucci), and Jill (Margaret Nagle). *TRIVIA TIME!* Tina Yothers went on to open for Menudo on their 1989 tour, and formed real band, Jaded, in 1996. See also **Eddie Dupre**; **The Polka Boys**.

PETTYBONE, JOHN IRVING — Cartoon character Droopy (voiced by Bill Thompson) plays this dog in the 1954 Tex Avery cartoon *Dixieland Droopy*. John loves Dixieland jazz, and with a little help ends up fulfilling his dream of playing at the Hollywood Bowl. See also **Pee-Wee Runt and His All-Flea Dixieland Band**.

PHILLIPS, BIBI — See **Alphie and Bibi**.

PHILLIPS, MOLLY — In the Disney channel show *So Weird* (1999–2001), daughter Fiona Phillips (Cara DeLizia) tours with her rock star mom, Molly Phillips (Mackenzie Phillips, daughter of real rocker John Phillips of The Mamas and the Papas). Fi finds some kinda supernatural bull hockey in every tour stop, investigates and posts about it to her Web site (www.soweird.com—now a Disney error page). This show was an odd combo of crappy, short-lived shows *Freaky Links* and *Dead Last*. Even odder, it predated them both! Even Disney was not immune to the *X-Files/Blair Witch/Sixth Sense/Buffy* supernatural boom of the turn of the century. *TRIVIA TIME!* Mackenzie did her own singing, which is even better than her acne medication infomercials.

PHILOUZA, JOHN BAPTISTE—A John Philip Sousa parody, and how often does that happen? In the 11/07/97 episode of sketch comedy *Mr. Show*, silly man-child Philouza (Bob Odenkirk) composes beautiful march after march to the dismay of his serious-minded rival, Salini (David Cross). It's an oompah parody of the 1984 movie *Amadeus*. See also **The Beetletown Players; Larry Black; Livingston Brewster; Willips Brighton; Dickie Crickets; Indomitable Spirit; Kid Jersey; Kill or Be Killed; C. S. Lewis Jr.; Horace Loeb; Marilyn Monster; Norma Jean Monster; Professor Murder; Puscifer; Salini; Smoosh; Old Swerdlow; Three Times One Minus One; Titannica; Sir Lloyd Wilson Webber; Wyckyd Sceptre; Daffy "Mal" Yinkleyankle**.

PHLEGM—In the 1995 *Brady Bunch Movie*, various plots (term used loosely) from *The Brady Bunch* TV show are integrated into the movie remake. So, borrowing from the "Amateur Night" episode, the Brady kids enter a talent show to raise money and put their sunny 70s pop up against this grunge-sounding band and their song "We Are Phlegm" (written by Steve Tyrell, Michael Landau, and Stephanie Tyrell). The Bradys win, because the judges are three-fourths of The Monkees. See also **The Banana Convention; The Brady Kids; The Brady Six; Johnny Bravo; The Silver Platters**.

PHOENIX—This is the lovely young female vocalist that evil Death Records impresario Swan (Paul Williams) can't wait to get his filthy mitts on, chew up, and spit out in the 1974 movie *Phantom of the Paradise*. She's also the object of desire of the disfigured Phantom of the title. Played by Jessica Harper, she sings "Special to Me" and "Old Souls." See also **The Beach Bums; The Juicy Fruits; The Undead**.

PICCOLO PETE—From the "My Music Rules" episode (11/08/99) of the animated PBS children's show *Arthur*. Piccolo Pete is the never-seen leader of a musical clown band who was scheduled to do a show at the Elwood City public library, but he ran away from the circus to join a family (rimshot, please). That's according to the librarian, Ms. Paige Turner (and another rimshot), voiced by Kate Hutchison. Fortunately, this kicks off the plot as the kids of the show cast about for a replacement musician. D. W. Read, the title character's little sister, talks an animated version of classical cellist Yo Yo Ma into performing. However, not knowing about Yo Yo Ma, Francine Frensky (voiced by Jodie Resther) has arranged for her uncle, an animated version of jazz saxophonist Joshua Redman, to play. When both show up, the kids take sides and butt heads over which is better, jazz or classical music. Redman and Ma teach them the painfully obvious lesson and jam together. See also **BINKY; The Squabs; U Stink; We Stink**.

PIGGY, MISS—An actress-singer hyphenate, Miss Piggy was the egocentric diva of *The Muppet Show* (1976–81) and subsequent Muppet specials and movies. Voiced by Frank Oz, she first appeared on *The Herb Alpert Special* (1974), and the 1975 *Muppet Show* pilot, "Sex and Violence." Her lust for fame and celebrity was only overshadowed by her lust for fellow Muppet Kermit the Frog, though it got pretty close sometimes. She may play at being a fainting violet to get her way, but make no mistake, she packs quite a wallop for a foam-rubber puppet, karate-chopping those who displease her with a vigorous "Hiiiii-ya!" She has appeared on various Muppet albums, but got only one all to herself, the bandwagon-jumping *Miss Piggy's Aerobique Exercise Workout Album* (1982). She has published two books, *Miss Piggy's Guide to Life* (1983) and *In the Kitchen with Miss Piggy* (a cookbook, 1996). *TRIVIA TIME!* She had her own TV special in 1982, *The Fan-*

tastic Miss Piggy Show, which guest-starred Andy Kaufman's fake singer, Tony Clifton! Also, when the character was first conceived, she was called "Miss Piggy Lee," the name a parody of singer Peggy Lee. This got dropped quickly and she was always officially referred to as just "Miss Piggy." See also **The Amazing Marvin Suggs and His Muppaphone; Tony Clifton; Dr. Teeth and the Electric Mayhem; Mahna Mahna and the Two Snowths; Rowlf the Dog; Wayne and Wanda**.

Miss Piggy
(voiced by Frank Oz)

PIMP FRANKLIN—Rapper mentioned in the 2002 season premiere of *King of the Hill*, "Get Your Freak Off" (11/03/02). According to prepubescent Bobby Hill (voiced by Pamela Segall), "He don't need your respect, 'cause he don't pay no man no mind." His raps drive Dad Hank (voiced by Mike Judge) to confiscate most of Bobby's CD collection. See also **The A Men; The Bluegrass Brothers; Cane and the Stubborn Stains; The Dale Gribble Bluegrass Experience; 4 Skore; The Harris Twins; John Redcorn and Big Mountain Fudge Cake; Pastor K.**

PINCIOTTI POLKA EXPLOSION, THE—Band mentioned (but not seen) in the "Nobody's Fault But Mine" episode (04/23/03) of *That '70s Show*, Bob Pinciotti (Don Stark) announces he's getting together with some old high school buddies and reforming the band in honor of his daughter's wedding. But dammit, we didn't get any polka.

PINE, BUCK AND HARRIET—Husband-and-wife country singing duo appearing on the 04/20/78 episode of talkshow parody *America 2-Night*, formerly *Fernwood 2Nite*, a spinoff of *Mary Hartman, Mary Hartman* (1976–78). Hank Penny played Buck, Peggy Conner played Harriet. See also **Denny and Brian; Pharoah Fawcett; The Friedkin Family Singers; Happy Kyne and the Mirth Makers; The Punk Monks; Tony Roletti.**

PINHEADS, THE—High-schooler Marty McFly's (Michael J. Fox) garage rock band from the beginning of *Back to the Future* (1985). They audition to play the school prom but are turned down for being "just too darn loud." The other, unnamed Pinheads were played by Paul Hanson, Lee Brownfield, and Robert DeLapp. *TRIVIA TIME!* The judge who turns them down is an uncredited Huey Lewis, of 80s faves Huey Lewis and the News, who performed the movie's theme "Back in Time." See also **Marvin Berry and the Starlighters**.

PINK—Oh, by the way, which one's Pink? Well it's singer Bob Geldof, of The Boomtown Rats, and later the man who cursed the world with insufferable rock benefit tunes by putting together the first one, England's Band Aid ("Do They Know It's Christmas") in 1984. Earlier, however, he starred in the seriously messed up movie *Pink Floyd The Wall* (1982), which opens with a dove exploding and goes downhill from there. Based on (and featuring the songs of) the most miserably depressing concept album ever, Pink Floyd's *The Wall* (1979), the movie is a look at this rock star's disintegrating life and mental state. It all starts when he finds out his wife (Eleanor David) is cheating on him. Various flashbacks take us through his life, segueing into bizarre and grotesque animations based on Gerald Scarfe's drawings and underlining Pink's screwed up relationships with um, pretty much everything. At one point, he flirts with fascism, imagining himself a Hitler-style leader. Soon, it's so bad he can only perform when drugged up to the gills. He's built up a wall around himself, you see—get it? Hanh? Hanh? It has never sucked harder to be a big, rich, successful rock star than this movie. The movie also has one of the all-time classic hotel-trashing scenes of all time, stunning even his manager (Bob Hoskins). The other amazing thing is that Pink gets through the movie with barely a single word of dialogue.

PINK SLIP—In Disney's 2003 update of the 1976 body-swapping movie *Freaky Friday*, teen Anna Coleman (Lindsay Lohan) has this suspiciously well-rehearsed high school garage rock band. Early on, Anna's teen histrionics are well preparing her for a life of spoiled rock-star tantrums, until she swaps bodies with her soon-to-be-remarried mom, icicle queen Tess Coleman (Jamie Lee Curtis). Naturally, the horrified duo assume the best thing is for them to try to lead each others lives, instead of oh, say, taking a sick day. After Anna-in-Mom's-body has her obligatory makeover-and-shopping montage, the pair start learning the whole a-mile-in-someone-else's-moccasins lesson. Eventually, the band's big opportunity to audition at The House of Blues for a local slot on Wango Tango seems shot, because the wedding rehearsal dinner is the same night. But the club miraculously turns out to be next door to the dinner, and Anna-in-Mom's-body gets Mom-in-Anna's-body to sneak out and gets her onstage. She stands there quite awkwardly until Anna-in-Mom ghosts the guitar solo from backstage and all's well that's rocked well ("Take Me Away"). Rest of the band: Peg (Haley Hudson), Maddie (Christina Vidal), Ethan (Chris Carlberg), and Scott (Danny Rubin). The cast learned to actually play the song for the movie, including Jamie Lee Curtis doing the solo.

Pink (Bob Geldof)

PINKUM, CARMEL— See **The Nice Neighbors**.

PLAGUE, THE— There were enough TV/movie rules-breakin', revenge-takin' vigilante cops by 1986 that TV hazarded a parody of the whole genre with the show *Sledge Hammer!* Too bad it wasn't funnier. In the "Sledge, Rattle, and Roll" episode (01/15/88), Det. Sledge (David Rasche) investigates the murder of your typical limey heavy-metal jerk singer, Rak Vulture (Dana Williams), leader of The Plague. The rest of the band (whot 'ave got 'orrible fake accents) set out on tour to cheerfully exploit his memory, but are all killed in a plane crash. Typical! Only, this time—it was no accident! After shooting some stuff, Sledge discovers the band's albums have, yep, damned backward masked messages promising all will pay. Turns out the killer is the band's much-abused and psycho-vengeful roadie, Rusty (Tommy Swerdlow), who turns out to be Rak's brother and who actually was writing all the songs. One fight scene later and justice is served. *TRIVIA TIME!* Monkees member Davy Jones played the band's slimy manager, Jerry Vicuna! The episode was directed by ex-Hulk Bill Bixby! Oingo Boingo member Danny Elfman composed the theme song for the series!

PLAVALAGUNA— Blue, hairless, presumably female alien opera singer from director Luc Besson's ridiculous 1997 sci-fi fairy-tale *The Fifth Element*. Aka "the Diva," she gives a concert at the opera hall in the floating hotel/spaceship *Fhlosten Paradise*, orbiting the Hawaii-like planet Fhlosten in the Angel System. She has an enormous head, like an elf shoe, with tendrils coming out of the sides, and sings "Il Dolce Suono" from Gaetano Donizetti's opera *Lucia di Lammermoor*, which then picks up a techno beat and becomes "The Diva Dance," written by Luc Besson. Moments after her standing ovation performance, the bad aliens (Mangalors) attack and she is shot in the gut. She exhorts Bruce

Willis to save the universe, love Milla Jovovich (how hard can that be?), tells him that the magic stones he seeks are IN her, and then dies. Whereupon Bruce has to root around in her ooey-gooey-bluey guts and pull out the four magic stones. Which raises the question: how was she originally intending to get the stones out? And the equally unpleasant question how did they get in there in the first place? Plavalaguna was played by Maïwenn Le Besco, who had a daughter with the director, Luc Besson. Hmmm. Plavalaguna's singing voice was Inva Mulla Tchako.

POINTLESS SISTERS, THE— From the "Singing Samurai Sensai-tion" episode (09/10/90) of Japanese anime show *Samurai Pizza Cats*. Talent agent Charlie Bird convinces anthropomorphic cats Polly Esther (voiced by Sonja Ball) and Lucille Omitsu (voiced by Susan Glover) that they have talent. They come up with the name "The Pointless Sisters" (obvious Pointer Sisters parody) and perform the pop song "We're Pointless Now" for screaming hordes. Unfortunately, Charlie Bird is really the villain Bad Bird (voiced by Rick Jones), and has hypnotized the crowd with the music, and uses them to power some giant robots that start stomping on Little Tokyo. The good guys can't attack, or the innocents inside will get hurt. But they manage to snap the citizens out of their trance, and get them out of the robots. Unfortunately for Polly and Lucille, none of the awakened citizens remembers their group now. Of course, the show was rewritten and redubbed for the U.S., so Lord knows what The Pointless Sisters were called in Japanese.

POLKA BOYS, THE— From the "Band on the Run" episode (02/26/87) of hit 80s sitcom *Family Ties*. They audition to play the Leland College 10th reunion. Only Alex Keaton (Michael J. Fox) likes them. They lose to Alex's sister's band, The Permanent Waves. See also **Eddie Dupré**; **The Permanent Waves.**

PONIES, THE — Dream-sequence band featured in the "Ginger's Solo" episode (06/30/02) of the cartoon *As Told by Ginger.* This power trio features Ginger Foutley (voiced by Melissa Disney) on guitar and the dynamite rhythm section of her pals Macie Lightfoot (voiced by Jackie Harris) and Dodie Bishop (voiced by Aspen Miller). In the dream, Ginger makes a "Born to Run"–esque connection with Sasha (voiced by J. Evan Bonifant), her summer crush. See also **The Wetheads**.

PONY — Pop star who's coming back to visit his former high school buds who are still stuck in suburbia and the movie *SubUrbia* (1996). Yep, Pony (Joyce Bartok) managed to escape this grim hellish land, suburbia. Yeah, it's right up there with the Holocaust. Where's a dad to smack some sense into an ungrateful brooding brood when you need one?! So Pony escaped by becoming a rock star, and now perversely envies the tiny, anonymous lives his friends lead and despise. Directed by Richard Linklater, and based on a play by Eric Bogosian, who also did the screenplay. Here's a good rule of thumb: movies based on plays stink. Everything that works for a play (pretentious dialogue, people standing around talking forever, no action) always comes off terribly in a film (pretentious dialogue, people standing around talking forever, no action).

POOVIE, LOU-ANN — Gomer's sometime (1967–69) girlfriend and singer at the Blue Bird Café, where Gomer and the gang hang out in *The Andy Griffith Show* spinoff, *Gomer Pyle, U.S.M.C.* (1964–70). Played by Elizabeth MacRae.

PORTER, KELLY — A Leslie Gore/Patty Duke–type early 60s square, hairspray-queen singer with her own TV show, played by Bridget Fonda in the 1996 movie *Grace of My Heart.* The two rival Brill-building songwriters, Cheryl Steed (Patsy Kensit) and Denise Waverly (Illeana Douglas) are assigned to write her a hit. They are loath to do so, because her material is usually dreck like "Dring Dring, Are You Home?" Then they find out she's really an emotionally troubled and heavily closeted lesbian, and write her the coded "My Secret Love," which Kelly sings beaming at HER secret love, Marion (Lucinda Jenney). *TRIVIA TIME!* The song was actually cowritten BY Leslie Gore, with Larry Klein and Dave Baerwald. See also **The Click Brothers**; **Little Tammy Lee**; **The Luminaries**; **The Riptides**; **The Stylettes**; **Denise Waverly**.

POWER STEVES, THE — In the prologue to the "Girls' Town" episode (07/16/94) of *Mystery Science Theater 3000*, Crow T. Robot (voiced by Trace Beaulieu) has hired this accordion-fronted trio to play, as mad scientist Dr. Forrester (Trace Beaulieu) has a big announcement. They play that soul-numbing fave of accordionists everywhere, "Lady of Spain." Where's Dick Contino when you need him?! The band was played by some of the show's writers: Paul Chaplin, Mary Jo Pehl, and David Sussman.

POWERPUFF GIRLS, THE — In *The Powerpuff Girls* cartoon episode "Mime for a Change" (02/03/99), the superheroines of the title form an impromptu but strangely well-rehearsed band to stop evil Mr. Mime from sucking the color and sound out of Townsville. Their bubbly power-pop number, "Love Makes the World Go Round" (composed by show creator David Smith), turns him back into lovable Rainbow the Clown (voiced by Tom Kenny), who he had been before the accident with the bleach turned him evil. Lineup: Bubbles (voiced by Tara Strong) on drums, Blossom (voiced by Cathy Cavadini) on lead guitar, and Buttercup (voiced by E. G.

Daily) on bass.

PROBLEM — From the very short-lived WB paranormal dramedy, *Dead Last* (08/14/01–12/08/01). This low-level rock trio finds the "Amulet of Sauryn," which gives them the very *Sixth Sense*-y ability to see and talk to dead people. So, in addition to rocking out, they are press-ganged into postlife-counselor jobs, helping the dead sort out their unfinished business. And no, they can't just chuck the amulet; they tried that and it always comes back. Lineup: bassist Jane Cahill (Sara Downing), drummer Scotty Sallback (Tyler Labine), guitarist and singer Vaughn Parrish (Kett Turton), and manager Dennis Budny (Wayne Pére).

PROBLEMS, THE — See **The Barbusters.**

PROFESSOR LA PLANO AND THE PLANOTONES — One of the artifacts of the 70s fad for 50s nostalgia was the 1978 flick *American Hot Wax*, which dramatized real-life Cleveland DJ Alan Freed's championing of rock and roll. Real rockers Jerry Lee Lewis, Chuck Berry, and Screamin' Jay Hawkins appeared as themselves, but for some reason, fictionalized versions of other real groups were created, like this one. Professor LaPlano and the Planotones were a doo-wop quartet of white, greasy-looking young men in matching suits. Kenny Vance played Professor La Plano, the rest of the band was played by Joe Esposito, Bruce Sudano, and Ed Hokenson. Their version of "Rock and Roll Is Here to Stay" (Danny and the Juniors) is on the soundtrack album. *TRIVIA TIME!* Kenny Vance, a member of real 60s band Jay and the Americans, reformed the fictional Planotones in 1992 and tours with them, performing doo wop. So now they're real! Ahhh! Vance also composed the song "Countdown to Love," performed by the fictional Sorels in the movie *Streets of Fire*. See also **The Chesterfields; The Delights; Clark Otis;**

Timmy and the Tulips.

PROFESSOR MURDER — From the "Oh, You Men" episode of HBO's *Mr. Show* (10/03/97). This African-American rapper (B. J. Porter) appears in a sketch about the East Coast/West Coast ventriloquist rivalry, which gleefully skewers the East Coast/West Coast rap rivalry. He appears on a news program about the two rivalries, and gets to face-shove an uppity ventriloquist dummy that accidentally calls him Professor Pickles. He also appeared in a later episode, "It's Perfectly Underdishable," as a ringer brought in by the campers at the Fat Kids' Camp to win a rap contest. See also **The Beetletown Players; Larry Black; Livingston Brewster; Willips Brighton; Dickie Crickets; Indomitable Spirit; Kid Jersey; Kill or Be Killed; C. S. Lewis Jr.; Horace Loeb; Marilyn Monster; Norma Jean Monster; John Baptiste Philouza; Puscifer; Salini; Smoosh; Old Swerdlow; Three Times One Minus One; Titannica; Sir Lloyd Wilson Webber; Wyckyd Sceptre; Daffy "Mal" Yinkleyankle.**

PRUIT, RAY — This musician character joined the pretty, pretty cast of overblown drama *Beverly Hills, 90210* in the "Rave On" episode (10/05/94). He (Jamie Walters) hooked up with show regular Donna Martin (Tori Spelling, daughter of the show's producer, Aaron Spelling) and became her boyfriend. He starts off as a construction worker with musical aspirations, and eventually tries his hand at performing, but suffers from stage fright ("Sentenced to Life," 01/04/95). In another episode, Martin's mom (Katherine Cannon) tries to bribe him with ten grand to stay the hell away from her daughter, but no dice. In "Little Monsters" (02/01/95), he actually gets the chance to sign with a record company. Then he has a fling with Valerie Malone (Tiffani-Amber Thiessen), who turns around and buys the club where he sings, and threatens to fire him unless he continues their relationship! He neatly sidesteps the issue by going on tour. Eventually Pruit's dark side comes out after he shoves Donna into a wall in Portland. They have more fights, which climax in his shoving her down a flight of stairs ("P.S. I Love You Part 2," 05/24/95)! They reconcile, but eventually Donna wises up and breaks up with him completely. But that (nor therapy) stops him from stalking and harassing her. His last appearance was in the "Courting" episode (11/29/95), after which Walters left the show, afraid

Ray Pruit (Jamie Walters)

his portrayal of an abusive character was hurting his real-life musical career. His fans wouldn't forgive him for pushing Donna down the stairs! *TRIVIA TIME!* Jamie Walters was also a member of fake band/show The Heights. See also **Cain Was Able**; **Jasper's Law**.

PUFF SMOKEY SMOKE—Tommy Davidson stars as this rapper in the shiznittizniznay movie *Juwanna Mann* (2002), about a basketball player who gets booted from the NBA, so he gets a horrible drag outfit and plays in the WNBA. Kinda like *Tootsie* meets *Basketball Diaries*. (Dear Lord, don't let that be the pitch that sold it!) Puff's stupid enough to fall for the drag getup and stupid enough to find her attractive, following that old sitcom rule—the uglier a man in drag, the more inexplicably he will be hit on by other men.

PUNK FLOYD—Dirk McQuickly's (Eric Idle) late 70s post-Rutles punk band, formed with his wife, French actress Martini (Bianca Jagger). He sings. She doesn't. From the 1978 documentary *All You Need Is Cash*. See also **Arthur Hodgeson and the Kneecaps**; **Les Garçons de la Plage**; **The Machismo Brothers**; **Ruttling Orange Peel**; **Blind Lemon Pye**; **The Rutles**.

PUNK MONKS, THE—Unusual act playing the 06/14/78 episode of talk-show satire *America 2-Night*. The band was played by Sandy Helper, Paul Ryan, Sandra Bernhard, and Maryedith Burrell. They sang "Karmic Love." See also **Denny and Brian**; **Pharaoh Fawcett**, **The Friedkin Family Singers**; **Happy Kyne and the Mirth Makers**; **Buck and Harriet Pine**; **Tony Roletti**.

PURPLE, TURNER—Real-life rock star/Rolling Stone Mick Jagger portrayed this famous, reclusive, eccentric bisexual rock star who takes in mob hood Chas

(James Fox) in the very, VERY strange 1970 film *Performance*. Jagger also wrote and sang "Turner's Song: Memo from T" used in the film.

Performance, featuring Turner Purple (Mick Jagger)

PUSCIFER — Real band Tool makes a cameo on "The Cry of a Hungry Baby," the first episode (11/03/95) of *Mr. Show*, as this band singing about pseudocelebrity Ronnie Dobbs (David Cross), the most-arrested redneck in the history of reality cop shows. Tool lead singer Maynard James Keenan is briefly interviewed in a hideous wig and also appears a bit later as a random dude staggering down the street drunk and shirtless with Ronnie. See also **The Beetletown Players; Larry Black; Livingston Brewster; Willips Brighton; Dickie Crickets; Indomitable Spirit; Kid Jersey; Kill or Be Killed; C. S. Lewis Jr.; Horace Loeb; Marilyn Monster; Norma Jean Monster; John Baptiste Philouza; Professor Murder; Salini; Smoosh; Old Swerdlow; Three Times One Minus One; Titannica; Sir Lloyd Wilson Webber; Wyckyd Sceptre; Daffy "Mal" Yinkleyankle.**

PUSSYCATS, THE — Hard-rocking female quartet from *The Adventures of Ford Fairlane* (1990), which hired the rock-and-roll detective of the title (Andrew Dice Clay) to find a stalker. Talk about coincidence: the lead singer's name is Josie! What are the odds?! The Pussycats were played by Delia Sheppard, Kimber Sissons, Monique Mannen, and Pamela Segall. See also **Black Plague; Disco Express; F. F. & Captain John; Slam; Kyle Troy.**

PYE, BLIND LEMON — African-American Mississippi Delta blues singer who learned everything he knew about music from the Rutles, instead of the more typical other way around, according to the 1978 documentary *All You Need Is Cash*. Played by Jerome Greene. See also **Arthur Hodgeson and the Kneecaps; Les Garçons de la Plage; The Machismo Brothers; Ruttling Orange Peel; Punk Floyd; The Rutles.**

QUADRATICS, THE — Crappy garage band of geeks in *Welcome to the Dollhouse* (1995). High-schooler Mark Weiner (Matthew Faber), the band's leader and clarinetist, hires older guy Steve Rodgers (Eric Mabius) as the singer. They do a version of The Rolling Stones' "(Can't Get No) Satisfaction." Rodgers's singing voice was Daniel Rey.

QUEENHATERS, THE — A running sketch on *SCTV* was a TV dance-show parody called "Mel's Rock Pile," with total dweeb Rockin' Mel Stirrup (Eugene Levy) as host. In the "Punk Rock Tribute" episode (03/18/83), this English punk band performed "I Hate the Bloody Queen," which gets in a dig about the Falkland Islands! The snotty lead vocalist was Martin Short. The rest of the nameless fivesome was John Candy on drums, Joe Flaherty on bass, Andrea Martin on guitar, and Eugene Levy on lead guitar. In a later *SCTV* show, the "It's a Wonderful Film" parody (12/20/83), a character is listening to the radio playing the unlikely collaboration of Jackie Rogers Jr. and The Queenhaters. See also **Vic Arpeggio; Big Momma; 5 Neat Guys; Happiness Unlimited; The Happy Wanderers; Lola Heatherton; The Lemon Twins; Linsk Minyk; Tom Munroe; The Ramblers; The Recess Monkeys; Russ Riley; Jackie Rogers Jr.; Jackie Rogers Sr.; Speed of Light; Dusty Towne; The Wally Hung Trio.**

RABBIT, JESSICA — Animated human female with a Veronica Lake hairdo and physics-defying anatomy in Disney's (well, Touchstone/Amblin) *Who Framed Roger Rabbit* (1988). The wife of Maroon Cartoons star Roger Rabbit (voiced by Charles Fleischer), she was voiced by an uncredited Kathleen Turner. She sang "Why Don't You Do Right?" backed by a band of nameless cartoon crows at The Ink and Paint Club, a disreputable "strictly humans only" joint with a "toon revue." She sings as sexy as she looks, too. Jessica's singing voice was actually Amy Irving, executive producer Steven Spielberg's then-wife.

Jessica also popped up in minor roles in the three subsequent animated Roger Rabbit shorts that fronted the theatrical release of various Disney movies: "Tummy Trouble" (*Honey, I Shrunk the Kids*, 1989), "Roller Coaster Rabbit" (*Dick Tracy*, 1990), and "Trail Mix-Up" (*A Far Off Place*, 1993).

Jessica Rabbit (voiced by Kathleen Turner) (r)

RACHEL TOOVEY BICYCLE CHOIR — From the eleventh episode (12/28/69) of now-legendary BBC sketch show *Monty Python's Flying Circus*. They appear briefly on the TV-show parody skit "Interesting People." Just six guys in rain slickers singing "Men of Harlech" and ringing their bicycle bells. Not your usual bell choir. See also **Arthur Ewing and his Musical Mice; Bolton Choral Society; Johann Gambolputty de von Ausfern-schplenden-schlitter-crasscrenbon-fried-digger-dingle-**

dangle-dongle-dungle-burstein-von-knacker-thrasher-apple-banger-horowitz-ticolensic-grander-knotty-spelltinkle-grandlich-grumble-meyer-spelterwasser-kurstlich-himbleeisen-bahnwagen-gutenabend-bitte-ein-nürnburger-bratwustle-gerspurten-mitz-weimache-luber-hundsfut-gumberaber-shönendanker-kalbsfleisch-mittler-aucher von Hautkopft of Ulm**; The Herman Rodriguez Four; The Hunlets; Jackie Charlton and the Tonettes; Arthur "Two Sheds" Jackson; Not Noel Coward; Not Tony Bennett; Inspector Jean-Paul Zatapathique.**

RADICAL POSTURE—In the "Oil" episode (11/16/82) of anarchic BBC comedy *The Young Ones*, the four mismatched flatmates discover oil in the basement. Mike (Christopher Ryan) immediately stages a fascist coup and enslaves Rick and Neil (Nigel Planer) to dig up the basement. Rick (Rik Mayall) turns revolutionary and hires this band to play a benefit concert in their living room to raise money for the oppressed workers (himself) and at the height of the concert, revolt! Lead singer of the trio, Alexei Yuri Gagarin Siege of Stalingrad Glorious Five Year Plan Sputnik Pravda Moscow Dynamo Back Four Balowski (his dad was a bit of a communist, doncha know), played by Alexei Sayle, sing-raps a l'il ditty about Dr. Marten's boots right before the scheduled revolution fails to happen. See also **Dicky and Dino; Il Duce.**

RAGING PUSSIES—Band that unknowingly precipitates a crisis in the cartoon town of South Park, Colorado, in "The Wacky Molestation Adventure" episode (12/13/00). Eric Cartman (voiced by Trey Parker) has four tickets to their concert, but Kyle's mom and dad won't let Kyle (voiced by Matt Stone) go. After he begs, they say he can go if ". . . you clean out the garage, shovel the driveway, and bring democracy to Cuba." Undaunted, Kyle writes a let-

ter to Castro SO heartwarming, Castro actually DOES bring democracy to Cuba. But his parents still won't let him go. Furious, he takes Cartman's suggestion to tell the cops his parents "molestered" him, so the cops will take them away. It works like a charm, and Kyle and Co. have a parentless blast at the concert, in their underwear even. Then every kid in town uses the "molestering" routine and soon the town is a creepy, adultless, *Children of the Corn/Lord of the Flies* wreck. See also **The Avenue Street Ghetto Boys; Faith + 1; Fingerbang; Getting Gay with Kids; The Ghetto Avenue Boys; Jerome "Chef" McElroy; MOOP; Reach for the Skyler; Sanctified; Sisters of Mercy Hold No Pain Against the Dark Lord; Timmy! and the Lords of the Underworld.**

RAISINETTES, THE—See **The California Raisins.**

RAMBLERS, THE—A Peter, Paul, and Mary–type 60s folk quartet in a greatest-hits commercial in an *SCTV* sketch (03/27/84). The voiceover lauds them for their political stance and activism while all they do is play twee nonsense songs like "Ricky Tippy Tin," "Bottle of Wine," and a parody of "Puff the Magic Dragon" called "Cliff the Magic Squirrel." Lineup: Eugene Levy on banjo, Andrea Martin as the female singer, Martin Short on stand-up bass, and Joe Flaherty on acoustic guitar. See also **Vic Arpeggio; Big Momma; 5 Neat Guys; Happiness Unlimited; The Happy Wanderers; Lola Heatherton; The Lemon Twins; Linsk Minyk; Tom Munroe; The Queenhaters; The Recess Monkeys; Russ Riley; Jackie Rogers Jr.; Jackie Rogers Sr.; Speed of Light; Dusty Towne; The Wally Hung Trio.**

RANCHBONE—This black country-western band was actually the real black ska-funk-punk band Fishbone. From the 1988 comedy *Tapeheads*. See also

The Blender Children; Cube Squared; The Swanky Modes.

RANDY WATSON AND SEXUAL CHOCOLATE—Eddie Murphy played the disturbingly fey Randy Watson and several other characters in the 1988 film *Coming to America*. The band was a sort of 70s soul-type band. They did a version of the Whitney Houston hit "The Greatest Love of All."

RAPID FIRE—Evil high-school rock band in the 1978 NBC made-for-TV movie *Cotton Candy*, an early, not-so-good, directorial work of Ron Howard. They cover Bob Marley's "I Shot the Sheriff." Very badly. See also **Cotton Candy**.

RAPPIN' RABBIS, THE—News anchorman Kent Brockman (voiced by Harry Shearer) reports on this act as "Springfield's answer to the Benedictine Monks," in the "Star Is Burns" episode (03/05/95) of *The Simpsons*. As the Rabbis are a shining example of Springfield's lack of high culture, Marge is then inspired to get the city to sponsor a film festival, judged by crossover character Jay Sherman (voiced by Jon Lovitz) of animated series *The Critic*. *TRIVIA TIME!* The Benedictine Monks of Santo Domingo de Silos' album of Gregorian chants, *Chant*, was briefly and inexplicably hip and popular in 1994. See also **The Beach Boys Experience; The Be Sharps; Johnny Bobby; Johnny Calhoun; Captain Bart and the Tequila Mockingbirds; The Crazy Old Man Singers; Cyanide; Gulliver Dark; Ferl Dixon and His Second Helping Boys; Funky C Funky Do; Garfunkel, Messina, Oates, and Lisa; Hooray for Everything; Kovenant; Krusty and the Krums; The Larry Davis Experience; Little Timmy and the Shebangs; Loggins and Oates; Lurleen Lumpkin; M. C. Safety and the Caution Crew; Melvin and the Squirrels; "Bleeding Gums" Murphy; The Party Posse; Red Breem and**

His Band of Some Esteem; The Satin Knights; The Steve Sax Trio; Testament; Blind Willie Witherspoon; The Ya-Hoo Recovering Alcoholic Jug Band; Yodelin' Zeke.

RASTA BILLY SKANK—Dave Lister's (Craig Charles) fave but never-seen artist in the U.K. sci-fi series *Red Dwarf*. Lister's fave song is "Don't Fear the Reefer, Man." Are puns supposed to be this painful? See also **Smeg and the Heads**.

RATS, THE—See **Curt Wild**.

RAW-D—Rapper played by real rapper Kurupt in cheapie rapsploitation comedy *Keepin' It Real* (2001), involving stolen master tapes and the label owner's (naturally) hot daughter.

RAY, BILLY—The honky-tonkin' hero of singer Mary Rose Foster (Bette Midler) in the 1979 movie *The Rose*. The Rose was a huge fan of Ray (Harry Dean Stanton) and even recorded some of his songs as tribute. At their fateful after-concert meeting, Billy Ray called her trash and asked that she never record his songs again. The Rose got her revenge, though, by stealing his limo. It doesn't matter how big a star you are, you never recover from your first stolen limo. See also **Mary Rose Foster; Monty's Band; The Rose Band**.

RAYTONES, THE—See **Floyd Burney**.

REACH FOR THE SKYLER—Extremely short-lived solo project of Skyler Moles after leaving band Timmy! and the Lords of the Underworld. So short, they may not have even played one show before Skyler rejoined his old band. Then again, they might have opened for Phil Collins. From the "Timmy! 2000" episode (04/19/00) of animated Comedy Central show *South Park*. See also **The Avenue Street**

Ghetto Boys; Faith + 1; Fingerbang; Getting Gay with Kids; The Ghetto Avenue Boys; Jerome "Chef" McElroy; MOOP; Raging Pussies; Sanctified; Sisters of Mercy Hold No Pain Against the Dark Lord; Timmy! and the Lords of the Underworld.

REBO TWELVE, THE — See **The Max Rebo Band**.

RECESS MONKEYS, THE — This band performs at the Preteen World telethon in a comedy sketch on the 04/23/82 episode of *SCTV*. They cover the Canadian band Chilliwack's "My Girl (Gone, Gone, Gone)," a #22 hit in the U.S. in 1981. Lineup: Stephan Seely (John Candy) on drums and backing vocals; Paul Rey (Eugene Levy) on guitar, backing vocals, and tambourine; and Steve Applebaum (Rick Moranis) on guitar and vocals. See also **Vic Arpeggio**; **Big Momma**; **5 Neat Guys**; **Happiness Unlimited**; **The Happy Wanderers**; **Lola Heatherton**; **The Lemon Twins**; **Linsk Minyk**; **Tom Munroe**; **The Queenhaters**; **The Ramblers**; **Russ Riley**; **Jackie Rogers Jr.**; **Jackie Rogers Sr.**; **Speed of Light**; **Dusty Towne**; **The Wally Hung Trio**.

RED BREEM AND HIS BAND OF SOME ESTEEM — Aging eleven-man swing band that plays the Springfield Community Center's senior citizens swing dance in the "Lady Bouvier's Lover" episode (04/12/94) of *The Simpsons*. (No, not that seniors' swing dance, the one right before the big Cat Spay-a-Thon that everyone's still talking about.) Breem and his band provide the musical background for Abe Simpson's and Montgomery Burns's competitive wooing of Jacqueline Bouvier (voiced by Julie Kavner). See also **The Beach Boys Experience**; **The Be Sharps**; **Johnny Bobby**; **Johnny Calhoun**; **Captain Bart and the Tequila Mockingbirds**; **The Crazy Old Man Singers**; **Cyanide**; **Gulliver Dark**; **Ferl Dixon and His Second Helping Boys**; **Funky C Funky Do**; **Garfunkel, Messina, Oates, and Lisa**; **Hooray for Everything**; **Kovenant**; **Krusty and the Krums**; **The Larry Davis Experience**; **Little Timmy and the Shebangs**; **Loggins and Oates**; **Lurleen Lumpkin**; **M. C. Safety and the Caution Crew**; **Melvin and the Squirrels**; **"Bleeding Gums" Murphy**; **The Party Posse**; **The Rappin' Rabbis**; **The Satin Knights**; **The Steve Sax Trio**; **Testament**; **Blind Willie Witherspoon**; **The Ya-Hoo Recovering Alcoholic Jug Band**; **Yodelin' Zeke**.

REDCOATS, THE — Real British Invasion rockers Chad (Stuart) and Jeremy (Clyde) pose as Ernie and Freddie, respectively, the members of this fictional British Invasion duo on *The Dick Van Dyke Show* episode "The Redcoats Are Coming" (02/10/65). The duo spark Beatlemania-like fervor in their fans; one fan screams "I'm breathing their air! I'm breathing their air!" They're in town to sing on *The Alan Brady Show* and promote their new album, *The Redcoats Are Coming*. Show flunky Mel Cooley (Richard Deacon) comes up with a convoluted plan to have them stay at show writer Rob Petrie's (Dick Van Dyke) house so the boys can avoid their fans and relax. It almost works, but the next morning the beans get spilled and the boys narrowly escape a locust-like swarm of crazed teen girls who take most of Rob's furniture for souvenirs. Singing on the show, the boys credit one song to . . . themselves! They "cover" a tune by Chad and Jeremy, their good friends!

REED, KITTY — Nightclub singer at a fancy restaurant/club in the 1944 sub-drive-in quality movie *I Accuse My Parents*. She's the moll of gangster Charles Blake (George Meeker). She falls for high-schooler Jimmy Wilson (Robert Lowell), whose many problems start with his negligent, gin-soaked parents, the most boozed-up onscreen couple since Nick and Nora Charles of *The Thin Man*. Shoe salesman and pathological liar Wilson gets mixed up in Blake's mob biz to earn money to take Reed out. When caught, he is way, way ahead of his time in blaming his parents to get off scot-free. Reed gets to sing THREE complete numbers in what can only be described as padding. This movie was also mocked on an episode of *Mystery Science Theater 3000* (09/04/93).

REESE, LINNEA — Comedienne Lily Tomlin plays the only white member of a black gospel choir in Robert Altman's 1975 character-driven film with too many characters, *Nashville*. She has an ill-advised affair with the Tom (Keith Carradine) of folkie group Tom, Bill & Mary. See also **Agnus Angst; Tommy Brown (II); Sueleen Gay; Haven Hamilton; Purvis Hawkins; Barbara Jean; The Smoky Mountain Laurels; Tom, Bill & Mary; Tommy Velour; Connie White**.

REGULARS, THE — From *This Is Spïnal Tap* (1984). This is the early 60s London band that was originally The Originals, forcing the Spïnal Tap precursor band, also called The Originals, to change their name to The New Originals. But then the original Originals changed their name to The Regulars. So, The New Originals could have gone back to the name The Originals, but they said screw it and became The Thamesmen instead. Got it? See also **Duke Fame; Lambsblood; Meconium; Spinal Tap**.

R.E.M. — Jesse (John Stamos) is having a grand reopening of the Smash Club in the "Another Opening, Another No Show" (11/2/93) of *Full House* (he inherited it a few episodes prior). Unfortunately, the band hired to play is not the R.E.M. he thought it was. It's Renee, Esther, and Martha! Real novelty act, The Del Rubio Triplets—a trio of singing, acoustic guitar–playing, identical triplets—played the band: Renee (Milly Del Rubio), Esther (Eadie

Del Rubio), and Martha (Elena Del Rubio). *TRIVIA TIME!* The Del Rubio Triplets made many TV guest appearances, also appearing on such shows as *Married with Children, Pee-wee's Playhouse*, and *The Golden Girls*. See also **The Diplomats; The Funky Tongues; Hot Daddy and the Monkey Puppets; Human Pudding; Jesse and the Rippers; The Wanker Triplets**.

REVERE, BO — In "The Zack Tapes" episode (12/02/89) of *Saved by the Bell*, that mischievous amoral bastard teen Zack (Mark-Paul Gosselaar) hides subliminal messages on a tape of this artist's song "Don't Leave with Your Love," so that Kelly (Tiffani-Amber Thiessen) would listen to it and dump Slater (Mario Lopez) and go to the dance with him instead. It backfires when EVERYONE listens to the tape and wants to go to the dance with Zack. Messing with people's minds? For a lousy dance? Dude, that's just sick. And a complete waste of mind control! See also **The Five Aces; Hot Sundae; Stevie; Zack Attack**.

RHONDA WEISS AND THE RHONDETTES — Sixties-looking girl group of Jewish-American princesses who sing "Goodbye Saccharin," an ode to their favorite low-calorie sugar substitute in the opening skit of the 03/19/77 episode of *Saturday Night Live*. At the time, saccharin was briefly under suspicion of causing cancer in lab rats. Now we know that you can safely eat up to twelve pounds a day! Gilda Radner was Rhonda Weiss. The Rhondettes were Jane Curtin, Laraine Newman, and that week's musical guest, Linda Ronstadt. Radner also used the character on her *Live in New York* album (1980).

RIB TIPS, THE — Soul duo from *The Steve Harvey Show* formed by T-Bone (T. K. Carter) and Clyde (Jonathan Slocumb), two former members of Steve Hightower and the Hi-Tops. In the episode "When the Funk Hits the Rib Tips" (10/29/97), The Rib Tips audition to be the house group for Club Mystique. When they find out their main competition is the Soul Teachers, they decide to win by sabotaging the Soul Teachers. However, as in every other sitcom in the history of mankind, the bad guys fail in the end. Hard cheese, Rib Tips. Mmm, hard cheese and rib tips. See also **Smitty Rollins; Soul Teachers; Steve Hightower and the Hi-Tops**.

RICARDO, RICKY — Desi Arnaz played the bandleading, club-owning, Cuban husband of that crazy, conniving, self-destructing redhead, Lucille Ball, in the classic 1951–57 sitcom *I Love Lucy*. Ricky, a talented conga drummer and arranger, owned the Tropicana Club, later the Babalu Club, where his talentless harridan of a wife kept scheming to get into the show. He also had to put up with her countless other antics that surely would have driven a lesser man to drink, or at least divorce. Arnaz started his showbiz career as a real bandleader, helping popularize the conga up through 1949, when he turned from music to films and TV. Novelty artiste Weird Al Yankovic produced a 1991 CD of tunes from the show, *Babalu Music: I Love Lucy's Greatest Hits*.

RILEY, RUSS — From the 50s-movie parody skit, "I Was a Teenage Communist," on the 07/16/82 episode of *SCTV*. Real rocker Dave Edmunds and his band appear in the film playing "From Small Things (Big Things One Day Come)" at the Coco Shack. Edmunds plays Russ Riley, the band's leader and secretly a commie no-goodnik trying to seduce normal teen Eddie Davis (Martin Short) into communism with rock and roll. Then Eddie tries reefer, turns into a werewolf, and is gunned down by the cops. So kids, remember: stay away from drugs, communism, rock and roll, and lycanthropy! See also **Vic Arpeggio; Big Momma; 5 Neat Guys; Happiness Unlimited; The Happy Wanderers; Lola Heatherton; The Lemon Twins; Linsk Minyk; Tom Munroe; The Queenhaters; The Ramblers; The Recess Monkeys; Jackie Rogers Jr.; Jackie Rogers Sr.; Speed of Light; Dusty Towne; The Wally Hung Trio**.

RIPTIDES, THE — Total Beach Boys stand-ins in the 1996 movie *Grace of My Heart*. Carole King–like main character, Denise Waverly (Illeana Douglas), meets up with the group's leader, Brian Wilson–like Jay Phillips (Matt Dillon), when her Don Kirshner–like boss, Joel Millner (John Turturro), gets him

The Riptides

to produce her single, to cheer her up after a couple of unhappy relationships. Jay gives her song "God Give Me Strength" a big orchestral sound, but it has "disappointing" sales. But they get married, so it all works out. She has a ringside seat as he moves the band from California surf ("Take a Run at the Sun") to theremin-driven symphonic rock ("Chewing and Waving"). But one member grouses, "Where are the cars, where are the surf boards?" Anyway, Jay, a bit of a space cadet, goes completely loopy, losing the kids and locking himself into the studio for three weeks. He gets talked out and, after telling Denise how much talent she has and how much he wants to help her make her album, walks into the ocean and drowns himself. Doofus. The rest of The Riptides were played by real band Redd Kross: Jeffrey McDonald, Steven McDonald, and

Brian Reitzell. The Beach Boys–pastiche songs were written by Dinosaur Jr.'s J. Mascis, who also had a bit part playing The Riptides' engineer. See also **The Click Brothers**; **Little Tammy Lee**; **The Luminaries**; **Kelly Porter**; **The Stylettes**; **Denise Waverly**.

RIVERS, DEKE — Young, hot-rodding, delivery-boy-turned-singing-sensation in *Loving You* (1957), the movie that is to Elvis what *8 Mile* is to Eminem. Rivers delivers beer to a Tex Warner and the Rough Ridin' Ramblers concert and ends up on stage, singing and ultimately wowing the crowd. Well, Tex (Wendell Corey) and his public relations genius ex-wife Glenda Markle (Lizabeth Scott) know a good thing when they see it, so they convince Rivers to join them, the Ramblers, and Sweet Susie Jessup

Deke Rivers (Elvis Presley) with Tex Warner and the Rough Ridin' Ramblers

(Dolores Hart) on tour. The tour goes well through the small towns, with Deke leading the way, of course. Over the course of the tour, he falls for Susie, enough to want to quit music and live on her family farm. Soon he becomes a headliner, with big-time fame just ahead. Except that he doesn't want fame and fortune, he just wants family, a family that he never had back when he was an orphan named Jimmy Tompkins. Oh yeah, and the influential wives in Freegate (just outside Dallas) don't want him corrupting the youth. Problems, problems, problems. You know what cures problems? The singing of Elvis! Well, in an Elvis movie it does. Deke finds the family he wants, the girl of his dreams, and career success, thanks to his friends—and, of course, his singing. See also **Tex Warner and the Rough Ridin' Ramblers**.

RIVERS, NICK — None other than Val Kilmer played this late 50s/early 60s–style teen rock idol in the 1984 Zucker-Abrahams-Zucker comedy *Top Secret!* Rivers is riding a crest of popularity singing about the latest fad—skeet-shooting while you surf. His Beach Boys parody "Skeet Surfing" is a smash hit, but, unfortunately, you never get to hear his duet with Loretta Lynn on "Your Skeetin' Heart." Rivers goes behind the Iron Curtain to perform a concert and also spy in a simultaneous spoof of Elvis flicks and WWII spy movies. He teams up with the French Underground (very strange, as he's in East Germany) to locate a kidnapped scientist (Michael Gough). *TRIVIA TIME!* This was Val Kilmer's first starring movie role. Kilmer actually sang the songs on the soundtrack as well: a parody

of "Are You Lonesome Tonight," a straightforward cover of Little Richard's "Tutti Frutti," as well as the period-type songs "How Silly Can You Get," "Straighten the Rug," and "Spend This Night With Me."

ROBERTS, BOB — Folk-singing, evil, right-wing Senate candidate from Pennsylvania portrayed by Tim Robbins in the 1992 movie *Bob Roberts*. He's running a shady campaign to get elected, capped by the orchestration of his own assassination attempt. He rigs it so it coincides with the release of his latest single/video, "I Want to Live." Tim Robbins wrote, directed, and starred in this political satire about the self-made millionaire who rebelled against his hippie parents, and releases albums that are parodies of Bob Dylan album titles: *The Freewheelin' Bob Roberts* (1987), *The Times They Are A-Changin' Back*

Nick Rivers (Val Kilmer)

(1988), and *Bob on Bob* (1990). The songs are so great, it's a crime no soundtrack album was released for this movie, but apparently Tim Robbins had an ethical problem with the right-wing songs being taken out of the context of the movie, and forbade it. The songs were written by Robbins and his brother David. When Tim Robbins guest-hosted *Saturday Night Live* (10/03/92), he performed in a sketch as Bob Roberts, which brought everything full circle, since the character originated in a short film Tim Robbins did for *SNL* in 1986.

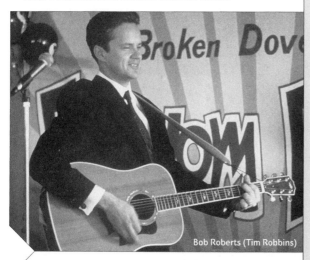

Bob Roberts (Tim Robbins)

TOP TEN FAKE BANDS FROM SONGS
BY GALEN BLACK

Fake bands flourish not just in the world of movies and TV, they're everywhere—in ads, books, poems, plays, radio dramas, the very occasional pamphlet, and even in songs themselves. There are plenty of songs that reference generic or unnamed "superstars" or "rock and roll bands," but here are a few of the best fake bands in songs that actually got a name.

1. **Sgt. Pepper's Lonely Hearts Club Band (featuring Billy Shears) from "Sgt. Pepper's Lonely Hearts Club Band" by The Beatles**—Sgt. Pepper's Lonely Hearts Club Band was invented as an alter ego for The Beatles on their 1967 concept album of the same name. At the end of the song the band introduces singer Billy Shears for the next number, "With a Little Help from My Friends." It's uncertain if Mr. Shears was a permanent member of the band,

but the band is certainly nothing more than a Founder's Day novelty act without him. Besides, in any music top ten list, The Beatles always get first place. Why should this list be any different?

2. **Johnny B. Goode from "Johnny B. Goode" by Chuck Berry**—The song tells the story of a hopeful young rock and roll guitarist who is so poor he has to carry his guitar around in a gunny sack. Damn, that's poor. But he can take heart from his mother's prophecy that her boy is destined for fame and fortune.

3. **Boogie Woogie Bugle Boy from "Boogie Woogie Bugle Boy" by The Andrews Sisters**—Although this song was recorded for the Abbott and Costello movie *Buck Privates* (which, alas, had no Boogie Woogie Bugle Boy) and the bugle boy of the song only plays reveille, we have to give the man a very patriotic shout out. Besides, getting those goldbrickers awake is an important job.

4. **Bennie and the Jets from "Bennie and the Jets" by Elton John**—Bennie and her posse, the Jets, are probably the only other fake band from a song that comes close to the name recognition of Sgt. Pepper and his crew. And snappy dressers, too, what with their mohair suits and electric boots.

5. **Ziggy Stardust from "Ziggy Stardust" by David Bowie**—Ziggy is special, because not only is there a song about him, but his creator BECAME him for a while. David Bowie invented Ziggy and the band Spiders of Mars for the concept album *The Rise and Fall of Ziggy Stardust*. Talk about losing yourself in a song!

6. **Willie and the Poor Boys from "Down on the Corner" by Creedence Clearwater Revival**—For some reason, successful musicians love to sing songs about unsuccessful musicians who play on street corners for pocket change. Singing about these bands sure beats BEING one of these

(continued)

bands, isn't that right, CCR?

7. **Gitarzan from "Gitarzan" by Ray Stevens**—The novelty song "Gitarzan" combined rock and roll with Edgar Rice Burroughs's character Tarzan and came up with an unlikely, ax wielding king of the jungle and his "homely" lead singer, Jane.

8. **Sultans of Swing from "Sultans of Swing" by Dire Straits**—Now here's a bar band if there's ever been one. A good bar band has to be ready with a little bit of all kinds of music. The Sultans of Swing play Dixie, Creole, jazz, and honky-tonk—quite a repertoire!

9. **The Little Drummer Boy from "The Little Drummer Boy" composed by Katherine Kennicott Davis**—Contrary to what many may believe, there is no mention of a drum solo during Baby Jesus' birth in any of the four books of the Gospel. Nevertheless, it takes guts to play for the Son of God, and talent not to make His infant self cry from the noise.

10. **Alexander's Ragtime Band from "Alexander's Ragtime Band" by Irving Berlin**—Great American songwriter Irving Berlin had his first big hit with this toe-tapper all the way back in 1911, practically inventing this genre of song! This band makes no bones about their talent, they're "the best band in the land." Plus, they have a bugle call "so natural that you want to go to war." Good thing, since WWI is only three years away.

ROBERTS, JAMES—Real rocker and 80s heartthrob Rick Springfield played this fictional rocker in the 1984 film *Hard to Hold*. He sang "Love Somebody" and "Bop 'Til You Drop," both of which charted for real in the U.S. top twenty. His ex-girlfriend Niki Nides (Patti Hansen) is still in the band, hindering his efforts to charm the woman of his dreams, social worker Diana Lawson (Janet Eilber), who never heard of him.

ROBIN, JACK—Real name Jakie Rabinowitz (Al Jolson), this is the title character of the first-ever talkie, *The Jazz Singer* (1927)! He defies his cantor father (Warner Oland) to become, duh, a jazz singer. He sings "Toot, Toot Tootsie," "Mother of Mine, I Still Have You," "Dirty Hands, Dirty Faces," "Kol Nidre," Irving Berlin's "Blue Skies," and, of course, "My Mammy." See also **Jerry Golding**; **Keith Lennox**; **Jess Robin**.

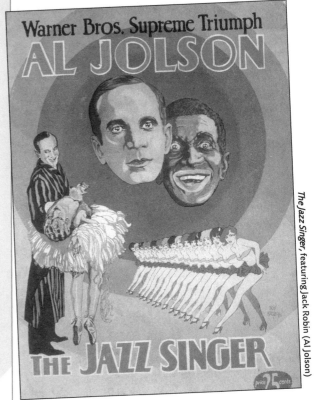

The Jazz Singer, featuring Jack Robin (Al Jolson)

ROBIN, JESS—In the 1980 Neil-Diamond-vehicle-slash-remake of *The Jazz Singer*, Yussel "Jess" Rabinovitch (Neil Diamond) becomes, well, not a jazz singer, but a pop singer, defying his tradition-bound cantor father (Sir Laurence Olivier, playing a Jew so stock the Anti-Defamation League should be notified). The movie works in some of the 1927 original's blackface routine when Robin has to sub in his black buddy's nameless foursome in a, uh, "black club." This naturally leads to a fistfightin' free-for-all when he's found out to be a white boy! Jess ditches his oppressively clingy wife (Caitlin Adams) and dad to go to Los Angeles, and manages to become a gold-album pop star—with no drugs, booze, or naked groupies in sight! Sheesh, what's the point, then?! When his father disowns him, he freaks out, berates his friends, and does what any man would do . . . hitchhikes to Texas to play country music in a redneck bar out in the boondocks. Fortunately, his buddy Bubba (Franklyn Ajaye) tracks him down so he can tell Robin about the son he didn't know he had. This movie stunk up the box office on release, but the soundtrack album shot to #3 on the charts, and spawned three top-ten singles, becoming Neil Diamond's last great musical highwater mark and songwriting triumph. See also **Jerry Golding**; **Keith Lennox**; **Jack Robin**.

ROBINSON, MANTRA—Long-haired rock artist (Neil Innes) being interviewed in "The Old Gay Whistle Test" sketch (06/02/75) on *Rutland Weekend Television*. He discusses how he's spent two years spelling the title of his new album, *Karmic Subtopian Protoplasmic Maximised Mantric Arcadian Intrusions*. He also talks about his bandmates: Brad, who's in prison; Ronnie, who's had a brain injury since 1957; Pete, whom he killed; and bass violinist Al Hutz, whom he dropped down an elevator shaft. See also **Stan Fitch**; **The Rutles**; **Splint**; **Toad the Wet Sprocket**.

ROCKHARD, KEITH—See **Mick Jagged and the Stones**.

ROD TORFULSON'S ARMADA FEATURING HERMAN MENDERCHUCK—See **Armada**.

ROD TORFULSON'S ARMADA FEATURING HERMAN MENDERCHUCK AND THE DUDETTES—See **Armada**.

ROGERS AND CLARKE—Warren Beatty was Lyle Rogers and Dustin Hoffman was Chuck Clarke, the singing/songwriting duo of the deservedly underrated 1987 movie *Ishtar*. The first twenty minutes or so, when they meet, team up, and start writing hilariously bad songs together, isn't actually that bad, but then the plot clumsily lurches into gear, ships them off to the Middle East, embroils them in spy crap, and everything goes straight to hell. Their awful songs, such as "Telling the Truth Is a Dangerous Business," "That a Lawnmower Can Do All That," and "Wardrobe of Love" are pretty funny. Diminutive 70s singer-songwriter Paul Williams penned many of the deliberately bad songs. Alas, this movie bombed so badly, so quickly, no soundtrack album was released!

Lyle Rogers (Warren Beatty) and Chuck Clarke (Dustin Hoffman) of Rogers and Clark

ROGERS, CHARLIE—Tough-guy club singer played by Elvis Presley in *Roustabout* (1964). After a fistfight against three college meatheads, Rogers hits the road. Literally, as his motorcycle is rammed off the road by Joe Lean (Leif Erickson), a crotchety carnie unhappy with the goo-goo eyes Rogers just made toward his daughter Cathy. The owner of the carnival, Maggie Morgan (Barbara Stanwyck), offers to fix Charlie's bike and smashed guitar, and even gives him a job as a roustabout while waiting. Well, he plays around the carnival, he tries to pick up Cathy (Joan Freeman), and—oh yeah—he starts singing and entertaining the teenagers. That helps the carnival, which is hurting for money. But things are never easy! He breaches the carnie code and storms out of the carnival, looking out for #1 and signing with a rival carnival for a lot of money. However, his desire for Cathy and a sense of family is too great, so he returns to Maggie's carnival and saves the day in song.

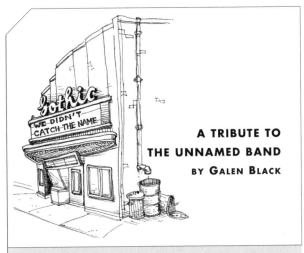

A TRIBUTE TO THE UNNAMED BAND
BY GALEN BLACK

Charlie Rogers (Elvis Presley)

Unnamed fake bands in movies and television shows are not mentioned in this book, because that would make the "U" chapter a volume unto itself. As a tribute to all the fake bands with no name we pay homage to one of the most famous unnamed bands of television history, the fake band from *Happy Days* (1974-84).

This 50s amateur rock and roll band featured Richie Cunningham (Ron Howard) on piano and sax, Warren "Potsie" Weber (Anson Williams) on lead vocals and guitar, and Ralph Malph (Don Most) on sax, piano, bass, and, on special Irish holidays, the squeeze box. The boys were a tight ensemble, but never got that big break. Of course not having a name hinders commercial success, but there were other contributing factors. A lack of originality no doubt played a big part in their failure at landing any big fat record contracts. The boys only played covers of the hits of the day and the occasional standard, if the situation called for it: "Great Balls of Fire," "Splish Splash," "Monster Mash," "Put Your Head on My Shoulder" and "When Irish Eyes Are Smiling"—on those special Irish holidays. Lack of management hurt also. If only they had found their Colonel Parker or Brian Epstein. But any chance of getting a talent agent or record producer interested was ruined during one of their early gigs at the Leopard Lodge dance in the "Fonzie Joins the Band" episode (03/04/75). The band had a tight set that night except they were forced to add another member, a certain bongo player named Arthur

"Fonzie" Fonzarelli (Henry Winkler). Fonzie's bongo playing wasn't an issue until the prima donna demanded a bongo solo during one of the band's best numbers. Any person who could have helped their career would have been put off by this uncouth street hoodlum and his "beatnik" instrument. It's ironic then that the band's best shot at fame came when Fonzie rejoined the band for one night as a replacement for Potsie in the "Fonzie the Superstar" episode (01/27/76). That magical night in Arnold's Fonzie's animal charisma had every female in the audience in a fit of hysteria worthy of Elvis or The Beatles. But Fonzie wasn't looking for fame, and traded in his microphone, tasseled jumpsuit, and potential fame, for his wrench, his old grease-stained mechanic's jumpsuit, and an endless supply of easy women.

A lack of a consistent rhythm section during the band's seven years together also prevented them from ever moving forward. The first drummer was Bag Zombroski (Neil J. Schwartz), but he was nothing more than the band's Pete Best. Outside of performing or rehearsing, his relationship with Richie, Potsie, and Ralph was contentious, to say the least, mostly due to his membership in a teen street gang, the Demons. After less than two years, Bag had been bagged. The band then tried to bridge the racial divide by adding a black drummer named Bill "Sticks" Downey Jr. (Jack Baker) to the band in the "Fonzie's New Friend" episode (11/25/75). But 1950s TV land racism and 1970s real American racism made sure the experiment in integration didn't "stick." The band didn't stop pushing the social envelope after "Sticks" was forced out—the boys started jamming with a female drummer ("Joanie's Weird Boyfriend," 03/01/77), although her presence in the band and show was negligible. Before the band broke up and the boys went their separate ways, they settled on the drumming of Fonzie's cousin, Charles "Chachi" Arcola (Scott Baio). But Chachi's interest in the band could have been solely to get in good with Richie, the brother of his future wife, Joanie Cunningham (Erin Moran).

Of course, the band's fate was really in the hands of the show's writers. Giving Richie, Ralph, and Potsie big-time music careers would have taken them out of Milwaukee and changed the entire complexion of the show, leaving behind its trademark family wholesomeness. Sure, a spin-off series about the band could have been an option, but that would have turned one good show into two bad shows. *Happy Days* would have become very crappy without Richie and Ralph, because *Happy Days* DID get very crappy without Richie and Ralph. And besides, they DID spin off Chachi and his band into a show, *Joanie Loves Chachi* (1983–84). And we all know how well that worked out! Don't cry, Richie—your band failed that your sitcom might live.

ROGERS, JACKIE JR.—Extremely bizarre and eccentric albino lounge singer portrayed by Martin Short. A somewhat fey extrovert, he prefers wearing silver lamé and constantly milks his famous father's tragic death for whatever it will get him. He has an annoying tendency to laugh through his teeth. Martin Short originated the character on *SCTV*, and afterward imported him wherever he was working: his *Saturday Night Live* tenure (1984–85); his two cable specials—*Martin Short Concert for the North Americas* (1985) and *I, Martin Short, Goes Hollywood* (1989); and another special, *The Show Formerly Known as The Martin Short Show* (05/20/95). See also **Vic Arpeggio**; **Big Momma**; **5 Neat Guys**; **Happiness Unlimited**; **The Happy Wanderers**; **Lola Heatherton**; **The Lemon Twins**; **Linsk Minyk**; **Tom Munroe**; **The Queenhaters**; **The Ramblers**; **The Recess Monkeys**; **Russ Riley**; **Jackie Rogers Sr.**; **Speed of Light**; **Dusty Towne**; **The Wally Hung Trio**.

ROGERS, JACKIE SR.—Best known as the father of Jackie Rogers Jr. Most of what is known of him is from the *SCTV* sketch "Jackie, We Hardly Knew Ye" (03/11/83), a mockumentary where Jackie Rogers Jr. (Martin Short) played his father. J.R. Senior had a vaudeville act and used his kids in it, until the state took 'em away and he hit the skids. He died after being mauled by a cougar in the middle of his 1970 comeback TV special, *Old Mother Nature, She Loves Me*. He was singing "Born Free." His son wrote a fictional tell-all about pops, *Damn You, Daddy, Sir*. Jackie Rogers Sr. was NOT an albino. See also **Vic Arpeggio**; **Big Momma**; **5 Neat Guys**; **Happiness Unlimited**; **The Happy Wanderers**; **Lola Heatherton**; **The Lemon Twins**; **Linsk Minyk**; **Tom Munroe**; **The Queenhaters**; **The Ramblers**; **The Recess Monkeys**; **Russ Riley**; **Jackie Rogers Jr.**; **Speed of Light**; **Dusty Towne**; **The Wally Hung Trio**.

ROLL, ROCK — Prehistoric rock star who sings the big hit "The Bedrock Twitch" in "The Twitch" episode (10/12/62) of the animated show *The Flintstones*. It's a parody of "The Twist," but Roll also features a swipe at Elvis's redneck accent. He gets sick, and Fred looks enough like him to be forced to lip-synch to the song on stage pretending to be him. Hal Smith was the voice of the cornpone-sounding Rock Roll. The song was written by William Hanna and Joseph Barbera. See also **Ann-Margrock**; **The Beau Brummelstones**; **Jimmy Darrock**; **The Flintstone Canaries**; **"Hot Lips" Hannigan**; **Hi-Fye**; **Pebbles and Bamm-Bamm**.

ROLLETTI, TONY — Talentless lounge singer played by Bill Kirchenbauer on the 1977 TV talk-show spoof *Fernwood 2Nite* and its 1978 successor, *America 2-Night*. A frequent guest, he got married on one episode à la Tiny Tim on *The Tonight Show*—then got divorced on the show in a later episode! *TRIVIA TIME! Fernwood 2Nite* was directed by Micky Dolenz of The Monkees! See also **Denny and Brian**; **Pharoah Fawcett**; **The Friedkin Family Singers**; **Happy Kyne and the Mirth Makers**; **Buck and Harriet Pine**; **The Punk Monks**.

ROLLING BOULDERS, THE — See **Mick Jadestone and the Rolling Boulders**.

ROLLINS, SMITTY — Jazz-legend-turned-high-school-janitor (Antonio Fargas) who is rediscovered in the "All That Jazz" episode of *The Steve Harvey Show* (02/11/99). See also **The Rib Tips**; **Soul Teachers**; **Steve Hightower and the Hi-Tops**.

RON NASTY AND THE NEW RUTLES — See **The Rutles**.

ROSE, THE — See **Mary Rose Foster**.

ROSE BAND, THE — The backup band for Mary Rose Foster in the 1979 movie *The Rose*. The band was played by Danny Weis (leader and guitarist), Steve Hunter, Robbie Louis Buchanan, Jerome Noel Jumonville, Norton Buffalo, Mark Leonard, Mark Underwood, and Pentti (Whitey) Glan. See also **Mary Rose Foster**; **Monty's Band**; **Billy Ray**.

ROUND POUND, THE — Pompadoured cartoon egomaniac Johnny Bravo (voiced by Jeff Bennett) meets up with this morbidly obese hip-hop trio in the "Hip Hop Flop" episode (08/18/97) of animated show *Johnny Bravo* on the Cartoon Network. The Round Pound's DJ has eaten his turntables, and Johnny finds them a new one. As payment, the group teaches him how to be down, def, and dope. Real rap star Chuck D. provides the voice of member CD Biggenz. See also **Johnny and the Deer Ticks**; **Berry Vanderbolten**.

ROWLF THE DOG — Piano-playing dog Muppet best known for his love of bad puns and stint as the house piano player for the 1976–81 TV series *The Muppet Show*, but his career goes back much further. His first gig was in a 1962 Purina Dog Chow commercial. He was a regular on the 1963–66 *Jimmy Dean Show*. In 1968 he hosted (!) *Our Place*, the summer replacement series for *The Smothers Brothers Comedy Hour*. Then he did a stint on the first (1969) season of *Sesame Street*. Rowlf was voiced by Jim Henson, and Henson's 1990 death put a serious crimp in Rowlf's style as he was subsequently relegated to the background in later Muppet movies and their 1996 TV series, *Muppets Tonight*. Some of Rowlf's performances were collected on the 1993 album *Ol' Brown Ears Is Back*. See also **The Amazing Marvin Suggs and His Muppaphone; Dr. Teeth and the Electric Mayhem; Mahna Mahna and the Two Snowths; Miss Piggy; Wayne and Wanda.**

Rowlf the Dog (voiced by Jim Henson) (r)

ROY MAXWELL AND THE CORSAIRS—See **The Wonders**.

R.U. DA 1?—See **Three Times One Minus One**.

RUFFEE—Parody of longtime children's musician Raffi in the "Ruffled Ruffee" episode (11/11/92) of *Tiny Toon Adventures*. Ruffee (voiced by Rob Paulsen) is holding a concert, singing twee praises to obedience, when he is upstaged by a guitar-playing Buster Bunny (voiced by Charlie Adler). See also **Def Zepplin; Fuddonna; Skinhead O'-Connell; Vanilla Lice.**

RULE, HAMLIN—From "The Pied Piper" episode (11/21/77) of TV adventure show *Wonder Woman*. Comedian Martin Mull plays this flute-playing rock star whose last three concert box-office receipts have been heisted midconcert by sonic-gun-wielding thieves. It turns out Rule himself has brainwashed some female fans into doing it for him, you know, with his flute-playing?! Because you know how you get hypnotized by the sound of a flute, right? Well, Elena Atkinson (*The Brady Bunch*'s Eve Plumb) does get hypnotized, and since she's the daughter of IADC (Inter-Agency Defense Command) honcho Joe Atkinson (Norman Burton) and Diana's boss, Diana Prince (Lynda Carter) is sent to investigate. As Wonder Woman, she kicks the necessary asses needed to wrap up the plot and reunite Elena with her father. The episode's writers David Ketchum and Tony DiMarco must have thought themselves clever; "Hamlin" is the town the Pied Piper story takes place in. See also **AntiMatter; Billy Dero; Jeff and Barbi Gordon; Lane Kinkaid; Kathy Meadows.**

RUSTY HINGES AND THE BOYS FROM THE BRIG—See **The Bird Brains**.

RUSTY WELLS AND HIS COMBO—Elvis Presley is Rusty Wells, leader of this combo playing Chicago's 77 Club in *Girl Happy* (1965). They can't wait to blow the snow for some fun in the sun and head to Fort Lauderdale, Florida, to play spring break. Mob-type club owner Big Frank (Harold J. Stone) nixes the idea, realizing how they can pack the place even during a blizzard. But when his daughter, cute coed Valerie Frank (Shelley Fabares), says she's heading there, too, Rusty cleverly hornswoggles Big Frank into sending the band there to secretly chaperone her, all expenses paid. They play the Sand Bar at night ("Wolf Call,") and follow her around every other waking moment, which puts a serious crimp in their tail-huntin' plans. Then Rusty really falls for her, but when she mentions his name to Dad, Dad spills the beans to her about his secret chaperone plan, driving her to a drunken walk down a strip-club runway and causing one of the largest and most elaborate of all the many, many Elvis-movie bar brawls. Dad bails her out of jail and makes her realize that Rusty is really in love with her. It's a happy ending as spring break ends and they all head back to freezing-cold Chicago. Lineup: Andy (Gary Crosby, son of Bing) on bass, Wilbur (Joby Baker) on drums, and Doc (Jimmy Hawkins) on guitar and occasional sax.

RUTH EDDING AND THE BLUEBELLS—See **Lila Rose Oliver**.

RUTLES, THE—The Rutles first originated on the U.K. BBC *Rutland Weekend Television* TV program—er, sorry, programme—Eric Idle's post-Monty Python sketch comedy show. The name of the band came from the show's name, and the show's name came from Britain's smallest county, Rutland, which the British government once tried to legislate out of existence. Strangely, America saw the skit first, a quick *Hard Day's Night* parody—the song "I Must Be in Love" (the piece aired on the 11/19/76 episode of *Rutland Weekend Television*). When Eric Idle hosted *Saturday Night Live* on 10/02/76, he brought along the clip, playing into a previous joke (04/24/76) where *SNL*'s producer Lorne Michaels offered The Beatles a whopping $3,000 to reunite on the show. Idle "tricked" Michaels out of the money, supplying not The Bea-

Rusty Wells and His Combo

tles, but The Rutles. Eric Idle hosted another *Saturday Night Live* (04/23/77), which was set up as a telethon on behalf of a cash-stricken Great Britain. Idle brought on ex-Rutle Ron Nasty (Neil Innes) to play the very Lennonesque "Cheese and Onions" on the show. It's a tribute to Innes's compositional ability that the performance later turned up on a Beatles bootleg, purporting to be the real thing! Idle wanted to turn The Rutles idea into a movie, and *SNL*'s producer Lorne Michaels helped get him a deal with NBC, which provided more money than the BBC would have. Thus the spoof was spun into the full-blown, prime-time TV mockumentary *All You Need Is Cash* (03/22/78). It mercilessly savaged The Beatles mythology from top to bottom and inside and out, yet in such a ridiculous and clever fashion as to be enjoyed by Beatle fans and detractors alike. It featured most of the then-current cast of *Saturday Night Live* in various roles, and even Beatle George Harrison himself had a role (he plays a financial reporter investigating reports of theft at Rutle Corps, who has his microphone stolen). Paul Simon and Mick Jagger appeared as themselves, reminiscing about The Rutles. A key component of the movie was Neil Innes's spot-on compositions that so successfully aped the real thing that ATV Music, The Beatles' publishing company, demanded (and got) half ownership! The movie charts the rise of Dirk McQuickly (Eric Idle), Ron Nasty (Neil Innes), Stig O'Hara (Rikki Fataar), and Barry Wom, real name Barrington Womble (John Halsey). It swiftly moves from their club days to becoming massive hitmakers under manager Leggy Mountbatten (Terence Bayler) to the band's disintegration into solo acts. A lavish gatefold soundtrack album with a twenty-page booklet inside was released, thanks to the efforts of Derek Taylor, The Beatles' former press officer and then a VP at Warner Bros. Records. It reproduced the covers of such prefab four albums as: *A Hard Day's Rut, Ouch!;*

Sgt Rutter Darts Only Club Band; Tragical History Tour; Shabby Road, and their final album, *Let It Rot*. Then, for a long time, nothing happened. *All You Need Is Cash* did poorly in the ratings, the album was remaindered, and everyone somehow managed to get on with their lives and other, non-Rutle aspects of their careers. The year 1990 saw a CD rerelease of the album on Rhino Records, as well as a tribute album, *Rutles Highway Revisited*, on Shimmy Disc. In 1994, Neil Innes teamed up with a Beatles tribute band, The Moptops, to play as Ron Nasty and the New Rutles at a Beatles convention and the Monty Python Lust for Glory retrospective festival. So well received was the band that Innes cooked up a new Rutles album, *Archaelogy* (1996), purporting to be the album The Rutles were working on when they broke up. A timely parody of *The Beatles Anthology* CDs, miniseries, and hoopla, it featured another batch of Innes-penned songs. There was a bizarre Rutles parallel to The Beatles' addition of backing tracks to old Lennon demos to make "new" Beatles songs. Ollie Halsall, who had played on all the original Rutles tracks, passed away in 1992, but Innes dug up some of the original sessions and used three of the tracks on *Archaelogy*, turning an unfinished backing track into the song "Unfinished Words." Two other songs "Shangri-La" and "Knicker Elastic King" from the album are actually songs from previous Neil Innes albums, Beatle-fied. Idle wasn't involved in the *Archaelogy* project, which was fine, as he had nothing to do with the music of the first movie. But in 2002, Idle wrote and produced *Can't Buy Me Lunch*, a sequel to the 1978 film, which analyzes the effect of The Rutles on the world, and spoofs innumerable Beatles documentaries and specifically the 1995 *The Beatles Anthology* miniseries. The Rutles tower in the fake-band universe, because they stand on the shoulders of real musical giants The Beatles. Being really funny also helps. See also **Arthur Hodgeson** and the Kneecaps; Les Garçons de la Plage; The Machismo Brothers; Ruttling Orange Peel; Punk Floyd; Blind Lemon Pye.

THE RUTLES
(1990, RHINO RECORDS)

WE HAVE RHINO Records to thank for the 1990 CD reissue of the soundtrack to *All You Need is Cash*, the 1978 TV special that detailed the finest Beatles spoof ever, The Rutles. The CD contains a whopping six bonus tracks that were not on the original vinyl album, which helps make up for the less impressive packaging of the CD. The original album came with a gatefold cover with a big, beautiful booklet, dense with pictures and album covers from all points of The Rutles' careers. The foldout CD booklet manages to cram the highlights in, if at necessarily reduced size. It's a shame they couldn't cram in two more bonus tracks as well, the original versions of "I Must Be in Love" and "Good Times Roll" from the *Rutland Weekend Television* soundtrack album. The CD covers the entire career of the pre-fab four, giving composer/mastermind Neil Innes a wide swath of pop history to cover, which he does with vigor. The spirited rocker "Goose Step Mama" spoofs The Beatles' early, high-energy, pill-popping Berlin days. So does "Blue Suede Schubert," but with bizarre nods to Chuck Berry's "Roll Over Beethoven" and Elvis's "Blue Suede Shoes." The Merseybeat era is showcased in "Number One," a sort of inside-out "Twist and Shout." The album tragically has no spoofs of the *Revolver*-era Beatles, jumping from the balladry of "Between Us" and "With a Girl Like You" to the psychedelic years with the perfect George Harrison satire, the sitar-heavy, Indian-influenced "Nevertheless." It's a lot more listenable (and, thankfully, shorter!) than his own "Within You, Without You" which it parodies. A couple of the later-era tracks, such as "Get Up and Go"

and "Doubleback Alley" are not quite as enjoyable, because they ape the song they're spoofing ("Get Back" and "Penny Lane," respectively) TOO closely, becoming one-note ponies. Lyrically, Innes goes out of his way to turn The Beatles' sunshine upside down into a frown, interjecting odd grimier moments while the music carries on cheerfully. "Hold My Hand" turns the pure teen innocence of "I Want to Hold Your Hand" into a sleazy pickup line as the narrator swoops in to pick up a bird with the claim ". . . I've just seen your date outside, he's with another." "Doubleback Alley" mentions ". . . the funny man in the ice cream van who talked so queer . . ." Run kids, run! In fact, run to the store and buy a copy of this CD already.

SACRED COWS, THE—From the "Groovy Guru" episode (01/13/68) of TV spy-spoof *Get Smart*. This drummerless "rock" trio were part of the Groovy Guru's (Larry Storch) evil plot to cause the youth of America to run wild, looting and killing. Sample lyrics: "Thrill, thrill, thrill. Kill, kill, kill." Compelling, isn't it? The band was played by session musicians Jerry Scheff (bass), John Greek (guitar), and Ben Benay (guitar).

SAINT HEX—See **Stillwater**.

SALINI—In the 11/07/97 episode of sketch comedy *Mr. Show*, turn-of-the-century march composer Salini (David Cross) seethes as his rival John Baptiste Philouza (Bob Odenkirk) effortlessly turns out brilliant works off the top of his head. It's an oompah parody of the 1984 movie *Amadeus*. Philouza's works consistently bring tears to Salini's eyes, so he has his tear ducts surgically removed. Salini's first name is never mentioned. See also **The Beetletown Players; Larry Black; Livingston Brewster; Willips Brighton; Dickie Crickets; Indomitable Spirit; Kid Jersey; Kill or Be Killed; C. S. Lewis Jr.; Horace Loeb; Marilyn Monster; Norma Jean Monster; John Baptiste Philouza; Professor Murder; Puscifer; Smoosh; Old Swerdlow; Three Times One Minus One; Titannica; Sir Lloyd Wilson Webber; Wyckyd Sceptre; Daffy "Mal" Yinkleyankle.**

SAMPSON'S BALLS — See **Stillwater**.

SANCTIFIED — A Christian punk-metal band that is sabotaged by Eric Cartman before they can play South Park's Christfest 2003 concert in the "Christian Rock Hard" episode (10/29/03) of *South Park*. See also **Faith + 1**.

SAND WAILERS, THE — A ten-piece, all-accordion, all-whale concert ensemble featured in the "Sand Whale Strikes" episode (11/09/01) of cartoon *Courage the Cowardly Dog*. One of the whales lost their accordion gambling with Eustace's father, Icket, and comes back years later to get it. Was it mentioned they were sand whales?

SASHAY — Amy Hunter guest stars as this R&B diva in the "We Don't Need Another Hero" episode (04/21/96) of the WB series *The Parent Hood*. Cast regular Zaria Peterson (Reagan Gomez-Preston) and her friends are picked to appear in a Sashay music video, but her dad, Robert (Robert Townsend), forbids her on the grounds the videos are offensive. Starstruck Zaria, in true sitcom fashion, sneaks out to be in the video, with the help of her aspiring-musician older brother, who hopes to give Sashay

his tape. But after Zaria sees the skimpy outfit she'll have to wear in the video, she gets cold feet, and her brother, defending her, sacrifices his chance to make it big. Sashay's hit song is "I Got Plenty of Booty (Boo-tay)."

SATAN'S PENIS — Contestants in the battle of the bands in the "That Thing You Don't" (11/26/97) episode of *The Drew Carey Show*. They are all attired in full 40s-retro-swing-gear—zoot suits with the reet pleat. Presumably they were one of the many jump blues/swing revival bands of the mid 90s. They are never actually shown playing. See also **The Horndogs; The Underprivileged; The Unreliables**.

SATIN KNIGHTS, THE — Never-seen Moody Blues tribute band playing the Quicksands Casino in Las Vegas in the "Viva Ned Flanders" episode (01/10/99) of *The Simpsons*. Obviously named after the Moody Blues hit "Knights in White Satin." Tragically, their opening act is the REAL Moody Blues, who have a surprise cameo in the episode as themselves. See also **The Beach Boys Experience; The Be Sharps; Johnny Bobby; Johnny Calhoun; Captain Bart and the Tequila Mockingbirds; The Crazy Old Man Singers; Cyanide; Gulliver Dark; Ferl Dixon and His Second Helping Boys; Funky C Funky Do; Garfunkel, Messina, Oates, and Lisa; Hooray for Everything; Kovenant; Krusty and the Krums; The Larry Davis Experience; Little Timmy and the Shebangs; Loggins and Oates; Lurleen Lumpkin; M. C. Safety and the Caution Crew; Melvin and the Squirrels; "Bleeding Gums" Murphy; The Party Posse; The Rappin' Rabbis; Red Breem and His Band of Some Esteem; The Steve Sax Trio; Testament; Blind Willie Witherspoon; The Ya-Hoo Recovering Alcoholic Jug Band; Yodelin' Zeke.**

SATINE—Singer Satine (Nicole Kidman), known as "the sparkling diamond," is the all-singing, all-dancing, all-whoring star attraction of Paris's Moulin Rouge (nightclub, dance club, and bordello), run by Harold Zidler (Jim Broadbent). Penniless Londoner writer Christian (Ewan MacGregor) falls in love with her, but alas, so does the Duke (Richard Roxburgh), Zidler's investor, who holds the deeds to the club as security for financing the new show starring Satine and written by Christian. Even more alas, there's a reason she's drop-dead gorgeous, cuz drop dead she does—of consumption. The Baz Luhrmann psychedelic extravaganza that is *Moulin Rouge!* (2001) brazenly

Satine
(Nicole Kidman)

raids twentieth-century culture to reimagine 1900 Paris as a burlesque hippie 60s farce through a kaleidoscopic MTV lens. In this musical, the cast sings songs kidnapped at random from the history of pop music, brainwashed and press-ganged into service as hallucinogenic yet coherent musical numbers. Oh, and composer Erik Satie (Matthew Whittet), painter Toulouse-Lautrec (John Leguizamo), and a narcoleptic Argentinian (Jacek Koman) are writing the *Sound of Music* as a bohemian revolutionary play. *TRIVIA TIME!* Aussie popster Kylie Minogue plays the Green Faerie, with Ozzy Osbourne as her singing voice!

THE SATURN 5—Sixties Ventures-type instrumentalists of the twangy guitar variety. They are credited as appearing in *That Thing You Do* (1996), but good luck spotting them anywhere in the movie. They have the instrumental "Voyage Around the Moon" on the soundtrack album. Allegedly played by Thomas Cleo, Ken Empie, Ron Jeffrey, Mike Piccirillo, and Chris Wilson. Mike Piccirillo helped craft the movie's carefully imitative period songs and sound. *TRIVIA TIME!* The band's name is a play on their being a quintet, and the NASA launch vehicle of the same name. The Saturn 5 got us to the moon! See also **Elizabeth Anne; Blue Spot Trio; The Chantrellines; Diane Dane; The Echoes; Freddy Fredrickson; The G Men; The Heardsmen; The Hollyhocks; Jon D and the Walkers; Legends of Brass; Marilyn Lovell and the Geminis; The Norm Wooster Singers; Del Paxton; The Tempos; The Trends; Two Eriks; The Vicksburgs; The Wonders.**

SAVAGES, THE—In the "Extracurricular Activities" episode of the Canadian coming-of-age teen drama *Degrassi High* (1989–91), Bronco Davis (L. Dean Ifill) lets leak to girlfriend Lucy Fernandez (Anais

Granofsky) that this rock band is coming to the school to shoot a music video. She blabs the secret to some gal pals and they sneak in to see the band, even if it means getting her boyfriend in trouble. Supposedly one of the band members is a Degrassi alum, which is why they're shooting there. See also **Gourmet Scum; The Zits.**

SAVANTE — African-American rap/R&B singer (Phil Lamarr) from at least three *Mad TV* sketches. In the first, "The R&B Meeting" (02/01/97), he meets with clueless execs to choose a song for a benefit album for sick kids, but all his songs are filthy sex fantasies. So they go with "Suck My Freak." In "Savante: Career Day" (01/31/98) he sings dirty songs at second-graders for career day. And in "Savante with Usher" (09/12/98) he and guest star/real hip-hopper Usher contribute songs to a Disney film. See also **Defcon One; Dr. Dazzle; The Eracists; Hoppy Potty; Darlene McBride; Michael McLoud and Jasmine Wayne-Wayne; Shaunda; Little Hassan Taylor; Willow.**

SCÄB — A two-man alternately hard rock, metal, and New Wave-y band originally featured in the "Director's Cut" episode (09/02/01) of animated show *Home Movies.* Third-grader and film auteur Brendon Small (voiced by Brendon Small) is hired by long-haired guitarist/mumbler Duane (also voiced by Brendon Small) to film his Queen-esque rock opera based on Franz Kafka's *Metamorphosis.* Brendon would rather work on his film *Louis Louis,* a fictional meeting of Louis Braille and Louis Pasteur. But none of Brendon's friends, who, more important, double as his crew, are interested, so he grudgingly makes the rock opera. Duane and his band (later expanded to a quartet) have occasionally appeared in other episodes ("Mortgages and Marbles," 09/30/01; "Law & Boarder," 10/07/01; "Hiatus,"

01/20/02) to contribute music to Brendon's latest project. *Home Movies* originally aired on UPN for a handful of episodes (April–May 1999) before cancellation and a second life on the Cartoon Network. See also **Alligator Shoes; Brendon Poppins and the Chimminy Sweeps.**

SCALLION, DILL — See **Dill Scallion and the Dillionaires.**

SCHIFFER, STEPHANIE — This professional singer is hired to replace Phoebe Buffay (Lisa Kudrow) at the coffeehouse Central Perk in the *Friends* episode "The One With the Baby on the Bus" (11/02/95). Schiffer (played by real singer Chrissy Hynde) sings a cover of "Angel of the Morning" and later performs a duet with Phoebe on her hit "Smelly Cat." See also **Phoebe Buffay; Ross Gellar; Leslie.**

SCHNEEBLY, NED — See **Maggot Death.**

SCHOOL OF ROCK — In *The School of Rock* (2003), rocker Dewey Finn (Jack Black in his most perfect role ever) gets kicked out of his band No Vacancy. When his substitute-teacher roommate bugs him for the rent, Dewey poses as his roommate to score a teaching gig and some cash. He plans to snooze through class at prestigious private Horace Greeley Preparatory. But after seeing the kids in their music class, and having an upcoming battle of the bands in the back of his mind, he hatches a scheme to turn the class into his band! He puts the uptight rich kids into a crash course in rock, amazingly finding positions for everyone, even if it's not in the band proper (security, roadies, groupies). It's all amazingly charming, and no one but the charismatic Jack Black could pull this trifle off. He soon has the classically trained kids rocking like pros, and after various shenanigans, including his getting exposed as a fraud to Principal Rosalie Mullins (Joan Cusack), the kids themselves sneak out to complete the plan and play the WROK Battle of the Bands. They kick out some excellent jams ("The School of Rock," written for the movie by The Mooney Suzuki) and although they don't win the contest, they have the crowd (including their stunned parents) chanting their name until they come back for an encore (AC/DC's "It's a Long Way to the Top"). Lineup: Zack Mooneyham (Joey Gaydos Jr.) on guitar, Katie (Rebecca Brown) on bass, bad boy Freddy Jones (Kevin Clark) on drums, shy Lawrence (Robert Tsai) on keyboards, backup singers Tomika (Maryam Hassan), Alicia (Aleisha Allen), and Marta (Caitlin Hale), and, of course, Dewey himself on lead guitar and vocals. The kids all did their own playing! Black and the kids also performed on *The Tonight Show* and *Live with Regis and Kelly*. See also **Maggot Death**; **No Vacancy**.

SCHROEDER — The Beethoven-loving, child-prodigy classical pianist from the comic strip *Peanuts*, and the many dozens of animated *Peanuts* TV specials. He first appeared in the strip as a baby on 05/30/51. His first TV appearance was in the *Peanuts'* first and now classic TV animated special, *A Charlie Brown Christmas* (12/09/65), where he was voiced by Chris Doran. Schroeder was in charge of the music for the kids' Christmas pageant, but screwed around at rehearsal, playing the now-trademark *Peanuts* song, the jazzy instrumental "Linus and Lucy" (really The Vince Guaraldi Trio), that got all the kids dancing and Snoopy jamming along on bass. Schroeder played amazingly well, especially when you consider that the black keys on his toy piano were just painted on. He frequently had to fend off Lucy Van Pelt, who had a crush on him. **TRIVIA TIME!** Is Schroeder his last name or his first name? There is

School of Rock

some scanty evidence in the strip that it is his last. However, his other name, first or last, has never been revealed.

SCISSOR BITCH — From the "Teddy Cam" episode (02/03/02) of animated show *Baby Blues*. Suburban middle-class mom Wanda MacPherson (voiced by Julia Sweeney) is introduced to the hummable tunes of this band by Johnny (voiced by *Angel*'s David Boreanaz), the current disreputable boyfriend of their baby-sitter Bizzy (*Mad TV*'s Nicole Sullivan). See also **Darryl and the Chaos, Roadkill Hoagie**.

SCOTT, WILHELMINA "WILLIE" — Pre-WWII American nightclub singer in the Shanghai nightclub Club Obi Wan (gratuitous *Star Wars* reference), played by Kate Capshaw in *Indiana Jones and the Temple of Doom* (1984), a prequel to first Indiana Jones movie. After she sings Cole Porter's "Anything Goes" in Chinese, she callously scrambles af-

ter a diamond mixed with ice on the floor of the club, instead of the antidote to the poison Indy just got slipped. As a fitting punishment, she spends the rest of the movie getting dragged by Dr. Jones (Harrison Ford) from one treacherous, exotic locale to another. Oh, and screaming. *TRIVIA TIME!* Kate Capshaw and her future hubby, Stephen Spielberg (who directed this film) met on the set of this film.

SCRATCH — An unseen artist (possibly rap) on rapper Massive Genius's label who illegally sampled the backing vocals from an old song owned by mob-connected Hesh Rabkin. When Rabkin finds out, it cuts the legs out from under Massive G's plan to sue Rabkin for back royalties he bilked another artist, Little Jimmy Willis, out of. From the "A Hit Is a Hit" episode (03/14/99) of mob-riffic HBO drama *The Sopranos*. See also **The Chablis**; **Massive Genius**; **Visiting Day**; **Little Jimmy Willis**.

Wille Scott (Kate Capshaw) (center)

SCREAMER, JET — High-energy rocker from the "Date with Jet Screamer" episode (09/30/62) of the animated TV show *The Jetsons*. Daughter Judy (voiced by Jane Waldo) writes a song to enter a contest to win a date with him, but disapproving daddy George (voiced by George O'Hanlon) sabotages her song, swapping it for his younger son Elroy's (voiced by Daws Butler) nonsensical secret code. The wacky code wins the contest, and Jet Screamer sings "Eep Op Ork Ah Ah" to an enthralled Judy, as suspicious George secretly tails them. Howard Morris was the voice of Mr. Screamer.

SCROOGE, EBONY—Nasty, unpleasant pop singer played by singer/disgraced former Miss America Vanessa Williams from the 2000 VH1 TV special, *A Diva's Christmas Carol,* yet another reworking of Charles Dickens's much reworked *Christmas Carol.* She gets visited by the ghost of her former band-mate in Desire, Marli Jacob (Rozonda "Chilli" Thomas of rap group TLC), and gets the standard three-ghost treatment before seeing the light and reforming her ways.

SCUM OF THE EARTH—Self-described "hoodlum rock" band from the "Hoodlum Rock" episode (10/09/78) of the sitcom *WKRP in Cincinnati.* Michael Des Barres played member Sir Charles Weatherbee, who preferred to be called "Dog." The other members were Blood (Peter Elbling) and Sir Nigel Weatherbee (Jim Henderson). They give grief to the station's employees while they're in town to do a concert. It takes a whole lot of hotel room–trashing to impress DJ Johnny Fever (Howard Hesseman) though; he's seen it all. *TRIVIA TIME!* Their music ("Got Enough Love") was by Michael Des Barres's real band, Detective. See also **Linda Taylor**.

SGT. PEPPER'S LONELY HEARTS CLUB BAND (I)—In the 1968 animated movie *Yellow Submarine,* four old-fashioned brass band musicians play in a gazebo in Pepperland, spreading peace, love, and all that bull. Then the Blue Meanies attack and it all hits the crapper. The Beatles are immediately called in (of course) to save the day. Forced to impersonate the band, they turn out to be dead ringers for 'em. What are the odds!? *TRIVIA TIME!* The roles of The Beatles were not voiced by The Beatles. What a ripoff! Paul Angelis did Ringo's voice; John Clive, John; Geoffrey Hughes, Paul; and Peter Batten, George.

A HARD DAY'S NIGHT

Blame The Beatles. Or at least *A Hard Day's Night* director Richard Lester. This seminal 1964 movie unknowingly stamped a mold on the face of pop music television that would take decades to shake off. You know: running around while the song plays. Director Richard Lester led the fab foursome through a half dozen or so proto-music videos in the wildly successful 1964 film.

On September 12, 1966, NBC debuted *The Monkees,* a television show formed as a direct, deliberate imitation of The Beatles film. The Beatles not being available for a weekly television show themselves, especially not for $450 each per show. Each *Monkees* episode featured, yup, at least one musical number with the band running, jumping, and standing still while the song played.

Once the formula had been established, cartoon studio Hanna-Barbera took it and ran with it—into the ground: *The Impossibles* (1966). *The Banana Splits* (1968–70). *The Cattanooga Cats* (1969–71). *Josie and the Pussycats* (1970–72). *The Pebbles and Bamm-Bamm Show* (1971–76). *The Amazing Chan and the Chan Clan* (1972). *Jabberjaw* (1976). Even shows without bands used the formula. Can you recall a single *Scooby Doo* (1969–72) chase scene without a limp pop tune playing? Didn't think so.

Basically, The Beatles and Richard Lester were ripped off right and left, culminating in that triumph of the short attention-span, MTV (debut: 08/01/81). On second thought, let's blame Hanna-Barbera for ruining a good idea with endless repetition, because Lester doesn't ac-cept the blame anyway:

"...I was sent a vellum scroll from MTV saying that I was the 'spiritual father' of MTV...and I demanded a blood test!"—Richard Lester from a 1999 interview with Steven Soderbergh.

Sgt. Pepper's Lonely Hearts Club Band (II)

SGT. PEPPER'S LONELY HEARTS CLUB BAND (II)—Dear Lord in Heaven. There are bad movies, but *Sgt. Pepper's Lonely Hearts Club Band* (1978) was not just an utter waste of celluloid, but also a cinematic black hole that marked an end or severe downturn in the careers of most people who appeared in it. In the movie, the original brass band of the title has magical instruments that make the soldiers lay down their arms to listen, and hence ends WWI. Why they then waste them merely entertaining troops in WWII while Europe and Indochina burn and Hitler slaughters six million Jews is quickly glossed over. Anyway, the last surviving member, the old Sergeant Pepper himself (Woody Chambliss), finally keels over dead on August 10, 1958. A new version of the band is needed and his grandson Billy Shears (Peter Frampton) becomes the new Sergeant Pepper, and he drafts his three friends, the Henderson brothers, Mark (Barry Gibb), Dave (Robin Gibb), and Bob (Maurice Gibb), to fill out the band. Frampton fronting The Bee Gees—it's a 70s nightmare come all too true. The plot, such as it is, leisurely creaks into gear and they all go to Hollywood to become big, debauched, drug 'n' booze–addled rock stars. Meanwhile, bad guys steal the magic instruments, the band tries to get them back, and it all leads into a nonclimactic confrontation with Future Villain Band (Aerosmith) and the only scene even mildly worth seeing—Peter Frampton fighting to the death with Aerosmith lead singer Steve Tyler. Then Sergeant Pepper magically appears, only NOW he's a totally different guy who's black (?!) (Billy Preston), and he makes everything all better. Now try to imagine all this happening with absolutely no dialogue and only the narration of ancient comedian George Burns, because that's exactly what happened! Robert Stigwood, the man behind this fiasco, has earned a special place in many peoples' private hell, if not the real one. See also **Future Villain Band; Lucy and the Diamonds**.

SENSATIONS, THE—In the unappealingly titled "Urine Trouble" episode (05/11/89) of *L.A. Law*, two African-American music groups go head-to-head in court. Thing is, they're the same group! The first group, old-time Motowners, decided to retire and sell their name and act to a bunch of new guys to keep the music alive. Trouble is, the new guys changed the songs; having "put in this ka-tonk, ka-konk," whereas The Sensations always stood for smooth, according to original member Malcolm Redding. New guy Mr. Wiltern ain't having none of it, calling the old stuff "sugary puke!" Now the old guys want to come out of retirement to sing their stuff the way it's supposed to be. The new guys want to slap an injunction on them—they don't want the old guys bleeding off potential revenue. Naturally, Judge Vance has no choice but to demand a sing-off, in the courtroom! The oldsters, in matching powder-blue suits, smooth up a storm with the pretty decent Motown pastiche, "Walking In the Rain With My Baby." "Notice the soothing nature of the performance" points out their lawyer/music-critic Michael Kuzak (Harry Hamlin). Wow, he must write for *Rolling Stone*. Then the new guys jump around in eye-hurting pink shirts and purple-sequined suits. They do the same song with a horrible 80s beat-box funk beat, featuring scratching and that mid-80s bane of musical goodness: the keyboard worn around the neck like a guitar. Nothing but "Smut! . . . Cheap smutty trash!" says Redding. After the performances, the judge shudders to think what the new guys may have done to "Bopping All Night With Betty" and finds the two acts too distinct to cause marketplace confusion. Injunction denied! The old Sensations were played by real 60s act The Rivingtons: Al Frazier, John "Sunny" Harris, and Andrew Butler. The new Sensations were played by Simply Raw, Theodore Miller, Ricky Wyrick, and Xavier Thomas.

7 DEGREES CELSIUS — Boy-band parody on *Saturday Night Live*. The band—Jeph (Chris Parnell), Samm (Chris Kattan), Sweet T (Horatio Sanz), and P-Nutt (James Van Der Beek, that week's guest star)—and their manager (Will Ferrell) were introduced in the "Teen Pulse" sketch (01/16/99). When the band resurfaces a year later (01/15/00) in the "Boy Band Blowout 2000" sketch, guest star Freddie Prinze Jr. plays the role of P-Nutt. When the show's musical guest is *NSYNC (03/11/00), they naturally bring out the band one more time, with *NSYNC playing another boy band, No Refund. In this last outing, P-Nutt has been replaced by Wade (Jimmy Fallon). See also **No Refund**.

SHARKS, THE — The number six artist on the top-ten board in the record-shop scene in the 1971 classic *A Clockwork Orange*. The song title is "Switch Me On." See also **The Blow Goes; Bread Brothers; Comic Strips; Cyclops; Goggly Gogol; The Heaven Seventeen; The Humpers; The Legend; Johnny Zhivago.**

SHASTA MCNASTY — An interracial hip-hop trio from the 1999–2000 UPN show of the same name, although not totally, because the show name was changed in the second season to just *Shasta*, but it

didn't help, and the show was canceled. The band all shared an apartment and had wacky, Monkees rip-off escapades, only with crude sexual innuendoes and gratuitous dirty jokes thrown in. Lineup: Scott (Carmine Giovinazzo), Randy (Dale Godboldo), and Dennis (Jake Busey). *TRIVIA TIME!* Jake Busey is the son of actor Gary Busey and man oh man does Jake look like Gary! Wow! It's creepy.

SHAUNDA — Female lounge-type singer (Alex Borstein) from at least three *Mad TV* sketches. In "Shaunda—Ladies Room" (01/09/99) she plays a ritzy women's restroom with her blindfolded pianist (it's a LADIES restroom), Phil Lamarr. In "Shaunda—Holding Tank" (05/01/99) she plays a Vegas jail and is joined by Wayne Newton (Will Sasso). In "Shaunda—Rock and Harpist" (12/09/00), she has a harpist instead of a pianist. See also **Defcon One; Dr. Dazzle; The Eracists; Hoppy Potty; Darlene McBride; Michael McLoud and Jasmine Wayne-Wayne; Savante; Little Hassan Taylor; Willow.**

SHEBANGS, THE — See **Little Timmy and the Shebangs**.

SHMENGE, STAN — See **The Happy Wanderers**.

SHMENGE, YOSH — See **The Happy Wanderers**.

SHOES 'N' SOCKS — From the "Rock of Ages" episode (11/15/92) of *Married with Children*. The Bundy family manages to get into the airport first-class lounge and hobnob with real rock stars Spencer Davis, Richie Havens, Robby Krieger, Mark Lindsay, Peter Noone, and John Sebastian. Father Al Bundy (Ed O'Neill) poses as "Axel Bundy" from this band. Appropriate, since Al is really a shoe salesman. The stars are such acid casualties they can't remember if they know him, so they assume they do. Later in the episode, the whole Bundy clan infiltrates the stars' "Old Aid" recording session, a "We Are the World" parody. See also **Burned Beyond Recognition**; **Jimmy Dick and the Night Sticks**; **Joanie and the Slashettes**; **Oozing Meat**; **Otitis Media**; **Tears and Vomit**; **The Tuxedos**; **The Wanker Triplets**; **The Why**; **Yodeling Andy**.

SHORT CIRCUS, THE — Rock band of kids on zany PBS children's show *The Electric Company* (1971–76). They sang educational songs. The lineup changed almost constantly, and included, at one time or another, June Angela, Todd Graff, Douglas Grant, Stephen Gustafson, Melanie Henderson, Rodney Lewis, Réjane Magloie, Janina Matthews, Denise Nickerson, and Irene Cara, who later came to fame with, uh, *Fame*.

SHORTER, STEVEN — Paul Jones, lead singer of Manfred Mann from 1963–66, portrayed this English singer in the odd 1967 British movie *Privilege*, set in a world where the British government manipulates the populace through pop singers and their lyrics, instead of TV, like now. The film's tagline: "A film so bizarre, so controversial, it shall crucify your mind to the tree of conscience." Jeez!

Steven Shorter (Paul Jones)

SHOYU WEENIE — Cartoon Network's hilarious series *Harvey Birdman, Attorney at Law* takes the channel's penchant for retreading old, unloved cartoon characters to new heights. Birdman, a forgotten superhero from Hanna Barbera's 1967–69 *Birdman and the Galaxy Trio*, has been made over into a lawyer who takes cases from other, well-known cartoon characters and argues them against a rogues' gallery of supervillains now serving as judges and lawyers. In the particularly surreal "Shoyu Weenie" episode (07/21/02), this Japanese pop band (portrayed by members of The Chan Clan from cartoon *The Amazing Chan and the Chan Clan*) hires Birdman to sue The Neptunes (from *Jabberjaw*). The Neptunes stole "Mochi Mochi" (Shoyu's number-one-in-Japan song), wrote new English lyrics, retitled it "Lovely Lovely," and rode it to the top of the fake-band pop charts. Band members included Kenji (voiced by Tony Masa), Seiko, and Miko (both voiced by Jeanne Mori). Did you get the band's name yet? See also **The Chan Clan**; **The Neptunes**.

SHY — Band fronted by lycanthrope Veruca (Paige Moss) who gets the hots for Oz Osbourne (Seth Green), another lycanthrope fronting his own band. Wow, what are the odds?! Well, on supernatural show *Buffy the Vampire Slayer*, pretty good, probably. Veruca first appears briefly solo in the "Living Conditions" episode (10/12/99), then with this band in the "Beer Bad" episode (11/02/99). In the "Wild at Heart" episode (11/09/99), it all hits the fan because Veruca's all-wolf, baby—she doesn't worry about her wolf rampage killing like Oz does, and goes after Oz's friend Willow Rosenberg (Alyson Hannigan) to get him all to herself. Oz has to put that puppy to sleep! Boo-yah! After killing Veruca, Oz/Seth Green leaves town/the show to "heal" himself/pursue other projects. Shy's music was done by real band THC. See also **Dingoes Ate My Baby**.

SID KNISHES AND HIS MOSH PIT-TATOES — Parody of The Sex Pistols' Sid Vicious and punk band of Muppet potatoes from the 06/23/96 episode of the all-too-short run of *Muppets Tonight*, an attempt to bring the Muppets back to television. In another feat of pun-ditry, Sid dedicates their song to his pal, Johnny Au Gratin.

SILLY RABBIT — Ska band that played at the Backwash club in the "Pilot (or, The Douchebag Aspect)," the first episode (07/21/99) of animated show *Mission Hill*. At least, it's assumed they played; the animators seemed to think lip-flapping by the brothers French was more important than a fake band. Anyway, the band's logo is a line drawing of a rabbit wearing black shades and a hat. This show was on the WB network for all of six episodes before being dropped and resurfacing on the Cartoon Network's Adult Swim lineup, like similarly abandoned cartoon shows *Baby Blues*, *The Oblongs*, and *Home Movies*.

SILVER PLATTERS, THE — Iconic 70s sitcom *The Brady Bunch* (1969–74) sets its sextet of siblings a-singing in the "Amateur Night" episode (01/26/73). The kids want to engrave a silver platter for their parents' anniversary gift, but Jan miscalculates the price. So they enter local TV show *The Pete Sterne Amateur Hour* (MC Pete Sterne played by Steve Dunne) to try and win the $100 first-prize money. They perform the Archies-esque "It's a Sunshine Day" to audition, but sing "Keep On" on the show. They come in third but learn some kind of valuable lesson about some heartwarming thing, I'm sure. You really should know this, but the Brady kids were: Marcia (Maureen McCormick), Jan (Eve Plumb), Cindy (Susan Olsen), Greg (Barry Williams), Peter (Christopher Knight), and Bobby (Mike Lookinland). In reality, the producers herded the Brady brood into the studio to record no less than four al-

bums of pop fluff and covers to cash in on the show: *Christmas with the Brady Bunch* (1970), *Meet the Brady Bunch* (1972), *The Kids from the Brady Bunch* (1972) (containing the above songs), and *The Brady Bunch Phonographic Album* (1973). MCA released an, ahem, "best of" compilation CD in 1993, *It's a Sunshine Day: The Best of the Brady Bunch*. See also **The Banana Convention**; **The Brady Kids**; **The Brady Six**; **Johnny Bravo**; **Phlegm**.

SILVER RUTLES, THE — See **The Rutles**.

SIMMONS, DON "NO SOUL" — From the 1987 sketch comedy movie *Amazon Women on the Moon*. Poor Don is the poster child in a commercial featuring blues great B. B. King appealing for donations for the "Blacks Without Soul" organization. Don (David Alan Grier), who "turned a terrible affliction into a recording career," is shown gleefully singing incredibly white-bread versions of white-bread songs like Tony Orlando and Dawn's "Tie a Yellow Ribbon," "Chim Chim Cheree" from *Mary Poppins*, and a seriously funk-impaired version of Three Dog Night's "Joy to the World."

SIMONE — From the 2002 movie *S1m0ne*. Director Viktor Taransky (Al Pacino) creates an artificial, computer-generated actress named Simone (played by model Rachel Roberts) to star in his troubled movie (*Sunrise, Sunset*). Only he knows the truth. When the movie turns out to be a hit, he keeps up the charade, turning the even more difficult trick of having Simone sing live in concert before a sell-out crowd (via holograms). The song? Why, Aretha Franklin's "(You Make Me Feel) Like a Natural Woman," of course.

SINCLAIR, BOBBY — Robert Carradine plays this acoustic guitar–strumming washed-up rocker who gets involved with aliens and the obligatory military cover-up in the 1982 stinker *Wavelength*. Unbelievably, the aliens tell him they like his music.

SIREENA AND THE SIRENS—When the best thing about a movie is Howie Mandel, you know you're in for a world of discomfort. Such it is with the 50s period Showtime channel movie *Shake, Rattle & Rock* (1994). Mandel is remarkably tolerable as cool, hip Danny Klay, host of *Danny Klay's 3 O'Clock Hop,* the local rock-and-roll show. Black female quartet Sireena and the Sirens are accidentally discovered by Klay, and get to perform "Look into My Eyes" on his show. Unfortunately, the station manager gets a lot of calls about putting Negroes on the air—you know, where white people might actually see them. Klay pulls a hitherto unknown set of principles out of his rectum, argues with the manager, and gets canned. Fortunately for Sireena Cooper (Latanyia Baldwin) and the rest of the nameless Sirens (played by Necia Bray, Josina Elder, and Wendi Williams), who should stop into her mom's restaurant but Thomas Taylor (Ron Jackson), VP of Scepter Records. *TRIVIA TIME!* The band's singing was done by group For Real, who also provided the singing voices of fake band The Luminaries in *Grace of My Heart.* Also, MTV metalhead VJ Rikki Rachtman has a cameo playing rock legend Eddie Cochran—aw man! Rikki should be rolling in his grave! Wait . . . no, that's accurate. See also **The Egg Rolls; The Luminaries.**

SISTERS OF MERCY HOLD NO PAIN AGAINST THE DARK LORD—Briefly shown competitor to band Timmy! and the Lords of the Underworld in the battle of bands from the "Timmy! 2000" episode (04/19/00) of animated show *South Park.* Their song is "Silk Blood on the Footsteps of My Mind—Revisited." See also **The Avenue Street Ghetto Boys; Faith + 1; Fingerbang; Getting Gay with Kids; The Ghetto Avenue Boys; Jerome "Chef" McElroy;**

MOOP; Raging Pussies; Reach for the Skyler; Sanctified; Timmy! and the Lords of the Underworld.

SKYE BAND, THE—Seventeen-year-old guitarist/leader of this band, Michael Skye (heartthrob Rex Smith), unexpectedly deals with his own pedophilia in the 1979 NBC TV movie, *Sooner or Later.* Skye, also a teacher at the Eddie Nova Guitar Institute, falls for student Jessie Walters (Denise Miller) who claims she's sixteen when she's really thirteen. She's totally crushing so hard on him she lied about her age to date him. Things move along and Jessie has to decide whether to reveal the truth. Insert your own crude remark about "finger exercises" here. The rest of the band was played by Emily Bindiger, Mark Cunningham, Lenny Mancuso, and Egleton Leroy Woodside Jr. *TRIVIA TIME! Dick Van Dyke Show* regular Morey Amsterdam plays guitar teacher Eddie Nova.

SKYLARK, CHIP—Pretty-boy teen sensation voiced by *NSYNC's Chris Kirkpatrick in the "Boys in the Band" episode (03/01/02) of cartoon *The Fairly OddParents.* Every woman in town, including Timmy's mom (voiced by Susan Blakeslee), is gaga over Chip's goateed, pink-hooded-sweatshirt-and-stocking-cap good looks. Timmy's dad (voiced by Daran Norris) is Chip's sole male fan. After Chip's big concert overshadows Timmy's birthday, the latter wishes for Chip to get kidnapped, *Misery*-style, by evil baby-sitter Vicky. But, as per usual in these kinds of situations, Timmy (voiced by Tara Strong) learns that Chip's not a bad guy, etc., etc., etc., and helps Chip escape in time for the big show and his crowd-pleasing new song "Oh Vicky You're So So Icky." Skylark returns in the "Shiny Teeth" episode (11/30/02), where he's shooting a new music video for his song "Shiny Teeth and Me." Alas, evil Dr. Bender (voiced by Gilbert Gottfried) steals his teeth, and Skylark's in danger of being replaced by rival Skip Sparklypants. Skylark made a third appearance in the "Chip off the Old Chip" episode (11/21/03), singing "Find Your Voice." See also **The Fairies**.

SLADE, BRIAN — From the homosexual glam-trash *Citizen Kane*, the 1998 movie *Velvet Goldmine*, which rewrites the David Bowie/Iggy Pop relationship as a gay-slash-fiction wet dream told in a series of flashbacks from the point of view of reporter Arthur Stuart (Christian Bale). Singer Brian Slade (real name Thomas Slade, played by Jonathan Rhys-Meyers) starts off as a hippie, playing London's Sombrero Club, introed by his Brit-afied American wife Mandy (Toni Collette). He gains manager Cecil (Michael Feast), and is soon playing twee folk tunes at an outdoor festival in a dress. American rocker Curt Wild of The Rats goes on next, jumping around with his pants down, flapping in the breeze, flipping off the audience, and it's infatuation at first sight for Slade. Eventually Cecil gets dumped in favor of flamboyant superagent Jerry Devine (Eddie Izzard), who quickly turns the now-glam Slade into a star, getting him on *Top of the Pops* to perform his hit "The Whole Shebang." Slade is now powerful enough to demand to go meet Wild in America, where Wild (Ewan McGregor) anticlimactically nods off on heroin. Slade's man-crush on Wild blossoms and Slade takes Wild, now on methadone, under his sheets, er, wing. Devine plays up their relationship for the publicity, as Slade throws stolen Oscar Wilde quotes at reporters. But it all turns ugly as Devine says Slade's wasting his time recording Wild's album, and the volatile Wild goes nuts, smashing stuff and stomping off. Meanwhile, for his new album, *The Ballad of Maxwell Demon*, Slade has come up with a new persona for himself and his band, Maxwell Demon and the Venus in Furs (think

Ziggy Stardust and the Spiders from Mars), dominating the charts for months. Eventually, the rockstar lifestyle catches up with him, and Slade loses his wife and Wild, and, at the start of a concert, gets shot on stage! But it's all revealed as a publicity stunt. A pissed-off public turns on Slade, and his career takes a nosedive. *TRIVIA TIME!* Michael Stipe of R.E.M. was executive producer of this movie. See also **Jack Fairy**; **The Flaming Creatures**; **Tommy Stone**; **Curt Wild**.

Brian Slade
(Jonathan Rhys-Meyers)

SLAM — Rapper played by real rapper Tone Loc in *The Adventures of Ford Fairlane* (1990). He's only a struggling rapper, however, and he needs Fairlane (Andrew Dice Clay) to use his industry contacts to make him a star. However, this doesn't happen, and he never performs onstage (he does bust rhymes on the sidewalk, however). See also **Black Plague**; **Disco Express**; **F. F. & Captain John**; **The Pussycats**; **Kyle Troy**.

SLICE, CANDY — Gilda Radner played this over-the-top parody of punk rock in general and Patti Smith specifically in a couple of *Saturday Night Live* skits. In the "Candy Slice Recording Session" skit (12/09/78), she's six hours late to record "If You Look Close." On the 02/17/79 show, she meets rocker Rick Nelson (for real, as he was hosting the show) at a serious contender for best celebrity-benefit parody, "Rock Against Yeast." Radner also used the character on her 1979 Warner Bros. *Live in New York* album, where she sang "Gimme Mick," as well as "If You Look Close," as Candy Slice and the Slicers.

SLIM CLAXTON AND HIS TRIO — Jazz trio that played the Gaslight Club in the Village in "The Drum Major" episode (02/04/88) of *The Cosby Show*. Xylophonist Claxton (Dub Taylor) is an old pal of Grandpa Russell Huxtable (Earle Hyman), who once loaned Claxton $100 for a wedding ring. Former members of the group included the now-deceased Freddy Collins and Claude Powers. Cliff (Bill Cosby) sings a song of theirs early in the show that goes something like "Baby don'tcha step on my face cause you got nails in your shoes." See also **Clyde; JT Freeze; The Icicles; The Jazz Caravan; The Lipsticks; The Maniacs; Walking Lemons; The Wretched.**

SLIME AND THE FAMILY STONE — See **Mick Jagged and the Stones.**

SMEG AND THE HEADS — In the "Timeslides" episode (12/12/89) of U.K. sci-fi series *Red Dwarf*, Dave Lister (Craig Charles) gets to glimpse his past self, as a 17-year-old practicing the song "Om" with his garage band, or whatever they use for garages in the future. "Om," also known as "The Om Song," had a very simple lyric (can you guess?), and a lot of noise. Bill Steer and Jeff Walker of real Liverpool grindcore act Carcass played, respectively, band members Dobbin and Gaz. Emile Charles played young Lister. See also **Rasta Billy Skank.**

SMOKY MOUNTAIN LAURELS, THE — Old-timey country trio that appears briefly in the 1975 film *Nashville* playing at Deemen's Den, a small club.

Member and acoustic guitar–session man Frog (Richard Baskin) was previously fired from a Haven Hamilton recording session. Sheila Bailey and Patti Bryant played the other, singing members. See also **Tommy Brown (II); Sueleen Gay; Haven Hamilton; Barbara Jean; Linnea Reese; Tom, Bill & Mary; Connie White.**

SMOOSH — An Oasis parody, featuring the two most bored, jaded English brothers in the world, Ian Shropshire (David Cross) and Clive Shropshire (Bob Odenkirk), in a sketch from the "Flat-Top Tony and the Purple Canoes" episode (10/10/97) of HBO's *Mr. Show*. They can't get excited about their album (*Space Age Super Suit*) going triple platinum, Ian's new baby, or about being the first rock band on the moon. See also **The Beetletown Players; Larry Black; Livingston Brewster; Willips Brighton; Dickie Crickets; Indomitable Spirit; Kid Jersey; Kill or Be Killed; C. S. Lewis Jr.; Horace Loeb; Marilyn Monster; Norma Jean Monster; John Baptiste Philouza; Professor Murder; Puscifer, Salini; Old Swerdlow; Three Times One Minus One; Titannica; Sir Lloyd Wilson Webber; Wyckyd Sceptre; Daffy "Mal" Yinkleyankle.**

SMOOTH DADDY — In "The Pig Whisperer" episode (04/08/00) of *Spin City*, supersquare NYC Mayor Randall Winston (Barry Bostwick) becomes friends with this African-American rapper (Kevin Mambo) who sampled one of his speeches. At the end of the episode, Smooth says it's nothing personal but his people don't think they should hang anymore. In a touching gesture, he gives the mayor one of his gold chains, even after the mayor ignorantly calls him "homo" instead of "homie."

SNARKS, THE — In the 1967 U.K. film *Smashing Time*, this fake U.K. band was played by real U.K. band Tomorrow (not to be confused with fake band

Toomorrow). The band members were John Alder, Steve Howe, John Pearce, and Keith West. *TRIVIA TIME!* Band member Steve Howe would later become a member of prog rockers Yes and then the Howe in Anderson, Bruford, Wakeman and Howe.

SNOW PINK — In the "Battle of the Bands" (01/31/82) episode of cop series *CHiPs*, Susan Richardson plays this artist who has her van broken into. She still manages to win a battle of the bands competition against the punk band Pain, who were the ones who robbed her van. The rest of her band was played by the real band Shepherd. See also **Moloch**; **Pain.**

SNOW WHITE — A one-joke band from the 1980 movie *Roadie*—they're all dwarves! Hanh?! Get it? Hanh?! When hot sixteen-year-old groupie/rock-philosopher Lola Bouillabaisse (Kaki Hunter) gets mad at the titular roadie, Travis W. Redfish (rocker Meat Loaf), she decides to get him off her mind by going to this band's trailer to see if they need servicing. A little later, she tracks him down watching *Asleep at the Wheel with Deborah Harry* from Blondie. Snow White comes with her and gets in a fight with the boys from Blondie. The African-American dwarf with the afro manages to pick up Deborah Harry, though. Lucky dwarf. The movie also features a mishmash of real artists as themselves: Blondie, Roy Orbison, Alice Cooper, The Pleasant Valley Boys, Asleep at the Wheel, Hank Williams Jr., and The Bama Boys. See also **Spittle (I).**

SOGGY BOTTOM BOYS, THE — Country/bluegrass singing group thrown together for a fast buck in 1937 by three on-the-lam convicts and a bluesman who sold his soul to the devil in the silly and charming 2000 movie *O Brother Where Art Thou*. Their song, the old standard "I Am a Man of Constant Sorrow," sung with tight harmonies and that "high lonesome sound" becomes a regional radio hit. They also sing

"In the Jailhouse Now" at an impromptu concert performance. Lineup: Ulysses Everett McGill (George Clooney) on lead vocals, Pete (John Turturro) on backup vocals, Delmar (Tim Blake Nelson) on backup vocals, and Tommy Johnson (Chris Thomas King) on guitar. *TRIVIA TIME!* The band's name is a spoof of the 1948–69 Foggy Mountain Boys, the famous group that featured bluegrass legends Lester Flatt and Earl Scruggs. See also **The Wharvey Gals.**

SOLIDS, THE — From the "Loyalties" episode (02/20/01) of the NBC primetime series *Ed*. The titular lawyer Ed (Thomas Cavanagh) loses a court case over singer Amanda Bays (Paige Price) getting kicked out of this band. Amanda was replaced by Vanessa (Diane Neal) at the instigation of Jordi Hasler, pet-store owner and rock manager. Amanda doesn't want back in, she just wants them to stop using her songs, but when her notebook goes missing, she can't prove authorship. After the trial, the band tries to get her to rejoin (Vanessa quits for a better gig in Jaspertown), but she refuses and watches them blow an audition for a record company exec. Their big song was "Watching Him Go" (Amanda wrote it about her ex-boyfriend Gideon, but in court guitarist Kerry Thomas testified that SHE wrote it about someone else). The actors portraying Kerry Thomas and drummer Barry Jessup (Carter Bays and Craig Thomas) are both staff writers for *The Late Show with David Letterman.*

SORELS, THE — African-American doo-wop group on their way to success, thanks to new manager Billy Fish (Rick Moranis), by the end of "rock 'n' roll fable" *Streets of Fire* (1984). Oddly, it's pronounced, "SIR-ells," not "sore-ELLS." Lineup: Bird (Stoney Jackson), B.J. (Mykel T. Williamson), Reggie (Grand L. Bush), and Lester (Robert Townsend, who was also in *The Five Heartbeats*). They performed "Countdown to Love" and "I Can Dream

About You." *TRIVIA TIME!* The song "I Can Dream About You," was a top-20 chart hit for Dan Hartman in the summer of 1984. See also **Ellen Aim and the Attackers**.

SOUL TEACHERS—Soul duo from *The Steve Harvey Show* formed by Steve Hightower (Steve Harvey) and his fellow teacher and best friend Cedric Jackie Robinson (Cedric the Entertainer). Soul Teachers first appeared in the episode "When the Funk Hits the Rib Tips" (10/29/97), when the duo decides to audition to be the house group for Club Mystique. They end up competing against (and beating) the Rib Tips, composed of two former members of the Hightower's first group, Steve Hightower and the Hi-Tops. See also **The Rib Tips; Smitty Rollins; Steve Hightower and the Hi-Tops**.

SOUND COMMITTEE, THE—What better barometer for how much the times had changed in the late 60s than for teen garage rock to rear its ugly head on the unlikeliest place outside of *Sing Along With Mitch*—*The Andy Griffith Show*. The timeless small town of Mayberry, North Carolina gets a small dose of the youth cultural revolution when teen Opie (Ron Howard) joins a local rock band as guitarist in the "Opie's Group" episode (11/06/67). But when Opie's grades start to slip, pop Andy worries, and Clara (Hope Summers) cuts a deal with him where she'll manage the group if he keeps his grades up. The rest of the band is Clifford (Jim Kidwell), Wilson (Joe Leitch), and Jesse (Gary Chase). See also **Carl Benson's Wildcats; The Darlings; Keevy Hazelton; Jim Lindsey**.

SPACE CADETS, THE—See **The Limp Lizards**.

SPACE GHOST—See **Zorak**.

SPARKLYPANTS, SKIP—See **Chip Skylark**.

SPEED OF LIGHT—From the recurring "Mel's Rock Pile" sketch on *SCTV*. A parody of teen dance shows, in the 11/21/80 episode, host Rockin' Mel Slirrup (Eugene Levy) has to deal with this band backing out of their appearance on his show. Duke, the singer, was played by Dave Thomas. See also **Vic Arpeggio; Big Momma; 5 Neat Guys; Happiness Unlimited; The Happy Wanderers; Lola Heatherton; The Lemon Twins; Linsk Minyk; Tom Munroe; The Queenhaters; The Ramblers; The Recess Monkeys; Russ Riley; Jackie Rogers Jr.; Jackie Rogers Sr.; Dusty Towne; The Wally Hung Trio**.

SPINAL TAP—Heavy-metal brain-dead hair farmers from the now-classic 1984 comedy *This Is Spinal Tap*, done up documentary-style by fake director Marty DiBergi (Rob Reiner). The movie captures every embarrassing moment of their disastrous tour as well as dips back in time to sample the band's mutation from early 60s skiffle to Merseybeat to flower power to finally the heaviest of metal. As other members come and go, and a seemingly endless list of drummers meet bizarre and unnatural ends, the band's core remains joined in mediocrity: lead singer David St. Hubbins (Michael McKean), lead guitarist Nigel Tufnel (Christopher Guest), and bassist Derek Smalls (Harry Shearer). Guest, McKean, and Shearer all dabbled in musical parody before *Spinal Tap*; McKean, Shearer, and *Laverne and Shirley's* David L. Lander were also all members of comedy troupe The Credibility Gap (1968–76) where they performed songs and sketches on L.A. radio station KRLA. Later, McKean and Landers became cast regulars on *Laverne and Shirley* and formed the duo Lenny and the Squigtones. Guest was musical director on National Lampoon's 1972 *Radio Dinner* album and also played guitar on the 1979 *Lenny and Squiggy Present Lenny and the Squigtones* album—under the alias Nigel Tufnel! In-

Spiñal Tap

terestingly, Spiñal Tap first appeared before the public a full five years earlier than the movie, in a glam-rock incarnation on the 1979 failed sketch-comedy show pilot, *The T.V. Show*, playing the still-unreleased song "Rock and Roll Nightmare." That version of the band included singer/songwriter Loudon Wainwright III on keyboards! After the movie premiered, Guest, McKean, and Shearer kept up the pretense to the hilt, appearing as the band in music magazines, in their own greatest hits album commercial, even on *Saturday Night Live* in 1984, playing "Christmas with the Devil"—in May. They had a cameo on the *Hear 'N Aid* album and video, the 1986 heavy metal "We Are the World." In 1992, they released a new album, *Break Like the Wind*, featuring guest musicians Jeff Beck, Cher, Steve Lukather, Joe Satriani, Slash, and Dweezil Zappa. They turned out the 1992 home video *The Return of Spiñal Tap*, featuring a full live concert and filmed inserts updating the where-abouts of the band and other characters from the movie. They even toured as the band in 2001. See also **Duke fame**; **Lambsblood**; **Meconium**; **The Regulars**.

THE MANY NAMES OF SPIÑAL TAP

Spiñal Tap didn't start out as Spiñal Tap. At least, not ac-cording to the meandering history woven in the movie. The band's history goes back to 1964, when singer/guitarist David St. Hubbins (formerly of The Creatures) and gui-tarist Nigel Tufnel (formerly of The Lovely Lads) formed The Originals. Unfortunately, there was already a band named that, so they became The New Originals. Then, in late 1964, they changed their name to The Thamesmen.

In late 1965 or early 1966, they went through rapid-fire personnel and name changes, including: The Dutchmen, Rave Breakers, Hellcats, Flamin' Daemons, Shiners, Mon-dos, The Doppel Gang, The Peoples, Loose Lips, Waffles, Hot Waffles, Silver Service, Bisquits, Love Bisquits, The Mud Below, and The Tufnel–St. Hubbins Group before fi-nally settling on Spiñal Tap in December 1966. In late 1967, bassist Derek Smalls (formerly of the bands Teddy Noise, Skaface, and Milage) permanently joined the lineup, re-placing Ronnie Pudding, who went off to form the group Pudding People.

In 1976 the band played under the names Anthem and The Cadburys while having legal difficulties with their record label, Megaphone. And, of course, they played at least one gig as Spiñal Tap Mark II when Nigel briefly walked out on their 1982 U.S. tour. Sheesh! These guys make this hard.

SPITTLE (I) — Punky rock band playing Los Angeles' Whiskey-a-Go-Go club in the rockin' 1980 movie *Roadie*. They refuse to go on when groupie Lola Bouillabaisse (Kaki Hunter) shows up with a box of real laundry detergent instead of the detergent box of cocaine she was supposed to bring. Their fat bitch manager (played by Helena Humann) says, "No snow, no show." The titular roadie, Travis W. Redfish (Meat Loaf), threatens the band into performing and chases them onstage! But when the band starts playing, Redfish sees Lola leaving unhappy and grabs a mic to talk to her. He can't hear her, so he throws her a mic and they oddly have a conversation over the PA while the band plays. Then there's an earthquake! Spittle was played by real band Standing Waves: Shona Lay, Bob Murray, Larry Seaman, Randy Franklin, and David Cardwell. The movie also features a mishmash of real artists as themselves: Blondie, Roy Orbison, Alice Cooper, The Pleasant Valley Boys, Asleep at the Wheel, Hank Williams Jr., and The Bama Boys. See also **Snow White.**

SPITTLE (II) — Industrial metal band from the 1998 independent movie *Bandwagon*. They had one song on the soundtrack, "Muddah Muddah Fadda." They are the evil rivals of good indie band Circus Monkey. See also **Circus Monkey.**

SPLINT — Pop band from "The Old Gay Whistle Test" sketch (06/02/75) on the U.K. comedy show *Rutland Weekend Television*. The band, who record for the Abattoir label, are shown performing "Bandwagon" live at the Gerard's Cross Pop Festival. The lead singer (Neil Innes) looks an awful lot like Elton John. See also **Stan Fitch; Mantra Robinson; The Rutles; Toad the Wet Sprocket.**

SPOINK — Matt McGuire (Jake Thomas) and Larry Tudgeman (Kyle J. Downes) name their three-piece Spoink in the "Facts of Life" episode (10/12/01) of *Lizzie McGuire*. Why? Because it shows they are "all about the issues" and "all about the music." Uh, sure. Along with Larry and Matt (on bass and guitar, respectively), the band features longtime session drummer Rick Marotta on skins. Of course, since the writers knew that none of the target audience of easily amused preteens would know who Rick Marotta was, they had to have Matt read off Marotta's credits (Linda Ronstadt, John Lennon, Steely Dan). Poor Rick. Actually, poor Jake and Kyle—they were the ones who had to act impressed about an old guy who played with artists who were already classic rock when their dad (Robert Carradine) was in high school. Anyway, in standard sitcom mode, they break up after a single show and likely never will mention the band again.

SPUMONI, DINO — A Sinatra-like crooner with plenty of attitude from several episodes of Nickelodeon's cartoon *Hey Arnold!* He first appeared in "The Old Building" episode (10/16/96). Later in the 1997 "Partners" episode, Spumoni and his lyricist Don Reynolds (voiced by Harvey Korman) split up. Spumoni also turns up in the "School Dance" (01/04/99) and "Dino Checks Out" (12/11/99) episodes. Some of Spumoni's song titles include: "You Better Not Touch My Gal," "Don't Count Me Out," and "You Broke My Heart." Spumoni is voiced by Rick Corso, his singing voice by Alan Paul and Michael B. Levin. See also **Ronnie Matthews.**

SQUABS, THE — In the hour long PBS *Arthur* Christmas special, *Arthur's Perfect Christmas* (11/23/00), spoiled rich kid—er, cartoon monkey kid, Muffy Crosswire (voiced by Melissa Altro)—boasts of this rock band she's hired to play her big Christmas party. At the party, the kids all rock out to the band playing "Boogie Woogie Christmas." Muffy blithely assumes her best friend Francine Frensky (voiced by Jodie Resther), also a cartoon monkey kid, will be there. However, the Frenskys are Jewish cartoon monkeys and goyim Muffy's party is on the same night as the last night of Hanukkah, so Francine can't make it, but dammit, Muffy just won't listen! See also **BINKY**; **Piccolo Pete**; **U Stink**; **We Stink**.

SQUARES, JOHNNY — *The Dead Pool*, a mediocre 1988 installment in the *Dirty Harry* series is enlivened by Jim Carrey's sublimely ridiculous, leather-pantsed performance as this metal star killed off in the first twenty minutes. He works his rubber face and wriggles to beat the band lip-synching to his song "Welcome to the Jungle" (really Guns 'n' Roses) in a music video shoot for limey jerk director Peter Swan (Liam Neeson!). Swan churns out cheapo horror flicks and has cut a deal where he shoots Squares's video and also gets the scene for his movie, *Hotel Satan*. Squares excuses himself for a quick heroin break, and nips back to the trailer for a syringeful. Only he's murdered by someone who stuffs even more drugs down his gullet. An appropriate end, as he made his career singing about drugs. See also **Eduardo Barlow**.

SQUAREY, CHUNK — Robot-boy Olie is the star of this Nelvana-animated, Disney channel show about robots, *Rolie Polie Olie*. In the "Chunk Squarey" episode (11/5/00), everybot's raising the roof to the tune of Squarey's new dance-craze song "The Twirl." Robots—always suckers for a novelty dance song, aren't they? In a follow-up episode, "Chunk

Sings the Blues," Chunk's in town for a concert but because he has a bimple (some kinda robot pimple) on his forehead, he wants to cancel, like a whiny spoiled little bitch. Olie and pal Billy refrain from pimp-slapping him and instead help him learn a valuable lesson, 'cause it's Disney.

SQUIRES, SHANNA — Blond, Britney Spears-esque popster whose performance of "Gimme Gimme All Your Love" during the second half of *Justice League*'s "Secret Society" episode (11/23/03) was cut short by the timely appearance of the Legion of Doom. Er, we mean, the Secret Society. Even though they have many, many of the same members of the Legion of Doom, and fly in a Legion of Doom building-shaped craft, they aren't the Legion of Doom. So anyway, the Legion of Doom kept us from hearing more than a couple of seconds of Squires's production music-quality warbling. But from what's heard, it's hard to understand how her last few albums went triple-platinum or why her latest album (*Underbelly*) isn't banned. Why do people on TV have such horrid taste in music?

STAINS, THE — Punk trio of pissed-off teenage girls whose meteoric rise and fall is chronicled in *Ladies and Gentlemen, The Fabulous Stains* (1981). Corinne Burns (Diane Lane) is a spunky girl from a dying Pennsylvania steel town who got fired from her fry-cook job on live TV. The response to her outburst from viewers was so strong that TV reporters decided a more in-depth interview was needed. During the interview, she tells the audience of her band, The Stains. Corinne, who calls herself Third Degree Burns, is the lead singer and manager; her little sister Tracy (Marin Kanter), introduced as Dee Pleeted, plays lead guitar; and cousin Jessica McNeil (Laura Dern) introduced as Dizzy Heights, plays bass. Based on that interview, the Stains get booked as the opening act for the tour of The Looters and

The Metal Corpses. Their music is terrible to start, but Corinne's skilled manipulation of the media, along with her new look of sheer outfits and skunk-like hair, begins the Stains' rapid climb to fame. Hundreds of fans, calling themselves Skunks, begin to dress and act like Corinne, and they create such a rabid scene that Billy, lead singer of The Looters, condemns the fans as little girls with no mind of their own who are seen as nothing but little cash machines by The Stains. The crowd angrily turns against the band, and it appears to be the end of The Stains, after only one amazing month! But in an impressively tacked-on ending, The Stains come back, changing their name to The Fabulous Stains, and their looks and sound to a more glamorous, MTV-friendly punk, à la The Go-Gos. *TRIVIA TIME!* The band tapped to replace The Stains as openers on the tour is Black Randy and the Metrosquad, a real L.A. punk band. See also **The Looters**; **The Metal Corpses**.

STATLIN BROTHERS, THE—See **Dill Scallion and the Dillionaires**.

STEEL DRAGON—The focal point of the 2001 movie *Rock Star*. Lead singer Bobby Beers (Jason Flemyng) gets the boot from this loud, 80s metal band. The band members replace him with Chris Cole (Mark Wahlberg), the lead singer of Blood Pollution, a small-time Steel Dragon tribute band. The plot is a fictionalized version of how Judas Priest frontman Rob Halford was replaced by Tim "Ripper" Owens. Beers's singing voice was Jeff Scott Soto (Yngwie J. Malmsteen's lead singer) and/or Mike Matijevic (Steelheart vocalist). Most of the rest of the band were played by various real rockers from the 80s: Kirk Cuddy (Dominic West) on guitar, A.C. (Jason Bonham, Led Zeppelin drummer John Bonham's son) on drums, Ghode (Zakk Wylde, Ozzy Osbourne's guitarist) on guitar, and

Jorgen (Jeff Pilson of Dokken) on bass. See also **Blood Pollution**.

STEVE AND THE APOCALYPSE—See **Darryl and the Chaos**.

STEVE HIGHTOWER AND THE HI-TOPS—The former funk/R&B band of music teacher Steve Hightower (Steve Harvey) from *The Steve Harvey Show* (1996–2002). They were popular in the 70s and even opened for Gladys Knight and the Pips, but then hard times came, and Steve Hightower had to make the tough choice: either stay on the road and struggle or return, *Welcome Back, Kotter*–style, to teach music at his alma mater, Booker T. Washington High School. He chose teaching and never looked back, until he tried to reunite the band in the episode "High Top Reunion" (11/17/96) for 70s Night at Club Mystique. Two members of the Hi-Tops later form The Rib Tips. The Hi-Tops are T-Bone (T. K. Carter), Pretty Tony (Ronald Isley), and Clyde (Jonathan Slocumb). *TRIVIA TIME!* Ronald Isley is a member of famed, long-running singing group The Isley Brothers. See also **The Rib Tips**; **Smitty Rollins**; **Soul Teachers**.

STEVE SAX TRIO, THE—From the "Homer at the Bat" episode (02/20/92) of *The Simpsons*. When Mr. Burns (voiced by Harry Shearer) needs a batch of baseball ringers for his company team to win a million-dollar bet, he sends his assistant Smithers (also voiced by Harry Shearer) to bribe up a batch. Smithers finds real ballplayer Steve Sax (voiced by himself) in an unlikely place, playing stand-up bass with this piano-drums-bass jazz trio in a jazz club. The episode also featured a bunch of other pro baseballers playing themselves: Wade Boggs, Jose Canseco, Roger Clemens, Ken Griffey Jr., Don Mattingly, Mike Scioscia, Ozzie Smith, and Darryl Strawberry. See also **The Beach Boys Experience**;

The Be Sharps; Johnny Bobby; Johnny Calhoun; Captain Bart and the Tequila Mockingbirds; The Crazy Old Man Singers; Cyanide; Gulliver Dark; Ferl Dixon and His Second Helping Boys; Funky C Funky Do; Garfunkel, Messina, Oates, and Lisa; Hooray for Everything; Kovenant; Krusty and the Krums; The Larry Davis Experience; Little Timmy and the Shebangs; Loggins and Oates; Lurleen Lumpkin; M. C. Safety and the Caution Crew; Melvin and the Squirrels; "Bleeding Gums" Murphy; The Party Posse; The Rappin' Rabbis; Red Breem and His Band of Some Esteem; The Satin Knights; Testament; Blind Willie Witherspoon; The Ya-Hoo Recovering Alcoholic Jug Band; Yodelin' Zeke.

STEVENS, DEREK — Dana Carvey played this procrastinating English piano-playing rocker/balladeer in a series of skits during his tenure at *Saturday Night Live* (1986–93). His big hit was "Choppin' Broccoli."

STEVIE — Female pop star from the "Stevie" episode (03/04/89) of *Good Morning, Miss Bliss,* the forerunner of *Saved by the Bell.* She comes back to her alma mater (JFK Junior High) to perform a farewell concert before "retiring" to go to college. Student Zack (Mark-Paul Gosselaar) pretends to be dying in order to scam a kiss off her in a bet he made with Nikki (Heather Hopper). But Stevie is filled in on Zack's tricks by their teacher, the titular Miss Bliss (Disney's Hayley Mills), whom Stevie is staying with, because obviously you can't expect pop stars to afford hotel rooms. The kiss goes to nerd Screech (Dustin Diamond) instead. Stevie's real name is Colleen Morton (Suzanne Tara). See also **The Five Aces; Hot Sundae; Bo Revere; Zack Attack**.

STEWIE AND THE COWTONES — The bluegrass band formed by precocious infant Stewie Griffin (voiced by Seth MacFarlane) in the *Family Guy* episode "To Live and Die in Dixie" (11/15/01). The Griffins are forced to enter the Witness Relocation Program after middle child Chris (voiced by Seth Green) identifies a convenience-store robber for the cops. The family moves to the Deep South, where Stewie falls in love with the dulcet tones of the banjo. Later, he forms Stewie and the Cowtones, which consists of Stewie on banjo and lead vocals, and some nameless hicks playing the jug, washboard, and the tub bass. They practice their song "My Fat Baby Likes to Eat" before playing later that night at the town social. See also **Billy Bob and the Nocturnal Emissions; Pearl Burton**.

STILLWATER — Early 70s rock band from Troy, Michigan, and a major part of the 2000 movie *Almost Fa-*

Stillwater

mous. The movie's name comes from the name of the band's 1973 tour. Incredibly lucky teen reporter William Miller (Patrick Fugit) gets picked to follow this band on tour and write about them for *Rolling Stone* magazine. There's a great scene where the band's plane flies into a lightning storm, and the panicky band members blurt out their sins to each other. The movie's Web site gave the band even more fictional history, including the members' former bands: Guitarist Russell Hammond (Billy Crudup) was formerly in Fizz Merchant and Blues Reduction; lead singer Jeff Bebe (Jason Lee) was formerly in The Juddson Brothers, Sampson's Balls, and The Jeff Bebe Band; drummer Ed Vallencourt (John Fedevich) was formerly in Saint Hex and Fellow's Fellows; and bassist Larry Fellows (Mark Kozelek) was also formerly in Saint Hex and Fellow's Fellows. *TRIVIA TIME!* The band's music ("Fever Dog," "Love Thing," "Love Comes and Goes,") was written by director Cameron Crowe and his wife, Nancy Wilson of real band Heart.

STINGERS, THE — Halfway into the last season of cartoon *Jem!*, the show caught Cousin Oliver Syndrome. The rivalry between Jem and the Holograms and The Misfits was getting stale, so the writers decided to add this third band into the mix to liven things up. This German band was composed of frontman Riot (voiced by Townsend Coleman), Rapture (voiced by Ellen Gerstell), and Minx (voiced by Kath Soucie). Riot's singing voice was done by Gordon Grody. Riot falls for Jem, but ends up signing with rival music company, Misfits Music. The band was introduced in the two-part episode "The Stingers Hit Town" (02/02/88, and 02/03/88). See also **Bobby Bailey**; **The Ben Tiller Orchestra**; **Jem and the Holograms**; **The Limp Lizards**; **The Misfits**; **The Tapps Tucker Quartet**.

STOKE, LENNY — See **The Lenny Stoke Band**.

STONE, TOMMY — A pop singer in 1984 America from the pretentious 1998 movie *Velvet Goldmine*. He has a ridiculous blond pompadour big enough for two televangelists, and talk about ugly . . . sheesh! Tommy (Alastair Cumming) is on his world tour with his shill Shannon (Emily Woof), who used to work for much cooler, much more rebellious 70s glam rocker Brian Slade. Come on, Stone even supports the president! Reporter Arthur Stuart (Christian Bale) manages to somehow link Stone with the now-disappeared Slade, but doesn't bother telling the audience how exactly. See also **Jack Fairy**; **The Flaming Creatures**; **Brian Slade**; **Curt Wild**.

STONEATRA, FRANK — See **Mick Jagged and the Stones**.

STOVALL, RED — Clint Eastwood is the titular character in *Honkytonk Man* (1982). He plays Red Stovall, a Hank Williams–like character who is suffering from tuberculosis and hopes to get to that Mecca of country music, the Grand Ole Opry, before he dies. Eastwood does his own singing, a gutsy but misguided move. Unless that's how you're supposed to sound singing with tuberculosis, in which case it's another stellar Eastwood performance!

STRANGE FRUIT — A chance encounter with the son of the Wisbech Rock Festival organizer reunites this 70s British classic rock band after twenty years in the 1998 Brit flick *Still Crazy*, to discover that people don't really change. Especially people carrying twenty-year-old petty rock-band grudges. Middle age and crappy day jobs have not been kind to keyboardist Tony Costello (Stephen Rea), bassist Les Wickes (Jimmy Nail), drummer David "Beano" Baggot (Timothy Spall), and singer Ray Simms (Bill Nighy). Nighy and Nail did their own singing in the movie. Thrown into the moody mix is flashy young guitarist Luke (Hans Matheson), a replacement for Brian Lovell (Bruce Robinson), a near genius on the guitar. Unfortunately, he's a near genius of the Brian Wilson/Syd Barrett stripe, and Brian's heroic intake of narcotics and his brother's death have left him fragile, missing, and presumed dead, until he pops up alive at the end of the movie in a poorly tacked-on subplot. There was also original singer Keith Lovell (Lee Williams), Brian's brother, who didn't make it out of the 70s alive, OD'ing in a Little Chef. In the flashbacks the band is played by Sean McKenzie (Beano), Rupert Penry-Jones (Ray), Matthew Finney (Brian), Alex Palmer (Les), Gavin Kennedy (Tony), and Lee Williams (Keith). The entire movie is unnecessarily narrated by their roadie Hughie (Brian Connolly). Never revealed is if the band is named after the Billie Holliday song. See also **Blind Fish**; **Thumbscrew**.

STREET SLIM—In *The Blues Brothers* movie (1980), real bluesman John Lee Hooker is seen playing on the street in a brief—well, "cameo" is such a strong word. Giving his character a name seems hardly worth the bother. See also **The Blues Brothers**; **The Good Ole Boys**; **Murph and the Magic Tones**.

STYLETTES, THE—African-American a cappella doo-wop quartet from *Grace of My Heart* (1996). They indirectly give the main character, songwriter Denise Waverly (Illeana Douglas), her big break, when their manager Joel Millner (John Turturro) brings them her song "In Another World" and it becomes a hit for them. Then they disappear from the movie completely. The song was really cowritten by 60s hitmaker Gerry Goffin and band Los Lobos. The Stylettes were played by vocal group Portrait: Eric Jerome Kirkland, Irving Eugene Washington

Strange Fruit

III, Kurt Jackson, and Michael Saulsberry. See also **The Click Brothers; Little Tammy Lee; The Luminaries; Kelly Porter; The Riptides; Denise Waverly**.

SUBURBANS, THE — An 80s one-hit wonder band tries the comeback trail in the 1999 film *The Suburbans*. The band is Danny (Donal Lardner Ward), Rory (Tony Guma), Mitch (Craig Bierko), and Gil (*Saturday Night Live*'s Will Ferrell). Cate (Jennifer Love Hewitt) is the record-company scout who tries to whip them into shape.

SUMMERS, STELLA — In the mediocre 1981 Disney film *The Devil and Max Devlin*, title character Max Devlin (Elliot Gould) gets hit by a busful of Hari Krishnas and goes to Hell. Hell's Souls Manager Barney Satin (Bill Cosby) cuts him a deal—get three fresh souls to sign their souls over to Satan in two months and Max gets his life back. Max returns to the mortal realm with bitchin' new satanic powers: teleportation, instant knowledge about his three targets, and magic powers. The downside: he no longer has a reflection (makes shaving a hassle), and his magic only works as long as he is in line of sight of his target. In true demonic tradition, one of his targets is a struggling singer. In less-than-demonic tradition, the other two targets are a nerd who sells his soul to become a motocross champion, and then-child star Adam Rich. Stella Summers (Julia Budd) is a struggling nobody with zero stage presence trying out at the kind of big, lush, well-attended open mic night that only exists in movies. Max's new powers enable him to give her weak warble the full 70s Barbra Streisand/Karen Carpenter treatment. Audience member and Blizzard Records A&R man Jerry Nadler (Charles Shamata) is suitably wowed, and soon her new self-titled debut album is #28 and she's out on tour playing to 25,000 people every night. Yet she finds fame a bit hollow

and lonely, and reveals she's really from square-ass Brooklyn and not supercool hippie Topanga Canyon like she said (say what?). She also reveals her real name—gasp—is . . . Stephanie Pepper. NOOOOOAARRGGHH . . . wait. What's wrong with that name? Max finally secures her signature just before her song "Any Fool Can See" (music by Marvin Hamlisch, lyrics by Allee Willis) wins a Grammy! When Max has a change of heart and burns the three signed contracts, you get to see Bill Cosby in full demon getup, complete with goat legs and horns, bellowing about pain, pain, pain! Stella makes an onstage announcement that she's quitting the biz to spend time with her family—yeah, that claims more promising rock star careers than drugs, doesn't it? Max gets off scott-free, being redeemed by his act of burning the contracts, and God being apparently able to afford better lawyers than Satan.

SUPER BWOING — An animated superhero screw-up who flew around on a flying electric guitar when he wasn't goofing off playing it. From the DePatie-Freleng-produced show *The Super 6* (1966). He wasn't actually part of The Super 6, but had his own separate segment. Voiced by Charles Smith.

SVEN HELSTROM AND THE SWEDISH RHYTHM KINGS — Horribly square polka band in *The Monkees* pilot, "Here Come the Monkees" (11/14/66). A hip, with-it teenager's nightmare, they play "Goodnight Sweetheart" to a much bored Vanessa Russell (Robyn Millan) at her sweet sixteen party. The Monkees get the band to leave by announcing Norway has declared war on Sweden, and patriotic Swedes should report to the embassy. Then The Monkees perform to the delight of teens and horror of parents. Also in this episode, you get to see Mike Nesmith throw a dart at a Beatles poster! See also **Fern Badderly; Irene Chomsky; The Foreign Agents; The Four Martians; The Four Swine;**

Honey and the Bear; **The Jolly Green Giants (I);
Lester Crabtree and the Three Crabs; The Swinging Android; The West Minstrel Abbies.**

SWANKY MODES, THE—Real-life 60s R&B legends
Sam Moore and Junior Walker played brothers Billy
Diamond and Lester Diamond, members of this
legendary 60s R&B duo fallen on hard, modern
times. Main characters, music video makers, and big
fans Josh Tager (Tim Robbins) and Ivan Alexeev
(John Cusack) try to revive their career. From the
1988 comedy *Tapeheads.* See also **The Blender
Children; Cube Squared; Ranchbone.**

SWEENEY SISTERS, THE—Jan Hooks is Candy
Sweeney, and Nora Dunn is Liz Sweeney, and
they're . . . the Sweeney Sisters, big-haired lounge
act and two of the more popular recurring characters from *Saturday Night Live* during the mid-
1980s. Whether in the lobbies of hotels or in their
trademark Blarney Stone Bar, dim-witted but ever-
cheery Candy and Liz were always there with the
right medley, complete with free-form scatting, and
a stirring rendition of "The Trolley Song." Their
usual accompanist was Skip St. Thomas (Marc
Shaiman). See also **The Culps; Nick the Lounge
Singer.**

SWEET SUE AND HER SOCIETY SYNCOPATORS—From
the classic 1959 comedy *Some Like It Hot.* Joe (Tony
Curtis) and Jerry (Jack Lemmon) are two down-on-
their-luck musicians who accidentally witness the
legendary 1929 Chicago St. Valentine's Day Mas-
sacre. Fleeing the mob, they hide out in drag as
"Josephine" (sax) and "Daphne" (violin) with this
all-female jazz orchestra on a train to Florida. Sweet
Sue was played by Joan Shawlee. The band's singer
("I Wanna Be Loved By You," "I'm Through with
Love") is Sugar Kane, played by the legendary
Marilyn Monroe.

Sweet Sue and Her
Society Syncopaters

SWERDLOW, OLD—Folk singer (David Cross) with a
big-ass fake beard, who practices the "Ozark mountain tradition of song-storying" with his dancing
puppet, Limberlegs, at the Valdosta Folk Fest and
Jelly Off. Senator Tankerbell (Bob Odenkirk) shuts
him down, 'cause Mr. Limberlegs ain't wearin' no
clothes. From the "What to Think" episode
(11/10/98) of HBO's sketch comedy program *Mr.
Show.* See also **The Beetletown Players; Larry
Black; Livingston Brewster; Willips Brighton;
Dickie Crickets; Indomitable Spirit; Kid Jersey;
Kill or Be Killed; C. S. Lewis Jr.; Horace Loeb;
Marilyn Monster; Norma Jean Monster; John
Baptiste Philouza; Professor Murder; Puscifer;
Salini; Smoosh; Three Times One Minus One;
Titannica; Sir Lloyd Wilson Webber; Wyckyd
Sceptre; Daffy "Mal" Yinkleyankle.**

SWINGING ANDROID, THE—The Frankensteinian creation of Dr. Mendoza (John Hoyt) in the "I Was a Teenage Monster" episode (01/16/67) of *The Monkees*. However, the monster android (Richard Kiel) can only sing "Goorah!" (an old Transylvanian folk song). So, the doctor naturally is forced to steal The Monkees' musical talent and transfer it into the monster. You know, with science. After the obligatory running-around-while-the-song-plays montage, The Monkees get their talent back. See also **Fern Badderly; Irene Chomsky; The Foreign Agents; The Four Martians; The Four Swine; Honey and the Bear; The Jolly Green Giants (I); Lester Crabtree and the Three Crabs; Sven Helstrom and the Swedish Rhythm Kings; The West Minstrel Abbies.**

SWINGING CORPORATE RAIDERS, THE—See **The Permanent Waves.**

TAMMY—Brainless singing female teen dance-pop sensation in several *Kids in the Hall* (1989–94) skits. Played by Bruce McCulloch in unsettlingly cute drag. Scott Thompson played her conniving manager. See also **Armada; Cancer Boy; Death Lurks; Mississippi Gary; The Noodles.**

TANG, POOTIE—In an odd spin-off from HBO's *Chris Rock Show*, the character of Pootie Tang (Lance Crouther) is given his own 2001 movie, *Pootie Tang*. Pootie is so dang cool he speaks his own bizarre patois that no one can fathom. Despite, or perhaps because of this, he is a towering figure in the entertainment world—actor, singer, and hero to ghetto children everywhere. In one inspired bizarre sequence, he cuts a new track that is pure silence which becomes a big hit. Move over, John Cage. Chris Rock is wasted as Pootie's posse member JB, but kicks ass in his dual role as Pootie's belt-wielding, tough-but-fair father, Daddy Tang. Pootie, gifted on Dad's deathbed with Dad's "magic" belt, invents an entire style of martial arts around it. The Man (Dick Lecter, played by Robert Vaughn) is gunning for Pootie though, because he's doing PSAs against all of society's evils, which kids are ACTUALLY LISTENING TO! The Man has a big stake in selling kids booze, cigarettes, and greasy fast food, so they try to take him out by stealing his belt. A loose parody of blaxploitation flicks, the movie is silly fun, but a bit thin in places.

TANGERINE CONSPIRACY, THE—See **Happiness Unlimited.**

TAPPS TUCKER QUARTET, THE—Jazz quartet reunited by rockers Jem and the Holograms in the "The Jazz Player" episode (10/15/87) of cartoon *Jem!* Somehow poor Tapps Tucker (trumpet) manages to get caught in Jem's long-running feud with record exec Eric Raymond. Jem and the Holograms and the TTQ unite to play "Jazz Has." See also **Bobby Bailey; The Ben Tiller Orchestra; Jem and the Holograms; The Limp Lizards; The Misfits; The Stingers.**

TARZAN, SGT. BLIND KIWI—The sock puppets of MTV's po-mo *The Sifl and Olly Show* held their First Annual Sifl and Olly Show Battle of the Bands in the 01/12/99 episode. Second up was this hairy, sunglassed puppet with a throaty blues voice. He sang an adult contemporary style song full of bizarre imagery: "I'm your greasy tiger lover, I'm fifty bucks worth of waffles, I'm your beefy tender serpent, I'm your ravioli ancient man, I'm your sexy

Chinese dentist, I'll meet you at tooth hurty." (Apparently, he's only ten years old.) The show is the brainchild of Matt Crocco and Liam Lynch, who do the voices and compose and record the music. See also **Clear Fog; Kee Kee and The P. P. Gang; Yeah; Zafo.**

TAYLOR, LINDA—In the "Love Returns" episode (11/06/78) of *WKRP in Cincinnati*, station manager Andy Travis (Gary Sandy) discovers that his ex-girlfriend Taylor (Barrie Youngfellow) is now a famous country singer coming into town on tour. They fall in love all over again, and he has to decide between joining her on tour or standing by his station and its staff of loveable misfits. Gee, what do you think happened? See also **The Scum of the Earth.**

TAYLOR, LITTLE HASSAN—Angry black 60s singer played by Phil Lamarr in a "best of" commercial parody on the 11/07/98 episode of *Mad TV*. Some song titles: "Open the Door, Honky" and "What the World Needs Now (Is More Dead White Folks)." He died mysteriously after his 1972 Republican National Convention performance. Hmmm. See also **Defcon One; Dr. Dazzle; The Eracists; Hoppy Potty; Darlene McBride; Michael McLoud and Jasmine Wayne-Wayne; Savante; Shaunda; Willow.**

TEAM SAMURAI—Basement teen rock band from the short-lived and not terribly original 1994 live-action kids' series *Superhuman Samurai Syber-Squad*. The band's members fit nicely into the standard television high school archetypes: the Cool Kid—Sam Collins (Matthew Lawrence), the band's leader, lead guitarist, and lead vocalist; the Cute Girl—Sydney "Syd" Forester (Robin Mary Florence) on keyboards. She dates the Jock, Tanker (Kevin Castro), who plays drums. Last and least is

the Spaz, Amp Ere (Troy W. Slaten) on bass guitar.

TEARS AND VOMIT—From the "Eatin' Out" episode (02/19/89) of *Married with Children*. The band is mentioned by son Bud (David Faustino) for the joke: "We want to see Tears and Vomit"—"You can see that when your mother cooks." The name is likely a play on real band Blood, Sweat and Tears. See also **Burned Beyond Recognition; Jimmy Dick and the Night Sticks; Joanie and the Slashettes; Oozing Meat; Otitis Media; Shoes 'n' Socks; The Tuxedos; The Wanker Triplets; The Why; Yodeling Andy.**

TECHNIQUES, THE—See **The Wonders.**

TEMPOS, THE—Some unseen and anonymous mid-60s teen garage band from the 1996 Tom Hanks–produced movie *That Thing You Do*. During the scene where the future Wonders discuss names, someone suggests this name, but guitarist Lenny Haise (Steve Zahn) says he was already in a band called The Tempos and they stank. See also **Elizabeth Anne; Blue Spot Trio; The Chantrellines; Diane Dane; The Echoes; Freddy Fredrickson; The G Men; The Heardsmen; The Hollyhocks; Jon D and the Walkers; Legends of Brass; Marilyn Lovell and the Geminis; The Norm Wooster Singers; Del Paxton; The Saturn 5; The Trends; Two Eriks; The Vicksburgs; The Wonders.**

TEMPTONES, THE—Sixties Motown-type singing group from the "Return of The Temptones" episode (11/13/96) of *The Wayans Brothers*. Shawn and Marlon get Pops' (John Witherspoon) old group back together, but not without problems. Like the baritone having had a sex-change operation. The rest of the band was Harold (Kene Holliday, former star of 70s show *Carter Country*), Albert/Alberta (Jazzmun), and Dewey (Jeris Poindexter).

TENETTA, VIC — Quickly seen crooner in the Coen brothers' movie *The Hudsucker Proxy* (1994). He sings "Memories Are Made of This" to the delight of the ladies at the Hudsucker company Christmas party. Played by Peter Gallagher.

TERMITES, THE (I) — See **Pebbles and Bamm-Bamm**.

TERMITES, THE (II) — See **The Bedbugs**.

TESTAMENT — Band just mentioned in passing by Reverend Lovejoy (voiced by Harry Shearer) in the "My Sister, My Sitter" (03/02/97) episode of animated comedy *The Simpsons*. He says parishioners can "party down in the church basement to the Jesus-rock stylings of Testament." To which Bart Simpson (voiced by Nancy Cartwright) scoffs, "All the best bands are affiliated with Satan." This Testament is not to be confused with the real 80s metal band Testament. See also **The Beach Boys Experience; The Be Sharps; Johnny Bobby; Johnny Calhoun; Captain Bart and the Tequila Mockingbirds; The Crazy Old Man Singers; Cyanide; Gulliver Dark; Ferl Dixon and His Second Helping Boys; Funky C Funky Do; Garfunkel, Messina, Oates, and Lisa; Hooray for Everything; Kovenant; Krusty and the Krums; The Larry Davis Experience; Little Timmy and the Shebangs; Loggins and Oates; Lurleen Lumpkin; M. C. Safety and the Caution Crew; Melvin and the Squirrels; "Bleeding Gums" Murphy; The Party Posse; The Rappin' Rabbis; Red Breem and His Band of Some Esteem; The Satin Knights; The Steve Sax Trio; Blind Willie Witherspoon; The Ya-Hoo Recovering Alcoholic Jug Band; Yodelin' Zeke**.

TEX WARNER AND THE ROUGH RIDIN' RAMBLERS — The country band that discovers Deke Rivers (Elvis Presley) in *Loving You* (1957). Tex (Wendell Corey) never wanted to be in a country band, but it seemed like the style of the time. So, he leads the Rough Ridin' Ramblers on the road, singing their twangy songs. After Rivers rocks the mic in a hometown concert, Tex brings him under the wing of the band. Soon, though, Tex and Co. become an afterthought to Rivers's success. See also **Deke Rivers**.

THORN, WRAY — From the short-lived "spinoff" of *That 70s Show, That 80s Show*. In the "Spring Break '84" episode (03/06/02), protagonist Corey Howard (Glenn Howerton) is depressed and jealous that this former classmate of his is now a horrible synth-pop sellout opening for The Smiths. Worse, Thorn asks punker June Tuesday (Chyler Leigh) to go out before Corey could get up the nerve to. But Corey eventually asks Tuesday out, and they go to the concert together and boo Thorn (Nathan West). He totally deserves it, his stuff is wussier than Howard Jones and Kajagoogoo combined. See also **Corey Howard**.

THORNE, JON — Big famous rock star who's ruining rock promoter Richard Muir's (Colin Friels) *Weekend with Kate* (1990). Richard wants to use the titular weekend at a quiet beach house to throw wife Kate (Catherine McClements) over for mistress Carla (Helen Mutkins). Wifey wants to use the weekend to get knocked up by hubby. Jon Thorne played by saucy Aussie Jerome Ehlers.

THREE BLAZES, THE — Tulsa McLean (Elvis Presley) plays in this combo with his fellow army buddies stationed in West Germany; Cookey (Robert Ivers) and Rick (James Douglas) in *G.I. Blues* (1960). Tulsa claims they're "the hottest combo this side of the Rhein" to get an audition for sceptical Rathskeller owner Poppa Mueller (Fred Essler). The trio (Tulsa and Rick on guitar, Cookey on stand-up bass) plays "G.I. Blues" with a house drummer bedecked in lederhosen, just in case you forgot the movie was set in Germany. There's a nice gag where a bored dogface cranks "Blue Suede Shoes" by Elvis Presley on the jukebox while the Blazes are creeping thru "Doin' the Best I Can" which leads to a good ole American bar brawl. Tulsa and Co. want to open "one of the hottest night spots on the Oklahoma turnpike," an oxymoron bigger than "army intelligence." But there's the little matter of the money. Unable to pull yet another Sgt. Bilko on his disgusting sleaze of a sergeant, Tulsa fortunately witnesses a couple GIs goad each other into a bet on which can be the biggest male chauvinist pig—er, spend the night with lovely ice queen Lili, a dancer at Frankfurt's Café Europa. Tulsa's money is on his Casanova buddy "Dynamite" Bixby (Edson Stroll) until the complaints of Der Vaterland fathers get Bixby's bed-hopping, sex-addicted ass shipped to Alaska. Tulsa reluctantly steps up to the plate to protect his bet so he can make the payment to close the club deal. He spends the middle of the movie wooing Lili with song all over scenic Germany, but

Tulsa McLean
(Elvis Presley)
of The Three Blazes

what should cinch the bet but . . . a baby! It's Three Blazes and a baby, as Tulsa is unwittingly stuck baby-sitting Rick's newborn and unwittingly uses it to spend the night with Lili—strictly platonic, mind you, but still meeting the terms of the bet. One of the oldest tricks in the book, boys—babies are better girlbait than chocolate, cheesecake, or puppies. Or chocolate-cheese puppycake. The movie ends with the three paired-off Blazes (Tulsa mit Lili, Cookey and Lili's roommate Tina, and Rick and his Marla) on the Armed Forces Show singing "Didja' Ever." Well? Didja?

THREE EASY PIECES, THE—Pity your dad. He had to make do with the ultra-low-quality, low-budget pornography of crud like the deservedly hard-to-find *Lust Combo* (1970), featuring some of the homeliest people ever convinced to doff all and get it (urk) on. Yup, porn can be boring, as this movie proves. It's not even worth watching once. Our interracial psych-rock-pop trio roll into a Tennessee nightclub, lip-synch unenthusiastically to a couple of numbers with an invisible horn section (titles might be "Catch as Catch Can" and "The Answer We've Been Looking For"), and then pair off with the local skank for an evening of grubby groping. Lineup: Vince, the sleazy singer and guitar player; Mike, the sleazy African-American drummer; and Jim, the sleazy, long-haired bass player. The band's name is an obvious reference to the Jack Nicholson movie, *Five Easy Pieces* (1970).

THREE LITTLE BOPS, THE—The three little pigs of storybook fame are transmogrified into a hopping, bopping jazz piano-drums-guitar trio in the Stan Freberg–narrated 1957 cartoon *The Three Little Bops*. The Big Bad Wolf just wants to jam with them on his trumpet, but the pigs can't stand his terrible "corny horn" playing, so they give him the boot. The angry wolf blows down the clubs they play in—that is, until the pigs play the House of Bricks. The wolf blows himself up trying to destroy the club, but his ghost comes back from hell with newfound talent, or, as one of the pigs puts it, "The Big Bad Wolf, he learned the rule! You gotta get hot to play real cool!" So they become The Three Little Bops Plus One.

THREE TIMES ONE MINUS ONE—White R&B duo from HBO sketch program *Mr. Show*, consisting of Pootie T (David Cross) and Wolfgang Amadeus Stallonies Von Funkenmeister the Nineteenth and Three Quarters (Bob Odenkirk). Their hit, "Ewww, Girl, Ewww," wins the Homage Award for most soulful single performed by a white duo, beating out "Wanna Freak You in the Ass" by R.U. da 1?, "Premium Soulsonic Megajive—The Love Theme from Brutal Enigma" by 2 Tru 4 U, and "Ewww, Girl, Ewww, Girl" also by Three Times One Minus One. Boy, are they disappointed when they lose to themselves. The other bands are just shots of the live studio audience. TTOMO's song is off their *Literacy for the People* album on Sloppy Seconds Records with the video directed by fake director Famous Mortimer. They're also a big hit on the WPCBCN (White People Co-opting Black Culture Network). Pootie T is a chest-beating R. Kelly parody. They originally appeared in the "Talking Junkie" episode (11/22/96), but also put in an appearance in Cross and Odenkirk's troubled production *Run Ronnie Run!* (2002), which was based on Ronnie Dobbs, another *Mr. Show* character. See also **The Beetletown Players; Larry Black; Livingston Brewster; Willips Brighton; Dickie Crickets; Indomitable Spirit; Kid Jersey; Kill or Be Killed; C. S. Lewis Jr.; Horace Loeb; Marilyn Monster; Norma Jean Monster; John Baptiste Philouza; Professor Murder; Puscifer; Salini; Smoosh; Old Swerdlow; Titannica; Sir Lloyd Wilson Webber; Wyckyd Sceptre; Daffy "Mal" Yinkleyankle**.

THUDPUCKER, JIMMY—A young, piano-playing, sensitive 70s singer/songwriter type, this character was invented by Garry Trudeau for the *Doonesbury* comic strip circa 1975, but also appeared in the animated NBC TV special, *The Doonesbury Special* (1977). An album, *Doonesbury's Jimmy Thudpucker— Greatest Hits*, was released in conjunction on the RCA subsidiary Windsong Records in 1977. **TRIVIA TIME!** The album was produced by R&B guitar legend Steve Cropper, who was also a member of The Blues Brothers.

THUMBSCREW—The first band space-case singer Ray Simms (Bill Nighy) was ever in, well before his stint as lead singer for Brit 70s classic rock middleweights, Strange Fruit. Just mentioned in passing in *Still Crazy* (1998). See also **Blind Fish; Strange Fruit**.

THURGOOD AND THE STUBB TONES—From the "Cruising for a Bluesing" episode (02/18/01) of first FOX, then WB "foamation" show *The PJs*. With Thurgood Stubbs's wife looking after a sick aunt, Thurgood (voiced by Eddie Murphy) and his buddies take a boys' night out trying to relive their youth back when they had this electric blues band. They pack up their instruments and head through darkest downtown to play Muddy Guy's Famous Barrelhouse Blues Club Amateur Night, but it's been closed since 1996, when Muddy Guy got in trouble with the law. Lineup: Thurgood on guitar and vocals, his buddy Walter (voiced by Marc Wilmore) on guitar, Jimmy Ho (voiced by Michael Paul Chan) on drums, Sanchez (voiced by Pepe Serna) on harmonica, and Smokey the crackhead (voiced by Shawn Michael Howard) as their roadie.

TIMMY! AND THE LORDS OF THE UNDERWORLD—In the "Timmy! 2000" episode (04/19/00) of the animated show *South Park*, Timmy—an enormous-headed retarded (sorry, but he is) kid in a wheelchair who can only say "TIMMAH!"—somehow joins unsuccessful metal trio The Lords of the Underworld as the lead vocalist. Thanks to him, they win a battle of the bands to open for Phil Collins. The band is such a big hit, soon Phil Collins is opening for them. An Oscar-toting Phil, jealous of the band, convinces Skyler, jealous of Timmy, to leave the band. Once the band breaks up, Phil is the headliner again, with Skyler's solo project, Reach for the Skyler, opening. Everyone is enjoying the Phil Collins concert, 'cause they're drugged to the gills on Ritalin, when Chef appears in the nick of time to deliver the antidote, Ritalout. Everyone wises up, boos Phil Collins off the stage, and demands Timmy! and the Lords of the Underworld, who quickly patch up their differences, reunite, and rock out. Band lineup: Skyler Moles, Jonesy, Maltsey, and Timmy. The Lords of the Underworld first appeared with no name in the episode "Cat Orgy" (07/14/99), where twenty-two-year-old leader Skyler was dating twelve-year-old hellion and baby-sitter Shelly Marsh. Only back then Maltsey was called Mark. See also **The Avenue Street Ghetto Boys; Faith + 1; Fingerbang; Getting Gay with Kids; The Ghetto Avenue Boys; Jerome "Chef" McElroy; MOOP; Raging Pussies; Reach for the Skyler; Sanctified; Sisters of Mercy Hold No Pain Against the Dark Lord.**

TIMMY AND THE TULIPS—One of the artifacts of the 70s fad for 50s nostalgia was the 1978 flick *American Hot Wax*, which dramatized real-life Cleveland DJ Alan Freed's championing of rock and roll. Real rockers Jerry Lee Lewis, Chuck Berry, and Screamin' Jay Hawkins appeared as themselves, but for some reason, fictionalized versions of other real groups were created, like this one, a sort of clone of The Fleetwoods. Played by Charles Irwin, Jeanne Sheffield, and Jo Ann Harris, they sing "Mr. Blue."

TRIVIA TIME! Future writer/director Cameron Crowe (who would later create the fictional band Stillwater for *Almost Famous*) has a tiny role in the film. See also **The Chesterfields; The Delights; Clark Otis; Professor La Plano and the Planotones.**

TITANICCA—Three-man late 90s heavy metal/industrial band from a hilarious, yet creepy *Mr. Show* skit where they go to see young fan Adam Jimmy (David Cross), who tried to kill himself while listening to their song "Try Suicide." Jimmy's hideous medical condition inspires the band to release "Try Again (Adam's Song)." The band was played by Bob Odenkirk (guitar), Brian Posehn (bass, vocals), and John Ennis (drums). From "The Return of the Curse of the Creature's Ghost" episode (12/5/97). In the *Mr. Show* straight-to-video movie *Run Ronnie Run!* (2002), Titannica reappears, but only on the soundtrack with the song "Ass Kickin' Fat Kid," sung by Maynard James Keenan, lead singer of Tool. See also **The Beetletown Players; Larry Black; Livingston Brewster; Willips Brighton; Dickie Crickets; Indomitable Spirit; Kid Jersey; Kill or Be Killed; C. S. Lewis Jr.; Horace Loeb; Marilyn Monster; Norma Jean Monster; John Baptiste Philouza; Professor Murder; Puscifer; Salini; Smoosh; Old Swerdlow; Three Times One Minus One; Sir Lloyd Wilson Webber; Wyckyd Sceptre; Daffy "Mal" Yinkleyankle.**

TOAD THE WET SPROCKET—A bunch of long-haired limey wankers doing what sounds like Pavement warming up from "The Old Gay Whistle Test" sketch (06/02/75) on the 1975–76 BBC comedy series *Rutland Weekend Television*, the show that spawned The Rutles. You might also remember the name from the "Rock Notes" track off the 1980 album, *Monty Python's Contractual Obligation Album*. There was also a REAL band who named themselves Toad the Wet Sprocket (1986–98). Also only briefly mentioned in the sketch are Rex Higgins, Steve Flea, The Wretched Admiral Sphincter, Grunties, Hot Nudges, Red Buttocks, and Vomit. See also **Stan Fitch**; **Mantra Robinson**; **The Rutles**; **Splint**.

TOM, BILL & MARY — Acoustic folk-pop trio on tour pushing their popular, self-titled first album in Robert Altman's 1975 take on the country music industry, *Nashville*. Acoustic guitar player and singer Tom Frank (Keith Carradine) is the male-slut member of the band who seems intent on sleeping his way through the female population of the city in question. He even sleeps with fellow bandmate Mary (Cristina Raines), unbeknownst to their other fellow bandmate, Mary's husband Bill (Allan F. Nicholls). *TRIVIA TIME!* Actor Keith Carradine somehow won an Academy Award for his original song for the film, "I'm Easy." See also **Tommy Brown (II)**; **Sueleen Gay**; **Haven Hamilton**; **Barbara Jean**; **Linnea Rees**; **The Smoky Mountain Laurels**; **Connie White**.

Tom Frank (Keith Carradine) of Tom, Bill & Mary

TOMPKINS, CYRUS — Second-string country star wannabe from Knoxville, Tennessee, from the "Sherman, Woman and Child" episode (03/05/95) of animated show *The Critic*. The philandering ex-husband of Alice, the critic's assistant, he sang "My Lyin' Heart," and "Daddy's Steppin' Out" and released the album, *I'm Being Unfaithful to My Wife, Alice Tompkins. You Heard Me, Alice Tompkins*. Voiced by Sam MacMurray. See also **Nuns in a Blender**.

TOMPKINS, JIMMY — See **Deke Rivers**.

TONY COCA-COLA AND THE ROOSTERS — In cult horror flick *The Driller Killer* (1979), artist Reno Miller (credited as Jimmy Laine, but really director Abel Ferrara) descends into madness, helped along with the subtlety of a boot in the butt by this obnoxiously loud punk rock band playing next door. But when he does snap and go on a poorly lit drilling spree, he does NOT kill the band! He must have been really nuts! Lineup: Tony Coca-Cola on guitar (Rhodney Montreal), Ritchy on bass (Dickey Bittner), and Steve on drums (Steve Brown). It's a good possibility that Pepsi paid NOT to have the band named Tony Pepsi and the Roosters.

TOOMORROW — A young Olivia Newton-John starred in the odd 1970 sci-fi/rock flick *Toomorrow*. Olivia's band of the same name is the target of aliens who want to kidnap the band to play for them. The film was masterminded by Don Kirshner, who helped birth *The Monkees* and *The Archies*. He hoped to make it the next *Monkees/Archies*, but it flopped. Olivia Newton-John, Ben Thomas, Karl Chambers, and Vic Cooper played respectively, um, band members Olivia, Ben, Karl, and Vic. A soundtrack album was released on RCA Victor Records. *TRIVIA TIME!* The real drumming was done by Chris Slade, whose colorful drumming career includes

Tom Jones's "It's Not Unusual," Manfred Mann's Earth Band, The Firm, AC/DC, and Asia.

TOTAL DEFIANCE—Rap group from the "Yoko, Oh No!" episode (10/04/94) of TV show *California Dreams*. They're up against the regular cast's band, California Dreams, in, yes, a damned battle of the bands. See also **Bradley and the Billionaires; California Dreams; Zane Walker.**

TOWNE, DUSTY—Female singer (Catherine O'Hara) of risqué songs in two *SCTV* sketches. First in a commercial for her appearance at Lucifer's Arena (10/23/81), and then in her own TV Christmas special, *Dusty Towne Sexy Holiday Special* (12/18/81). On both occasions she's backed by The Wally Hung Trio. See also **Vic Arpeggio; Big Momma; 5 Neat Guys; Happiness Unlimited; The Happy Wanderers; Lola Heatherton; The Lemon Twins; Linsk Minyk; Tom Munroe; The Queenhaters; The Ramblers; The Recess Monkeys; Russ Riley; Jackie Rogers Jr.; Jackie Rogers Sr.; Speed of Light; Dusty Towne; The Wally Hung Trio.**

TRACE AND GINA—In the short-lived 1985 sci-fi TV series *Otherworld*, the Sterling family is transported to an alternate Earth divided into weird, worlds-unto-themselves provinces. In the "Rock and Roll Suicide" episode (02/16/85), they stick around in the Midwest-esque Centrex province. Bored Sterling siblings Trace (Tony O'Dell; guitar, vocals) and Gina (Jonna Lee; drums, vocals) form a two-piece band to compete in a talent show at "Developmental Thought Center 47" (i.e., school), covering The Beatles' "I Want to Hold Your Hand." Since rock and roll was never invented in this universe, their crazy, wimpy, derivative 80s beat is a hit with the kids and a menace to Principal Dromo and local head of the Church of Artificial Intelligence, Dr. Klaxon (i.e., "The Man"). They sign with impressed

booking agent Billy Sunshine (i.e., Brian Epstein), whose inexplicable English accent is inexplicably bad and comes and goes. Inexplicably. The kids, with the help of a few extra studio musicians, cut a "repo disc" (i.e., album), of the greatest rock songs ever, such as Quiet Riot's "Cum on Feel the Noize" and Flatt and Scruggs' *Beverly Hillbillies* theme. Trace and Gina, obviously drunk on their own success, even try writing their own songs (eep!), including The Beatles' tribute "Rock City." Soon, the kids are expelled and Dr. Klaxon (convinced the album has hidden backward messages!) is burning dolls and albums on their lawn. Not for "Rock City" specifically, but it should have been. Worse, the Sterlings' nemesis, evil Zone Trooper Commander Nuveen Kroll (perennial heavy Jonathan Banks), shows up in town to check out the menace, and the family is forced to flee the province, leaving poor Billy Sunshine with only a hit repo disc and a dozen newly inspired bands to manage.

TRENDS, THE—From *That Thing You Do* (1996). They play Boss Vic Koss the Mattress King's (Kevin Pollack) rock and roll show in Pittsburgh, which opens with a lackluster performance by protagonists, The Wonders. This band's name is just briefly glimpsed on the marquee, you never actually SEE the band or anything. See also **Elizabeth Anne; Blue Spot Trio; The Chantrellines; Diane Dane; The Echoes; Freddy Fredrickson; The G Men; The Heardsmen; The Hollyhocks; Jon D and the Walkers; Legends of Brass; Marilyn Lovell and the Geminis; The Norm Wooster Singers; Del Paxton; The Saturn 5; The Tempos; Two Eriks; The Vicksburgs; The Wonders.**

TRINITY—A Christian rock band playing *South Park*'s Christfest 2003 concert in the "Christian Rock Hard" episode (10/29/03). See also **Faith + 1; Sanctified.**

TROVADOR, EL—Never-seen singer at the Chapulte-pec Room of the ritzy Hotel Acapulco Hilton in ole May-hee-co in the 1963 Elvis flick *Fun in Acapulco*. His sign in the lobby says he's "diariamente!!" Which is Spanish for, um, "daily." But El Trovador (Spanish for "The Troubador") is a bit of a prima donna, getting headaches and illnesses caused by se-vere salary deficiencies. So plucky preteen Raoul Almiedo (Larry Domasin) convinces the manager (who is also his cousin) to hire on gringo-in-need Mike Windgren (Elvis Presley) to fill in and see if some free-market competition can't cure El Trovador. El Trovador gets to keep his job; singing was just Mike's way to earn some cash until he could get up his nerve to return to his first love, trapeze artist. A-humma-humma-what? See also **Mike Windgren.**

TROY, KYLE—Groomed to be the next big thing by Grendel Records in *The Adventures of Ford Fairlane* (1990), Troy (Cody Jarrett) is nothing but Clay Aiken minus the talent (shudder!). He can't sing, he can't dance . . . he can barely stand in place! Rock-and-roll detective Ford Fairlane (Andrew Dice Clay) tried to show him how to rock, but obviously the lesson didn't stick. In fact, at his big CD-release party, his own label head (singer Wayne Newton) slams Troy's abilities in the obligatory bad-guy rant of what evil misdeeds he is currently plotting. That makes Troy cry. Cry, baby, cry! See also **Black Plague; Disco Express; F. F. & Captain John; The Pussycats; Slam.**

TRUCK SHACKLEY AND THE TEXAS CRITTERS—Over-sized Muppet–type band from the 1980–82 variety show *Barbara Mandrell and the Mandrell Sisters*. This five-piece country band and their dog were created not by Jim Henson, but by Sid and Marty Krofft, since, hey, they were producing the show. Some of the puppeteers involved were: Tony Ur-bano, Sandey Grinn, and Carl Johnson. Apparently the band occasionally actually performed on the show. One song was called "Cowboy's Valentine."

TRUCKSTOP—The 1994 low-budget indie flick *Half-Cocked* follows a bunch of friends who steal a van of band equipment and then attempt to become a band, touring from Louisville to Chattanooga to Memphis. The band members were played by musi-cians from the actual indie-type bands Rodan, Crain, and Ruby Falls.

TWITTY-STEVENS CONNECTION, THE—In the "Battle of the Bands" episode (11/24/00) of the Disney chan-nel's sitcom *Even Stevens*, rivals The Alan Twitty Project and The Louis Stevens Experience combine to create this band. They are then prominently fea-tured in the "Band on the Roof" episode (05/03/02). Lineup: Alan Twitty (A.J. Trauth) on guitar, Louis Stevens (Shia LaBeouf) on drums, his sister Ren (Christy Carlson Romano) on vocals, Tawny Dean (Margo Harshman) on keyboards, and Artie Ryan (Jerry Messing) on bass, although Artie gets replaced by Beans Aranguren (Steven Anthony Lawrence). They want to perform on their school's roof, like the famous Beatles' scene in *Let It Be*. Or U2's rooftop scene in their video for "Where the Streets Have No Name." Naturally, Principal Wexler (George An-thony Bell) says no. So they do it anyway and all get detention. See also **The Alan Twitty Project.**

TWO ERIKS—Never-seen band in *That Thing You Do* (1996). They play Boss Vic Koss the Mattress King's (Kevin Pollack) rock and roll show in Pittsburgh, which opens with an embarrassingly bad perfor-mance by The Wonders. But you never actually SEE the band or anything, their name is just briefly glimpsed on the marquee. Presumably, the group is two guys named Erik. Or not. See also **Elizabeth Anne; Blue Spot Trio; The Chantrellines; Diane**

Dane; **The Echoes; Freddy Fredrickson; The G Men; The Heardsmen; The Hollyhocks; Jon D and the Walkers; Legends of Brass; Marilyn Lovell and the Geminis; The Norm Wooster Singers; Del Paxton; The Saturn 5; The Tempos; The Trends; The Vicksburgs; The Wonders.**

2 FINE—Real-life boy band 98° appeared on the "A Night at the Plaza" episode (10/19/00) of sitcom *Just Shoot Me* as this fictional band put together by *Blush* magazine employee Dennis Finch (David Spade). They perform their then-current hit "Give Me Just One Night (*Una Noche*)," and kick Finch out of the group. Probably because he's one of the most annoying characters on television. 98° are Justin Jeffre, Drew Lachey, Nick Lachey, and Jeff Timmons. See also **Simon Leeds.**

2 TRU 4 U—See **Three Times One Minus One.**

TWOBADORS, THE—See **The Folksmen.**

2GETHER—A spoof of those damned MTV "boy bands"—on MTV! They were in a TV movie of the same name, which was then turned into a short-lived series. When manager of boy band Whoa!, Bob Buss (Alan Blumenfeld), is fired, he turns around and starts this boy band. The members—Jerry O'Keefe (Evan Farmer), Mickey Parke (Alex Solowitz), Jason "QT" McKnight (Michael Cuccione), Chad Linus (Noah Bastian), and Doug Linus (Kevin Farley)—all live in a house paid for by their record label. They actually released two albums: the *2gether* soundtrack album (2000) and *2ge+her: Again* (2000). Tragically, Michael Cuccione died of respiratory failure on January 13, 2000—just days after his sixteenth birthday. Kevin Farley is the younger brother of deceased *Saturday Night Live* alumnus Chris

Farley. See also **Unity; Whoa!**

TUXEDOS, THE—Mentioned in the "Rock and Roll Girl" episode (02/04/90) of *Married with Children*, this is Steve Rhoades's (David Garrison) old band when he was in high school. That Steve was in a band is implied in the earlier episode, "Dead Men Don't Do Aerobics" (09/10/89), but no name was given. Real band The Gutter Cats appear in this episode as themselves. See also **Burned Beyond Recognition; Jimmy Dick and the Night Sticks; Joanie and the Slashettes; Oozing Meat; Otitis Media; Shoes 'n' Socks; Tears and Vomit; The Wanker Triplets; The Why; Yodeling Andy.**

TYRONE GREEN AND HIS REGGAE BAND—Eddie Murphy played the running character angry felon Tyrone Green on *Saturday Night Live* in the early 80s. In a skit from the 11/13/82 episode, an apparently released Tyrone Green and his reggae band play "Kill the White People" at the VFW Annual Talent Show, horrifying the MC (Tim Kazurinsky) and the white, middle-class audience.

TYRONNE, JOHNNY—Yeah, the King really stretched his acting chops on this one. In perhaps the dumb-

Harum Scarum, featuring Johnny Tyronne (Elvis Presley)

est of Elvis's thirty-something movies, *Harum Scarum* (1965), Elvis Presley plays a singer/actor who stars in the movie-within-a-movie *Sands of the Desert*, a cheesy musical adventure that debuts in Babalstan, a fictional Arabian country in northern Africa. A group of assassins watching the movie see Tyronne kill a cheetah with a single karate chop and are so impressed they kidnap him to slay King Toranshah (Philip Reed), the leader of Lunarkand. Now, most singer/actors who are kidnapped by assassins because of a karate chop in a movie would tell the assassins that it was just a movie trick, right? Not Johnny Tyronne. He tells them the chop is only for bad people. That just gets him more mixed up in the conflict, confronting him with belly dancing, thieves, princesses pretending to be slave girls, and Billy Barty. Feel free to just read this entry and not see the movie.

U STINK — From the prime-time animated PBS children's show special *Arthur: It's Only Rock and Roll* (09/01/02). Francine Frensky (voiced by Jodie Resther) gets a bug up her butt about the upcoming Elwood City appearance of boy band The Backstreet Boys (playing animated versions of themselves). Considering them sellouts, she creates this, her own, authentic group. Lineup: Binky Barnes (voiced by Bruce Dinsmore) on clarinet, Molly (voiced by Maggie Castle) on electric guitar, lunchroom lady Mrs. McGrady (voiced by Bronwen Mantel) on keyboards, and Francine herself on drums and lead vocals. Alas, she can't sing and play at the same time. The rest of the band want shy Fern Walters (voiced by Holly Gauthier-Frankel), who sports a

surprisingly good voice. But when the band actually garners some popularity, Francine gets disgusted and quits. Then there's a whole lot of willing suspension of disbelief as U Stink gets to duet with The Backstreet Boys. See also **BINKY**; **Piccolo Pete**; **The Squabs**; **We Stink**.

UNDEAD, THE — The latest, hottest act on Death Records in the 1974 movie *Phantom of the Paradise*. A sort of KISS-like band with outrageous stage antics, its frontman is Beef (Gerrit Graham, singing voice Ray Kennedy), who is menaced by the Phantom of the title (William Finley). The rest of the band was played by Archie Hahn, Jeffrey Commanor, and Harold Oblong. See also **The Beach Bums**; **The Juicy Fruits**; **Phoenix**.

UNDERPRIVILEGED, THE — The hard-rockin' bar band (played by real band Reverend Horton Heat, plus one actor guy) that defeats Drew's band in a battle of the bands at the Warsaw bar in the "That Thing You Don't" episode (11/26/97) of *The Drew Carey Show*. Herb (the actor guy, Joseph D. Reitman) is the gang's arrogant old high-school rival. His band has been playing a Holiday Inn for twenty years. They sing "Now, Right Now." See also **The Horndogs**; **Satan's Penis**; **The Unreliables**.

UNITY — Third boy band from the MTV boy band spoof TV movie *2gether*. They have a song on the soundtrack album, "Breaking All the Rules." See also **2gether**; **Whoa!**

UNRELIABLES, THE — One-joke contestants in the battle of the bands in the "That Thing You Don't" episode (11/26/97) of *The Drew Carey Show*. They don't show up—get it?! See also **The Horndogs**; **Satan's Penis**; **The Underprivileged**.

UNTITLED — The mixed-gender, interracial, guitar-drums-bass-vocals Chicago rock quartet whose van breaks down in the hick town of Hereabouts, Alabama, and has to deal with the eccentric inhabitants. From the 2000 indie movie *Stalled*, the brainchild of writer/producer Mindy Weinberg, based partially on her experiences in real band 40th Day. The movie won an award at the Telluride Indiefest film festival.

VAINES, KIRK—The art-house flick *Scarlet Diva* (2000) was written, directed by, and stars Asia Argento as Anna Battista, an Italian actress who bounces around Europe and America before landing in Los Angeles and having a fling with this rock star (played by Jean Shepard) who knocks her up and dumps her. In reality, Asia Argento is an Italian actress and has a kid by a member of the Italian band Bluvertigo. *TRIVIA TIME!* Rapper Schooly-D has a cameo as a drug dealer.

VALENTINE, JIMMY—Prefab pretty boy teen idol (Jeff Yagher) in the Fabian or Frankie Avalon mold who sings and acts in the period movie *Shag* (1989). He's in town to judge the Myrtle Beach Sun Queen beauty contest in 1963 Myrtle Beach, South Carolina. Pudge (Annabeth Gish) says he "... can't even sing. Did you see *Paradise Anew?* Made me puke." But slut Melaina (Bridget Fonda) sees him as her meal ticket—she knows she's not going to college. She plans to win the contest and seduce the hell out of him. Unfortunately, she follows staid Luanne's advice on choice of swimwear and talent-show act. She loses big time. Furious, she makes Luanne (a senator's daughter) invite Valentine back

to the senator's house for a nonexistent party so she can seduce him. It works! Mostly because Valentine's manager (Paul Lieber) is a control freak: "My manager's like a priest, man, you think I get to go to parties?" Unfortunately, the manager comes the next morning to escort the hungover Valentine away from Melaina's clutches. He spent a lot of money on turning Valentine into a star, "So don't think I'm going to let some piece of Dixie ass parade in here and crap all over my dream." Melaina's down, but not out, and later she tarts herself up and seduces the manager, wisely understanding the importance of the power behind the throne. Valentine and Luanne's parents judge the big shag dance competition in the finale, and Pudge wins! Maybe someone should take back the nasty things she said about Valentine, hmmm? See also **Big Dan and the Sand Dollars**.

VALLENS, DOROTHY—Tortured torch singer (played by Isabella Rossellini) in David Lynch's bleak, twisted take on small-town America circa 1986, *Blue Velvet*. Our chanteuse croons the title track (a #1 hit for Bobby Vinton in 1963) in a Lumberton, North Carolina, lounge before going home to be sexually abused by Frank Booth (Dennis Hopper at his most evil), who holds her true-love hostage. Jeffrey Beaumont (Kyle MacLachlan) is the stout young lad who finds a severed ear in a field and eventually comes to her rescue. Isabella Rossellini actually sang the title track and another song, "Blue Star," herself; both can be found on the soundtrack album.

VAN CARTIER, DELORIS—African-American casino lounge singer from the movies *Sister Act* (1992) and its sequel, *Sister Act 2: Back in the Habit* (1993). In the first movie, Van Cartier (Whoopi Goldberg) has the misfortune to accidentally witness her boyfriend Vince LaRocca (Harvey Keitel?!) making a mob hit. She successfully flees to the police, where the witness protection program puts her in a nunnery! Van Cartier, now Sister Mary Clarence, takes charge of the nunnery's crappy choir, and turns them around. She soon has them singing Motown oldies like "My Guy," with the lyrics changed to "My God." Unfortunately, their new success gets them and Van Cartier on TV, where she's recognized by the mobsters. And then there's some chase stuff. In the second movie, the nuns come to Van Cartier to get her to repeat her success by teaching music to a bunch of parochial-school students whose school is going to be closed by some jerk. *TRIVIA TIME!* The second movie starred Fugees' singer Lauryn Hill as a student whose mother won't let her sing.

Deloris Van Cartier, aka Sister Mary Clarence (Whoopi Goldberg)

VAN CLIBURN SUMMER ORCHESTRA, THE—See **The Dale Gribble Bluegrass Experience**.

VANDERBOLTEN, BERRY—In the "Berry the Butler" episode (12/01/97) of the Cartoon Network cartoon *Johnny Bravo*, Johnny's mother (voiced by Brenda Vaccaro) wins a contest where her favorite singer becomes her butler for a day. Johnny (voiced by Jeff Bennett) makes the bum really work. See also **Johnny and the Deer Ticks**; **The Round Pound**.

VANILLA, JADE AND EBONY—A white, Asian, and black trio (one of each, can you guess who's who?) of high schoolers who perform the supposed-to-be-awful "Graduation Rap" at the beginning of the 2001 movie *Ghost World*. Vanilla (Lindsey Girardot), Jade (Joy Bisco), and Ebony's (Venus DeMilo Thomas) song is on the soundtrack album. *TRIVIA TIME!* Daniel Clowes, who did the comic book the movie is based on, wrote the lyrics. Later, at the graduation party, the crappy top forty is supplied by real band Orange Colored Sky. See also **Alien Autopsy**; **Blueshammer**; **Fred Chatman**.

VANILLA LICE—From the "Toon TV" episode (11/09/92) of cartoon *Tiny Toon Adventures*. Intro'ed by Buster Bunny (voiced by Charlie Adler) as the "world's hippest little louse," Vanilla Lice (voiced by Rob Paulsen) raps the song "Toon Out, Toon In," with rap cameos by characters Plucky Duck (voiced by Joe Alaskey), Elmyra Duff (voiced by Cree Summer), and Gogo Dodo (voiced by Frank Welker). This vermin with the high-top fade and goatee is, yes, every bit as talented as the artist whose namesake he parodies. The rap song sucks major rectum, a shame, since the lyrics to the show's theme are pretty good. See also **Def Zepplin**; **Fuddonna**; **Skinhead O'-Connell**; **Ruffee**.

VANILLA SHERBET—See **N.W.H.**

VELOUR, TOMMY—Sleazy, Vegas-style lounge singer who wore one of those little two-part, French-looking, pencil-thin mustaches that were the epitome of suave in the 30s, but in the latter half of the twentieth century became excellent shorthand for "creep." He also has a hairy chest, which is impressive when you consider the character is played by comedienne Lily Tomlin. He appeared in the TV special *Lily: Sold Out* (1981) and probably some other things. Cough. *TRIVIA TIME!* Tomlin wrote to Prince Charles and Lady Diana in 1981 to try and have Velour sing at their wedding. See also **Agnus Angst**; **Purvis Hawkins**; **Linnea Reese**.

VELTRI, DAVID "DAVE"—Veteran character actor Steve Buscemi shows up at the beginning of the 1998 Adam Sandler vehicle *The Wedding Singer* as a drunken wedding guest. He staggers between misery and violence before being talked down by Adam Sandler's good-guy title character, Robbie Hart. In a nice little twist, David Veltri reappears at the end of the movie as the wedding singer for Hart's own wedding! The other members of Dave's band were played by Robert Hackl, Joshua Oppenheimer, and Gabe Veltri. Waitaminute, Veltri? Veltri isn't just a goofy name they made up for the movie?! See also **Robbie Hart**; **Jimmy Moore**.

VELVET VULTURES, THE—Oft-mentioned but never-seen band from disgustingly nice 60s sitcom *Family Affair*. Older sister Cissy Patterson-Davis (Kathy Garver) was a big fan, dropping mentions of this "epitome of folk-jazz" throughout the 1966–71 run of the show. The band features most prominently in the episode "The Baby Sitters" (04/01/68), where Cissy abandons her baby-sitting duties and fobs disgustingly cute younger siblings Jody (Johnny Whittaker) and Buffy (Anissa Jones) off on someone else when a boy shows up with tickets to one of their shows.

VENEER—Hunky Dawson Leery (James Van Der Beek), the title character of *Dawson's Creek* has the slightest of tiffs with his girlfriend Jen Lindley (Michelle Williams) in the "In a Lonely Place" episode (02/20/02), when he bails on accompanying her to a Veneer concert. She has to attend and interview the band for WBCW, the college station. The band can't be that good; she got stuck interviewing them because no one else wanted to. But he already promised to take Joey Potter (Katie Holmes) to a movie, and doesn't want her to be alone, as she just got mugged the previous night. So Jen takes gal pal Audrey Liddell (Busy Philipps) instead. Jen finds the band's music ". . . awful. It was puerile and gimmicky." But she quickly changes her tune to "really good" when face-to-face with band members Steve (Drew Wood) and scruff-faced Wynn (Nick Cornish). Veneer is on tour opening for the band North America, which Wynn sarcastically calls a "totally rockin' band." They get interviewed for all of about two minutes and then hang around the station for hours as Steve hits on Jen and Audrey hits on Wynn. But Wynn loves his girlfriend back in Charlottesville, Virginia, and Jen sees through Steve's pathetic come-on crap about "clicking" with another person and acting on sudden passion. Plus she gets a free Veneer T-shirt! Score!

VENUS IN FURS, THE—See **Brian Slade**.

VERNON-WILLIAMS, ALLISON—The Peggy Lee–like singer who falls for the rebel in the 1990 John Waters period 50s movie *Cry-Baby*. Allison (Amy Locane) has a happy, albeit square, life: she's beautiful, rich, a good singer and the girlfriend of Baldwin (Stephen Mailer), the lead singer of the doo-wop band The Whiffles. Yet when she sees Cry-Baby

(Johnny Depp) shed that single tear, she knows she wants to leave the safety of her world behind to be with him. She's readily accepted by the rebels, and even gets to sing with Cry-Baby and the Cry-Baby Combo, before a riot breaks out and Cry-Baby gets sent to jail. Allison tries to put Cry-Baby behind her, but their love is too strong. Let's hear it for strong love! See also **The Cry-Baby Combo; The Whiffles.**

VERSIS—White tough-guy rapper from the short-lived 2003 UPN drama *Platinum*, about the daily struggles of two brothers running their rap label. Basically, an Eminem clone. Played by real rapper Vishiss. Since he's the biggest seller on the Sweetback label, his antics are tolerated—such as shooting his video director in the butt, who then has to be paid off. Versis also gets shot up by rivals and survives to be taunted by a label employee who slept with his wife. Bonus rap-career points for getting shot three times, but minus a few for surviving, and minus a few more for getting shot in a department store. See also **Camille FaReal; Lady Bryce; Mace.**

VICKSBURGS, THE—Never-seen band in *That Thing You Do* (1996), a movie chock full of bands, both seen and unseen. Their song "Drive Faster" comes on the radio right before The Wonders' "That Thing You Do" and The Wonders all go crazy hearing their own song on the radio. They're also a big enough band to headline Boss Vic Koss the Mattress King's (Kevin Pollack) rock and roll show in Pittsburgh, which opens with a disastrous performance by The Wonders. But you never actually SEE this band or anything. "Drive Faster" was composed by Scott Rogness and Rick Elias. See also **Elizabeth Anne; Blue Spot Trio; The Chantrellines; Diane Dane; The Echoes; Freddy Fredrickson; The G Men; The Heardsmen; The Hollyhocks; Jon D and the Walkers; Legends of**

Brass; **Marilyn Lovell and the Geminis; The Norm Wooster Singers; Del Paxton; The Saturn 5; The Tempos; The Trends; Two Eriks; The Wonders.**

VICTOR, LAURA—Demi Moore plays a singer in *No Small Affair* (1984). *Cheers'* George Wendt is Jake, the owner of the club where she sings. Jon Cryer plays Charles Cummings, the Matthew Broderick stand-in who falls for her. Chrissy Faith was the singing voice of Laura. See also **Cassandra Eldrich.**

VILLAGE FOLK ENSEMBLE, THE—See **The New Main Street Singers.**

VISITING DAY—In the "A Hit Is a Hit" episode (03/14/99) of mob-tastic HBO drama *The Sopranos*, Christopher Moltisanti's girlfriend Adriana (Drea de Matteo) is inspired/encouraged by her casual acquaintance, rapper Massive Genius (Bokeem Woodbine) to produce a demo tape for this band of Adriana's old boyfriend Richie Santini (Nick Fowler). Christopher (Michael Imperioli), who ponies up the dough, quickly realizes that Santini's band sucks, and sucked in its previous incarnation as Jersey metal band Defiler. He also realizes that Adriana has no producing skills and that Massive Genius is just trying to get in Adriana's pants. See also **The Chablis; Massive Genius; Scratch; Little Jimmy Willis.**

VIVIAN, JOHN "LONG JOHN"—Purple-Nehru-jacketed rocker who sings "Wooly Bully" and "the national anthem of Vietnam," Eric Burdon's "We Gotta Get Out of This Place" at a Vietnam War USO show in the "USO Down" episode (01/21/88) of Vietnam war drama *Tour of Duty*. Alas, their chopper crashes on the way to the next gig, killing half the band, and worse, some of their hot go-go dancers. After the crash, they meet up with Bravo Company, but they're not out of the woods yet. Long John's (Patrick O'Bryan) sax man Larry Carlin (Stuart Fratkin) drags his sax everywhere, 'cause his dad bought it from Charlie Parker. Larry freaks out when they accidentally leave it behind, so he and Long John go back for it and Larry and his sax get riddled with bullets by the Viet Cong. Everyone's a music critic! This helps turn Long John all kill-crazy (much like the writers of the show, racking up a body count of at least five), as he wanted to join the army and waste some Cong, but his epilepsy kept him out. Long John nobly sacrifices himself like a guest star should, by throwing himself on a grenade meant for a major character—in this case, Sgt. Zeke Anderson (Terence Knox).

VON SHTUPP, LILI—Oversexed German cabaret-type chanteuse touring the Wild West and played by Madeline Kahn in Mel Brooks's classic Western parody *Blazing Saddles* (1974). She vamps her way through "I'm Tired."

VOX POPULI—See **Bleeding Eardrum**.

WAILING FUNGUS—Misshapen alien lump of . . . something with a bandana and an acoustic guitar advertised playing the Bend-Aid benefit concert for broken robots. From the "Bendin' in the Wind" episode (04/22/01) of *Futurama*, the animated sci-fi FOX comedy set in the year 3000. See also **Cylon and Garfunkel**; **Leaf Seven**.

Lili Von Shtupp (Madeline Kahn)

WALKER, CLARENCE—Comedian Eddie Murphy played this hilarious character angrily trying to persuade the host (Joe Piscopo) of talk show/comedy skit *Rock and Roll and Then Some* that he was an original member of The Beatles (on sax), that he wrote all the songs, molded the group, and that they stole his stuff and kicked him out. And, best of all, that the band was originally called The Clarences. From the 02/11/84 episode of *Saturday Night Live*.

WALKER, WADE "CRY-BABY"—See **The Cry-Baby Combo.**

WALKER, ZANE—Successful musician from the "Fallen Idol" episode (10/14/95) of TV show *California Dreams*, a sort of sub-*Saved by the Bell*. He's Jake's (Jay Anthony Frake) idol, but ends up stealing a song from Jake's band, California Dreams. Played by Julian Stone. See also **Bradley and the Billionaires; California Dreams; Total Defiance.**

WALKING LEMONS—Not a Smashing Pumpkins parody, if that's what you're thinking, cause they wouldn't even form for three more years. This is an unseen band mentioned in the "Jitterbug Break" (01/31/85) episode of *The Cosby Show*. Denise Huxtable (Lisa Bonet) wants to camp out for tickets, a plan that is quickly negged by her father (Bill Cosby). The show concludes with a dance contest between breakdancing youngsters (including a very young, very uncredited Blair Underwood) and jitterbugging oldsters (including choreographers Judith Jamison and Donald McKayle). See also **Clyde; JT Freeze; The Icicles; The Jazz Caravan; The Lipsticks; The Maniacs; Slim Claxton and His Trio; The Wretched.**

WALLY HUNG EXPERIENCE, THE—See **The Wally Hung Trio.**

WALLY HUNG TRIO, THE—Backup band for bawdy Dusty Towne (Catherine O'Hara) on two *SCTV* sketches. First in a commercial for her appearance at Lucifer's Arena (10/23/81), and then on her own TV Christmas special, *Dusty Towne Sexy Holiday Special* (12/18/81). Lineup: Ricky on drums (Rick Moranis), Wally Hung on organ (Paul Flaherty, Joe Flaherty's brother), and an unnamed bassman (Dick Blasucci). They also appear in the *Ocean's 11* parody skit, "Maudlin's 11," playing the Blue Angel Burlesque Strip Tease Club. They also appeared as The Wally Hung Experience on the 1982 RCA *Count Floyd* EP, which added Gene Martynec as synth programmer, Mike Short on keyboards, Rick Gratton on drums, and Memo Acevedo on timbales. See also **Vic Arpeggio; Big Momma; 5 Neat Guys; Happiness Unlimited; The Happy Wanderers; Lola Heatherton; The Lemon Twins; Linsk Minyk; Tom Munroe; The Queenhaters; The Ramblers; The Recess Monkeys; Russ Riley; Jackie Rogers Jr.; Jackie Rogers Sr.; Speed of Light; Dusty Towne.**

WANKER, REGGIE—None other than Malcolm McDowell played this decadent, self-indulgent, Mick Jagger–like rock star in the 1983 movie *Get Crazy* (aka *Flip Out*). McDowell does a surprisingly good job doing his own singing on "Hot Shot!" Later in the movie he has a heart-to-heart chat with his penis. See also **Auden; King Blues; Nada.**

WANKER TRIPLETS, THE—Identical singing triplets from the "All in the Family" episode (05/01/88) of *Married with Children*. Played by REAL identical singing triplets, The Del Rubio Triplets (Milly, Elena, and Eadie). Visiting relatives of wife Peggy Bundy (Katey Sagal), they sing "You Are My Sunshine," and Al gives them bad advice. See also **Burned Beyond Recognition; Jimmy Dick and the Night Sticks; Joanie and the Slashettes; Oozing**

Meat; **Otitis Media**; **Shoes 'n' Socks**; **Tears and Vomit**; **The Tuxedos**; **The Why**; **Yodeling Andy**.

WARREN CHESWICK EXPERIENCE, THE — Amateur band of, duh, Warren Cheswick (Justin Long) in "The Whole Truth" episode (12/07/00) of NBC's *Ed*. They audition to play an open mic night at the Stuckeybowl, but Phil (Michael Ian Black), who's running the show and is mad with power, will only let them play if they do his song ("Soothe My Soul, Stuckeybowl") and let him sing it. See also **The Solids**.

WARTS, THE — Kick-ass garage rock and roll band from the "How Not to Manage a Rock Group" episode (04/28/68) of *The Mothers-in-Law*. How can they rock so hard? Because they're played by real kick-ass garage rockers The Seeds. They get to kick out the jams on their song "Pushin' Too Hard." Unfortunately, son Jerry Buell (Jerry Fogel) somehow gets managing duties taken away from him by his folks and his wife's folks. These fogies think they know from music, and pepper the band with old-school advice, like wearing matching suits, nice haircuts, and a nice name. The band gets scared off by the squares, becoming no-shows at their own recording session. The two sets of parents decide to record themselves singing, and grab band The Friends Indeed off the street to provide music. That doesn't work so well either. *TRIVIA TIME!* This series was directed by Desi Arnaz, Ricky Ricardo himself. See also **The Friends Indeed**; **The Mamas and Papas-in-Law**.

WASHINGTON, BOBBY — See **Del Paxton**.

WASHINGTON, HOWLING BLIND LUTHER — See **King Blues**.

WAVERLY, DENISE — Sixties Brill Building songwriter who wants to be a singer, and central character of the 1996 movie *Grace of My Heart*. Her real name is Edna Buxton (played by Illeana Douglas), of the rich Philadelphia family that owns Buxton Steel. She enters the 1958 McMartin Singing Competition and wins with Rosemary Clooney's "Hey There." First prize is a recording contract with McMartin Records, but it never goes anywhere. She sings all over New York only to be told, "We've already got someone like you." A producer takes pity on her and gives her recording of her original song "In Another World" to manager Joel Millner (John Turturro), who wants it for his group The Stylettes. It becomes a hit, and he gives her a job songwriting. She spends the 60s writing hit singles for various artists, having unhappy love affairs, and sporting an endless parade of awful period hairdos. Finally, in 1970, Joel ousts her from the hippie Idyllwyld Commune to help her record her long-dreamed-of solo album, titled *Grace of My Heart,* which goes platinum. Her life is loosely based on that of real Brill hitmaker Carole King. The movie's original period songs were various collaborations with Brill vets and younger writers. Denise's big ballad, "God Give Me Strength," was cowritten by Elvis Costello and Burt Bacharach, at director Allison Anders's instigation, and sparked further collaboration that led to their 1998 album *Painted from Memory*. Kristen Vigard was Waverly's singing voice. See also **The Click Brothers**; **Little Tammy Lee**; **The Luminaries**; **Kelly Porter**; **The Riptides**; **The Stylettes**.

WAYNE AND WANDA — This pair of singing and dancing human Muppets always had the worst luck during their nine or so appearances on the 1976–81 *Muppet Show*. No sooner would they get a few bars into a piece of wholesome (and boring) American music than something would usually fall on them. Wayne was voiced by Richard Hunt; Wanda by Eren Ozker. See also **The Amazing Marvin Suggs**

and His Muppaphone; **Dr. Teeth and the Electric Mayhem**; **Mahna Mahna and the Two Snowths**; **Miss Piggy**; **Rowlf the Dog**.

WE STINK—From the prime-time animated PBS children's show special *Arthur: It's Only Rock and Roll* (09/01/02). Guest stars The Backstreet Boys (playing cartoon versions of themselves) are coming into town and pissing off tomboy Francine Frensky (voiced by Jodie Resther). So she starts her own damn band, U Stink. Her rejects go on to form this, their own painfully bad band with the truth-in-advertising name. Lineup: Arthur Read (voiced by Mark Rendall), Buster Baxter (voiced by Daniel Brochu), and George (voiced by Mitchell David Rothpan). See also **BINKY**; **Piccolo Pete**; **The Squabs**; **U Stink**.

WEBBER, SIR LLOYD WILSON—Unseen composer (and obvious Andrew Lloyd Webber parody) of the delightful *Rap: The Musical!*, which contains all the fun and joy of rap, without all that rap music. From the "A Talking Junkie" episode (11/22/96) of HBO's sketch comedy show *Mr. Show*. See also **The Beetletown Players**; **Larry Black**; **Livingston Brewster**; **Willips Brighton**; **Dickie Crickets**; **Indomitable Spirit**; **Kid Jersey**; **Kill or Be Killed**; **C. S. Lewis Jr.**; **Horace Loeb**; **Marilyn Monster**; **Norma Jean Monster**; **John Baptiste Philouza**; **Professor Murder**; **Puscifer**; **Salini**; **Smoosh**; **Old Swerdlow**; **Three Times One Minus One**; **Titannica**; **Wyckyd Sceptre**; **Daffy "Mal" Yinkleyankle**.

WELLS, RUSTY—See **Rusty Wells and His Combo**.

WEST MINSTREL ABBIES, THE—From the cross-dressing episode of *The Monkees*, "Some Like It Lukewarm" (03/04/68). The boys want to compete in the KXIW Rockathon, but it's for mixed-gender groups only. Boom, they put Davy in drag and

they're in. The bands tie and have to have a rematch. Unfortunately, the contest's MC, Jerry Blavat (a real DJ, playing himself), gets the hots for Miss Jones, following the iron law of sitcom logic that men in drag are inexplicably attractive to whoever's most inconvenient. Davy escapes his clutches (still in drag) to meet and wind up falling in love with "William McCochrane" from this band. At the rematch, they discover this band is really an all-girl band and that "William McCochrane" is member Daphne (Deana Martin, daughter of Dean Martin!), in drag for the same reason Davy is! Davy confesses his chicanery to Blavat, who's ready to disqualify The Monkees, but then the girls of TWMA join The Monkees for their number, technically making them (if only temporarily) a mixed-gender group! The West Minstrel Abbies' uncredited other members are Harmony, Melody, and Caphophone. See also **Fern Badderly**; **Irene Chomsky**; **The Foreign Agents**; **The Four Martians**; **The Four Swine**; **Honey and the Bear**; **The Jolly Green Giants (I)**; **Lester Crabtree and the Three Crabs**; **Sven Helstrom and the Swedish Rhythm Kings**; **The Swinging Android**.

WETHEADS, THE—Unseen and unheard band mentioned in passing in the "Love with a Proper Transfer Student" episode (4/14/02) of the cartoon *As Told by Ginger*. Joaquin Cortez (Mathew Valencia), the new kid at Lucky Jr. High and the object of affection for best friends Ginger (Melissa Disney) and Dodie (Aspen Miller), says they're his favorite. See also **The Ponies**.

WHARVEY GALS, THE—The four young daughters of Penny Wharvey (Holly Hunter) who sing ("In the Highways") briefly in the Coen brothers's movie *O Brother Where Art Thou* (2000). The Wharvey Gals were played by Georgia Rae Rainer, Marianna Breland, Lindsey Miller, and Natalie Shedd. Their singing was done by real singing group The Peasall Sisters (Sarah, Hannah, and Leah). See also **The Soggy Bottom Boys**.

WHIFFLES, THE — Foursome of 50s white-bread kids who perform soulless, Pat Boone–style doo-wop in the 1990 John Waters period film *Cry Baby*. As leader Baldwin (Stephen Mailer) says, ". . . we're proud to be square!" They sing "Sh Boom" and "Mr. Sandman." Baldwin even battles Cry-Baby (Johnny Depp) for the affection of the same girl, Allison Vernon-Williams (Amy Locane). The rest of the group was played by Drew Ebersole, Kenny Curtis, and Scott Neilson. Their singing voices were done by Timothy B. Schmit, Gerry Beckley, and Andre Gold. *TRIVIA TIME!* Timothy B. Schmit was a member of 70s groups Poco, and The Eagles. Gerry Beckley worked on *The Simpsons Sing the Blues* album (1990). See also **The Cry-Baby Combo; Allison Vernon-Williams**.

WHISKEY KITTEN — A garage band made up of former members of State of Contusion and teenager/alien-in-disguise Tommy Solomon (Joseph Gordon-Levitt) on sitcom *Third Rock from the Sun*, in the "Tricky Dick" episode (10/08/97). They play either speed or death metal (there's some confusion among the band members as to their exact genre, but all agree that it's not about labels man, it's about the music). They only have one song, which is another bone of contention among band members. *TRIVIA TIME!* When he shuts down the band mid-practice, Dick Solomon's (John Lithgow) antirock sermon reprises the same speech Lithgow's Rev. Moore character made in *Footloose* (1984).

WHITE, CONNIE — Rising country singing star played by Karen Black in Nashville (1975). She has two enormous . . . talents, nudge, nudge. Black does her own singing on the tunes "Memphis" and "Rolling

Stone," which she also wrote. See also **Tommy Brown (II); Sueleen Gay; Haven Hamilton; Barbara Jean; Linnea Reese; The Smoky Mountain Laurels; Tom, Bill & Mary**.

Connie White (Karen Black)

WHITMAN, JUDD — See **Ted Jackson**.

WHOA! — From the MTV boy-band-spoof TV movie *2gether*. Rival lip-synching boy band of 2gether, Whoa! fires their manager, Bob Buss (Alan Blumenfeld), who then goes out and creates 2gether. Whoa! have a song on the soundtrack album, "Rub One Out." See also **2gether; Unity**.

WHY, THE — From the two-part "Married . . . with Queen (Part 1)" (04/23/89) and "Married . . . with Queen, The Sequel" (04/30/89) episodes of *Married with Children*. They play the Polk High School reunion, where Peg (Katey Sagal) renews her high school feud with Connie Bender (Lisa Raggio). Obvious play on the name of real band, The Who. See also **Burned Beyond Recognition**; **Jimmy Dick and the Night Sticks**; **Joanie and the Slashettes**; **Oozing Meat**; **Ottis Media**; **Shoes 'n' Socks**; **Tears and Vomit**; **The Tuxedos**; **The Wanker Triplets**; **Yodeling Andy**.

WILD, CURT — This thinly veiled version of Iggy Pop from *Velvet Goldmine* (1998) is first shown playing an English outdoor festival circa 1970. He's the leader of The Rats, an American garage band formed from the trailer parks of Michigan. Wild (Ewan MacGregor) is alleged to have been discovered servicing his brother as a teen and sent off for electroshock therapy. Which might explain his pants-dropping, weenie-flopping, crowd-inflaming antics. Future rock star and thinly fictionalized version of David Bowie Brian Slade (Jonathan Rhys-Meyers) is entranced by Wild's performance, wishing he'd thought of it. Several years later when Slade is a big androgynous glam rocker, he goes to meet Wild in America and signs him to do a record that Slade will produce. It's all 'cause Slade has a big ole gay man-crush on Wild. But the album doesn't go well, and consumes too much of Slade's time for his manager's liking. It all falls apart and Wild ends up in Berlin with Jack Fairy (Micko Westmoreland), another cartoonish, androgynous glam rocker. The Rats were played by Alan Fordham on bass guitar, Jono McGrath on lead guitar, and Perry Clayton on drums. See also **Jack Fairy**; **The Flaming Creatures**; **Brian Slade**; **Tommy Stone**.

WILLIS, LITTLE JIMMY — From the "A Hit Is a Hit" episode (03/14/99) of HBO drama *The Sopranos*. Hesh Rabkin (Jerry Adler) is an old mob guy who used to have a record company (F-Note Records) back in the 60s, and who bilked this now-deceased singer out of his royalties. When rapper Massive Genius (Bokeem Woodbine) finds out, he threatens to sue on behalf of Willis's widow. Clever Rabkin does a little research and finds out that one of the acts on Massive G's label sampled a song from another artist on Rabkin's old label that he still owns all the rights to. Rabkin would have to, of course, countersue. Check and mate, my friend. Be grateful he didn't have you whacked. See also **The Chablis**; **Massive Genius**; **Scratch**; **Visiting Day**.

WILLOW — Female folk singer in the "Lowered Expectations—Folk Singer" sketch on the 02/10/96 episode of *Mad TV*. She sings about the type of man she's seeking, while sporting some, uh, au naturel underarms. Played by cast member Nicole Sullivan. See also **Defcon One**; **Dr. Dazzle**; **The Eracists**; **Hoppy Potty**; **Darlene McBride**; **Michael McLoud and Jasmine Wayne-Wayne**; **Savante**; **Shaunda**; **Little Hassan Taylor**.

WINDGREN, MIKE — Mike Windgren (Elvis Presley) starts off *Fun in Acapulco* (1963) working on some rich gringo's boat and fending off the advances of the owner's bleached-blond, frisky, jailbait daughter (Mike: "I'm sure I got neckties older than you are"). While hanging at the bar El Torito's, he sings an impromptu number just before that bitch daughter gets him fired. With not enough money to get home, he is befriended by homeless orphan hustler Raoul Almeido (Larry Domasin), a pint-sized, precocious, prepubescent Colonel Parker with cousins everywhere. He takes it on himself to manage Mike's singing career. One incredibly unlikely meeting with the manager of the ritzy Hotel Acapulco Hilton later, and Raoul's got Mike a job occasionally filling in for never-seen house singer El Trovador. While Raoul is hustling up gigs, Mike is pissing off hotel lifeguard/famous cliff diver Moreno (Alejandro Rey) by muscling into his lifeguard job, and wooing his gal, the hotel social director Marguerita

(Ursula Andress). And occasionally switching it up by dating lady bullfighter Dolores Gomez (Elsa Cárdenas). But Mike has a dark secret, revealed in a flashback scene so oddly done, it seems you've briefly switched channels to a completely different movie. You'll get the same feeling a bit later watching a goofy cameo by Howard McNear, better known as Floyd the Barber from *The Andy Griffith Show*. Mike's singing career is going like gangbusters, thanks to Raoul's incessant hustling. Elvis should have fired the colonel and hired this kid! But it turns out Mike's singing is just to earn enough money to get home to Florida and rejoin the family business: The Flying Windgrens, a trapeze artist act, so the rousing finale song "Guadalahara" is undoubtedly his last performance. Which is good, because Mike will need the time to figure out how he's going to smuggle Raoul across the border, since he promised to take him with him. See also **El Trovador**.

Mike Windgren (Elvis Presley) and Marguerita Dauphin (Ursula Andress)

WINSLOW'S WOPPERS—A doo-wop group featured in the "Doo Wop Diggety" episode of Nickelodeon's cartoon *CatDog* (1998–2001). The band, which was formed by blue mouse/musical entrepreneur Winslow T. Oddfellow (voiced by Carlos Alazraqui), featured CatDog (voiced by Jim Cummings and Tom Kenny) and the Greasers—Cliff (Kenny), Lube (Alazraqui), and Shriek Dubois (voiced by Maria Bamford). After a dispute about hats and dressing rooms, the band fell apart and were replaced by stagehands-cum-rappers Mervis and Dunglap (both voiced by John Kassir).

WINSTEAD, CHASE—From *The Giant Gila Monster* (1959). This teen has problems. His dad's dead, his little sister's crippled, he works a dead-end job at a towing business as his family's only means of support, local rich jerk Wheeler (Bob Thompson) wants his ass on a platter, the local sheriff (Fred Graham) is leaning on him to keep his hot-rodding friends in line and below the speed limit, AND, to top it all off, there's a damned giant gila monster running around killing folks. But Chase gets a break when he gives a tow to one drunk drivin' Horatio Alger Smith, better known 'round town as hot rock and roll DJ "Steamroller" Smith. Smith repays the favor by arranging for Chase to cut a demo disc of a rock and roll song he's written and to DJ the kids' barn dance. Smith plays the demo at the dance, and gets Chase to sing another of his compositions, when dammit if that giant gila monster doesn't crash the party, literally. Chase demonstrates himself the pluckiest teen in all of monster moviedom when he nobly sacrifices his sweet hot rod (packed with nitroglycerin) to blow up the beast. This movie was also used as fodder for an episode of *Mystery Science Theater 3000* (06/13/92).

WINTERS, BARBARA—Famous, short-haired, female American pop singer (Lauri Peters) in Paris, who disguises herself as a fourteen-year-old boy named Bobby and stows away on a passing doubledecker bus to get away from her horrible, horrible showbiz mother, Mrs. Stella Winters (played to the hilt by Madge Ryan). It's an indication of how awful a mother she really is that her daughter would rather take her chances with a busful of strangers in a foreign city. Fortunately, it's the early 60s, the movie is the musical *Summer Holiday* (1963), a G-rated Cliff Richard vehicle, and his vehicle is a doubledecker bus stuffed with lovable, vacationing English lads and lasses. Her cover is eventually blown and bus driver Don (Cliff Richard), a confirmed bachelor who doesn't want a woman to "own" him (". . . date them once, and then run . . ."), falls in love with her for no apparent reason. Unless it was the fourteen-year-old-boy getup. She rejects his advances originally ("I don't want to own you. I don't even want to rent you") until the plot apparently puts a gun to her head between scenes and she swoons for him. Meanwhile, her mother conspires with manager Jerry (Lionel Murton) to milk the publicity of the missing singer and play the role of the worried mother. Somehow this involves boneheaded attempts at getting the whole busload arrested on one flimsy pretext or another at her instigation. So the bus hits one plot hole after another, always squeaking out of legal jams. Finally it all comes to a head in Athens, where Mommy dearest has them all busted for kidnapping, and quavers her voice righteously at a big press conference. Don and Barbara, mysteriously locked in four-star-hotel rooms instead of cells, escape and interrupt Stella with the news they're getting married! Obviously, poor Barbara is a victim of Stockholm syndrome. *TRIVIA TIME!* Cliff Richard is the G-rated Elvis of England, you ignorant Yank, with more hits than you've had hot dinners. Unfortunately, his movies aren't any better than Elvis's. See also **Do Re Mi**.

WINTERS, PAUL — My Lord. For TWENTY-NINE years, *The Wonderful World of Disney* (1954–83) aired, as reliable as Johnny Carson or Mr. Rogers. Of course, it was really just a bunch of unconnected movies-of-the-week. In "The Sultan and the Rock Star" episode (04/20/80), pop singer Paul Winters (Timothy Hutton) runs off to Sportsman's Island and befriends Sultan, a Bengal tiger. Wow. Rock stars—is there anything they can't do?!

WITHERSPOON, BLIND WILLIE — In the "Round Springfield" episode (04/30/95) of *The Simpsons*, running character saxman "Bleeding Gums" Murphy (voiced by Ron Taylor) is killed off, but not before a flashback takes us back to his beginnings in the 50s. This blind saxman (voiced by Hank Azaria) had been in the jazz biz for thirty years and couldn't make a go of it, so he gives his sax to Murphy. But it turns out his sax is really an umbrella, which explains his trouble playing it. Everyone else let him do it 'cause they all thought it was funny. Alas, it isn't, and neither is the finale of this most maudlin of *Simpsons* episodes. See also **The Beach Boys Experience; The Be Sharps; Johnny Bobby; Johnny Calhoun; Captain Bart and the Tequila Mockingbirds; The Crazy Old Man Singers; Cyanide; Gulliver Dark; Ferl Dixon and His Second Helping Boys; Funky C Funky Do; Garfunkel, Messina, Oates, and Lisa; Hooray for Everything; Kovenant; Krusty and the Krums; The Larry Davis Experience; Little Timmy and the Shebangs; Loggins and Oates; Lurleen Lumpkin; M. C. Safety and the Caution Crew; Melvin and the Squirrels; "Bleeding Gums" Murphy; The Party Posse; The Rappin' Rabbis; Red Breem and His Band of Some Esteem; The Satin Knights; The Steve Sax Trio; Testament; The Ya-Hoo Recovering Alcoholic Jug Band; Yodelin' Zeke**.

WIZZLETEATS, STINKY — The Burl Ives–resembling

vocalist (voiced by Bob Camp) who sings the insane li'l ditty "Happy Happy Joy Joy" in *The Ren and Stimpy Show* cartoon "Stimpy's Invention" (02/23/92). He also shows up on their 1993 *Crock O'Christmas* CD.

WONDERS, THE—Mid-60s pop band protagonists from Erie, Pennsylvania, in Tom Hanks's noncautionary tale about the nonproblems of fame, *That Thing You Do* (1996). Tom Hanks produced, wrote, and directed this period piece, as well as starred in it as slightly unsavory Play-Tone label rep Mr. White. The band's original lineup is Jimmy Mattingly (Johnathon Schaech) as lead singer and rhythm guitar, Lenny Haise (Steve Zahn) on lead guitar, T. B. Player (Ethan Embry) on bass (give yourself a cookie if you guess what T. B. stands for), and Chad (Giovanni Ribisi) on drums. But when Chad breaks his arm leapfrogging a parking meter shortly before a talent show, they recruit Guy Patterson (Tom Everett Scott), who drums along to jazz records in his basement. During the naming scene, they try out and reject The Echoes, The Corvettes, The Chordvettes, The Tempos, The Heardsmen, and Jimmy and the Heardsmen. Guy inadvertently names the group saying the word "wonder," giving Jimmy's girlfriend Faye Dolan (Liv Tyler) the idea to call the band that, and Jimmy the bad idea of spelling it "Oneders." Thanks to Guy's muscular, sped-up beat, their song "That Thing You Do" (supposed to be more of a ballad) wins the boys the 1964 Mercyhurst College Talent Show. You better like this title track, 'cause it's played about NINE BILLION times in the movie. The talent show win leads to a club gig, which leads to the idea of cutting a 45. Which leads to recording session in a church! Guy's uncle Bob (real singer Chris Isaak) records church choirs and sermons and does his nephew a favor recording their song and its B-side, "All My Only Dreams." They are then approached by creepy guy Phil Horace (Chris Ellis) who apparently lives in a pickup with a camper top and fortunately wants to manage them, not rape and kill them. He also gets their record on the radio, which has the band squealing like little twelve-year-old girls. Despite their disastrous Pittsburgh gig at the Boss Vic Koss show, they still get offered a deal by record company shark Mr. White. On signing, the idjit bass player reveals he has joined the Marine Corp but has a couple months before boot camp. White changes their name from Oneders to Wonders ("It's confusing"), and whisks them away to the 1964 Play-Tone Galaxy of Stars package tour with a bevy of other label-mates, playing state fairs and the like. Their song hits the charts at #93 and keeps shooting up as they tour fair after fair. Finally, in Illinois, they actually play a song that's NOT "That Thing You Do"—"Dance with Me Tonight." Savor the moment, because there's still about four and a half billion renditions of "That Thing You Do" left. When the song jumps from #21 to #7, becoming the fastest-rising single in Play-Tone history, White flies them out to Los Angeles to appear in the cheesy beach movie *Weekend at Party Pier*, playing the fake band Cap'n Geech and The Shrimp Shack Shooters (whoa! double fake band!). The Wonders also play *The Hollywood Television Showcase*, hosted by Troy Chesterfield (Tom Hanks's costar from the old *Bosom Buddies* sitcom, Peter Scolari). When Player disappears before the big TV gig, White pulls a new bass player out of thin air: Scott "Wolfman" Pell (Larry Antonio), who's played with The Techniques and Roy Maxwell and The Corsairs and can easily handle the bass line for their piece of teen-garage fluff. Unfortunately, after the show, Jimmy flips out because they put up a "Careful, girls, he's engaged" caption when they cut to him during the performance. This leads to him breaking up with girlfriend Faye, partly because he's a sensitive artist, but mostly because he's an insensitive jerk.

Then it all comes to a head in the recording studio when Mr. White lays down the law: they WILL cover only Play-Tone songs, they WILL record "That Thing You Do" in Spanish, etc. So Jimmy quits on the spot! Here endeth the band, literally one-hit wonders. At least Guy gets to record with his jazz hero, Del Paxton. In a "where are they now" ending, Guy and Faye get married and he founds the Puget Sound Conservatory of Music, Lenny manages a Vegas casino, Jimmy forms The Heardsmen, and T. B. Player gets the Purple Heart in 'Nam. The important thing is that nobody learned a sappy lesson about life, and nobody OD'ed, or any other standard rock cliché. See also **Elizabeth Anne; Blue Spot Trio; The Chantrellines; Diane Dane; The Echoes; Freddy Fredrickson; The G Men; The Heardsmen; The Hollyhocks; Jon D and the Walkers; Legends of Brass; Marilyn Lovell and the Geminis; The Norm Wooster Singers; Del Paxton; The Saturn 5; The Tempos; The Trends; Two Eriks; The Vicksburgs**.

The Wonders

WOODCHUCK, YANCY — See **The Frogtown Hollow Jubilee Jug-Band**.

WORTHY, BILLY — From the very, very first episode of very, very short-lived show *A Year at the Top* (August to September of 1977). This country-fried rock star speaks with a cornpone accent, sports a beige nudie suit and a poop-eatin' grin, and looks like a steroided John Denver. And he's supposed to be THE biggest rock star in the little ole U.S. of A? Well, it is 1977. And he also has the satanic assistance of Frederick J. Hanover, head of Paragon Records, and the quite literal son of the devil. Guess the old man got tired of hanging out at mysterious crossroads, and fast-tracked his son straight to where the action is. Hanover demonstrates his soul-buying modus operandi on Worthy: pump 'em up fast, then threaten to take away all the fame, money, and adulation unless they sell their soul for one more year at the top (thus the name of the show). When Hanover gives Worthy back his REAL voice (Mickey Mouse–squeaky!), Worthy collapses like a house of cards and signs. See also **Greg and Paul; Hogwash**.

WRETCHED, THE — From *The Cosby Show*'s "Off to See the Wretched" episode (04/05/90), appropriately enough. Never-seen band that Vanessa Huxtable (Tempestt Bledsoe) sneaks out to go see in Baltimore with her pals Janet (Pam Potillo), Kara (Elizabeth Narvaez), and Susan (Lisa Rieffel). The trip turns into a nightmare as their car gets stolen, a swindler cheats them out of their tickets, and Janet gets robbed. It all hits the fan when their folks find out. And they never got to even see the band! See also **Clyde**; **JT Freeze**; **The Icicles**; **The Jazz Caravan**; **The Lipsticks**; **The Maniacs**; **Slim Claxton and His Trio**; **Walking Lemons**.

WYCKYD SCEPTRE — From a hilarious and tasteless skit on the "Show Me Your Weenis" episode of HBO's *Mr. Show*. This gay metal band is in serious, serious denial. They think their casual gay sex with each other is just part and parcel of their hard-partying rock and roll lifestyle, until they get set, um, straight by their manager (Tom Kenny). Bob Odenkirk, David Cross, and John Ennis played the band members. See also **The Beetletown Players**; **Larry Black**; **Livingston Brewster**; **Willips Brighton**; **Dickie Crickets**; **Indomitable Spirit**; **Kid Jersey**; **Kill or Be Killed**; **C. S. Lewis Jr.**; **Horace Loeb**; **Marilyn Monster**; **Norma Jean Monster**; **John Baptiste Philouza**; **Professor Murder**; **Puscifer**; **Salini**; **Smoosh**; **Old Swerdlow**; **Three Times One Minus One**; **Titannica**; **Sir Lloyd Wilson Webber**; **Daffy "Mal" Yinkleyankle**.

WYLD STALLYNS — Cheesy metal garage band of the main characters from *Bill and Ted's Excellent Adventure* (1989) and the 1991 sequel, *Bill and Ted's Bogus Journey*. Keanu Reeves played Ted "Theodore" Logan and Alex Winter played Bill S. Preston Esquire, a pair of cheerfully dumb California Valley dudes. In the first movie, the band is just the two of them wanking around on guitar in the garage, until Rufus (comedian George Carlin) shows up in a time machine from a future where Wyld Stallyns' music and philosophy ("Be excellent to each other") has provided the template for a world of peace and harmony (!?). However, if they flunk their upcoming history presentation, that world will never exist. So the trio adventure through time, meeting historical figures, all for a school project! The second movie is

Bill S. Preston, Esq. (Alex Winters) (l) and Ted Logan (Keanu Reeves) (r) of Wyld Stallyns

more band-centric, as Bill and Ted must triumph over space, time, robot duplicates of themselves, and Death himself (William Sadler) to win the San Dimas Battle of the Bands. They pick up a pair of keyboard-playing medieval princesses, who become their girlfriends and band members. Rufus's time machine comes in extra handy when they need to go back in time and rehearse for sixteen months.

THE FAKE BAND SUPERGROUP: INAUTHENTICA

BY **CHARLES REMPEL**

With all the great fake musicians in the fake world, it sure would be something to see the best of the best together in one supergroup. We're not talking a "We Are the World" collection of stars, where Phoebe Buffay and The Rose share a microphone to sing why we should give our hard-earned fake money to help Starvin' Marvin, the fake undernourished Ethiopian from *South Park* (although the idea is intriguing, if for no other reason than seeing the multitude of near-identical singers Elvis played all dancing and swaying together). No, we're looking for the dream team of fake musicians to come together in a band we'll call Inauthentica. Ladies and gentlemen, introducing the members of Inauthentica:

Lead Vocals: Plavalaguna—There are plenty of worthy singers in this book, but the female alien opera singer of *The Fifth Element* gets the nod. Not only does this intergalactic diva wail across several octaves and fight for the good forces of the universe, but having a hot, blue-skinned alien babe as frontwoman is the penultimate visual hook for the band! All she needs is a rock makeover to up her sex appeal.

Lead Guitar: Nigel Tufnel (Spiñal Tap)—Tufnel goes to eleven. ELEVEN. That's all that needs to be said.

Co-Lead Guitar: The Kid—This *Purple Rain* heartthrob is here for sexiness and funksmanship. He'll take lead vocals on some songs in a blatant attempt to get the screaming girlies in the door.

Rhythm Guitar: Russell Hammond (Stillwater)—This *Almost Famous* ax-slinger normally plays lead guitar, but since he's a self-proclaimed golden god, he surely can adapt. Besides, Tufnel and The Kid both have a tendency to quit bands or ride off in a sexy sulk, so the band will need a top-notch backup in case one's a no-show.

Bass: Death (Wyld Stallyns)—Sure, there are better and funkier bass players than Death, from *Bill and Ted's Bogus Journey,* but are you going to tell him he's out of the band? He is Death! THE Death! You don't mess around with Death. Death could play the glockenspiel and still be in the band.

Drums: Animal (Dr. Teeth and the Electric Mayhem)—This is the easiest decision to make. One drum solo from Animal, the madman Muppet, and the band becomes legendary! Of course, the tour bus would have to have a healthy supply of restraints and sedatives onboard, and

not for recreational purposes.

Keyboards: Max Rebo (The Max Rebo Band)—Technically, this stubby alien plays the Red Ball Jett organ, but that instrument has to be even tougher to play than ordinary keyboards, right? He should have no problems. As the head of Jabba the Hutt's house band in *Return of the Jedi,* he's seen some tough places, so playing in dives should be no problem for Max. Plus, a second alien will help make Plavalaguna feel right at home. And perhaps might there be a Billy Joel/Christie Brinkley–Tommy Lee/Pamela Anderson–beauty/beast–type romance in the air . . . ?

X-PRESIDENTS, THE—Cartoon versions of Gerald Ford, Jimmy Carter, Ronald Reagan, and George Bush the Elder from *Saturday Night Live*'s animated "TV Funhouse" segments (later spun off to its own show on Comedy Central) masterminded by Robert Smigel. They first appeared 01/11/97, but showed up about half a dozen times since then. After a hard day fighting supervillains, they kick back with a little Archies-style pop rock. Carter gets the wimpy tambourine, hee hee! Groovy!

XT—A now-he's-dead, now-he-isn't, now-he's-maybe-a-zombie rapper from the "Subject: Still I Rise" episode (01/12/01) of the short-lived and shameless *Blair Witch/X-Files* ripoff series, *Freaky Links.* XT's real name is Gregory Purdell. Played by Reno Wilson.

YA-HOO RECOVERING ALCOHOLIC JUG BAND, THE—In the "Colonel Homer" (3/26/92) episode of *The Simpsons,* Homer Simpson (Dan Castellaneta) discovers and promotes Lurleen Lumpkin, a country singing star voiced by Beverly D'Angelo. He gets her on the *Ya-Hoo!* TV show, an obvious parody of long-running cornpone fare *Hee-Haw*, featuring this house band. See also **The Beach Boys Experience; The Be Sharps; Johnny Bobby; Johnny Calhoun; Captain Bart and the Tequila Mockingbirds; The Crazy Old Man Singers; Cyanide; Gulliver Dark; Ferl Dixon and His Second Helping Boys; Funky C Funky Do; Garfunkel, Messina, Oates, and Lisa; Hooray for Everything; Kovenant; Krusty and the Krums; The Larry Davis Experience; Little Timmy and the Shebangs; Loggins and Oates; Lurleen Lumpkin; M. C. Safety and the Caution Crew; Melvin and the Squirrels; "Bleeding Gums" Murphy; The Party Posse; The Rappin' Rabbis; Red Breem and His Band of Some Esteem; The Satin Knights; The Steve Sax Trio; Testament; Blind Willie Witherspoon; Yodelin' Zeke.**

YEAH — MTV's po-mo sock-puppet extravaganza, *The Sifl and Olly Show*, held their First Annual Sifl and Olly Show Battle of the Bands in the 01/12/99 episode. The third and last entry was this four-piece prog/art rock band in silver jumpsuits. Their influences are Yes, King Crimson, and Medusa. They win, but their lead singer says, "We do not make music for it to be judged. We make art for the mind, not the ears. And in protest of sound, we shall not accept this award, break up, and live in silence forever." The show is the brainchild of Matt Crocco and Liam Lynch who do the voices and compose and record the music. See also **Clear Fog; Kee Kee and The P. P. Gang; Sgt. Blind Kiwi Tarzan; Zafo.**

YINKLEYANKLE, DAFFY "MAL" — A "Weird" Al Yankovic parody, which is a mind-bending concept. He does a brief parody of Li'l Davey Cross's "Superstar Ma-chine" called "Sushi Bar Machine." Played by Bob Odenkirk, from the "Rudy Will Await Your Foundation" episode (11/30/98) of HBO's *Mr. Show*. See also **The Beetletown Players; Larry Black; Livingston Brewster; Willips Brighton; Dickie Crickets; Indomitable Spirit; Kid Jersey; Kill or Be Killed; C. S. Lewis Jr.; Horace Loeb; Marilyn Monster; Norma Jean Monster; John Baptiste Philouza; Professor Murder; Puscifer; Salini; Smoosh; Old Swerdlow; Three Times One Minus One; Titannica; Sir Lloyd Wilson Webber; Wyckyd Sceptre.**

YODELIN' ZEKE — In the "Colonel Homer" (3/26/92) episode of *The Simpsons*, Homer Simpson (Dan Castellaneta) visits the redneck Beer-n-Brawl bar out in Spittle County and discovers a waitress with the potential to be a country singing star. Zeke is the act that goes on just before her. Yodelin' Zeke is just back from the hospital. After a few notes of yodelin', we quickly learn why he was there, as he is hit with a chair. He pops up again at the end of the episode on the *Ya-Hoo!* TV show, appearing with a big bandage on his head. See also **The Beach Boys Experience; The Be Sharps; Johnny Bobby; Johnny Calhoun; Captain Bart and the Tequila Mockingbirds; The Crazy Old Man Singers; Cyanide; Gulliver Dark; Ferl Dixon and His Second Helping Boys; Funky C Funky Do; Garfunkel, Messina, Oates, and Lisa; Hooray for Everything; Kovenant; Krusty and the Krums; The Larry Davis Experience; Little Timmy and the Shebangs; Loggins and Oates; Lurleen Lumpkin; M. C. Safety and the Caution Crew; Melvin and the Squirrels; "Bleeding Gums" Murphy; The Party Posse; The Rappin' Rabbis; Red Breem and His Band of Some Esteem; The Satin Knights; The Steve Sax Trio; Testament; Blind Willie Witherspoon; The Ya-Hoo Recovering Alcoholic Jug Band.**

YODELING ANDY—Artist seen in a commercial in the "Master the Possibilities" episode (02/07/88) of *Married with Children*. He has the albums *Yodeling Andy's Yodel Songs, Yodeling Andy Yodels the Blues, Yodeling Andy Yodels the Hits*, and *The Best of Yodeling Andy*. According to Bud Bundy (David Faustino), he's a mix of Burl Ives and Trini Lopez, which is strange, as neither of them yodel. See also **Burned Beyond Recognition; Jimmy Dick and the Night Sticks; Joanie and the Slashettes; Oozing Meat; Otitis Media; Shoes 'n' Socks; Tears and Vomit; The Tuxedos; The Wanker Triplets; The Why.**

YOUNG CAUCASIANS, THE—Parody of 50s whitebread acts covering black music, à la Pat Boone. From the 11/12/77, Ray Charles–hosted episode of *Saturday Night Live*. The group sings their version of "What'd I Say" for Ray Charles, who wrote the song! They probably made Ray wish he was deaf instead of blind.

YOUNG SAVAGES, THE—From the "Valentine's Day" (aka "The Valentine") episode (02/14/86) of *Mr. Belvedere*, a sitcom so mind-numbing it was only left on the air to send coded messages to our spies. Okay, YOU think of a more plausible reason for why it was on the air for five years. Teen drummer hopeful Kevin Owens (Rob Stone) joins this band that, to his disappointment, is nowhere near as cool as their name. It's merely named for members Stan Young (Howard E. Writwright) and the three Savage brothers, Herb (Johnny Bisaha), Bud (John Glaudini), and Ernie (Eric Peterson).

ZACK ATTACK—From the lightweight comedy series *Saved by the Bell*, and named for the band's (and show's) pretty-boy egomaniac preppie leader, Zachary "Zack" Morris (Mark-Paul Gosselaar). The band exists because having a band is just something that high schoolers in TV land do. In the most band-centric episode, "Rockumentary" (11/30/91), Casey Kasem guest-stars as himself and narrates a dream sequence where the band become big and famous. But usually the band just shows up playing the occasional school dance. Lineup: drummer Albert Clifford "AC" Slater (Mario Lopez), bassist Lisa Turtle (Lark Voorhies), guitarist Zack Morris, keyboard player Samuel "Screech" Powers (Dustin Diamond), and sometimes Kelly Kapowski (Tiffani-Amber Thiessen) or Jessica "Jessie" Spano (Elizabeth Berkley) on vocals. The *Saved by the Bell* soundtrack album features several Zack Attack tracks: "Love Me Now," "Make My Day," "Friends Forever," and "Did We Ever Have a Chance?" See also **The Five Aces; Hot Sundae; Bo Revere; Stevie.**

ZAFO—Puppet rock star from two episodes (02/23/99 and 03/02/99) of MTV's oh so po-mo sock-puppet hoedown, *The Sifl and Olly Show*. He did a concert on top of Mt. Rushmore. Sifl and Olly idolize him, and rightfully so, as a meteor headed straight for Earth decided not to collide with us after hearing about Zafo. The show is the brainchild of Matt Crocco and Liam Lynch, who do the voices and compose and record the music. See also **Clear Fog; Kee Kee and The P. P. Gang; Sgt. Blind Kiwi Tarzan; Yeah.**

ZATAPATHIQUE, INSPECTOR JEAN-PAUL—The singing forensic expert from the Monaco Murder Squad, played by Graham Chapman. He sings the bouncy 'n' nonsensical "Bing Tiddle Tiddle Bong" in a Eurovision Song Contest–like competition he's won at the end of the "How to Recognise Different Parts of the Body" episode (11/24/70) of the now probably legendary BBC sketch show *Monty Python's Flying Circus*. See also **Arthur Ewing and His Musical Mice; Bolton Choral Society; Johann Gambolputty de von Ausfern-schplenden-schlitter-**

crasscrenbon-fried-digger-dingle-dangle-dongle-dungle-burstein-von-knacker-thrasher-apple-banger-horowitz-ticolensic-grander-knotty-spelltinkle-grandlich-grumblemeyer-spelterwasser-kurstlich-himbleeisen-bahnwagen-gutenabend-bitte-ein-nürnburger-bratwustle-gerspurten-mitz-weimache-luber-hundsfut-gumberaber-shönendanker-kalbsfleisch-mittler-aucher von Hautkopft of Ulm**; The Herman Rodriguez Four**; **The Hunlets**; **Jackie Charlton and the Tonettes**; **Arthur "Two Sheds" Jackson**; **Not Noel Coward**; **Not Tony Bennett**; **Rachel Toovey Bicycle Choir**.

ZEKE BENNY AND HIS MAD MOUNTAIN BOYS — Ozarks combo on the 11/04/51 episode of *The Jack Benny Program*. An overall-clad Benny leads the band, whipping and sawing his famous fiddle through "You Are My Sunshine." Afterwards, he intros the band, tossing in hick jokes: Charlie Bagby on concertina, Wayne Songer on clarinet, Frank Remley on guitar, his singer "wife" (some thirteen-year-old-looking girl—a seriously non-PC hick joke!), and his "son" Sammy (Weiss) on percussion. Those are their real names; Benny's band is really his real band, albeit in bumpkin drag. Then they play a medley of Gershwin's "Fascinatin' Rythym" and "Puttin' on the Ritz." The country-fried theme was in honor of their guest star, singer Dorothy Shay, the "Park Avenue Hillbilly," who also sang and introduced this combo. *TRIVIA TIME!* Seven years later (04/20/58), the show reused this footage, as Benny's manager reminisced about Benny's early days as Zeke Benny and His Ozark Mountain Hillbillies.

ZEKE BENNY AND HIS OZARK MOUNTAIN HILLBILLIES — See **Zeke Benny and His Mad Mountain Boys**.

ZHIVAGO, JOHNNY — Number two artist on the top-ten board in the record shop scene in the 1971 sci-fi classic, *A Clockwork Orange*. The song title is "Really Play." Pretty teenybopper Marty (Barbara Scott) asks her pretty teenybopper friend Sonietta (Gillian Hills), "Who you gettin' bratty? Goggly Gogol? Johnny Zhivago? The Heaven Seventeen?" just before evil ole Alex (Malcolm McDowell) sweet-talks them back to his place for sex. Johnny's name and much of the teen slang throughout the movie is to indicate a Russian influence on teen culture in the future. See also **The Blow Goes**; **Bread Brothers**; **Comic Strips**; **Cyclops**; **Goggly Gogol**; **The Heaven Seventeen**; **The Humpers**; **The Legend**; **The Sharks**.

ZILLA, ROCK — Superpopular, green-haired billionaire heavy metal rocker in the animated 2003 show *My Dad the Rock Star*. Concerned about his family, he's decided to semiretire to the suburbs of Silent Springs. This comes as a relief to son Willy Zilla, (voiced by Joanne Vannicola), who just wants to be a normal tween. Rock Zilla is voiced by Lawrence Bayne. Willy's mom, Crystal Zilla, is voiced by Kathleen Laskey, and his older sister, Serenity, by Stephanie Anne Mills. Believe it or not, this show is based on KISS lead singer Gene Simmons's 2001 kids' book *My Dad the Rock Star: Rebel Without a Nose Ring*. Simmons originally pitched a KISS cartoon show to animation house Nelvana, but they came out (probably wisely) with this instead. From despised and feared rock-star monster to children's author. Only in America! Or possibly Canada, where this show airs on the Canadian cartoon channel Teletoon.

ZIT REMEDY, THE — See The Zits.

ZITS, THE — Joey Jeremiah (Pat Mastroianni) on vocals and keyboards, Archie "Snake" Simpson (Stefan Brogren) on guitar, and Derek "Wheels" Wheeler (Neil Hope) on bass form the New

Wave-y trio originally named The Zit Remedy in the low-budget, Canadian-produced, coming-of-age show *Degrassi Junior High* (1986–89). They had only one damn song, "Everybody Wants Something," available on their 1988 homemade album (or cassingle, to be more accurate), *The Zit Remedy: LIVE!* After Wheels's parents' tragic death, he drifted in and out of the band and was briefly semi-replaced on bass by Simon Dexter (Michael Carry). Eventually Wheels sold his bass and it seemed the band was dead. But when the show changed its name and setting to *Degrassi High* (1989–91), the boys resurrected the band, decided a new, more mature moniker was needed, and so changed their name to The Zits. Yeah. Much more mature. They tried to get their song on radio station CRAZ, got shot down, made a music video, and committed other such antics until the writers ran out of stereotypical high school band plots and the band faded from the show. See also **Gourmet Scum**; **The Savages**.

ZORAK — Never has a repurposed cartoon brought such joy. Zorak (originally voiced by Don Messick), an evil, mantislike alien, once tried to kill hero Space Ghost (originally voiced by Gary Owens) in the original mindless 1966 Hanna-Barbera *Space Ghost and Dino Boy* sci-fi adventure cartoon series. But in 1994, the Cartoon Network launched ever-zany *Space Ghost: Coast to Coast*, recycled from the original animation. Space Ghost (voiced by George Lowe) is now a talk-show host and Zorak (voiced by C. Martin Croker) is forced to serve as his keyboardist and occasional singer. Host Space Ghost and idiot sidekick Brak (voiced by Andy Merrill) are also known to step up to the mic on occasion. Rhino Records released two CDs of their sublime ridiculousness, *Space Ghost's Musical Bar-B-Que* (1997) and *Space Ghost's Surf & Turf* (1998).